The McGraw-Hill
# 36-Hour
# Real Estate
# Investing
# Course

## Other Books in The McGraw-Hill 36-Hour Course Series

# The McGraw-Hill
# 36-Hour
# Real Estate
# Investing
# Course

## Jack Cummings

### McGraw-Hill, Inc.

New York   San Francisco   Washington, D.C.   Auckland   Bogotá
Caracas   Lisbon   London   Madrid   Mexico City   Milan
Montreal   New Delhi   San Juan   Singapore
Sydney   Tokyo   Toronto

**Library of Congress Cataloging-in-Publication Data**

Cummings, Jack.  Date
  The McGraw-Hill 36-hour real estate investing course  /  Jack
Cummings.

        p.     cm.
    Includes index.
    ISBN 0-07-015047-8      —ISBN 0-07-015048-6 (pbk.)
      1. Real estate investment—United States.    2. Real estate
investment—United States—Examinations, questions, etc.    I. Title.
II. Title: McGraw-Hill thirty-six-hour real estate investing course.
HD1382.5.C844   1993
332.63'24—dc20                                                    92-39185
                                                                    CIP

        5 6 7 8 9 0   DOC/DOC   9 8 7 6 5

ISBN 0-07-015047-8 {HC}
ISBN 0-07-015048-6 {PBK}


*The sponsoring editor for this book was Theodore Nardin, the editing supervisor was
Valerie L. Miller, and the production supervisor was Suzanne W. Babeuf. This book
was set in Baskerville by North Market Street Graphics.*

*Printed and bound by R. R. Donnelley & Sons Company.*

# Contents

# Acknowledgment

When a writer sits down to write a book there is an anticipation that a love affair is about to start, and no matter how tedious the work may be, the affection for the manuscript is steady and faithful.

When the work is completed there is a period of absolute mixed emotion—an elation that the child is born, a sadness that the love affair has ended, and worst of all, despair that the writer is now out of work.

When finally asked to "dedicate" the book to someone, there is a moment when all writers scramble to find the person they should acknowledge as a primary driving force for the book, while at the same time not stepping on toes, hurting feelings, or cutting off possible loan sources when times might get tough.

Fortunately, for this book at least, this dedication is made with a clear conscience and sincere thanks. Many years ago, my first editor for the first book I was to sell was a young man who called me one day to ask me if I would be interested in writing a book. That book turned out to be *The Real Estate Financing Manual*, and that man was to teach me a great deal about the writing profession, and myself.

It is because of his continual faith in me that I dedicate this book to my good friend and first editor, Ted Nardin.

# Introduction

*Now is the time to invest in real estate—lenders are ready, interest rates are down, sellers are motivated, prices are the lowest in 18 years—what are you waiting for? This book is your guide to wealth.*

Are you new at the Real Estate Game, or have you been investing in real estate for years? Either way, this book is for you. In fact, this book is the best place for any real estate investor to begin because it is designed to deal with the modern problems that real estate investors encounter—and it will show you how to arrive at the proper solution to best attain your desired goals, whether they are modest, such as to get out of renting and to own your own home, or more lofty, as to become wealthy and financially independent through real estate investing.

This book will get the novice started in the right direction and help the knowledgeable investor to maximize his or her efforts to reduce risk and to produce more profitable results from their investments.

Are you concerned or confused about timing? Do you wonder: **Is now the right time to get into real estate**? The simple answer is "yes." Now may be the very best time in your entire life—because the real estate market is about to bust wide open. The mortgage interest rates indicate it, the mood of the market is in favor of the buyer, and "now" is here. All you need to do is to learn how to invest successfully in real estate, not just learn some tricks that worked for someone else, but *learn the solid foundation that the "insiders" always knew.*

But don't be surprised and don't be misled. To learn this art properly is not as simple as some TV promotions and Saturday night lecturers would like you to believe. Let's face it, learning how to become wealthy requires effort, study, and determination. This *McGraw-Hill 36-Hour Real Estate Investing Course* will be your college education into real estate investing—the graduate work is up to you.

Real estate investing is, as you will discover, a study of history. The history of why the real estate market goes up and down will give you the inside track of where your local market is headed. Successful real estate investing is nothing more than seeing opportunities, realizing they are the right ones for you to grasp, and knowing what to do next.

You will find that the factors which govern the rise and fall of real estate values are relatively simple. Most of the forces that affect the real estate market and control this rise and fall of values are evident for everyone to see and follow. The key is to know where to look, how to read the signals, and what to do to take advantage of the situations and opportunities as they present themselves to you. The idea of becoming an expert in the real estate market is not a complex task of knowing 100 techniques or being able to calculate mortgage interest rates in your head. The ultimate key is to know what your goal is and to become the *local* expert on the kind of real estate that can help you attain that goal.

> *This book is a unique approach to the idea of "learning" how to become a real estate investor.*

All real estate fluctuates in value and is governed most dramatically by local situations, such as local economy, population growth, and so on. Wider-based secondary forces, such as nationwide building starts or national unemployment figures, can often be more misleading than helpful unless you know and understand the local picture of things. It is quite possible that your local area defies the national or even countywide trends.

This book is a unique approach to the idea of "learning how to become a real estate investor." It is unique in several ways: First and most important is that this book provides an easy-to-follow course of study that will establish a sound platform for you to launch your real estate investment career.

## How to Use This Book

This book is divided into four main parts plus the final examination. Each of the four parts contains chapters that relate to the main topic of that section. These divisions are shown below:

Part 1: How to Get Started in Real Estate Investing

Part 2: How and Why Property Values Go Up and Down and What You Can Do About It

Part 3: How to Find The Right Property to Buy

Part 4: How to Buy and Sell Real Estate for a Profit

Final Examination

## How the Book Is Designed to Work with You

Each of the chapters follow the outline shown below:

1. Chapter goals
2. Key terms
3. Chapter concepts
4. Case studies

## How to Get the Most out of Each Chapter

In the approach to writing this book, the author has drawn on over 30 years of solid and very successful real estate investing experience. The material provided within this book is based on varied experience as an investor, developer, financial advisor, realtor, and a widely published author of many real estate investment and finance books.

As you examine this book you will discover that segments 1 through 4 of each chapter provide the basis for this 36-hour course. These are the primary elements of this text, which, within an average of 36 hours, will give you the fundamentals needed to approach real estate investing as a knowledgeable insider.

Below you will see the breakdown of each segment of the chapters you will encounter.

**Chapter Goals.**  This segment lists the goals of the chapter and what you should expect from them. Review this segment both at the start of the chapter and after you have read it thoroughly. If, when rereading the chapter goals, you are not sure you have a good understanding of them, then you need to review the chapter material prior to moving on.

**Key Terms.**  Each chapter contains several key terms that aid you in understanding and later making use of the concepts of the chapter. These key terms will build on one another as you progress through the book so that you expand your knowledge in a systematic and useful way.

**Chapter Concepts.**  These are the basic concepts or steps that you will discover are essential to obtain the goals established for each chapter. These are presented in the building-block method, which allows you to broaden your base of information and knowledge continuously. At the same time, you are developing a solid understanding of what makes real estate "tick," how you can reduce risk in investing, and how you can determine which of the opportunities you discover will best help you attain your goals.

**Case Studies.**   There are only a few case studies in this book. These are designed to direct your attention to potential problem areas for real estate investors. At the end of most chapters, there are assignments that allow readers to compile their own Real Estate Investor's VIP List. This list, which follows Chap. 20, should be filled out faithfully as described in the chapter exercises. When you finish the book, there will still be some blank areas, which readers can complete at their leisure. The investor who has a fully completed list will have the edge over any other potential investor in the same community. This list is to be *used*. Its sole purpose is to help you build personal confidence in the real estate arena. Its success depends on you to obtain the data called for. Do not skip this important part of the book— your future may depend on it.

# PART 1

# How to Get Started in Real Estate Investing

# 1
# Sound Investment Strategy Starts with a Good Plan

## Chapter Goals

This chapter is the foundation for all that follows, and its purpose is to help you establish a positive outlook on the task of real estate investing. It will do this by illustrating that **determination** and **attitude** are the two most important qualifications needed to become a successful real estate investor. Without these two characteristics as part of your approach to real estate investing, you will become frustrated with the roadblocks in your way and will become bored with the tedium of the work required to become an expert in the local real estate market. This chapter also tackles the problem of **risk** in real estate investing and shows the reader the key to reducing that element from the investment portfolio. The ultimate aim of this chapter is to show the reader the importance of establishing sound and meaningful goals.

This chapter and those that follow are directed to the goal-oriented investor. The problem is that most novice investors are not **goal oriented**, and consequently most investors are not very successful. The importance of good goals is essential for sustained success in any venture, so real estate investing should not be an exception. The connection between a firm focus (a goal clearly in sight) and a winning attitude is very important, because it will shape the self-confidence of an individual and provide a road map for the future. The result will enable you to overcome needless frustration and to dispel the idea of fruitless effort.

Take everything one step at a time and let your mind begin to sort out the pieces of the puzzle.

## Key Terms

- Success-oriented attitude
- Apparent opportunity
- Attainable opportunity
- Positive failure alignment
- Successful elasticity
- Comfort zone

Review each in detail.

### Success-Oriented Attitude

The *little train that could* is the basis of this concept. Knowing that you can succeed is the driving force that results in effective and worthwhile effort. When virtually every task begun is completed, strong **self-confidence** is generated. This self-confidence is the inner reflection of the right kind of success-oriented attitude. In person-to-person contact, this self-confidence *must* be so positively charged within you that it shows in everything about you. In sports this kind of self-confidence is what gives one player the edge over another. In essence, the loser gets "psyched out." The positive attitude keeps the winner charged with the vision of success right from the beginning. It pays off in sports and also in real estate investing.

In the business world this simple element is often the only thing that separates a closed contract, a signed order, or a profitable venture from failure. It is a natural course of events. People *want* to do business with people who exude success and who have the confidence to prove it.

The idea is to look and think the part. It takes both aspects to really work. Just thinking success and not playing the role is not enough. It is important to dress smartly, to have good manners and taste, and to be respectful and punctual.

You will discover that you can develop a success-oriented attitude about real estate investing that will really work for you by following these simple steps.

- Know that you can and will learn the tools needed to be a success in real estate investing. Right now you might feel like the student pilot, taking a look at the dashboard filled with strange gauges, switches, and dials with no idea of how they function. But just as the pilot learns to fly, you will learn the keys and the insider techniques in real estate investing and you will be a success—if you want it to happen.

- Don't rush anything. Take this book step by step and become comfortable with the concepts and your ability to apply them as they relate to your goals. Building your own self-confidence is an essential part to building a success-oriented attitude.

## Apparent Opportunity

The moment you begin to learn anything new you will have the urge to grasp what jumps out at you as an **apparent opportunity**. It's like the budding psychiatrist who first learns of a mental disorder and begins to see it in everyone. Learning about real estate investing is *learning how to take advantage of opportunities that may have been around all the time;* the only difference is that you did not have the ability to see them, so they went unnoticed. Apparent opportunities are both *dangerous* and *worthy*. The key is for you to make the ultimate determination about which end of the scale any apparent opportunity is from the point of view of the attainment of your goal.

Novice investors often jump at a deal that looks good for the wrong reason. For example, dealing with highly motivated sellers is a very good source for making excellent deals. However, to acquire property from a seller simply because he or she will sell it for nothing down may not be an opportunity at all because that property may not serve to move you closer to your desired goals. Many investors armed with a little information or who try to make investments without having solid goals firmly in mind have quickly overburdened themselves with debt and/or management problems beyond their abilities.

Every purchase or acquisition should be part of an investment plan. If the property can fit into that plan and can be purchased or acquired in such a way that the obligation does not overburden you or sidetrack you from your goals, then you have examined the apparent opportunity and determined it is a **worthy opportunity**.

## Attainable Opportunity

Not every worthy opportunity will be attainable. The reason is that not every seller will be willing to meet your acquisition requirements. One of the elements of being successful as a real estate investor is to convert *obstinate sellers to willing sellers*. A success-oriented attitude will help. This book is designed to help you concentrate on attainable opportunities rather than waste your time trying to acquire properties that are owned by property owners who are not motivated or who are unrealistic about property values. Sometimes the roadblock is not the owner of the property but his or her agent, lawyer, family partner, friend, or other confidant. You need to make an early decision about whether the property is right for you, and, equally important, whether the owners will work *with* you. If not, move on.

## Positive Failure Alignment

Don't be concerned about the word **failure**. Failure is not your enemy. Failure is not the opposite of success. Failure is an essential part of the attainment process of every goal. Without failure along the way, you will not have that sweet taste of success at the end of the path. Use failure as a sign that you are getting sidetracked and may need to step back a bit, readjust your goals, or simply apply a new tactic and try again.

## Successful Elasticity

A football running back knows the advantage of being able to make sudden changes in direction and speed. In real estate investing, the ability to make sudden adjustments to your goals and your plans will enable you to move with the changing trends. In this way you can avoid economic disaster when outside factors have a negative influence. Fixed and unbending goals and plans must be avoided. However, do not be too quick to make changes until you have thought out the new plan or the adjusted goal. Change for the sake of change is not wise.

## Comfort Zone

An investment comfort zone for real estate is the combination of a geographic area and a specific type of property in which an investor decides to specialize. This concept is unique, and later chapters are devoted to providing details on how to establish and maintain an investment comfort zone. However, the development and proper utilization of an investment comfort zone are so important that almost everything the investor does to increase his or her knowledge and the expansion of investment techniques must be directed to the function of the comfort zone. A typical comfort zone is shown below.

**A Typical Comfort Zone.**   Charles has decided that he will buy and fix up homes as his first venture into real estate investing. Because Charles worked as a carpenter before becoming a mortgage loan officer at a local savings and loan institution, he is handy with building tools and can take advantage of his skills.

Charles blocks out an area of several hundred homes in an old part of town that is coming back into vogue and is conveniently located between where he currently lives and the savings and loan institution where he works. The geography of his comfort zone is a single subdivision that consists of a variety of categories of properties. The specific category to which Charles will direct the majority of his efforts will be the single-family homes within that subdivision. Because the nature of the real estate market within that subdivision is governed by the same factors affecting all property in the immediate area, Charles will follow the general trends for the whole immediate area. In general, Charles will learn everything there is to know about his comfort zone and the local events and people that can have an influence over the rise and fall of the real estate market there. All that Charles learns will increase his confidence and expand his ability to recognize an opportunity.

## The Elements to Getting Started as a Real Estate Investor

### The Importance of Self-Confidence and How to Build It

The key to a success-oriented attitude in real estate investing is to build your self-confidence to the level where you can deal with total involvement of buying and selling real property. It is logical, then, that the first part of your plan to become a successful real estate investor should be to outline all the steps needed to obtain the necessary knowledge and tools of the trade. You must expand your knowledge to the point where your self-confidence becomes evident not only to those around you but, more importantly, to you.

### Five Steps to Building Self-Confidence

1. Accept the fact that by the time you complete this 36-hour course you will have the basic foundation on which to build your investment portfolio.

2. Anticipate that you will have strong points from which you can build, and weak points that you will either have to strengthen or circumvent.

3. Set down clear and attainable long-range goals and work to refine them.

4. Establish intermediate *need to accomplish to improve* goals and timetables. These minigoals are set by you as steps you need to take to attain, increase, or fine-tune your knowledge and abilities so you can succeed at longer-range goals. The list of minigoals or steps should never have more than three or four items at any given time, and only when one is completed can another be added. Keep your timetable short. No item should be on the list if you cannot complete the maximum of four items within 12 months. You can begin this list with item 1: Complete this *36-Hour Real Estate Investing Course.*

5. Celebrate each intermediate step you attain. Pat yourself on *your own back* and be proud of your accomplishments. By continuing to set intermediate minigoals that can be reached in relatively short time periods, you are setting a pattern for success. Continual achievement creates a strong success-oriented attitude and helps build your self-confidence quickly.

## How Much Time Is Needed to Get Started in Real Estate Investing?

The amount of time needed to become a real estate investor is divided into two segments.

- Preparation
- Implementation—start your comfort zone plan

Study in detail the following explanation of the two segments.

### Preparation

This is a combination of active study, such as reading this book and the case studies provided, and development of investment habits that will become a natural part of your everyday life. Much of this "awareness building" will not take additional time from your current activities, but can become a part of them. For example, instead of merely driving to work, get to know the neighborhood. Look at properties on the market or for sale, jot down phone numbers from *for sale* or *for rent* signs, and so on. The key is to take as much time as necessary to accomplish the minigoals set. Time is on the side of the real estate investor.

### Implementation

Following the completion of the *McGraw-Hill 36-Hour Real Estate Investing Course,* this book can become a guide to investing. The book is designed to take the investor through a step-by-step process and is an ideal reference guide.

One morning each week plus one full day during the weekend is a reasonable time to devote to field work. Field work is the time spent driving around the community, getting to know it better than any taxi driver ever could. This means not only knowing the streets, but knowing the zoning, neighborhood boundaries, schools districts, churches, and so on. A few hours one or two evenings each week should be devoted to paperwork and additional reading to continue to expand your sphere of knowledge and reference.

*Warning:* You should not attempt to put this book into practice until you have completed the whole course and taken the final examination.

## How to Reduce Risk in Real Estate Investing

If there was a way to eliminate risk entirely, that secret would bring a very high price tag. It will be impossible to remove the element of risk completely from real estate investing. However, the prudent investor who follows simple and proven rules can greatly reduce the element of risk to acceptable levels. To understand how this is accomplished one must first realize that risk is a relative term that does not apply to everyone for the same situation or circumstance. It should be obvious that a trained pilot with 1000 hours of flight time in a Boeing 747 jet has much less risk of making a mistake in landing that giant of an aircraft than would a part-time single-engine student pilot. Likewise, the real estate investor who knows his or her comfort zone like the back (and front) of his or her hand and has astutely followed the market for several months or more is better equipped to deal with investments in *that area*. This investor knows what property has been sold and rented for in the past, and is aware of the current market conditions.

As the investor's knowledge of the local area increases, opportunities that would never have been seen before start to stand out, almost as though they have a neon sign that blinks "buy me." At first, the investor will have to be cautious and fight the urge to take advantage of every apparent opportunity that comes along. Soon, the investor gains confidence in his or her own knowledge and information. Once this begins to happen the investor feels his or her success-oriented attitude take over, and then all effort is directed toward the long-range goals. The apparent opportunities will give way to attainable opportunities, and a real estate investment portfolio can be built.

## The Importance of Meaningful Goals

Your goals are the shortcuts to the desired destinations of your life. Goals are not essential for life, as many people never grasp the advantage of setting meaningful goals or never set any kind of goal at all. Not having any goals or setting the wrong kind of goals does not mean you will not arrive at a destination. However, it leaves the choice of that destination and the timetable you will follow to others or to indecision.

## What Is a Meaningful Goal?

For a goal to work for you it must have four qualities. It must be attainable, measurable, tied to a timetable, and clearly defined.

A goal that is more distant in time than one year should be divided into intermediate minigoals that lead you in the right path continually toward the attainment of the end goal. A person who sets a long-range goal to become a medical doctor would establish intermediate minigoals for the current 12 months that must be obtained one after the other as essential steps toward the medical degree. As each step is completed, within a defined timetable that the person sets for him or herself, another minigoal can be added. Ideally, no more than four minigoals should be on the list at any single time, and no goal should be discarded once it is placed on the list without careful reexamination of the long-range goal.

Constant attainment of these minigoals strengthens the self-confidence level and promotes a healthy outlook and success-oriented attitude.

### Goals Should Be Attainable

The fastest route to frustration is to set goals that are not attainable at all or not within the timetable set. The "I want to be a millionaire by the end of this year" goal, while an interesting approach to the desire for financial independence, may not be attainable to begin with, and surely each intermediate minigoal will equally be unattainable.

Goals should be set to be both challenging as well as attainable.

### Goals Must Be Measurable

All goals must have a scale that allows for readjustment and fine-tuning. This means that there should be a way to tell how close a goal is to being attained. For example, if a long-range goal set a few years ago was to own 100 rental apartment units and there are currently 50 rental apartments in the portfolio, the long-range goal is 50 percent attained. Minigoals that may have established a minimum number of units to acquire each year can be adjusted either up or down to keep the timetable in line. Or, if the long-range goal itself is adjusted to increase the number of units now set as the long-range goal, say to 150 apartment units, the current level is only one-third toward the goal and new plans need to be implemented to meet the new long-range goal.

Esoteric goals that have no measure can create chaos in setting the minigoals, and frustration is bound to occur. These kinds of goals are often not easily spotted at first, as they seem to have measure at the time they are set. *Financial independence* as a goal, for example, becomes unmeasurable later on because financial needs change.

## Goals Should Be Tied to a Timetable

The timetable serves several functions. First, it requires time management and the prioritization of effort. Most people work better if they know they must complete something by a deadline. The key to setting a timetable is to allow a reasonable time for taking into account the other items placed on the list. Because you must keep the list down to no more than four principal items, you are required to be very selective with these four goals you must accomplish.

Avoid putting things off. This is a self-established timetable, and if the deadlines are constantly pushed ahead, the whole concept of setting goals and attaining them will be defeated. Goals are chosen by the person who must then establish the deadlines and work to meet them. Frequent measures must be taken to judge the progress in accomplishing the task and if adjustment is needed. If any part of the goal is changed, there must be a very good reason.

## Goals Must Be Clearly Defined

A vague goal can cause more problems than it is worth. Consider the goal of 150 apartment units mentioned earlier. Is that a clearly defined goal? I think not. It needs further definition so that the investor is not lulled into thinking that the end goal has been attained when in reality it is even farther away. A more precise definition could be to own 150 rental apartments free and clear of any debt. Naturally, further definition can be given to any goal, but it is important to avoid locking a goal into an unattainable status. One element of a goal being clearly defined is essential—the goal must be written down.

A verbal goal is only as good as one's memory, and if the only recorded place is in one's mind, recollection of exactly how it was originally stated is subject to frequent interpretation. Written goals placed where they can be seen become an important force in setting daily priorities.

### Case Study

Assignment

1. Fill out your own Personal Assessment sheet (see p. 16). Save it for future reference.
2. Turn to *The Real Estate Investor's VIP List* following Chapter 20 and complete the first three items:
   (1) City hall
   (2) City manager
   (3) Mayor
   Be sure to get the name of the secretary. She or he may be your primary contact with that principal.

## PERSONAL ASSESSMENT

**Name:**_____

**Date:**_____

**Age:**____

**Education:**_____

**Jobs held:**_____

**Abilities:**_____

**Strengths:**_____

**Weaknesses:**_____

**Financial data—**

   **Cash in the bank:**_____

   **Monthly salary:**_____

   **Debt items:**_____

   **Fixed expenses to cover debt:**_____

   **Other monthly expenses:**_____

   **Monthly savings:**_____

**Time—**

   **Hours worked each week:**____

   **Days off:**____

**Five-year long-range goal:**_____

_____

_____

**First-year intermediate minigoals:**_____

_____

_____

# 2
# Basic Real Estate Terminology

## Chapter Goals

This chapter introduces the reader to the basic terminology that any savvy real estate investor would be expected to know and understand. The primary goal of this chapter is to acquaint the reader with these basic terms so that the reader will be able to move easily through this book. The terms contained within this chapter are by no means a full glossary of real estate terminology; however, they are the most basic elements dealing with real estate investing.

Before reviewing this, or any list of terms, the reader should be aware of the following three factors that govern most terminology.

## Key Terms

- KISS
- Not universal
- Due diligence

Review each in detail.

## KISS

*Keep It Simple Silly* is a good rule of thumb in any kind of business activity. When it comes to doing business, every investor should get into the habit of using plain English and not fancy or legal-sounding terms. Lawyers are well known to flow with the stilted grammar of legal language. While all real estate investors should be able to understand the technical and legal terminology as it applies to real estate, it is not essential that investors actually use the same language themselves. In fact, only lawyers seem to understand their own language.

With the concept of KISS firmly in mind, the reader should become absolutely comfortable with all the terms that are mentioned in this book. At the same time, every potential investor should anticipate that most of the people they deal with may not be as fluent in these terms as they are.

### Not Universal

Not every term is used universally. This factor makes it even more important to understand when a term is used properly and when it is not.

### Due Diligence

*The single most important aspect in real estate investing is due diligence.* The best description of this term or concept is that **due diligence** is the focused attention given to research and study about a specific property being considered for acquisition or sale. The focus given by the investor must be from the point of view of that person's goals, and the research and study should answer the question: "Does this transaction move me closer to my goals?"

Effort extended in research and study without this clear, yet narrow focus can cause many hours, days, or even weeks of wasted time. This time can give other investors the opportunity to go to contract first.

Misdirected due diligence, that is, study and research that is not properly focused, often causes investors to make a decision that directs them away from their goals rather than closer to them.

The complex nature of real estate has made it imperative that the *due diligence* process be completed prior to making any final decisions to buy or sell. The reader will discover that much of this book is dedicated to showing investors how to maximize this due diligence effort.

## The Basic Real Estate Terminology

This chapter divides the basic real estate terminology into five segments, as follows:

1. Getting started
2. Property values
3. Finding the best property to buy

4. Buying and selling techniques

5. Pitfalls in real estate investing

## Getting Started

**acre:** The standard land term. An acre consists of 43,560 square feet (sq ft) of land area. Farm land, commercial sites, and other real estate are often referenced by acre. Prices are also given in this format. For example, a tract of land that consists of 100 acres may be priced at $500 per acre, giving a total price of $50,000.

Home sites are often shown as a quarter of an acre, half an acre, and so on. Developmental land may have a density allowed by the local government, often seen as 5 units per acre, 25 units per acre, and so on. If a developer were to acquire a tract of 100 acres with a density of 10 units per acre, he or she could, without any modification and after obtaining appropriate approvals, build up to 1000 dwelling units on that tract.

A square lot consisting of 1 acre is equivalent to 208.71 ft by 208.71 ft (the square root of 43,560 sq ft). No investor will ever find a lot of this size, but every investor should have a mental image of it. It is a good idea to find a parking lot or other open area that has two sides against a structure (walls, buildings, even hedges will do). Mark off 209 sq ft and walk around this square. Have a friend walk opposite you so you can get the feel and vision of what this simple acre looks like.

**ad valorem tax:** The real estate tax on any specific property. This tax differs from other assessments or charges that may occur. The amount of the tax for any given year is found by multiplying the tax assessment (after any deductions for homestead exemption) by the tax millage rate.

**building codes:** The rules and regulations that govern the methods, materials, and designs used in construction. Each community may vary the overall standards from neighboring communities.

**building permits:** When construction has been approved according to the local building codes, the local authorities usually require that a building permit be obtained (and paid for). This permit may require the contractor to have inspections made at various stages of the work. These periodic inspections ensure that work is being done according to the building codes.

The building and zoning department normally has detailed records of all building permits taken out for work at any specific location or site. If an investor discovers that construction has been done without a permit, a flag of caution should be raised, and the matter should be cleared through the building and zoning department prior to buying the property.

**contingency clause:** Any clause or condition put into an agreement or contract that allows one or both of the parties to the agreement to modify or withdraw from the agreement. One such clause that can be used to deal with possible building and zoning problems could be the following:

> This agreement is conditioned on there being no building code or zoning violations on the property being purchased. The buyer, therefore, has a period of 10 working days to obtain assurances in writing from the governing building and zoning office that there are no existing code violations. Should any violations exist, the seller has a period of no more than 30 days from the date the violations are revealed, and notice thereof given to the seller, to remedy those violations. Without such remedy the buyer has the option to withdraw from this agreement anytime prior to closing, which if elected, will cause this agreement to become null and void.

**demised premises:** The term that describes **leased property**.

**duplex:** This word has two distinct meanings.

1. A duplex may be a building that has two residences under one roof. This two-family building is a good starter home for many investors who live in one part and rent out the other.

2. A duplex is often a home or apartment with two or more levels. In this term there is only one residence referenced.

In the case of a duplex apartment the actual building could comprise any number of residences.

**Federal Housing Administration:** The FHA is an agency within the U.S. Department of Housing and Urban Development that administers many different loan and loan guarantee programs, which can often be a prime source for maximum financing at reasonable interest rates. Mortgage brokers and bankers are the usual source for these loans.

**Federal National Mortgage Association:** The FNMA, which is often called Fannie Mae, is a corporation that buys mortgages from banks, savings and loans institutions, and other loan sources. Most long-term residential financing arranged by banks and other thrift institutions are sold to FNMA or other similar mortgage holders.

**GI loan (also VA loan):** Loans that are insured by the Veterans Administration (810 Vermont Ave., Washington, D.C. 20420) and are available to qualified and eligible veterans (usually 120 days of active duty in the armed forces qualifies). This loan program can provide up to 100 percent of the acquisition funds for a home loan.

**lien:** The name for any obligation that must be discharged that is against a property or person. A lien that is recorded against a property must generally be paid to obtain a clear title.

**market analysis:** A detailed study of an area showing the condition of the market. In the case of real estate, a study should include the following data:

Selling information: A list of all similar properties within the area that have been sold over the past 12 to 24 months. Helpful statistics would indicate how long the property was on the market and the spread between the asking price and the actual selling price.

Available on the market: A list of all similar properties within the area that are currently on the market, their price, and how long they have remained unsold.

Rental data: A list showing available rental and rented properties that are similar to the subject property. Helpful information would be the square footage under roof and the rent prices. This information is a good indicator of value trends because every property has an economic value based on the possible rental income it can produce. A strong rental market with high rent prices indicates a good sales market. Declining rental prices and/or many vacancies of similar properties show a soft sales market.

**master plan:** Most communities have what is called a **master plan**, which is the overall comprehensive plan for the development or redevelopment of the community. This plan goes through frequent change and modification and must be checked periodically. The master plan is a key to the future of any community, as it establishes the priorities for growth. Generally a copy of the master plan can be obtained through the local building and zoning department. Master plans indicate the zoning that is allowed for each area of the community and, where applicable, the density allowed for development of residential units.

**metes and bounds:** A method to describe a parcel of land that details all the boundary lines and the terminal points and angles, an example of which follows.

> From the South West Monument of Section 7, Township 49 South Range 42 East, Broward County, Florida, go 1200 feet due North to a point of Beginning, thence westerly along the right-of-way of McNab Road 300 feet, thence due South 600 feet, thence due East 300 feet, thence due North 600 feet back to the point of beginning.

**offer and counteroffer:** The process by which most real estate is acquired. The art of making an offer and negotiating to a satisfactory conclusion is learned through practice. Each party in a contract needs to keep its own goals clearly in focus and look for the benefits in the transaction rather than be ruled by emotions.

**ordinances:** Each community has "laws" that govern everything from the size of signs to the setbacks from streets. These laws will vary according to many different reasons and are critical, as they govern many aspects of property use. Investors are warned that logic does not always apply in the administration of these rules and regulations. For example, what is being done across the street may not be allowed anymore but has been "grandfathered in" to that specific location and nowhere else. Violations of these laws (which include building and zoning rules and regulations) must be cleared before buying any property.

**PITI:** The principal, interest, taxes, and insurance portion of a mortgage payment. Most institutional lenders collect all four of these items as part of the mortgage payment, escrowing the taxes and insurance to ensure that those two items will be paid when they come due. Some mortgages may only show a P&I payment that excludes the taxes and insurance portion.

**planned unit development:** A zoning classification, also called a PUD, that allows flexibility of design within a subdivision, usually set to a maximum density for the overall property, but which allows the developer to cluster or concentrate the residential buildings to specific parts of the overall site.

**plat:** The actual drawing of a subdivision or part of a subdivision. Most areas of the country require a developer to record a plat of any subdivided land showing the divisions or lots within that property.

**plot plan (site plan):** A drawing showing the footprint of the buildings on a specific property. Excluded in this drawing are any details of the building itself or elevations of buildings. The plot or site plan shows all boundaries and should therefore indicate any encroachment of construction from or to the specific property in question.

**prime rate:** The lowest commercial interest rate charged by banks on short-term loans to their best customers. Many loans are based on a level over the prime rate; for example, a bank may make a commercial loan at 2 points (percentage points) above the prime. If the prime is, at that moment, 6 percent, then the loan would carry an interest rate of 8 percent until the prime either went up or down, requiring an adjustment in the loan rate.

**square foot:** A size that is 12 inches squared. Square footage is a standard measurement and pricing term for anything from land to rental area within a building. It is critical as a measurement of acreage, as 43,560 sq ft = 1 acre. A tract of 10 acres contains 435,600 sq ft. If the price is $2.00 per sq ft, the total price is $2.00 × 435,600 sq ft = $871,200. Rental prices for commercial buildings are usually quoted in either a monthly or annual price per square foot of the area rented. Every investor should be able to recognize the approximate size of 1 acre of vacant land and 1000 sq ft of building size.

**square yard:** An area that is 3 feet squared. Both square yards and cubic yards (3 feet cubed) are used in construction. Concrete, sand, and other similar material are sold by the "yard," which is a cubic yard of material. Carpets are sold in rolls but are priced by the square yard. A square yard is 9 sq ft.

**subdivision:** An area of a community that has been platted independently of adjoining areas. Investors should learn everything about one subdivision prior to expanding to an adjoining one as the best way to become an expert on property in their areas.

**zoning ordinances:** Zoning is the law that establishes the parameters of use to any property. Zoning is not absolute, however, as it can be changed under some circumstances. Zoning varies among communities, and the classifications used to describe zoning use may not be universal. No property should be acquired unless the investor knows the full extent of the zoning ordinances as they apply to that specific property.

## Property Values

**appraised value:** The value established by an appraiser. Appraisals are subject to differing opinions by appraisers, depending to some degree on the intent of the appraiser. If the appraisal is being accomplished by the local real estate tax authority, the resulting value may only take into account the property size, building square footage, and age of the construction, whereas an appraisal ordered by a property owner to show maximum value possible usually shows comparable properties that are on the market or that have been sold which support a higher value. Investors should not trust any appraisal offered by the seller as justification of value; while such an appraisal may be accurate, investors need to examine other information as well.

**basis:** The term that describes the "book value" of any asset. In real estate, basis is the price you paid for a property *plus* any capital improvements made to it, *less* any depreciation (or asset write-off) taken for tax purposes. Basis is important because it is the amount that establishes your capital gain. If you buy a building for $100,000 and add a second floor at a cost of $30,000, you have an adjusted basis of $130,000. Subtract the depreciation you took of $20,000, and your final basis is now $110,000. If you sell the building for $200,000, your gain is $90,000 ($200,000 − $110,000 = $90,000).

**buyer's market:** The market condition that is favorable to the buyer.

**cash flow:** The amount of cash from an income-producing property left at the end of any period (monthly or annually) after all expenses and debt service have been deducted. This is one of the major benefits obtained from investing in income-producing property.

**economic conversion:** The act of converting one property use to another. This is one of the best ways to increase rental income in a property and is measured against the cost to effect the conversion. For example, after a study of the rental market, an investor realizes that the income from an apartment building can be tripled by a conversion to offices. If the cost to convert allows a greater yield after the conversion, then this economic conversion would be worthwhile. However, the added cost to convert plus additional management may reduce the overall yield and total benefits to the property owner and may not be worth doing.

**loan-to-value ratio:** A term used by lenders that shows the ratio of the debt to the actual value of a property. If a home is worth $150,000 and there is a total debt of $75,000 outstanding, the loan-to-value ratio is $75,000/$150,000, or ½ loan and ½ equity. This term may be quoted as a percentage, the above example being 50 percent loan to value.

**market value:** A term that describes the presumed value for which a specific property will sell in any given market condition.

**seller's market:** The market condition that is favorable to the seller.

**tax assessment:** The actual annual ad valorem tax that the local taxing authority levies on any given property. It is worthwhile to compare this assessment and the corresponding tax appraisal value to those of surrounding properties of similar nature to see if these values are in line with each other. If the tax assessment is greater than the general average, it is possible that the tax assessment can be reduced through negotiations with the taxing authority. In any event, any shift from the average should be examined to determine the reason for the shift. Perhaps the taxing authority has information that could be important to any prospective investor.

**title insurance:** A form of insurance designed to protect the buyer against title problems following the acquisition of a property. This is a very important form of insurance, and most lenders require that it be in place for their own protection. However, this insurance is also very tricky in that, unless carefully examined, it may leave the insurer loopholes to avoid payment to the investor if certain problems arise. Recent surveys and plot plans are generally required to close any of the insurer's loopholes.


## Finding the Best Property to Buy

**broker versus realtor:** Registered real estate brokers and salespeople are licensed by the state and are not necessarily realtors. Realtors are brokers or salespeople who also belong to a local board of realtors. Realtors agree, among themselves, to abide by rules that can offer some additional protection to their clients and prospects over and above state regulations. Other in-house services that the local board of realtors provide to their members can also be an aid to investors in buying or selling their property. In terms of effectiveness, dealing with a broker, whether a realtor or not, becomes a personal relationship, the success of which depends on the qualifications of the salesperson more than anything else.

**builder-developer:** Often the best source for property in a buyer's market. These people are in the business of selling their own real estate, and if they have an inventory of unsold property that is eating a hole in their pockets because of high interest payments and carrying costs, they can become highly motivated sellers capable of working out a good deal for any buyer.

**code violations:** A violation on a current city building code can occur when the building was constructed to conform to an older code—or the builder "cut corners" and an inspector found the violation. Many such violations must be corrected. This is a problem for the owner, but perhaps an opportunity for the buyer; for example, when a property has a building code violation that can cause hardship for the current owner, he or she may suddenly become a motivated seller. Because codes change from time to time, this kind of situation can catch a property owner at a difficult time. For example, the state changes the building code for fire protection and now requires buildings of a certain category to have fire sprinklers installed. A sudden added investment of $20,000 to accomplish that work may be more than an owner wants or has to spend. The property is put on the market at a reduced price—or, to raise the $20,000, the owner decides to sell off another property at a bargain price.

**foreclosure:** A lender forecloses on a delinquent loan and the property is "sold" at a foreclosure sale. This sale is a form of auction, usually advertised in the local newspaper's legal announcement section or in legal publications available to the public. One or more of the lenders may bid at the auction to cover or protect their investment (via the loan) in the property. If the lender is the high bidder, then the title to that property goes to the lender, who later attempts to resell it or put it into use and operate it. All institutional lenders, including VA and FHA, end up with "real estate owned" (REO), or foreclosure properties, and are a prime source for good buys.

**FSBO:** **For sale by owner** is often the first sign that a property is for sale. Many owners feel they are better equipped to sell their own property than listing it with a real estate agent (broker or realtor), to avoid paying a commission. Many buyers feel that they can make a better deal dealing directly with the seller because there is no commission in the way. The reality is usually different, however, as direct confrontation between buyer and seller can create problems when emotion gets in the way of a successfully negotiated deal. Nonetheless, when properly handled, FSBOs can be a good source for good buys.

**management problems:** One of the prime reasons people sell income property. It is not uncommon for professionals to invest in income property only to discover later that they do not have the time to manage the property themselves and that the cost of management is too expensive to maintain the desired return on their cash invested. The proper function of a comfort zone will enable investors to discover who owns the property within that zone. The investor can find and approach such owners before the property is actually placed on the market and exposed to every possible buyer in the area.

## Buying and Selling Techniques

**addendum:** An attachment to any offer or counteroffer, often containing additional terms and conditions to the deal. In a series of counteroffers, care must be taken to ensure that each contract is complete and that each party has all the addenda that may become attached during the back-and-forth negotiating process.

**adjustable rate mortgage (ARM):** Any mortgage with an interest rate that is adjusted during the loan term. Usually the adjustment is tied to a periodic (quarterly, annual, etc.) change in the prime or another commonly acceptable interest rate.

**annual cap:** In adjustable rate mortgages it is important to the borrower that the loan have an annual or even a maximum cap under which the rate can be adjusted upward. This protects the borrower from excessive interest rates.

**balloon mortgage:** A mortgage that becomes due and payable in advance of the payment schedule set. For example, Able borrows $400,000 from Brown and sets up a 20-year repayment plan as though he were going to pay back the money over that length of time. However, the mortgage note requires all unpaid principal to **balloon**, that is, become due and payable at the end of a shorter period of time, say, 5 years. Able must then either pay Brown out of his own pocket, or refinance the loan with Brown or another lending source.

**blanket mortgage:** A mortgage that covers more than one property. Often, lenders want additional security when an investor borrows against a new acquisition. The lender wants to lower the loan-to-value ratio and to do that may insist on other property added as security.

**closing:** In real estate terms, this is the moment when the contract is transacted and each person fulfills his or her role under the terms and conditions of the agreement. In a sale, it is the moment when the title is deeded to the buyer and the seller gets the proceeds of the sale.

**escrow deposit:** The amount of deposit held by another party. In buying or leasing, the owner or his or her lawyer or agent generally holds a deposit in escrow from the buyer or tenant. Realtors are required to provide a separate bank account to hold such deposits; they are responsible for these accounts and must keep careful records. In the event of a dispute over the disposition of an escrow deposit, some third party—a court or arbitration board—may be called upon to intervene prior to either party to the agreement being able to use or recover the escrow deposit. Investors should never place a deposit in escrow unless they know the legal obligations of the holder of those funds and what is necessary for the investor to get the money back in the event the contract is not accepted or fails to close.

**first mortgage:** The mortgage that is recorded first or that has a previously recorded mortgage subordinated to it. The bold banner that says *First Mortgage* may not actually describe the document itself. The law provides that mortgage liens are ranked in the order they are recorded, unless there is an agreement that allows a subsequently recorded mortgage to have priority over a previously recorded mortgage (subordination occurs when a lien holder allows a subsequent lien holder to have a superior claim on the security). This aspect is important because an unscrupulous person may actually have more than one "first mortgage" on a property with each mortgagee (the lender) thinking they are first in order of priority when in reality they are not. All investors should have a title search to show all liens of record both before the closing and immediately prior to recording their own title to ensure that no additional liens have been recorded in the interim.

**fixed rate mortgage:** A mortgage that has a fixed interest rate for the whole term of the mortgage.

**graduated payment mortgage (GPM):** This is a mortgage in which the payment changes over the term of the mortgage. Often the payment starts out lower than it ends up, to enable an investor time to get situated in the property. If the payment is less than would be sufficient to pay interest, the unpaid interest is added to the principal due, and the mortgage amount owed can actually grow over a period of time until the payment increases sufficiently to start to reverse that trend. These mortgages must be fully understood by the investor, and the investor should be aware that the presumed positive leverage of these mortgages is due to payments that are actually less than the interest rate charged.

**installment sale:** This is a method of a sale allowed by the Internal Revenue Service that allows the seller to spread the tax due on a gain over the period of time from which the seller receives that gain because he holds a purchase money mortgage. If Brown holds a $400,000 mortgage from Able that provides for $40,000 per year of principal payments, then Brown will pay tax on the percentage of that $40,000 which is gain. The installment sale is a good tool for a seller to use when there might be a large tax to pay on a gain, and the interest rate the seller can get from the buyer is more attractive than taking cash and reinvesting it into the market.

**institutional lender:** Any lender who is a public entity licensed to lend money, such as savings and loans institutions, commercial banks, thrift institutions, mortgage bankers, insurance companies, credit unions, etc.

**kicker:** Something a party to a contract wants over and above the terms offered, often in the form of extra security or benefits. Lenders may want a percent of income over and above a set or flexible amount. Sellers may want to stay on in the property for a period of time rent-free, and so on. There are numerous forms of kickers.

**loan assumption:** When an investor assumes a loan, he or she relieves the mortgagor of the obligations they have on that loan. When property owners go to banks to get loans, they give the banks or other lenders mortgages. The mortgage is evidence of the security given and is accompanied by a mortgage note, which is the document that details the repayment of the loan. The lender (the mortgagee) looks to the original borrower (the mortgagor) as the responsible and liable party to that loan. With the sale of that property, the mortgagor will want the new buyer to assume the loan. Some lenders restrict or prohibit assumption, so each loan must be reviewed to ascertain what, if any, restrictions the lender can or will impose. Frequently lenders require a fee and extensive documentation to allow loan assumption. Investors should never rely on verbal assurances from any source on this or any loan information and should review the actual mortgage document and note as well as obtain an **estoppel letter** (legal assurance of the status), showing the circumstances of the loan.

**mortgage constant rate:** A shortcut insiders use to calculate mortgage payments. The constant rate is a combination of principal payback and interest. A 20-year self-amortizing loan of $100,000 at 9 percent interest will be paid off at the end of 240 equal payments of $899.75 (per month). This is found by looking at the mortgage interest constant rate Table A-1 in the Appendix of this book for a 20-year term at 9 percent. The constant rate shown is 10.797. This rate is based on 12 monthly payments of both principal and interest. To get the actual monthly payment, an investor would multiply the constant rate times the principal amount owed at the start of the term (20 years). Remember that we are dealing with percentages, so the math would look like this: 0.10797 × $100,000 = $10,797. Divide $10,797 (the annual total) by 12 to get the monthly payment of $899.75. All investors should memorize several constant rates applicable to the current market place so that quick calculations can be made to arrive at payments for self-liquidating mortgages. Below are four such rates.

| Mortgage | Constant rate |
|---|---|
| 8 percent for 15 years | 11.468 |
| 8 percent for 25 years | 9.262 |
| 9 percent for 15 years | 12.171 |
| 9 percent for 25 years | 10.070 |

**purchase money mortgage (PMM):** Any mortgage the seller takes back in a transaction. If Able sells his home and there is both a first and second mortgage already in place that the buyer is to assume, and Able holds a third mortgage, then Able has taken back a 3 PMM.

**second mortgage:** The mortgage that is in second place in the recording of mortgage liens. Unless there are other provisions that subordinate (cause it to become inferior) this mortgage to future debt, the second mortgage will automatically become the first mortgage on the satisfaction (payoff) of existing first mortgage liens.

**subject to:** A phrase used in contracts of great importance. A buyer who takes a property "subject to" the existing debt does not assume that debt but merely acknowledges that he or she is aware of the debt and the rights of the mortgagee. Because the buyer has not legally assumed the obligations of the seller (or existing mortgagor), if the buyer were to default on the payments and the lender had to foreclose, the buyer could lose the property but would not be liable for any deficiency if a foreclosure sale did not produce sufficient funds to cover the debt and cost. The last mortgagor to assume the obligation could be held liable.

## Pitfalls in Real Estate Investing

**accrued interest:** Outstanding interest that has not been paid, either by agreement or in default. When buying any property, obtain an **estoppel letter** from the lender. This letter will indicate the status of the mortgage and show the outstanding principal and any unpaid interest or other charges.

**adverse possession:** A function of law that varies from state to state. Because a title can ultimately be transferred to another person by adverse possession, investors should be aware of the possible danger. Because **adverse possession** must be *actual, hostile, notorious, exclusive, continuous, and under claim of right,* the claim is very hard to impose, but it can be raised against an absentee owner who may not be aware of what is going on. With an inspection of the site and a recent survey or plot plan showing locations of buildings and possible encroachments from neighbors, most adverse possession problems are quickly spotted. If any problems are evident they should be rectified prior to closing on a sale *even if there is no claim being made by the adverse party at that time.*

**cloud on title or title defect:** When the chain of title (history of ownership) to a specific property is examined by the buyer's closing agent (lawyer or title company), it is possible to discover an unsatisfied lien or an improperly executed document from a prior sale, mortgage satisfaction, or other legal action. These items represent a cloud or title defect that should be remedied prior to the buyer's taking title. In some cases the defect is so minor that the buyer may close and take title, aware of the problem.

**closing costs:** The cost of preparation of all the documents between the buyer and seller to effect a transfer between the two parties. There may be a "normal" division of these costs between the two parties, but in reality whatever is mutually agreed to in the contract is what is followed.

**cost of living (COL):** Found in many leases and in some mortgage interest calculations; also called COLA for cost of living adjustments. Its purpose is to make periodic adjustments in payments to adjust for increases (or less likely decreases) in the annual cost of living. The U.S. Bureau of Labor Statistics publishes a monthly Consumer Price Index that tracks the changes in the cost of living. This index is rather comprehensive and is divided by regions of the United States as well as by specific services and commodities. The usual index to be used in COL adjustments is the *All Item Index.*

A lease that called for annual COL adjustments in rent to begin at the end of the 10th year of a 30-year lease could have a massive increase in rent for the 11th year on if the adjustment went back to day one of the lease. On the other hand, if the adjustment at the end of the 10th year only took into account the increase between the start of the 10th year and the start of the 11th year, a modest and likely acceptable increase would occur. The key in understanding COL adjustments is to know which index and what base year (the start of calculations) are being used.

**due on sale clause:** A clause any lender can insert into a mortgage. This provision requires a seller to pay off a loan (unless the lender agrees to some other circumstance at the time) when the property is sold. If this provision is in any existing mortgage, the prospective buyer must satisfy the lender's requirements. Most lenders expand on this clause by including **long-term lease** as an event that would cause the mortgage to become due and payable. Provisions such as this in mortgages are good examples why every detail of a mortgage and the corresponding promissory note should be read and understood prior to assuming the obligations of that loan.

**emotion:** Emotion is the human factor that can get into the way of making a sound business decision. Salespeople love to "push the buttons" that turn buyers on, and smart buyers know their own weaknesses and try (often unsuccessfully) to keep emotion out of their decision making.

**government controls:** Regulatory controls in the real estate business abound from the federal level down to local subdivisions. Every real estate investor must be aware that governmental controls and bureaucracy can greatly affect the use of and cost to use real property.

**grandfather clauses:** When changes in local rules and regulations are enacted, it is not uncommon that the prior use, which is now nonconforming (not permitted under the changed rule or regulation), is allowed as a "grandfather right." For example, a building being used for auto repair may be in an area rezoned to allow only clean business activities. As long as the "grandfather right" is in effect, the auto repair shop can continue to operate. But the owner may not be allowed to alter the building in any way, including replacement in the event of a fire or other casualty, without now conforming to the current laws.

**land lease:** The land lease is a financing technique that is frequently used by both buyers and sellers to good effect. However, when using this technique or acquiring a property that has a land lease in effect, it is important to understand all the terms and their ramifications contained in the lease. The seven critical areas are as follows:

1. Cost of living adjustments

2. Subordination clauses

3. Default remedy

4. Options to buy

5. Exact dates of required notices

6. Renewal options

7. Termination provisions

**management:** Most real estate requires some form of management, and real estate investors of income properties will quickly discover that management problems can be the number one reason why that category of property is offered for sale. Investors who own income-producing real estate are most successful when they have solved management problems.

**percolation:** Refers to the drainage of water into the ground. Some areas of the country have very poor percolation. If a property under consideration had to have a septic tank (because sanitary sewers were not available), or "green" areas to absorb rain water within the property, problems could occur or greater than anticipated expenses could be incurred due to poor percolation.

**rising interest rates:** Adjustable mortgages can look very attractive when the rates are low, but they can rise suddenly when economic conditions change. Investors should know and fully understand the maximum that any rate can reach. Most adjustable mortgages have a cap that the rate cannot exceed over any period or for the life of the loan.

**tax liens:** Evidence that there is unpaid tax owing as a result of IRS or another taxing authority's actions against the property owner.

**subordination:** A provision that allows a lien to become payable ahead of one already recorded. Baker sells a vacant lot to Allen and holds back a $100,000 mortgage. Allen plans to build an office building on the lot and needs to get a first mortgage to finance the construction. Baker agrees to subordinate the $100,000 mortgage to another first mortgage to finance the building. If Allen later defaults on the new first mortgage and the property goes into foreclosure, Baker may not be able to collect anything on the $100,000 she is owed. Many land leases have subordination provisions that allow the lessee to finance over the land lease by pledging the land as security to the desired financing. A default on that mortgage could cause the landowner to lose the land in foreclosure.

# Review Items

The reader should review each term that is not clearly understood. In addition, the reader is requested to work on the exercises that follow each of the terms listed below.

**due diligence:** Why would "homework" be the most important factor in real estate investing?

**prime rate:** Check with a local commercial bank in your area or in the local newspaper and make note of the current prime rate.

**subdivision:** Call the local building and zoning office for your city. Give them the address where you live or work and ask for the legal address and if one exists, the name of the subdivision where that address is located.

**economic conversion:** Because this concept is very important and will be discussed in more detail in this book, while talking to the building and zoning office personnel, ask what the zoning is for that same address and what is allowed in that zoning.

**foreclosure:** Get into the habit of looking in the legal section of the classified advertisements of the local newspaper and see if there are any upcoming foreclosures near your address or within your subdivision. If you have time, attend the foreclosure sale (always double-check prior to going to make sure it will be held as scheduled).

**FSBO:** On your way to work take a new route and see if you can find an FSBO. Write down the phone number and find out what is offered and the details of the property.

# 3
# Real Estate Mathematics Made Simple

## Chapter Goals

This chapter divides the elements of real estate math into five segments, and then tackles each to illustrate that real estate math need not be complex. By using charts, tables, an inexpensive battery-operated calculator, the reader can learn how to perform the majority of all math needed to solve real estate investment problems. The primary goal of this chapter is to acquaint the reader with the different kinds of problems that confront investors, to illustrate why the solutions to the problems are so important, and to show how to arrive at simple solutions.

A simple battery-operated calculator can be used for any of the problems contained in this chapter, or for that matter, in this book. However, it is recommended that a calculator capable of printing be used. It is very easy to enter the wrong amount on any calculator, and without a printed record of all entries, checking for errors requires the calculation to be repeated.

Prior to continuing with this chapter, the reader should be comfortable with the operation of the calculator to be used. Special care should be taken to ensure that the decimal is being inserted in the proper location to show dollars and cents.

## Key Terms

- Gross revenue
- Net operating income
- Cash flow

Review each in detail.

## Gross Revenue

This is the total sum of all revenue produced by any income property. Some property owners divide the gross revenue into departmental income; for example, for a hotel the income could be segmented as room revenue, food and beverage revenue, telephone revenue, sundry income, and so on. Rental apartments may divide income between rents collected and miscellaneous income (laundry, shops, etc.).

When reviewing income and expense documentation, it is important to know the difference between actual gross revenue and total gross revenue possible. Actual gross revenue reflects the collections for the period, whereas gross revenue possible assumes that the maximum income possible occurred. Neither of these amounts may reflect normal vacancy factors.

Because most rental apartments have occasional vacancies as leases expire, it is rare for the actual gross rent collected for the year to equal the gross revenue possible for the year. However, when these sums are equal it indicates a **zero vacancy factor**, which is either the sign of very good management or a **unit rental price** that is below the market. The unit rental price can reflect any given factor depending on what is being rented. In the example of rental apartments, the unit rental price would be the price asked per apartment (either monthly or annually). Commercial rentals for office space are usually quoted by the square foot (either monthly or annually), whereas the unit rental price for land is usually given by the square foot or by the acre.

## Increasing Gross Revenue

> *There are only two methods to increase gross revenue from a fixed number of rental units: first, increase the amount of rent; second, reduce the vacancy factor.*

A combination of these two methods is the usual way to achieve maximum results.

When an investor sees a high vacancy factor or a great spread between the potential gross revenue and the actual gross revenue collected, it is likely that some or all of the following problems exist.

*Possible Problems with Rental Properties*

1. Mismanagement

2. Deferred or needed maintenance

3. Temporary problems in area

4. Overstated potential gross revenue

5. Current unit rental prices are too high

An investor would apply due diligence to ascertain which of the five problems existed. Clearly, problems 4 and 5 would suggest an overstated value in the property being reviewed. The first three problems, on the other hand, are exactly the problems that investors often like to see because they are indications that there is potential for the investor to increase the revenue.

## Net Operating Income (NOI)

The NOI of any income property is the resulting sum of money left after the operating expenses have been deducted from the actual gross revenue collected. Once an investor has satisfied himself or herself that the actual income collected is reported properly, the review then shifts to the expenses to be deducted.

> *To increase the net operating income once the annual income is fixed, decrease operational expenses.*

The problem with decreasing expenses is that it is easy to cut down on expenses by forgoing the needed new roof for less expensive, yet temporary roof repairs, or to let other normal maintenance chores fall behind. Savvy investors look closely at several years' expenses of any income property to see if there has been a trend of poor or neglected maintenance. In most cases sellers either understate their expenses or fail to account for their own time and effort, which in turn does not represent a *real* cost of operations. The result is a misrepresented NOI.

Potential investors usually need to determine the amount of increase of the actual expenses when they acquire the property rather than ways in which they can be reduced. The best way for an investor to approach the deferred maintenance aspect of the property is to ascertain the cost to put the property into good shape and then add that cost to the intended capital investment. If the investor estimates that repairs and deferred maintenance will cost $50,000, the investor should add that $50,000 to the cost of the investment. Once a property has been upgraded, the annual expense to maintain the property in good repair can more easily be estimated.

## Cash Flow

Cash flow is also called **the bottom line**, and is found by deducting the actual debt service from the net operating income. The debt service is the actual cost of the repayment of borrowed funds, including the principal portions of any mortgage. Cash flow is strictly the accounting for actual money taken in, less those funds paid out. It does not show the true yield on the invested funds because other factors, such as income tax and equity buildup, are not taken into account. However, cash flow is an important factor for all investors.

> *To increase cash flow with a fixed NOI, the cost of debt must be reduced.*

This approach generally uses **creative financing** as the primary technique to reduce the actual cost of debt service. Clearly, if a $100,000 mortgage with an annual debt service of $17,000 can be reduced (or refinanced) to a total annual cost of only $12,000, the resulting cash flow would be increased by $5000. This modest increase in the cash flow could increase the total value of that same property by $50,000 to an investor intent on earning 10 percent on his or her invested capital.

## The Five Sectors of Real Estate and Simple Math Techniques to Solve Their Problems

1. Property
2. Building
3. Financing
4. Yield
5. Equity buildup

### Property

Land has value primarily because of its location and use allowed. The value of land is usually given in one of these three basic terms:

1. Square footage
2. Front footage
3. Usable area

**Square Footage Price.**  (Remember that an acre consists of 43,560 square feet.) Commercial lots and building rental prices are usually quoted per square foot.

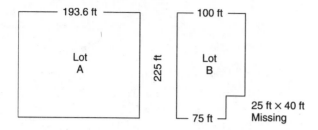

*To find the square footage of lot A:*

Multiply 193.6 × 225 = 43,560 sq ft

The price is $5.00 per square foot. To find the total price of lot A:

Multiply 43,560 sq ft × $5.00 = $217,800

If the price was quoted as $200,000 and the price per square foot needed to be determined:

Divide $200,000 ÷ 43,560 = $4.59 per sq ft

*To find the square footage of lot B:*

Multiply 100 × 250 = 25,000 sq ft

Deduct the missing corner:

Multiply 25 × 40 =   1,000 sq ft

Resulting square footage = 24,000 sq ft

The price quoted is $5.00 per sq ft:

Multiply 24,000 × $5.00 = $120,000

which is the total price. If the price was quoted as $100,000 and the price per square foot needed to be determined:

Divide $100,000 ÷ 24,000 = $4.16 per sq ft

**Front Footage Price.**   In an area where all the property is more or less the same depth, prices are often quoted per front foot.

If in the above drawings for lots A and B, the road frontage was 193.6 and 100 ft, respectively, these tracts, each having more or less the same depth, could be priced per front foot.

Lot A: Priced at $217,800. Find the front footage price:

Divide $217,800 ÷ 193.6 = $1,125.00 per front foot

Lot B: Priced at $120,000. Find the front footage price:

Divide $120,000 ÷ 100 = $1,200.00 per front foot

**Usable Area Price.**   This method of finding a price is one of the *best* ways
to compare similar properties that may have different **usable area** due to
setbacks or other restrictions. This is important because it is possible for two
identically sized lots to vary in the actual land area available to construction. A corner lot, as an example, may have greater setbacks from the two
streets it fronts than an inside lot of the same dimensions. Look at the following lot size and the setback rules described.

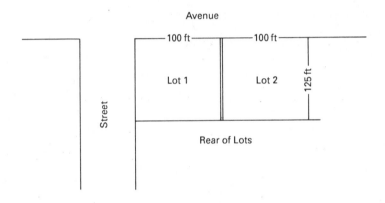

Setbacks for the above two lots establish how close to the lot lines a building
can be constructed.

*Setbacks According to Local Ordinances for These Lots*

From any street or avenue: 35 ft

From any side lot line: 10 ft

From any rear lot line: 20 ft

The following drawing on p. 39 shows the usable area within each lot.

If lots 1 and 2 were commercially zoned and equally priced, the investor
would have to weigh the advantage of being on the corner versus the loss of
usable area on which a building could be constructed. Initially one might
conclude that corner lots are not worth as much as inside lots, but for commercial use there can be substantial advantage to corner exposure because
of ease in access and visibility. However, access by car can often be restricted
at corners due to heavy traffic at some intersections, making corner lots
even less attractive. In such circumstances, the traffic flow may be better
toward the middle of the block, the inside lots, especially if there is a double left-turn lane that enables traffic to turn left or to make U-turns from
either direction.

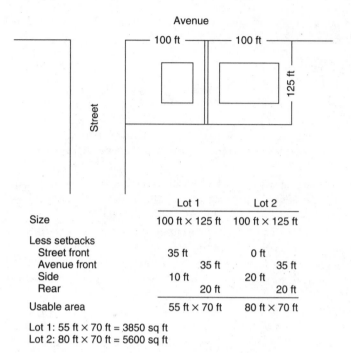

| | Lot 1 | Lot 2 |
|---|---|---|
| Size | 100 ft × 125 ft | 100 ft × 125 ft |
| **Less setbacks** | | |
| Street front | 35 ft | 0 ft |
| Avenue front | 35 ft | 35 ft |
| Side | 10 ft | 20 ft |
| Rear | 20 ft | 20 ft |
| Usable area | 55 ft × 70 ft | 80 ft × 70 ft |

Lot 1: 55 ft × 70 ft = 3850 sq ft
Lot 2: 80 ft × 70 ft = 5600 sq ft

If building size was the most important criteria to an investor, then lot 2 would be a better buy if the price per square foot was the same. If the price per usable area was the same and the allocated area of lot 1 sufficient for the required construction, *and the street access acceptable,* then the corner lot would be more attractive in a near-price comparison.

Investors should be aware that setbacks are not the only element that can restrict the amount of usable land that a property owner ends up with. Other factors can include the following.

- Utility easements: These areas are reserved for public utilities, usually within front or side setbacks but can run through a property.

- Density allowed: Often a property that fronts along one street or avenue has a different set of requirements from its adjoining neighbor that fronts another street or avenue.

**Calculating Square Footage of Odd-Shaped Lots.** Sometimes the odd-shaped lot is really a rectangle with one or more pieces missing. Such was the case of lot B shown earlier that had a 25 ft by 40 ft corner missing. In this example the square footage for what would be the whole lot is found and the missing area is subtracted from the whole. However, many odd-shaped lots are not as simple and follow property lines that are on unusual angles or curves. Signing up for a course in geometry is not necessary for these calculations, because in almost every situation you will be able to rely on one of three simple solutions.

1. Look at county deed records.
2. Tie the price to verifiable square footage.
3. Tie the price to usable area.

*County Deed Records.* In most areas of the United States, the local county property records contain information that is very helpful to real estate investors. One such bit of information that, when available, is usually accurate is the gross size of the property. This information may be stated in square footage or in acreage. In the case of lots that are smaller than 1 acre, the acreage shown will be in a decimal fraction, such as 0.624 acres.

When the area is shown in square feet you need go no further in your calculation, but if shown in acreage you may want to convert to square feet.

*How to convert acreage to square footage:* One acre contains 43,560 sq ft. Therefore the number of square feet in any acreage size would be the result of multiplying 43,560 by the number or fraction of acres.

A tract of land consisting of 0.624 acre would contain 27,181.44 sq ft ($0.624 \times 43,560 = 27,181.44$ sq ft).

A quarter of a section (a section is a tract of land approximately one mile squared) would contain 80 acres or $80 \times 43,560 = 3,484,800$ sq ft. Because a quarter of a section is 80 acres, keep in mind that a *whole section* will contain approximately 320 acres. Use of the word *approximately* will be clarified shortly. The United States is divided into **townships**. Each township contains 36 sections and is a square (more or less) six miles on each side. Because of the curvature of the earth, adjustments are made to some of the sections within a township that cause a slight variation in their size. However, every property in the United States is defined within a specific section or sections located in a specific township.

*How to convert square footage to acreage:* There are times when the square footage is known and the amount of acres is desired. To convert square footage to acreage, divide the amount of square feet by 43,560.

*Problem: Find the number of acres in a tract of land that is 4000 ft by 1360 ft.*
1. Find the square footage: $4000 \times 1360 = 5,440,000$ sq ft.
2. Convert to acreage: $5,440,000 \div 43,560 = 124.88$ acres.

*Problem: Find the number of acres in a lot that is 250 ft by 300 ft.*
1. Find the square footage: $250 \times 300 = 75,000$ sq ft.
2. Convert to acreage: $75,000 \div 43,560 = 1.72$ acres.

*Tie the Price to Verifiable Square Footage.* Assume that an investor has done his or her due diligence and is satisfied that if a property can be bought for no more than $4.00 per square foot, the investment will be very attractive. The problem is that due to the shape of the property, no one, including the county property record keeper of really odd-shaped property, may provide the exact square footage of the property. In these situations the investor may draw an offer based on the seller's estimation of the square footage but limits the offer so that it does not exceed a set per square foot price.

For example, Charlie wants to buy the whole end of a block to build a medical office building. The property fronts three meandering streets and contains two wide arcs at each of two corners. The seller states that the site is approximately 4.5 acres.

Find the total square feet in this tract.

$$4.5 \text{ acres} \times 43,560 \text{ sq ft} = 196,020 \text{ sq ft}$$

Charlie knows he cannot pay more than $4.00 per square foot and have the project succeed, so he offers $784,000 ($80.00 less than what $4.00 × 196,020 would equal). He puts the following condition in the agreement:

Said price to be adjusted at closing to be the lesser of $784,000 or $4.00 per square foot of the actual square footage of the property being purchased. Said square footage to be calculated by a certified property surveyor.

In this provision Charlie has set the maximum he will pay as $784,000 even if the property turns out to be slightly larger than the 4.5 acres the seller believes it to be.

*Tie the Price to Usable Area.*    In situations when the property must be *platted* or when *site plans* must be approved, the investor may not know in advance what the end usable area will be. This uncertainty occurs because in each of these two situations local governing authorities, such as the Department of Transportation, school boards, environmental groups, utility corporations, etc., may require easements or dedications or additional setbacks. As this process can be long and expensive, the investor may want to have a provision that would tie the price of the land to the final **usable product**.

If Charlie knew that in this approximately 4.5-acre commercial site for his medical office building he needed an absolute minimum area of 4.1 acres of usable land, then he would tie the offered price to that smaller number.

1. Find square footage: 4.1 acres × 43,500 sq ft = 178,596 sq ft.
2. Find square footage price at a gross price of $784,000 (divide price by square feet): $784,000 ÷ 178,596 sq ft = $4.38.

This indicates an increase to the per square foot price, but in the original contract Charlie had tied the final price to the usable land area which was allowed as a result of platting. Naturally, Charlie would show the price as "not to exceed $784,000."

## Building

The square footage of a building is found in the same way as that of vacant land. However, many buildings are not simple rectangles, but in essence a combination of rectangles. To find the square footage of a typical home may require dividing the home into its rectangular parts and adding them once each box or rectangle has been measured.

**Gross versus Net Area.**   With most commercial rental property, there are two areas that are important to know. The **gross area** is the total floor space of any building. This area can be found by taking the outside measurements of a building, finding each floor's gross area, and multiplying that area by the number of floors.

For example, the outside measurements of a building 100 ft by 150 ft would give a gross floor area of 15,000 sq ft. If the building had five stories and each floor was the same size, then $15,000 \times 5$ would indicate the building had a total gross area of 75,000 sq ft.

If this were a rental building, note that not all the area in a building is rentable. There are corridors, stairwells, elevator shafts, equipment rooms, maintenance areas, and the like. Each of these nonrentable areas need to be calculated and deducted from the gross area to arrive at the **net rental area**.

In a simple, single-story building, such as a strip shopping area or **free-standing building**, the gross area and the net rental area can actually be equal. In comparing the values of different properties, knowing the spread between the gross area and the net rental area can be important. Two buildings that appear identical, with the same gross area, may vary substantially in the net rental area. Because rents are usually based on the net rental area, a price comparison based just on gross area could be misleading. Everything else being equal, a greater net rental area would be a selling factor.

## Financing

Begin with the concept of borrowing money. If Patrick borrows $100,000 there will be someone (the lender or mortgagee) who gave him the money. This person or institution expects to get a return in the form of interest to be earned. In addition to interest the lender usually insists on a principal payment against the amount of the loan outstanding. In the case of institutional lenders (banks, thrift organizations, savings and loans institutions, etc.) there may also be a payment from which the lender saves to pay the annual real estate tax and often property insurance as well as other charges such as loan insurance, etc.

If Patrick's $100,000 loan was at an annual interest rate of 9 percent per annum and nothing more, Patrick would pay $9000 of annual interest each year with the outstanding balance of $100,000 still due at some future date. Some mortgages are stated in those terms, as in the following.

> Said $100,000 shall accrue interest at the rate of 9% per annum payable on the anniversary of the closing of said loan for a period of XX years. At the end of said term the total outstanding principal shall be due and payable.

To calculate the amount of the annual payment in a mortgage such as that just described is simple math.

Principal owed: $100,000

Interest due: 9 percent

Amount of annual interest is found by multiplying the amount of principal ($100,000) by the mathematical equivalent interest (0.09).

$$\$100,000 \times 0.09 = \$9,000.00$$

A more conventional mortgage requires a payment that is a combination of principal and interest. Under the common method used within the United States, investors can use tables of computed values to determine the mortgage payment for most interest rates used for nearly any period of years, from 1 to 40, divided into six-month increments.

Two amortization schedules (Table A-1 for mortgages with monthly payments and Table A-2 for mortgages with annual payments) are provided in the Appendix of this book.

Review the following mortgage example.

> *Loan terms:* $100,000 is lent for a period of 5 years at 9 percent interest per year with five equal annual installments of principal and interest according to Annual Table A-2: Payment is $25,709 per year. (The constant rate of 25.709 is found in Table A-2 in the Appendix under Constant Annual Payments. This constant rate is a combination of interest at 9 percent and the amount of principal needed to make up five equal annual payments to retire the loan.)

Table 3-1 is an example of an annual mortgage with equal annual payments. However, not all mortgages are computed this way. The same amount borrowed could be paid back in an interest-only annual payment with no principal repayment, or could have equal annual principal reduction, which will greatly change the debt service payments. Watch how this simple change from **equal annual payment** to **equal annual principal reduction** changes the amount of each year's payment.

**Table 3-1.** Example of an Amortization Table
Equal Annual Payment

| Principal at start of year | Amount of payment | Interest due end of year | Principal payment due | Principal due at year end |
|---|---|---|---|---|
| $100,000 | $25,709 | $9,000 | $16,709 | $83,291 |
| 83,291 | 25,709 | 7,496.19 | 18,212.81 | 65,078.19 |
| 65,078.19 | 25,709 | 5,857.04 | 19,851.96 | 45,226.23 |
| 45,226.23 | 25,709 | 4,070.36 | 21,638.64 | 23,587.59 |
| 23,587.59 | 25,709 | 2,121.41 | 23,587.59 | 0 |

**Using Amortization Tables.** Take a look at Tables A-1 and A-2 in the Appendix. Table A-1 is used for monthly payment mortgages which call for equal monthly payments with the annual interest rates shown in the tables for the period of years (six-month increments from 0.5 to 40 years). The interest is given in ¼-percent increases, from 8 to 20.25 percent. For example, see the 9 percent line:

| Interest, % | 24.5 yr | 25 yr | 25.5 yr | 26 yr | 26.5 yr |
|---|---|---|---|---|---|
| 9 | 10.126 | 10.070 | 10.018 | 9.969 | 9.922 |

These numbers under the years are the annual constant rates for any loan of the interest rate shown for the years illustrated. In the above example, a $100,000 loan with equal monthly payments at 9 percent for 25 years would have a total annual payment made up of 12 monthly installments with an annual constant rate of 10.07 percent. This means that the total annual debt service, each year for 25 years, would equal the constant rate times the amount of the loan at day one.

$$\$100,000 \times 0.1007 = \$10,070 \text{ annual total}$$

But remember two important factors:

1. Table A-1 provides the total for 12 monthly installments—this means the annual amount must be divided by 12 months to find the monthly payment: $10,070 ÷ 12 = $839.17 per month.

2. When using the constant rates shown in either Table A-1 or Table A-2, convert the percent from 10.07, for example, by moving the decimal two places to the left to obtain 0.1007 in the mathematical equation. If the interest rate was 9 percent for 26 years, the constant would be 9.969. To find the monthly payment would be a similar two-step process.

First multiply the mortgage amount by 0.9969:

$$\$100,000 \times 0.9969 = \$9,969.$$

Second divide the result by 12:

$$\$9,969 \div 12 = \$830.75 \text{ per month.}$$

**Constant Rates.** Savvy investors and most mortgage lenders think in terms of constant rates. These are the actual interest percents that are shown in both Tables A-1 and A-2, which were just discussed. Because the rate is a combination of principal and interest, it will cover the total debt service cost (except for taxes and insurance when applicable). The total debt service is important in arriving at the final **cash flow**, which was discussed earlier in this chapter, so learning several of the more common **constant rates** that will reference the interest rate and term which is currently being offered in the marketplace will help to give a mental picture of financing.

**Preview of Things to Come.** In later chapters the reader will learn how to use the Amortization Tables A-1 and A-2 to find mortgage balances in future years, discount mortgages, and other interesting and helpful shortcuts to real estate financing.

## Yield

Of all the terms used in real estate investing the term **yield** is the most misunderstood and most improperly used. It is therefore important that the reader understand that yield is relative to the point of view or focus.

In general terms, yield is a stockbroker term that references the annual dividend or interest an investment will pay back to the investor. If you invest $10,000 and expect a 10 percent yield at the end of the year, then you should get back a bonus, dividend, or interest of $1000.

As with any investment, if some of the cash to invest is received from someone else (you borrow the money) you have **positive leverage** and can increase your yield by paying less for the borrowed money than you earn.

To be specific, there are two kinds of yield we will discuss:

- Cash on cash yield
- After tax yield

Examine each in the following example.

Bradford buys a 10-unit apartment building at a total price of $300,000. He borrows $225,000 from a local savings and loan institution at 9.75 percent interest for 30 years with equal monthly payments. He invests $75,000 of his cash plus another $5000 of closing cost. His cash out of pocket is $80,000. The apartment complex gives off a solid $33,000 NOI at the end of his first year. Bradford, due to other investments and income, expects to be in the 25 percent income tax bracket. Consider that in this investment $50,000 was land value and $250,000 was in buildings and other items that Bradford can write off for the first year as $11,500 (with IRS approval and blessing). How did he do on his investment?

1. Determine the debt service with the following formula.

Mortgage amount × constant rate = Total annual payment

Look at Table A-1 under the 30 year column for 9.75 percent interest. This shows a constant rate of 10.31 percent. This means that the total annual debt can be found by multiplying the mortgage amount of $225,000 by 0.1031 and dividing the result of $23,197.50 by 12 to get the monthly payment of $1,933.12.

2. Find the cash flow.

| NOI: | $33,000 |
|---|---|
| Less debt service: | 23,197.50 |
| Cash flow: | $ 9,802.50 |

3. Find the cash on cash yield. There is a total of $80,000 invested. What interest rate would pay a dividend of the cash flow, which is $9,802.50? Use the following formula:

$$\text{Cash on cash yield} = \frac{\text{cash flow}}{\text{cash invested}}$$

$$\$ 9,802.50 \div \$80,000$$

The cash flow yield equals 12.2531 percent.

4. Find the after tax yield. To find the actual after tax yield it is necessary to find the actual taxable income from this property. To do this it is necessary to determine three other factors:

   *a.* The mortgage interest paid
   *b.* The principal portion of the mortgage
   *c.* The actual tax that is applicable to the income from the property

To find the mortgage interest and principal, look at Table A-1 under the column for one year less than the years remaining in the mortgage term, in this case, under year 29. The constant rate shown for the 9.75 percent interest is 10.371. The investor wants to find the actual principal outstanding of a mortgage that has 29 years remaining. Use the following formula:

$$\text{Principal outstanding} = \frac{\text{total annual payment}}{\text{annual constant rate}}$$

Because the actual payment is known ($23,197.50 per year), divide by the constant found, which is 10.371 percent.

   *a.* $23,197.50 ÷ 0.10371 = $223,676.60

| Original loan: | $225,000.00 |
|---|---|
| End of year 1: | 223,676.60 |
| Principal paid: | $1,323.40 |

How much of the payment was interest?

|                          |             |
|--------------------------|-------------|
| Total payment:           | $23,197.50  |
| Less principal:          | 1,323.40    |
| *b.* Total interest paid:| $21,874.10  |

*c.* Find the taxable income

Deduct the total interest paid from NOI:

| NOI:                      | $33,000     |                       |
|---------------------------|-------------|-----------------------|
| Less interest on debt     | 21,874.10   |                       |
| Profit:                   | $11,125.90  | (before depreciation) |
| Less depreciation:        | 11,500.00   |                       |
| Profit:                   | (375.90)    |                       |
| Tax bracket:              | × 0.25      |                       |
| Tax benefit from shelter: | 93.97       |                       |
| Add cash flow:            | 9,802.50    |                       |
| Cash benefit after tax:   | $9,896.47   |                       |

Find the yield after tax.

$$\text{After tax yield} = \frac{\text{cash flow after tax}}{\text{amount invested}}$$

$$\text{After tax yield} = \frac{\$9,896.47}{\$80,000.00}$$

$$\text{Yield} = 12.37 \text{ percent}$$

(*Note:* The actual mathematical result will be 0.123705875, which is rounded off and converted to a percent by moving the decimal two places to the right.)

The difference between these two yield calculations simply points out how the debt service is taken into account as well as the introduction of **depreciation**, which is a legal deduction for the economic decline of the value of an asset. To be accurate and true to themselves, all investors should consider the fact that the replacement of assets is a real part of real estate investment. Air conditioners, appliances, roofs, windows, etc., some day will need to be replaced. While the IRS allows investors to deduct a percentage of this ultimate replacement cost every year, many investors do not take the ultimate capital cost to make those replacements into consideration. Why? Because most investors bank on appreciation of value to exceed the actual depreciation. Appreciation is *not* guaranteed, however, and when the economy slows down or when real estate goes through a slump, property values can decline dramatically.

**What Else Is There to Real Estate?**   In certain economic conditions an investor may look to different benefits that result from real estate investments and attempt to structure their investments to maximize those benefits over others. Each of these benefits will affect the yield as well as the concept of that yield. Examine the different benefits that an investment in real estate can generate.

*Twenty Benefits That Can Come with Real Estate Investments*

| | |
|---|---|
| Income stream | Perks from type of investment |
| Financial security | "Free living" |
| Pride of ownership | Family jobs |
| Equity buildup | Great way of life |
| Image desired | Retirement dream |
| Payment for staff | "Free travel" |
| Shelter for other income | Security |
| Something for you to do | Appreciation of value |
| You are your own boss | Responsibility |
| Roots are established | Increase in self-confidence |

While many novice real estate investors do not think beyond the cash flow aspect of real estate or the "roof over their head" concept, the above 20 benefits as well as others that may relate individually to a given investor can become a primary reason why one property will appeal to any specific investor. Each person is, after all, different and each goal unique.

## Equity Buildup

One of the best benefits that comes from some real estate investments is the buildup of equity through the systematic reduction of debt by collection of other people's money in the form of **rent**.

Consider Charlie's apartment complex that cost $305,000 (described earlier in this chapter). He invested $80,000 of his own cash and borrowed the remainder of $225,000. As long as there is sufficient income from the apartment rentals to pay the expenses of the property as well as make the mortgage payment, Charlie can anticipate that when the mortgage has been paid off (30 years in this example) he will have an equity buildup of $225,000. That is an average principal reduction of $7500 per year for 30 years. ($225,000 ÷ 30 years = $7500 per year). Considering that Charlie's investment was $80,000, the equity buildup results in an average of 9.375 percent return (return of $7500 ÷ investment of $80,000).

Some investors choose to pay off debt faster at the sacrifice of cash flow. The end result can be that the investor will end up with debt-free property much sooner. In Charlie's case, if he applied all the current NOI to pay off the loan, it would take less than 11 years to have a free and clear property.

His cash flow at that time, without considering any increased rent along the way, would be $33,000.

**Appreciation.** Appreciation is the increase in value that occurs when the market value of a property increases. This happens for several reasons, which will be discussed in detail in Sec. II, Chap. 7, but the end result of appreciation is that wealth is being created that did not exist before.

If a property goes up 6 percent per year for each year there is a compounding effect to the extent that in approximately 12 years, the value would double.

At 6 percent a $300,000 property would be worth $600,000 in 12 years. This kind of appreciation averages $25,000 per year over the 12-year term.

The actual yield that any investment will generate should not be the sole criteria in selection of which property to acquire, nor should a drop of yield signal the time to sell or otherwise dispose of that investment. In the final analysis each investor should buy or sell based on whether or not the investment moves the investor closer to his or her desired goals.

### Case Study

Roberta Jones has decided she will buy a small apartment building and remodel it to increase the number of rental units it contains. Her plan is to do this so that she can increase the income from the property and build its value. At the same time, Roberta Jones believes that the improved property will command a greater per unit rental rate, adding to her income.

She has narrowed the property selection to the following property.

*Jake's units:* Four units consisting of two 600-sq ft one-bedroom apartments and two 900-sq ft two-bedroom apartments. Each of the one-bedroom apartments is rented for $500.00 per month, and the two-bedroom units are rented for $700.00 per month.

There is a two-car garage in the back of the building and a utility room attached to the garage; this building has a total of 700 sq ft. Roberta has reviewed the owner's operating expenses and believes them to be accurate at $14,800.

All buildings have flat roofs. The property is on a lot that is a 75 ft by 140 ft inside lot with the front 75 ft on the street and an alley in the rear, serving the garage. Building setbacks are as follows: front 25 ft, and parking is allowed within this setback; sides 15 ft; and rear 20 ft. The building location is shown on p. 50.

The price is $120,000. There is a first mortgage of $75,000 payable in equal monthly installments over 20 years at 8 percent interest. The seller has indicated he would take back a second mortgage for as much as $25,000 payable over 8 years at 8 percent interest with equal monthly installments.

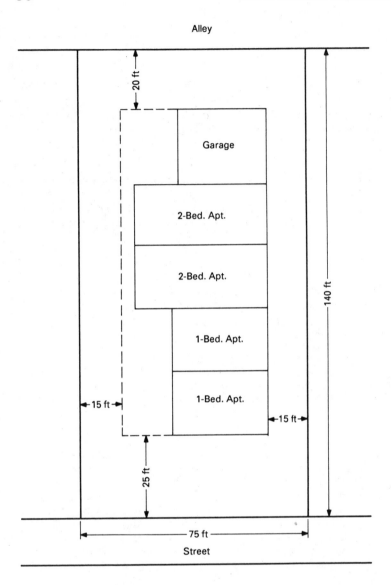

Complete the following:

1. What is the gross income possible?
2. With a 5 percent vacancy, what is the NOI?

Gross income possible:     _____

Less vacancy factor:     _____

Collectable income:     _____

Less operating expenses: _____

Net operating income: _____

3. With the current debt service and the NOI with 5 percent vacancy factor, what is the cash flow?

Net operating income: _____

Less debt service: _____

Cash flow: _____

4. Assume Jones was able to convert the garage and utility room into two studio apartments that would rent for $400 per month each, and *if* the seller took back the second mortgage as indicated. There is an additional $3000 per year of operating expenses due to the added units. Calculate the new cash flow using the debt service as is offered by the seller.

Gross income possible: _____

Less vacancy factor: _____

Collectable income: _____

Less operating expenses: _____

Net operating income: _____

Existing debt service: _____

Seller-held mortgage: _____

Less total debt service: _____

Cash flow: _____

5. If Jones buys the property for $120,000 by putting $20,000 down and assumes the existing debt, with the seller holding the balance with ten interest-only payments each year at 7.5 percent at which time he will pay off the total debt, and Jones spends an additional $5000 to make the needed improvements. Calculate the following:
   *a.* New cash flow
   *b.* Cash on cash yield

*New Cash Flow*

Net operating income: _____

Existing debt service: _____

Seller-held mortgage: _____

Less total debt service: _____

Cash flow: _____

## *Cash on Cash Yield*

Cash down:                     _____

Remodeling expenses:           _____

Total investment:              _____

$$\text{Cash on cash yield} = \frac{\text{cash flow}}{\text{cash invested}}$$

Cash on cash yield = ____ percent

# 4

# Why Local Government Officials Are Important and How to Deal with Them

## Chapter Goals

This chapter introduces the reader to the local bureaucracy that affects real estate usage and ultimately real estate values. The goal of this chapter is to indicate which officials within local government are important to real estate investors and how the investor can develop a working relationship with these people.

## Key Terms

- Building codes
- Building permit
- City manager
- Department of Transportation (DOT)
- Public safety officials
- Utilities

Review each in detail.

## Building Codes

These are the rules and regulations that govern construction procedures and materials for an area. If construction on a property does not meet the required code, violations could be costly to remedy. Virtually every area in the United States has a basic building code developed for the area by the state. Local authorities can and frequently do provide their own enhancements to the state or building codes designed for that part of the state.

## Building Permit

A **building permit** is the official authorization and license needed for construction within most communities. This is issued by the appropriate governing authority (usually the building department), which generally requires plans and drawings showing that the desired construction meets all the rules and regulations that would apply. In almost every instance a fee is paid by the property owner to one or more governing authorities. A building permit to construct a home can be very involved and could require separate approvals and inspections from many departments and agencies such as the fire department, water department, environmental agencies, Army Corps of Engineers, and state and county DOT. In most areas of the country a building permit is required for any work that exceeds a base cost. This cost can be as low as $50.00 and covers virtually anything from minor repairs to major construction. If several contractors or subcontractors are involved, it is also likely that each will have to apply for permits separately. The ultimate purpose for these permits is to ensure that work is done according to the building codes. This is protection for the property owner.

## City Manager

The city manager (or county manager) is a professional hired by the city or county to be the head of business operations. This person is not an elected official but is hired by the city council or county commission, which consists of elected officials. These professionals often retain their position for many years and are very influential and powerful within the community.

## Department of Transportation (DOT)

This authority controls and regulates the roadways in any community. Generally there is a DOT for the local city, another for the county, and a third for the state. If there are toll roads, such as turnpikes, there may be a DOT that specifically deals with those roadways as well.

Road systems are very expensive to build and maintain, and much effort of any Department of Transportation agency goes toward the planning of future needs for any road system. Therefore DOT offices are a wonderful source of growth information. New roadways are one of the primary events that can cause property values to either skyrocket or plummet.

## Public Safety Officials

Public safety officials such as the police, fire fighters, and other ancillary providers such as paramedics compose what is frequently called the Department of Public Safety. These departments are an important source of information about an area. Every investor should know how "safe" a potential investment area of town is. Of these offices, usually only the fire department is directly involved with real estate concerns. Generally, all new construction must meet certain local or state fire codes, and it is the responsibility of the fire department to approve the plans and "sign off" on a set of plans. This signifies that the department has approved the plans pending the final inspections it will make during construction. The fire department also makes periodic inspections of existing buildings to ensure that the property meets the necessary fire protection and fire safety rules and regulations. Every investor would want to know that a property they are about to purchase complies with fire codes either currently imposed or about to come into being.

## Utilities

Utilities (both public and privately owned) consist of water, sewage, garbage and trash removal, gas, electricity, phone, bus and other public transportation, and in some cases, cable TV companies. Each of these utilities has its own structure and plans for the future; each also has its own department heads and bureaucracy. These utilities can affect the values of real estate in a community positively or negatively. Clearly the most dramatic effect would be the lack of an essential utility such as water or sewage. Each of these departments or companies is an excellent source for information about community growth.

# The Four Most Important Areas of Real Estate Bureaucracy

- Building and zoning department
- Elected officials
- Planning department
- Tax assessment office

Review each in detail.

## Building and Zoning Department

Personnel from this office administer the rules and regulations that are contained in the city ordinances directed to the real estate within a community. Almost everything that concerns property will come under the jurisdiction of the building and zoning department at one time or another. Therefore the people who work in this department (it may actually be separated into two departments, one for building and the other for zoning) are excellent sources for any information about property. Even if they cannot answer a question, they usually can direct the inquirer to the right source.

Building permits are issued by this department, and it is also responsible for inspections during building progress as well as ensuring that property is used according to the laws of the community. Within this department will be all the data necessary to discover how a property *can* be used as will be the process for making a change in the zoning that governs property use.

## Elected Officials

In a typical community there are several levels of elected officials, many of whom are very important with respect to real estate. It is helpful for real estate investors to know which of these officials are influential for their type of property investments in order to maximize the benefits that can be obtained from these officials, both directly and indirectly. Virtually all elected governmental officials are chosen by voters from districts: state legislators from certain counties, county commissioners from certain parts of the county, city councilpersons or commissioners from various parts of the city, and so on. Generally an individual would want to know and have the closest relationship with the elected official from the district in which the investor lives, and the next closest, in which he or she invests. Because elected officials vote on matters that affect the whole community, getting to know all officials is helpful. The critical part of getting the most out of a relationship with any elected official is not knowing that person, but that person *knowing you*. Because this process takes time, the reader should start with the most influential areas and expand from there.

But first, look at the total structure of the government for a given area. The following is by no means a complete listing of every possible elected official, but is the list from which readers should focus their efforts to become an "insider" to the system.

*Federal level*—U.S. congresspersons—both senators and representatives from the districts within the state in which the investor lives and invests.

*State level*—state legislators—both senators and representatives from districts in which the investor lives and invests.

*County level*—county commissioners, port authorities (air, sea, river, etc.), school board—all are important but the investor should concentrate on officials who are given special duties within the county commission that gives them influence over specific areas of government that affect the investor the most, such as specific road projects, and water and sewage expansions. In the absence of such circumstances, the investor should begin with the commissioner from the investor's district and expand from there.

*City level*—mayor, vice-mayor, city councilpersons—all are important as are the county commissioners. The investor should be selective in the same way as with the county officials.

## Planning Department

At both the city and county level, an investor should seek out the head of the departments that deal with planning for the future. The development of new roads, widening of existing roads, building of bridges, development of new intersections, changes in zoning rules and regulations, and the like are all key factors in real estate growth. All road planners, for example, take into consideration many growth trends, and most of that information is available to any investor who will take the time to get it.

Road development involves very-long-range planning, partially due to the fact that new roads may require long and costly acquisition of new road rights-of-way and eminent domain procedures. Also, the raising of funds, detailed plans and development drawings, and selection of contractors can give an investor an idea about what is planned or being contemplated for the future.

## Tax Assessment Office

The department heads within the tax assessment division or department of a local government are helpful to know because this department maintains detailed information on all real estate in the county. Data on property owners, prices paid, legal descriptions, and much more is at their fingertips.

Many tax assessors provide much "data search" information to people within the real estate industry. Title insurance companies and real estate lawyers as well as real estate investors can and do use property records sections of the tax assessor. Within these records information is maintained that allows investors to track the ownership of a property, discover the tax assessment, and acquire a wealth of other information about the property and the property owner.

It is not essential for a budding investor to get to know the tax assessor; however, because the tax assessor is another local VIP, adding him or her to the investor's sphere of reference is not a bad idea. The most important aspect of using the tax assessor's department for investment purposes is to know what data is available and how to obtain it.

Fortunately most tax assessor's offices are very patient in teaching newcomers how to get maximum use of the data available. All real estate investors should spend a few days at the tax assessor's office to learn how to tap this vital information source.

## How to Build a Working Relationship with VIPs

### Crystallize Your Self-Image

Any real estate investor who wants to establish working relationships should start with the development of a self-image. This is important because the goal of developing a working relationship is not just to know the mayor or the head of the building department, but *for VIPs to know the investor.*

Credentials are helpful, and a personal card showing the investor's name along with address and phone number provides a future communication link. Equally important is quality stationary, which is an impressive reminder of whom the investor is and how he or she can be reached. Almost any print shop can design and print these items at a modest cost.

Bringing the investor's own name to the attention of important people is what is essential. Remember that KISS strategy works all the time, so when it comes to name cards and personalized stationary, fancy is not the way to go—but quality of paper stock and good taste are.

### Identify the People to Meet

The local newspaper usually publishes (at least once a week) a list of the local elected officials. If that source is not available, then see the county clerk of the court, who has a record of all elected officials within the county. Names of federal and state officials are available as general information from the nearest state government offices. Obtaining the name of building and zoning department heads and the heads of utility departments may require a direct phone call to those offices.

Prior to selecting the first person to meet, the investor should attend a county commission meeting and a city council meeting. This affords the quickest opportunity to see the people in question and to tie their names and faces together.

Seeing people in their workplace—the public meeting—will also provide insight into the type of people they are. Such insight plus later research on the background of these people at the local city library will quickly put the investor at an advantage for that impending first meeting.

### Develop a Plan

Every person on the **plan to meet list** will be responsive to the request for an appointment. However, a sound reason for the appointment is necessary to avoid the awkwardness of wasting a busy person's time. To solve this problem, the investor should approach the situation in a clear, straightforward, and truthful manner. After all, the goal is to establish a good working relationship with the VIP because the investor wants to buy and sell and possibly develop property within an area in which the elected official or other parties have obvious interest.

## Setting up the First Appointment

Start with an elected official within the county sector of government. The commissioner from the investor's own district would be the best place to start. The investor should already know what the commissioner looks like, and will have done some due diligence homework about that person's background. Information that should be discovered are things such as:

- Family background
- Party affiliation
- Years in office
- Other offices or positions held
- Current responsibility and authority

To set up the appointment, call the official's office in a businesslike manner and provide the following information for the appointment secretary:

- Name of the person requesting an appointment.
- Statement that the appointment should not take longer than 15 minutes.
- Reason for the appointment: the caller intends to make investments in the official's district and would like to meet him or her first.

## The First Appointment

The goal of the first appointment is to meet the elected official (or other party). With this firmly in mind, the attainment of that goal is ensured because the follow-up is firmly in the hands of the investor and nobody else's.

**Eight Tips for Success at the First Appointment.**   During the first appointment, follow these tips.

1. Be prompt.
2. Find something to praise immediately.
3. Look successful.
4. Ask a few questions about the future for the official's district.

5. Ask for the name of two (only two) people that the official believes would be important for the investor to meet. It is likely that more than two names will be given.

6. Tell the official that you will keep in touch with the official to apprise him or her of your plans or progress.

7. Do not overstay the visit.

8. Follow up immediately with two thank-you notes: one to the secretary for making the appointment, and the other to the official for sharing his or her busy time.

**What to Do at the Appointment.**    Review the above tips. Most are obvious, but three are absolutely critical for long-range success in becoming an insider as quickly as possible. The first is the element of praise extended at the start of a meeting. A sincerely delivered complement is sure to start any meeting on the right track. Flattery, unfortunately, often comes across as insincere even when it is given with the best intentions. If nothing flattering can be found after due diligence in reviewing the official's history and background prior to the meeting, then praise the secretary, the decor of the office, the official's reputation, or perhaps his or her attending the local university (which would become evident immediately from the framed graduation certificate hung on the wall next to the desk).

The second important element of the first appointment is the request for *two* names of people the official feels would be worth your meeting. I guarantee that any such request will be answered with more than two "important" names. Yet, asking for two people is reasonable. Regardless of the number of names actually offered, care should be taken to obtain their correct titles, the correct spelling of their names, and the best way to reach them.

Later, these persons can be contacted with the honest approach, saying that their names were personally given by "so and so." Name-dropping does play a useful role in becoming an insider.

The third and most essential aspect of any contact is the follow-up. The desired result for the first meeting is to begin the process whereby a working relationship is developed. Nothing will actually come from the first meeting unless the investor initiates an active follow-up program.

## Keys to Make the Follow-up Work

Follow-up occurs in several ways. The most effective follow-up involves the supportive people around the official with whom you met, which is why the thank-you note to the secretary is so critical. Establishing a solid contact with the right hand of the important person is often far more effective and beneficial than having a "so so" relationship with the official. This is not as easy as it might sound, however, as many secretaries consider themselves the first and primary barrier that cannot be breached by anyone other than God. The very best approach is sincerity, which should not be difficult if the primary goals are kept firmly in mind.

The follow-up to the official takes time and should not be rushed. One excellent technique is to draw attention to a relevant newspaper or magazine article during the first appointment and then promise to *send* it to the official. This forms a solid link that serves two very good purposes: (1) It sets up a natural follow-up that does not seem forced. (2) When the follow-up occurs it proves that the investor keeps his or her word.

After the first follow-up note, the next correspondence should be brief notes describing your meeting(s) with those who were recommended as important people to meet. This simple approach will let the official know that (1) you appreciated the introduction, and (2) you are living up to your word to keep him or her informed about your progress.

It should be obvious that if two people are recommended from each appointment, the sphere of reference VIPs will continue to grow for a long time. This method of personal contact is the best and is simply accomplished.

## Long-Range Contact Development

Insurance salespeople are the best at long-range contact development, and their normal routine is a lesson for any prospective real estate investor. The following three steps will ensure the success of long-range contact development.

### Three Steps to Successful Long-Range Contact Development

1. Clip flattering articles and send them to interested parties. Anything that would be of obvious interest to any person you have met will do. Naturally this should not be overdone, but with little effort four articles per year can be found in some local publication that would be of specific interest to a person recently met or who is on the long-term contact list.

2. Put the contacts on a "personal" Christmas list. A personalized card, along with a photograph of you and your family, will ensure they remember what you look like.

3. Maintain respect for the positions of the VIPs. It's okay that they call you by your first name, in fact, you should encourage it, but never drift away from respectful communication.

Review the following case study.

### Case Study

You decide to make your first VIP appointment with the county commissioner that represents your district. With the help of one of the librarians at the city library, you find several articles on the commissioner, providing background information. One point of interest is that the commissioner graduated from one of the state universities. A week prior to the appointment you attend a county commission meeting so you can see how the public meeting is conducted and what the commissioner looks like.

At the appointment you ask the commissioner to recommend two people in city hall who could be helpful to a "new real estate investor to the area." The commissioner gives you two names: (1) the head of the DOT for the city and (2) an official in the building department who "has been around forever."

*Complete the following:*

1. At the first appointment with the commissioner, you should _____.
   *a.* Make sure to get the name of the commissioner's secretary.
   *b.* Mention an article you clipped out of a recent magazine about the university the commissioner attended.
   *c.* Make sure to get the correct spelling and phone numbers of the people the commissioner recommended.
   *d.* All of the above.
2. Your *primary* goal at this meeting was to _____.
   *a.* Build a sphere of contacts with local VIPs.
   *b.* Establish a solid rapport with the commissioner.
   *c.* Make sure to get the secretary's phone number.
   *d.* Begin the process of building a rapport with the commissioner.
3. Turn to The Real Estate Investor's VIP List at the end of this book and fill in the names and details for each of the city council members for your city.

# 5

# How to Use the Public Forum to Find the Best Real Estate Investment

## Chapter Goals

Almost everything that happens in a community that can affect the value of real estate passes through the public forum. The primary goal of this chapter is to illustrate the importance of becoming a spectator and participant in the various policy- and decision-making events that occur in a community. There are few countries in the world that possess the open form of government practiced in the United States, and yet many people in the United States take this kind of government for granted.

Many policy- and decision-making meetings are held within every community. Some of the meetings are **workshop** meetings in which differences of opinion among developers and building departments are resolved, or discussions on upcoming events are made public so that local residents can have time to make formal requests or prepare proper counterproposals. Other meetings are scheduled on an as-needed basis as a result of problems that come up in city council or county commission meetings. In almost every case there is an agenda published in advance of the meeting.

> *Reduce risk by expanding knowledge.*
> *Expand knowledge by being involved in community affairs.*

Risk is reduced in any form of investing through knowledge of the subject and the causes of its value changes. A key to success in real estate investing is knowing everything possible about the growth trends of an area, the local problems, upcoming new investments, and changes in zoning or other regulations or rules that affect real estate both directly and indirectly. By being selective about which local meetings to attend, a newcomer to a community can, in a very short time, develop a keen sense of awareness about that community. On the facing page are examples of typical newspaper clippings that provide the reader with details on upcoming meetings.

## Key Terms

- Consent agenda
- Feasibility study
- Highest and best use
- Homeowner's association
- Homestead exemption
- Indemnify
- Injunction
- Land use regulation
- Performance bond
- Rendering
- Tax-exempt property
- Unincorporated area
- Variance
- Zoning board

Review each in detail.

### Consent Agenda

Most city or county council or commission meetings follow a prepublished agenda that lists the events taking place or items to be discussed at the

# NOTICE OF PUBLIC HEARING
## TOWN OF DAVIE, FLORIDA

THE TOWN COUNCIL OF THE TOWN OF DAVIE WILL CONDUCT A PUBLIC HEARING ON WEDNESDAY, JULY 22, 1992 IMMEDIATELY FOLLOWING ITS REGULARLY SCHEDULED MEETING AT 7:30 P.M. IN THE TOWN HALL. THIS MEETING IS TO PROVIDE A FORUM FOR THE RESIDENTS OF THE TOWN OF DAVIE TO DIRECT QUESTIONS AND EXPRESS CONCERNS ON ISSUES THAT AFFECT THE WELL BEING OF THE TOWN OF DAVIE AND ITS RESIDENTS.

ANY RESIDENT THAT WISHES TO ADDRESS THE TOWN COUNCIL SHOULD DELIVER THE TOPIC FOR DISCUSSION, INCLUDING THE SPEAKERS NAME AND ADDRESS, TO THE TOWN CLERK'S OFFICE NO LATER THAN 5:00 P.M. ON JULY 15, 1992.

FOR ADDITIONAL INFORMATION, CONTACT THE OFFICE OF THE TOWN CLERK, 797-1023.

ANY PERSON WISHING TO APPEAL ANY DECISION MADE BY THIS BOARD OR COMMITTEE WITH RESPECT TO ANY MATTER CONSIDERED AT SUCH MEETING OR HEARING WILL NEED A RECORD OF THE PROCEEDING, AND FOR SUCH PURPOSES MAY NEED TO ENSURE THAT A VERBATIM RECORD OF THE PROCEEDING IS MADE, WHICH RECORD INCLUDE THE TESTIMONY AND EVIDENCE UPON WHICH THE APPEAL IS MADE.

Town Council of Davie
by: Gail Reinfeld-Jacobs, CMC
Town Clerk

---

### City of Parkland Fla.
**Public Hearing**

There will be public hearings before the City Commission of the City of Parkland, Florida on July 1, 1992 and on July 15, 1992 at 7:00 P.M. at Parkland City Hall, 6500 Parkside Drive, Parkland, Florida. To be considered for final adoption on second reading on July 15, 1992 will be the following:

ORDINANCE NO. 92-13
AN ORDINANCE OF THE CITY OF PARKLAND, FLORIDA REZONING A PARCEL OF PROPERTY ON THE SOUTHEAST QUADRANT OF HOLMBERG ROAD AND UNIVERSITY DRIVE FROM A-1 AND AE-1 TO RS-3 WITH A LIMITATION TO 55 UNITS MORE PARTICULARLY DESCRIBED IN EXHIBIT "A" ATTACHED HERETO AND MADE A PART HEREOF; PROVIDING FOR SEVERABILITY; PROVIDING FOR CODIFICATION; PROVIDING FOR AN EFFECTIVE DATE.

ORDINANCE NO. 92-16
AN ORDINANCE OF THE CITY OF PARKLAND, FLORIDA REZONING APPROXIMATELY 55 ACRES OF PROPERTY LOCATED AT THE NORTHEAST QUADRANT OF HOLMBERT ROAD AND PINE ISLAND ROAD INTERSECTION FROM A-1 TO RS-3 ZONING DESIGNATION WITH A LIMITATION OF 105 UNITS, MORE PARTICULARLY DESCRIBED IN EXHIBIT "A", ATTACHED HERETO AND MADE A PART OF; PROVIDING FOR SEVERABILITY; PROVIDING FOR AN EFFECTIVE DATE.

Notice: Please be advised that if a person decides to appeal any decision made by the board, agency, or commission with respect to any matter considered at such hearing or meeting, he will need a record of the proceedings, and for such purpose he will need to ensure that a verbatim record includes the testimony and evidence upon which the appeal is to be based.
Susan Armstrong CMC
City Clerk
**June 22, July 3, 1992**

---

### CITY OF PLANTATION COMPREHENSIVE PLANNING BOARD
**SPECIAL MEETING**
CITY HALL, COUNCIL CHAMBERS, 7:30 P.M. TUESDAY, JUNE 30, 1992

1. CALL TO ORDER/ROLL CALL
2. APPROVAL OF MINUTES OF SPECIAL MEETING OF JUNE 2, 1992
3. PET. #R-1240: Consideration of request for approval to REZONE 1.01 plus or minus acres from B-3P (General Business) to CF-P (Community Facility) with a governmental PAROLE OFFICE as a permitted governmental Administrative Service use. Property lying in Section 1, Township 50 South, Range 41 East, and described as Tract "A", Brons Plat, according to the Plat thereof, as recorded in Plat Book 73, at Page 14, of the Public Records of Broward County, Fl. (Suite #101, 4121 NW S St.)
4. Consideration of an ordinance creating a new section 27-613.5 to the Plantation Code of Ordinances; pertaining to uses permitted in the State Road 7 SPI District; so as to clarify same and so as to permit auto wash, self-service, coin-operated, with the ancillary uses of auto detailing and self-service vacuum, as a conditional use in B-3P Districts within such SPI-2 District.
5. PET. #R-1309: Consideration of request to REZONE 12.46 Plus or minus acres from PRD-11.6Q (Planned Residential Development at 11.6 dwelling units per acre) to B-3P (General Business). Property described as a parcel of land in the North ½ of Section 6, Township 50 South, Range 41 East, said parcel including a portion of Block 1, according to the Everglades Plantation Company Amended Plat of said Section 6, as recorded in Plat Book 2, Page 7, of the Public Records of Dade County, Florida and including a portion of Tract 1, according to the Plat of Jacaranda West Parcel F, as recorded in Plat Book 113, at Page 32, of the Public Records of Broward County, Florida. Property better known as the unrecorded plat of Jacaranda West Parcel 12 and located at the NW corner of Nob Hill Road and Cleary Blvd.

---

### (PLANTATION FAMILY CENTER)

6. PET. R-401: Consideration of request for approval to Rezone 12.469 plus or minus acres from PRD 11.6Q (Planned Residential Development at 11.6 dwelling units per acre) to B-7Q (Planned Commercial Development). Property described as a parcel of land in the North ½ of Section 6, Township 50 South, Range 41 East, said parcel including a portion of Block 1, according to the Everglades Plantation Company Amended Plat of said Section 6, as recorded in Plat Book 2, at Page 7, of the Public Records of Dade County, Florida, and including a portion of Tract 1, according to the Plat of Jacaranda West Parcel F, as recorded in Plat Book 133, at Page 32, of the Public Records of Broward County, Florida. Property better known as the unrecorded plat of Jacaranda West Parcel 12 and located at the NW corner of Nob Hill Road, (PLANTATION FAMILY CENTER)

7. PET. R-529: Consideration of request to REZONE 12.46 plus or minus acres from PRD-11.6Q (Planned Residential Development at 11.6 dwelling units per acre) to OP-L (Office Park - Limited District). Property described as a parcel of land in the North ½ of Section 6, Township 50 South, Range 41 East, said parcel including a portion of Block 1, according to the Everglades Plantation Company Amended Plat of said Section 6, as recorded in Plat Book 2, at Page 7, of the Public Records of Dade County, Florida and including a portion of Tract 1, according to the Plat of Jacaranda West Parcel F, as recorded in Plat Book 113, at Page 32, of the Public Records of Broward County, Florida. Property better known as the unrecorded plat of Jacaranda West Parcel 12 and located at the NW corner of Nob Hill Road and Cleary Blvd. (PLANTATION FAMILY CENTER).

8. ADJOURNMENT
9. BOARD COMMENTS/DISCUSSION
10. REPORT BY DIRECTOR OF PLANNING
11. ADJOURNMENT
**June 22, 1992**

---

### NOTICE

Of Special Meeting for the Purpose of Reviewing the Indian Trace Community Development District's Special Assessment Formula and to Consider Public Comment on Same.

The Board of Supervisors of the Indian Trace Community Development District will hold a special meeting on Monday, June 29, 1992 at 7:30 P.M. in the Cafetorium of the Tequesta Trace Middle School, 1800 Indian Trace Road, Fort Lauderdale, Florida for the purpose of reviewing the District's special assessment formula and to consider public comment on same.

If any person decides to appeal any decision made by the Board with respect to any matter considered at the meeting is advised that person will need a record of the proceedings and that, accordingly, the person may need to ensure that a verbatim record of the proceedings is made, including the testimony and evidence upon which such appeal is to be based.

Gary L. Moyer
Manager
**June 22, 1992**

meeting. Some straightforward, "everyday" kinds of items that need to be voted on will usually be lumped together into what is called the **consent agenda**, in which they are voted on en masse. Any voting member can request an item be removed from the consent agenda if that member wants to hear discussion on that item.

## Feasibility Study

A study that examines the results which can be anticipated from any specific development or proposal. Such studies are usually done for the purpose of showing the success potential of a project with the goal to enhance the developer's chances to obtain financing. However, feasibility studies can also be made for presentations before various public forums.

## Highest and Best Use

The best economic use of a property with respect to what is legally and physically possible at any given time. A change in zoning or other regulations may dramatically change the highest and best use. When an investor can find and acquire a property that can easily and economically be converted to the highest and best use, the property value can be increased dramatically.

## Homeowner's Association

Members of an area of town or a specific condominium or cooperative building frequently form homeowner's associations to concentrate their influence within a community and for other mutual benefits. Representatives from homeowner's associations are frequent participants at public meetings.

## Homestead Exemption

Available in some parts of the country, this is a law that enables a resident property owner to, on application, receive a reduction from the real estate tax assessment. Its effect is to reduce the annual real estate tax on that property by providing an exemption from tax for a base value. Often this value increases because of years of ownership or residency in the community or for other reasons, such as age or medical handicap of the property owner.

## Indemnify

To agree to hold harmless. When Charles is given authorization to place a sign in a city right-of-way, the city may require that Charles indemnify the city against any claims or damages that are a result of the sign.

## Injunction

To get a court order to stop a process or procedure from continuing.

## Land Use Regulation

Most areas of the country have detailed land use rules that are frequently changed. Much of the discussion in the public forum deals with these and other regulatory changes. These changes can be very comprehensive or only minor. The problem with them is that public notification in the newspaper may not be explicit enough for everyone to understand the real changes. Any land use regulation change in an area where property is owned should be reviewed in detail by all concerned property owners. Many land use changes have the effect of **reducing land values**.

## Performance Bond

When construction work is contemplated, frequently the lender and/or the city or other governing body will require a performance bond, which ensures that if the contractor fails to complete the work, the insurer will. Property owners can also require the contractor to furnish a **completion or performance bond**.

## Rendering

An artist's illustration of a proposed development or building. The developer, in making his or her best case possible before the required boards and the public, often uses renderings that are designed to win over public and board support.

## Tax-Exempt Property

Certain types of ownership within a community may be tax-exempt in that the owner is not required to pay real estate tax on that property. Property owned by the community itself would be tax-exempt, and if declared surplus land, the city may place it on the market in an attempt to convert it from tax-exempt to taxable.

## Unincorporated Area

A part of a community that is outside legal city boundaries. These areas are governed solely by county government and may not have all the public services that are available to other parts of the county. Property in an unincorporated area often has a greater flexibility of use. This occurs because the county building and zoning rules and regulations are often more lax than those of the cities in that same county. For that reason industrial businesses, junkyards, and less attractive commercial businesses are frequently found in unincorporated areas.

## Variance

A variance is an approval granted by the city or county commission to enable a property to be used contrary to one of the building codes or sometimes contrary to a zoning regulation. A variance may be easier to obtain than a complete change of zoning, but each circumstance will vary.

## Zoning Board

A board that is usually compiled of nonelected community leaders appointed to the position. Their duties require them to hear and vote on zoning issues within the community. They often are the first step for a variance or request for zoning change. Developers interested in major projects within a community often request zoning changes so that the project will have more flexibility over the current zoning. As this request may precede the actual project by a year or more, following the proceedings of the zoning board (sometimes a combined building and zoning board) can give an investor advance information that could be very beneficial, for example, in acquiring property that may go up in value due to the proposed project.

# How to Become an "Insider" to Real Estate Investing

Consider for a moment the people who attend the different public meetings that are held in every community. First, there are the people who run the meetings: the elected officials, the city manager, city lawyers, department heads, and the appointed citizens. These are the people who establish policy, make decisions, and play a major role in the growth trends and other aspects that affect the value of real estate in the area. All these people are in a position to be helpful to the real estate investors in the area, so it is very important that some time and effort be devoted to getting to know these people as well as something about the position they hold.

Second, and of equal importance to the real estate investor, there are the people who attend the meetings. Review the following list.

### People in the Audience at a Public Meeting

Local developers

Homeowner's association members and directors

Local lawyers who specialize in real estate

Other real estate investors

Local residents who are concerned

People in favor of what is being discussed

People who are against what is being discussed

No matter who they are, many people attending a public meeting will be worth knowing. Some of them are the real "insiders" in the real estate investing circles.

Every meeting can provide some information that can be used to improve the chance of success in real estate investing. The key is to know which meetings to attend, what to look for, how to behave in these meetings, and how to follow up and take advantage of the information learned.

The first step is to find out what meetings occur plus the critical data of when and where they take place. The second step is to get advance copies of the meeting agenda by either placing your name on a mailing list or picking one up from the source. The **schedule of topics** is informative about what will be presented at the meeting, but it is suggested that the investor attend several meetings without trying to be selective. Sometimes the agenda is not very explicit about the nature of the topic, and the investor may need to experience how the meeting is run before relying on this schedule as the sole criterion to attend or skip the meeting.

## Eight Steps for Making the Best Use of the Public Forum

1. *Contact the city and county clerks.* For each of the cities or counties of interest, find out the following information from these clerks about every meeting that is open to the public.

- Name of meeting (city council, zoning board, traffic workshop, etc.).
- Schedule of meetings—date and time.
- Usual content of these meetings.
- Location of the meeting—address and, if needed, detailed directions of where to go and where to park once there.
- Name of the chairperson of the meeting (mayor, county commissioner, chairperson of the zoning board, etc.).
- Names of all members attending the meeting.
- Procedure for obtaining an agenda.

2. *Compose a 90-day calendar of meetings.* Start with city council and county commission meetings first, then go to the zoning board and workshop meetings later.

3. *Build contacts.* After attending a few meetings, the names and faces of the other "players" (those who are already insiders) will begin to appear time and time again. These insiders will eventually be known by anyone at the meeting who is observant. At breaks or through personal appointments that can be arranged outside of the public forum, the investor should add these people to the growing list of contacts. It would be very rare for one of these important people to avoid giving an appointment to a person who calls and says, "I saw you at the county commission meeting last week while you were presenting your development plan for the private airport, which I think would be a great economic plus for the area, and wonder if I could meet with you for about 10 minutes one day this coming week?"

4. *Follow-up with praise.* Not everything may appear praiseworthy, and you may find your elected officials voting on issues contrary to the way you might have wished them to vote. However, the goal of all this work must be etched in your mind. **Make contacts and develop a working relationship with the insiders.** There will be time later to take a stand on something important to you. Nonetheless, for example, even a personal note to the vice-mayor, who voted against the wishes of an angry mob that packed the council chambers, can praise the vice-mayor for keeping his or her poise in the face of such adverse circumstances without any mention that the sender of the note was one of those angry mob members.

5. *Make notes of all potential adverse players.* These are the local lawyers, the architects, land planners, department heads, and so on, who do not feel the same way as you. There may be a time when they will be representing or be a spokesperson for an angry mob that turns out to protest something you are trying to get passed. Keep in mind that these professionals may *not* actually have the same convictions as their clients.

6. *Learn the procedures of the meeting.* Each item that comes before any of these meetings will follow a set procedure. These procedures are worth knowing. The clerk who provides the agenda usually has the details on these procedures. Even if a zoning petition is never filed, knowing the details that go into petition filing can be important in following an event from start to finish.

7. *Attend the meeting with the goal to meet people and make a good impression on them.* It may be impossible to know who may turn out to be an important player when attending these meetings. There is one simple goal that can be attained every time, however, that is,

> *Do everything possible to make a good impression on everyone at the meeting.*

This sounds overly simplified, but it can be very important. This means that when attending these meetings one should treat the meeting as though it was a "first appointment" with everyone in the room.

Of specific importance will be the dress and demeanor of the investor. Showing respect for the speakers and the other people in the room and sincere interest in what is going on will be recognized by many people. They may view you as an "insider" right away.

8. *Avoid taking sides.* In some meetings emotions can get very hot, and because you weren't there last week, the issue may appear to be more one-sided than it is. Also, more people against an issue usually turn out to voice their opinion than those who may be in favor of that same issue. For this reason an audience may commonly be "packed" with people who are there for the sole purpose of using public opinion to sway the elected or appointed officials and their decision. This tactic often works.

## Important Things to Look for in Public Meetings

### The People

This has been mentioned before and is worth mentioning again. A successful real estate investor can increase his or her chances for success and reduce risk by knowing who has great influence within a community, and by knowing what events are being planned that is not general knowledge to "outsiders." This is where the "people" part of the public forum comes into play. Be observant at who is doing what.

Some public meetings can be very entertaining and are frequently filled with gut-wrenching emotion and hardship stories, sex, and violence and are rarely boring.

### The Agenda

What is the issue before the panel or council, and how does it affect you or the property in the community? Often what is decided will have no effect at all on anything other than the problem being dealt with. To reduce the number of meetings to attend, look for matters that deal with the following topics. What to look for when these items are brought up at the meeting is also listed below.

**Zoning.** What is the problem with the existing zoning, and who wants to change it? Sometimes the government wants a change in land use (thus the zoning must be changed). Other times a property owner or prospective buyer requests a change of zoning to "improve" the neighborhood or to get a better economic return from an investment. Any change of zoning may have an impact, positive or negative, in property distant from that which is being discussed. Follow zoning matters carefully and get all the details. If a change is going to be made because a project will have a very positive overall result, then being privy to that information early might be all that is necessary to make an investment in the path of progress.

**Planning.** Like zoning, planning can have far-reaching effects. Usually planning changes are slow in coming to fruition and occur only after many public meetings and much political "give and take." Planning changes can be so distant in the future, in fact, that changes often occur along the way that keep some aspects of long-range planning in a constant flux.

**Variances.** These are specific changes usually to a zoning regulation that are not technically (either legally or physically) possible. Sometimes workshop conferences within a building department are all that is necessary to avoid a need for a variance, but when a variance request is made, the reason for the modification to the rules should be investigated to see if this would set a trend that could either be a benefit or hindrance later on.

**Platting or Site Plan Approvals.** This is usually of major import, and any developer who has a major project on the drawing boards may spend years in the government bureaucracy getting approvals for plats and site plans. Being aware of these approval processes right from the start is the insider's real benefit.

**Traffic Control or Roadwork.** Each of the DOT offices in an area may hold meetings that either are a part of long-term road and traffic planning or deal with specific plats or site plans that are submitted before them. No new hospital, school, or factory, for example, is built today without preliminary discussions about meeting the needs of affected traffic and roadways. Knowing where new roads, bridges, highways, and the like are to be built is one of the keys to getting the jump on the investment competition.

**Taxes (Any Topic).** *Taxes*—just the very word should increase the attendance of any public meeting.

**New Construction Works (Any Topic).** When the state, county, or city plans new construction, all real estate investors should pay attention. A new hospital, expanded airport or seaport, new public buildings, etc., will have an impact on property values in the immediate area of the construction. As is true of any prolonged construction project, there can be a temporary setback to existing businesses in the area of construction due to disrupted traffic flow, noise, dirt, and other problems that come from a change in the normal conditions in the area. Although these disturbances are temporary it is not uncommon for businesses to fail while such activities are underway simply because overhead costs continue to accrue even when business income falls to zero. Owners of now vacant stores may be forced to sell, all in the face of a temporary setback that a new investor can take advantage of.

In addition, the allocation of a major block of public monies to one project may mean that other projects, some of which an investor may be counting on, will be cut or put on hold. This can have a compounding effect for the investor who has made financial commitments based on a different timetable.

**Land Plan Changes.**　Like zoning, a change in the overall land plan is often very comprehensive and can take a long time to be worked out. Of specific interest is how the density is altered. Most land plans control the amount of residences that can be put in a community or area of the county. These density regulations may establish a total cap, that is, a set number of people or a maximum number of residences per acre. As vacant property is developed, this density regulation is often changed up or down to fit the needs of other services available or changes of other kinds of development in the area. These changes can make or break the value of property in any given area, so investors are cautioned to be very wary of land plan changes.

**Building Moratoriums and Water or Sewer Hook-up Moratoriums.**
The nightmare of all real estate developers is a moratorium that will limit development. These moratoriums can be used by insider investors as an opportunity to purchase property that suddenly drops in value.

**Case Study**

You see an announcement in the local newspaper of the different governmental meetings for the week and are trying to decide which meeting to go to next. You have already been to a county commission meeting and want to try something different while at the same time maximize the little time you can devote to these public meetings.

You pick out several of the more important meetings that week shown below:

*County Department of Transportation:* To discuss a possible new turnpike overpass in an area more than 20 miles from any of your investment interests.

*City council meeting:* To present several rezoning requests. One involves the change from duplex zoning to multifamily zoning.

*Building department workshop:* To discuss the site plan for a new shopping center to be built within two miles from where you are looking to purchase property.

Complete the following:
1. If you are trying to buy an apartment building to remodel, what would be the best meeting for you to attend and why? _____

_____

2. Turn to The Real Estate Investor's VIP List at the end of the book and complete the following items:
   (11) Head of the city building department
   (12) Head of city zoning department
   (13) Head of city planning department
   (14) City clerk
   (15) Head of city Department of Transportation
   *Tip:* Call the city hall and ask for the required data.

# 6

# How to Find the Right Real Estate Broker Who Will Help You Buy and Sell

## Chapter Goals

This chapter introduces the reader to the real estate brokerage side of real estate investing and shows what to expect from real estate brokers and salespeople and how to get the most out of them. The goal of this chapter is to enable the reader to select the best agent and to get the most out of that relationship.

## Key Terms

- Buyer's broker
- Commission
- Deed search
- Exclusive listing
- Exclusive right of sale
- Licensed broker
- Lock box
- Market dominant

- Market analysis
- Multiple Listing Service (MLS)
- Open listing
- Preview
- Realtor

Review each in detail.

## Buyer's Broker

The buyer's broker represents the buyer and not the seller. This differs from the common broker–client relationship in which the agent legally represents the seller and is obligated by law to make every legal attempt to get the best deal for the seller.

Unless there is a *specific agreement* between the buyer and the agent that establishes a buyer's broker relationship, one must assume that all real estate agents work for the seller. In a **buyer's broker agreement** the buyer agrees to pay his agent a fee and that agent agrees not to collect a fee from the seller. This arrangement establishes a *fiduciary* obligation between the agent and the buyer. Under this situation the buyer's broker is obliged to act in the best interests of the buyer and can use his or her knowledge and experience to help the buyer obtain a property at the lowest price, under the best terms, or both.

More and more smart buyers are realizing that in using a **buyer's broker**, they do not end up paying any more for the property even though they pay a fee directly to the buyer's broker. In addition, as an added bonus, they may actually be able to save money by allowing the astute buyer's broker to work for them in doing the needed due diligence to buy the property at a bargain price.

## Commission

In most situations the seller pays the fee to the broker or brokers involved. When a buyer's broker is involved the seller still pays the broker representing him or her, but the amount is usually reduced, as that broker no longer has to split a commission with another broker. In addition, the exact details on the commission split should be specified in the sales contract. There should also be notice that the buyer's broker solely represents the buyer.

## Deed Search

This is a search of property records. These records contain much information that is helpful to buyers and sellers alike. Brokers who have computer access to the county property records can easily access this information and can provide this data to prospective buyers or sellers. The data contained in property records may vary from place to place, but the usual information available should include the following.

**Legal Description.**   A typical legal description would be: Lot 10 of Block 5 of Royal Hills Subdivision, Unit A, as recorded in Plat Book (PB) 22, page 108 of Winston County Records, North Dakota. This legal description follows the usual lot and block format of recorded (or unrecorded) subdivisions. A subdivision is the result of a vacant tract of land having been divided into blocks, which are then divided into lots. Subdivisions are the usual nucleus of neighborhoods, and a move from one subdivision to an adjoining one can frequently mean a change in the kinds of buildings and property values as well as the demographics of the people who live there.

**Street Address.**   The actual street address of the property, as well as the address of the owner, if different.

**Owner's Name.**   The name of the person or entity registered as the legal holder of title to the subject property. This can be a person, a corporation, or another form of legal entity. When a name is followed by the letters TR, such as "Paula Robins, TR," this indicates that the property is held by Paula Robins as trustee for someone else.

**Owner's Phone Number.**   Not always available, but this can be a very important part of the information when provided. It is possible that the owner is a corporation, which may not have a published phone number.

**Date Owner Acquired the Property.**   Generally the deed search will show the actual date the current owner acquired the property. If the property had been purchased when it was vacant and the owner later built on it, the deed search should indicate the improvements made and the date of those improvements.

**Price Owner Paid.**   There are several different methods by which property records report the price last paid. In some cases this is done by showing the deed transfer stamps that were affixed to a deed when it was recorded. This often occurs when local or state authorities require that a tax, in the form of deed stamps, be paid on a sale. To translate the amount of the stamps into a price paid, one would have to know the formula for such deed stamps. A call to the county clerk in charge of property records would be the quickest way to ascertain the formula.

**Square Footage or Front Footage of Property.**   In property records it is rare for actual property dimensions to be given, but the total square footage of both the property and the improvements are frequently part of the property records. This data is used by the tax assessor's office in determining the tax assessment of the property. Commercial and other unique properties may be listed with front footage, the dimension that the property fronts on a specific road, waterway, or other important boundary. All of this information is important in property value comparisons and can be a shortcut for an investor who is reviewing multiple properties.

**Property Tax Data.**   The most recent ad valorem tax amount would be the usual information provided, as well as the most recent tax assessment value. Property taxes can vary greatly, and a greater sales price does not necessarily mean a higher assessed value. This occurs for many reasons: different tax zones, changes in the millage (rate charged on the assessed value) among cities or unincorporated areas within the county or different counties, etc. Tax data can become a very important factor in choosing between two nearly adjoining properties that front on the same highway but are in different tax zones.

**Previous Owner's Name.**   When the current owner cannot easily be reached, it may be possible to contact the present owner through the previous owner.

## Exclusive Listing

An agreement between a property owner and a real estate agent showing the terms and conditions whereby the owner will pay a fee to that agent if that agent, or any other agent, performs the contract (to sell, lease, exchange, or all three). Any other agent is bound to work through the exclusive agent, but under this form of agreement the seller is free to deal with prospective buyers on his or her own without paying a fee to the exclusive agent.

## Exclusive Right of Sale

An agreement that expands on the exclusive agent contract that obligates the seller to pay the listing agent a fee in the event of a sale, lease, exchange, or any of the three as per contract, regardless of who brings in the other party. This does not prohibit the seller from dealing directly with a prospective buyer, but this form of listing obliges the seller legally to pay the fee to the listing agent, even if the seller goes to contract with a buyer he or she found without the agent. This form of listing is the usual contract between sellers and real estate agents.

## Licensed Broker

Any licensed real estate broker or salesperson will have a valid document issued by the state showing that the person has met the requirements to act as a real estate agent. State law generally imposes greater qualifications on brokers than salespeople; each is bound by state rules and regulations governing this profession. A licensed agent who acts as a salesperson (and not a broker) must have his or her license placed under the umbrella of a licensed broker. That broker is responsible for many of the actions of those salespeople working under his or her brokerage license. Most states require that a licensed broker or salesperson acting on their own account, or buying or selling their own property, must disclose the fact that they are licensed real estate agents.

## Lock Box

A lockable container that is often placed on the front door of a listed property in which a key to that door is placed to provide real estate agents access to a property. These boxes usually are combination locks that have a special code for that specific box. In theory, the real estate agent gives the combination to known agents so that the property can be easily shown. In practice, many lock boxes are used with the factory combination (usually the initials of the manufacturer), or are simple combinations composed of numbers or letters that the agency uses for all their lock boxes. Sellers should insist that specific and unique codes be used for any lock box used on that seller's property to narrow the risk of unauthorized entry.

## Market Dominant

When any real estate agency or broker has a share of listings in a specific area of town that is greater than all other agencies or brokers who have listings in that area, then that firm or broker is deemed to be **market dominant**. This would mean that any firm or broker with more than the average number of listings could be given that label. So if the agencies in town dealing in a specific area all had one listing each, the first to get a second listing in that area could (and most likely would) label itself the **dominant agency**. If an agent uses this term, a prospective seller should ask the following questions.

1. How many properties similar to mine within my price range are currently listed by all agencies combined?

2. How many of those properties are listed by your firm?

3. In the past 12 months, how many properties similar to mine has your firm *sold* in this area?

The answers to these three questions should help you separate the firms into active and not so active categories. It is often the case that the firm with the most listings is not the firm that makes the most sales.

## Market Analysis

Most real estate agents, in their attempt to obtain an exclusive right of sale from a prospective seller, will make a presentation to the seller that should contain an analysis of the condition of the market and a probable market range for which the specific property should sell. This analysis should include the following details:

- Similar property that has been sold in the past 12 months.
- Similar property currently on the market.
- Average time the sold property was on the market.
- Price comparisons on sold and available properties.
- Market plan that agent proposes to implement.
- Information about the salespeople and the firm.

## Multiple Listing Service (MLS)

In most communities the local board of realtors has a publication called the *Multiple Listing Service*. All exclusive right of sale properties listed by the subscribers to this service are printed and distributed among those subscribing firms. Some of these services are limited to realtors only, so a prospective buyer or seller who feels that the service would be important should find out if the agent they are working with has that service available to them.

## Open Listing

This is a listing that occurs when a seller agrees to pay an agent a fee but the agreement does not establish any form of exclusive relationship. Sellers should be aware that this kind of listing does not have to be in writing and can exist under very simple conditions. Many courts have found that an obligation to pay a fee existed even though the seller thought otherwise. If an agent can prove that there was an *implied listing agreement* by virtue of activity, by showing of the property, by letters of registration, etc., a fee could be due that agent in the event of a sale, lease, or exchange. Therefore, sellers should document their intentions exactly when dealing with any real estate agent. If there is already an exclusive right of sale, the seller need only refer other agents to the listing agent to avoid the possibility of paying two commissions.

## Preview

This is the act of looking at a property prior to showing it to a prospective buyer. Sellers should encourage a listing agent to hold **open houses**, which are specifically for other agents to preview the property.

### Realtor

A realtor is a licensed broker or salesperson who is a member of the National Association of Realtors, which has a local Board of Realtors in the area. Realtors pay a fee to the association, which in turn provides training programs as well as many marketing and research services for those agents. Local MLS programs may be one such service. Realtors also must agree to function under a **Realtors Code of Ethics**. This code of ethics allows realtors to police each other over and above the laws of that specific state.

## The Four Stages of Understanding Brokers and Agents and How to Get the Most out of Them

1. How real estate brokerage works—how to use brokerage methods to your advantage.
2. What investors need from their broker or salesperson.
3. How to interview brokers and salespeople.
4. How to get maximum benefits from a real estate agent.

Begin with the first stage.

### How Real Estate Brokerage Works— How to Use Brokerage Methods to Your Advantage

Most real estate brokerage firms are divided into the following categories:

1. Residential only
2. Commercial only
3. Residential and commercial

Regardless of the above category, firms generally specialize in specific geographic areas and often in specific types of property.

The critical aspect that buyers and sellers should look for within any category of firms above mentioned is the method that the real estate firm uses as the primary procedure to obtain listings in any given area. There are only two fundamental methods: the shotgun method and the farming method.

**The Shotgun Method.** This is the usual method real estate salespeople use to obtain listings. Real estate salespeople are, for the most part, independent contractors. As such, they may have no real supervision within the office, and as long as they meet quotas and bring in revenue to the company, many real estate firms use a "hands off" policy with their salespeople. Salespeople who like this aspect of the business gravitate to firms that operate in this way. Using the shotgun approach, these salespeople ramble about town or within large areas and attempt to list and sell property. They are frequently in constant competition with salespeople within their own office, and partially because of this, a well-run listing and sales team rarely is developed. An office full of "loners," no matter how knowledgeable they might be, is usually an office in which each salesperson keeps to him or herself.

**The Farming Method.**   On the other hand, an office that properly uses the farming method develops into a smoothly knit team of people who function well together because they add to each other's effort rather than compete against each other for the same listing. With the farming method, each salesperson (or a team of two or three salespeople working together) picks an area of town—usually a subdivision or two. He or she becomes an expert in every aspect of that area. The salesperson obtains full property records from the local authorities of each property in that area and is keenly aware of local events and happenings that could affect the value of property in that area.

The salesperson who uses the farming method is, in essence, doing what smart real estate investors do, but for different reasons. The salesperson who "farms" knows that by selecting a specific area of town, within a short time he or she will know more about the property in the area than do the property owners. This creates a great deal of personal confidence within that salesperson, who is then able to demonstrate that confidence as knowledge of the product at hand.

## What Investors Need from Their Broker or Salesperson

Once the investor has a clear understanding of his or her own goals, these needs should be broken down into basic elements to be obtained. Factors that can be delegated to the real estate agent will be the foundation for the selection of the best agent for that investor.

For example, Roberta Jones decided that to meet her goals she must acquire a number of small single-family homes that could be converted into free-standing office buildings. Her geographic area would be narrowed considerably to areas that either presently permit such conversion or would allow such conversion with changes in the zoning rules. Because this kind of investment direction combines both single-family and commercial aspects of real estate, it is likely that the best real estate firm to assist in finding this kind of property would be one that dealt in both residential and commercial real estate.

In the selection of members of any investment team the following six elements are the most important services that a broker or salesman should render:

1. Computer access to property records.

2. Possession of area zoning maps.

3. Knowledge of zoning rules and regulations.

4. Access to MLS listing services.

5. Time to assist you.

6. Willingness to be a member of your investment team.

## How to Interview Brokers and Salespeople

Every investor should interview real estate brokers with the idea of finding the salesperson best suited to become a part of your investment team.

Locating the right real estate brokerage firm is not that difficult. A drive through an area will provide the clue: "for sale" signs. In any given part of town where such signs are allowed (some parts of town or certain subdivisions may not allow "for sale" signs to be placed in the yard or on buildings), the real estate firms that obviously deal in that property quickly become evident. The second source is the local classified newspaper advertisements. A review of the firms advertising the geographic area and type of property desired will limit the number of firms to contact.

Keeping in mind the kinds of firms and the two methods of listing and selling, ask the following eight questions. Positive responses will be important in selecting a salesperson to represent you.

### First, the Firm

1. Does the firm specialize in both the geographic area and the type of property needed?

2. Does the firm encourage and support their salespeople in a farming method?

3. Does the firm have computer access to property records?

4. Is the firm a member of the local MLS service?

### Second, the Salesperson

5. Is there rapport between you and the salesperson?

6. Does the salesperson have the *time* to help you?

7. Does the salesperson understand your investment goals and needs?

8. Is the salesperson familiar with the geographic area and the kind of property needed?

A negative reply to any of the above eight questions will weigh against the selection of the firm or the salesperson in question. The most important question is number 5. Regardless of positive responses to other questions, unless there is a good rapport between the investor and the salesperson, a productive relationship will not develop.

### How to Get Maximum Benefits from a Real Estate Agent

Many factors are important for maximizing positive results when dealing with real estate agents. Review the different areas of service the real estate agent provides and how you can increase the productivity and get positive results from the agent.

**General Representation.**   Once a firm and agent have been selected to become a member of your investment team, you should immediately make sure that:

- The agent knows the investment goals you desire to accomplish.

- The agent concentrates his or her efforts on the kind of property you want to have information on.

- The agent understands what you expect from the agent.

### Finding Property

- You explain to the agent why certain properties presented are not satisfactory or do not meet your criteria.

- You have not exaggerated your financial capability.

- The agent understands that he or she is not the only agent you are working with.

### Presenting Offers

- The agent knows how to negotiate offers and counteroffers.

- You expect the agent to maintain an "urgency" about the offer without giving signals that you are anxious.

- The agent will absorb the heat that is generated in an offer–counteroffer situation and vent the seller's frustration away from you.

## Selling Your Property

- The agent seeks all viable options—especially those not evident or obvious to you.

- The agent will network the property to all logical firms and agents dealing with that kind of property in the area.

Dealing with real estate agents is a two-way street. Agents makes their living by being successful at closing transactions and collecting the resulting commission from the sale, lease, or exchange. A good agent knows that high priority must be given to the time spent on qualifying a prospect. If the agent determines that the prospective investor is not ready, willing, and able to close a deal, then the agent may simply move on to another prospect. An investor who finds a hard-working agent should make an effort to keep that agent interested in serving the investors needs.

## Case Study

Complete the following. Turn to The Real Estate Investor's VIP List at the back of this book and complete the items listed below:

(123)  A local realtor

(124)  Another local realtor

*Tip:* Get these names from signs in your area and fill in the other details when you call.

(125)  Property insurance company

(126)  Another property insurance company

*Tip:* Pick one of these from the Yellow Pages telephone directory: State Farm, Allstate, Aetna, or Prudential.

(127)  Title insurance company

(128)  Another title insurance company

*Tip:* In the Yellow Pages, look under Title Insurance Companies or Escrow Agencies.

(133)  Barter company

(134)  Another barter company

*Tip:* In the Yellow Pages, look for Barter and Exchange. If you do not find a barter company, then check with several real estate brokers to see if they know of one.

(135)  Real Estate Exchange Club

*Tip:* Call the Board of Realtors and ask the executive vice president for the closest Real Estate Exchange Club.

# PART 2

# How and Why Property Values Go Up and Down and What You Can Do about It

# 7

# Why Property Values Go Up and Down

## Chapter Goals

Understanding the principal reasons real estate values go up and down is an obvious key to successful real estate investing. The purpose and primary goal of this chapter are to introduce the reader to the concepts that affect real estate values. The basic elements that cause values to go up and down are relatively simple and generally predictable once the rules of the game are clearly understood. In fact some of these factors telegraph their coming well in advance of the actual event. The reader will be surprised that more people do not recognize these factors and take advantage of these situations in buying or selling at the right moment. Yet, despite the simple and uncomplicated history that illustrates past increases or decreases of value, many different factors often hide the obvious or cause sudden diversions from the predictable. This chapter shows many of these factors so that the reader will be better equipped to assess the situation and thereby reduce their own investment risk.

## Key Terms

- Concurrency
- Economic obsolescence
- Highest and best use
- Land lease
- Tax basis
- Tax shelter

Review each of these following key terms.

## Concurrency

This is a relatively new term that strikes terror in the hearts and pockets of real estate investors. Concurrency means **current needs.** When a county or city government decides that the level of services (road, water, sewer, school, police, parks, etc.) cannot be maintained for the population currently in an area, the government labels these regions as areas that do not meet concurrency. As a result owners of property in this area cannot build on vacant property or add to improved property. Under certain circumstances property owners can "buy their way out" of the moratoriums by paying **impact fees** that should go into the county fund to help solve the deficient service or services. Most investors argue that the impact fee is nothing more than a property tax that is not equally levied on all the property holders in the tax area. All real estate investors must be very alert to any move on the local governing agency's part to impose concurrency rules.

## Economic Obsolescence

Many buildings and most of what goes into a building will, at some time in the future, reach a point of economic obsolescence. Refrigerators, elevators, boilers, mechanical, electrical, and plumbing parts, etc., will reach a point in time when they become outdated and will be a burden to the value of a property by virtue of the *cost* it will take to replace those items with modern equivalents. This cost can be so onerous that modernization of a building is more costly than razing it and starting over.

## Highest and Best Use

This is an economic approach to define the best use of any site or building. The approach is to ascertain what can be done with a specific property, either vacant land or an existing building, to obtain the maximum value based on the current economic situation. The mathematics of this approach will vary greatly due to local restrictions, building setbacks, green area (area exclusively used for landscaping and/or ponds) requirements, parking codes, etc., to the extent that each property is apt to have a completely different end result. Because the highest and best use determination will require assumptions to be made for future rents that can be collected, as well as estimates for future operational expenses, it is very easy for an investor to exaggerate the ultimate highest and best use of a property. A conservative approach to rents and a generous operations budget will, on the other hand, produce a far more viable project.

## Land Lease

Land that is leased and not owned is an investment tool used by investors to maximize their investment return by reducing the investment capital needed to acquire a property. Often sellers keep the land and sell the buildings subject to a land lease. This can be a very attractive "seller's tool" to avoid paying a large capital gains tax on the land that may have increased in value many times over the original cost.

### Tax Basis

This is the book value of a property. The tax basis is found by taking the price paid for a property and adjusting for any capitalized costs, such as closing costs, and other expenses that are added to the value. This beginning tax basis is then adjusted each year of ownership by deduction of any allowed depreciation and the addition of the cost of any improvements. The final adjusted tax basis is deducted from the net proceeds of the sale of that asset to discover the realized gain.

### Tax Shelter

Any investment or investment plan that will produce a legal way to reduce annual or ultimate income taxes is called a **tax shelter**. The use of tax loopholes or legal maneuvering of ownership, depreciation, etc., generally convert present income into tax-free income with the requirement that the tax must be paid in the future when the property is ultimately sold. Land is not a depreciable tax item, so many investors interested in the maximum shelter from an investment will acquire property with a land lease, as mentioned earlier.

## The Six Reasons Property Values Go Up

Inflation

Improved infrastructure

Economic conversion

Increased bottom line

Capital improvements

Supply and demand

Each of these six factors can cause a rise in the value of some real estate in an area independently of other circumstances that may also have an effect on the value of that same property. In most situations a combined effect of more than one of these factors creates the local market for property. The reader should avoid looking at too big a picture because that viewpoint may distort the events occurring in any specific area. Real estate is local in nature and most of the factors that govern its value are often contained within that community. What happens in New York City may have absolutely no effect on what happens in Philadelphia. Even with widespread recession or depression, the economy of the local marketplace and some pockets of the country can be booming. Conversely, even when values are skyrocketing around the country, there will be areas where values are plummeting.

> *The key to getting the most out of market conditions is to understand the big picture and to concentrate on the comfort zone.*

Review each of the six factors in detail.

## Inflation

Inflation is the increase in the value of any object solely due to the increased cost of replacing that item. In the example of improving real estate, the combination of acquiring the location and then building the structure today in comparison to an existing building takes into account many different factors. The cost of the land, the design of the building, building permits and fees required prior to construction, and the actual cost of construction can be more complicated and costly than in the past.

Even with the long-term increase of the cost of living, inflation has not been universal in its effect on real estate values. Other factors, discussed later in this chapter, can cause real estate values to remain steady or even decline in value despite sizable increases in the cost of living.

## Improved Infrastructure

The changes in infrastructure of a community produce the most predictable effect on the value of real property. It should be obvious that if a new hospital is planned to be built, then the result of this facility should have a positive effect on the value of surrounding property. The development of a major public attraction such as Disney World would have an even greater impact on property values in the surrounding area. Roads, public buildings, public services such as electricity, water, and sewer systems, police and fire protection, bridges, parks, schools, hospitals, employment opportunities, and so on, have a major effect on the value of a property, usually in a positive way.

The changes that can occur following the development or expansion of any infrastructure within a community can be anticipated, and the investor can take advantage of these changes due to the following two reasons.

**Why Changes Following New Infrastructure Can Be Anticipated**

1. Long lead time.
2. Historic examples available.

A long lead time from the early planning stage to the final completion of the project occurs with almost all public works projects and most major private developments. The public forum within which all such projects generally pass gives the investor ample time to examine all the aspects of the project. A historical review of other communities that have had similar projects can give very accurate predictions of the results of the new project.

Changes in traffic systems, such as new roads, the expansion of existing road systems, and additional intersections or access to highways, open areas that were not accessible before and can create the greatest increase in value over the shortest period of time.

## Economic Conversion

Economic conversion is when the **use** of a property changes. This change can be **voluntary**, as would be the case if the property owner decides to make a change in the property to improve the income from rent or services, or **involuntary**, which would occur when the property owner has no control over an event that causes an economic change. An example of an involuntary change is a governmental change in the zoning or permitted use of the property. If this change allowed for use that would generate greater income, then that change would be favorable.

The voluntary change from one use to another with greater economic reward is one of three factors in which the increase of value is within the direct control of the investor. The other two factors, increased bottom line, and capital improvements, will be discussed shortly.

Several good examples of voluntary economic conversion are as follows: an investor buys a small apartment building and converts it to offices; a single family home is converted into three apartments; a vacant lot is turned into a U-Pick-It Strawberry Patch; a motel is converted to antique shops. In each case the conversion is possible because either the zoning permits it or the investor obtains permission to make the changes from the governing authorities.

Voluntary economic conversion is what development and redevelopment of real estate is all about. This form of real estate investment has the greatest success potential for several reasons.

1. The investment is based on current economic conditions rather than a long-term hold as would be the case with land speculation.
2. Because a conversion from one use to another that will produce a greater income is the basis of this form of investing, the investor would acquire the property at a reduced value and turn it into a higher value with solid predictable results.

Naturally, it is assumed that the investor has the ability to perform the required due diligence needed to determine what kind of conversion will work in the area, and then to follow through with the legwork. Much of this book is devoted to providing the reader with the knowledge of how to accomplish economic conversion.

## Increased Bottom Line

An income property increases in value if the income increases. An investor who is able to increase the bottom line (cash flow) will increase the resale value of the property assuming other factors have not changed. Good property management requires an in-depth understanding of many aspects of real estate and the people involved. Once a property has reached its maximum gross income possible, the operating expenses and cost of debt service are the elements that reduce income and thereby have an effect on the ultimate value of the property. The investor must pay close attention to and make every effort to reduce the following seven expenses:

- Utility charges
- Vacancy factor
- Carpet replacement
- Plumbing repairs
- Advertising cost
- Janitorial and cleaning
- Bad debt and collections

## Capital Improvements

Value generally goes up when capital improvements are made. This assumes, however, that the total value of a property will be the combination of values of both land and buildings. When the land value increases to the point that capital improvements are superfluous to the total value, then they are not a factor in value enhancement. Also, in some situations the improvements are such that the actual cost can never be recovered—as might be the case in remodeling a home that does not appeal to prospective buyers and will likely be redone by any buyer.

Because the investor has absolute control over the improvements made to a property, care must be exercised in the planning of these improvements. If the sole reason for making the improvements is to increase the value of the property, such as adding apartment units to an apartment building or adding a bedroom or extra bathrooms when the market demands such amenities, then the cost of the improvement must be weighed against the predictable increase in value. If the increase does not support the cost, then the choice to make the addition may not be sound.

Remodeling properties, with or without economic conversion, does not always require major capital expenditures. Many investors have been very successful looking for structurally sound properties that simply need some tender loving care, which may be nothing more than a fresh coat of paint, some innovative landscaping, or minor decor changes and improvements.

## Supply and Demand

This is the theory that dictates that the value of everything will rise as the demand for that item, product, service, or property rises. The theory also provides that with a steady demand, values will rise as supplies decrease, or that values will rise as long as a supply decreases faster than the demand goes down. In real estate this theory has great limitations due to the local nature of real estate values. There can be an overabundance of one kind of real estate, for example, condominium apartments in south Florida and southern California and resort areas along the Gulf coast. If the supply in those areas exceeds a reasonable absorption rate, then the values could actually decline. However, at the same time that Florida and California have problems with the condominium market, other areas of the country could be having a boom in condominium apartments. More difficult to assess is the fact that even within south Florida, southern California, and other areas that may be "overbuilt" in a specific property, there would be a demand for specific locations and price ranges that are contrary to the general market.

Real estate values should not be viewed as a **national statistic**. Gold, silver, and stock in IBM are but three items that can be purchased anywhere, and the influences on their values are independent of any general location where the item is purchased. Real estate is absolutely local and investors must be careful to distinguish between national events or circumstances that can affect the real estate market and national trends or statistics that may give the impression of a rise or fall in real values.

A general statistic that the media is fond of using when discussing real estate is **housing starts**. If there is a general decline in the percentage of new housing being built, this can give the impression that all real estate markets are in a decline. Because this statistic is based on a total marketplace, investors need to look at their own local marketplace to see what is happening. The very fact that new homes are being built suggests that somewhere there is a "hot" market. The likelihood is that within every community, except in severe recessions and depressions, there is some location and category of property in demand.

Any given market, such as a town or a collection of nearby towns or cities, can absorb only so much of any type of service. Successful businesses pay close attention to the market absorption for their product and avoid areas where there is excessive competition.

In real estate development there is a contradiction to the prudence of avoiding excessive market proliferation. There are, for example, more office buildings and retail commercial spaces in most communities than the current market of those areas can support. The result is a high percentage of vacant office and commercial space, which results in a reduced value of those properties with high vacancies and loss of rent potential.

The contradiction is that even in these areas, almost always new construction of more office buildings and more commercial buildings occurs. There are several reasons for this: (1) Lag time—Some projects take years to go from planning table to construction; many projects are caught in the middle of economic hard times and high vacancy percentages for similar uses. (2) "New is better" theory—Some developers believe that even if there are high vacancies in the same type of use, a new building, center, complex, etc., will attract tenants who will want to move out of older buildings in areas of town that have no longer become viable for those tenants. This concept works at times but is in direct opposition to the supply and demand theory. Developers who go headlong against the traditional concepts of the supply and demand theory are taking a risk that may not be prudent.

## The Seven Reasons
## Property Values Go Down

Decline of neighborhoods

Adverse effects of infrastructure change

Governmental controls and regulatory changes

Economic obsolescence

Supply and demand

Lack of proper maintenance

Urgency to sell

Each of these factors can cause drastic decline in property values. In general, circumstances work together to the ultimate effect that eventually all of these factors can occur. Review each in detail.

### Decline of Neighborhoods

Every property occupies a location within the community that is going through a change. This change occurs because of a wide variety of events that occur, some of which may be beneficial to the community and that location, while other events may have adverse effects on the location.

When areas of town begin to experience a decline in the economic via-
bility of property, property owners are faced with increasing vacancy factors,
which lead to reduced rents. A reduction of income from any property
often means that maintenance will be reduced, and the whole neighborhood begins to slip into decline.

The initial reason these slides begin is usually a lack of good long-range
planning within communities. If the infrastructure of a city is planned
around sound zoning ordinances and building restrictions, areas are less
likely to suffer major declines.

However, to meet the needs of a growing community, less attractive facilities such as prisons, sewer treatment plants, airports, and city dumps must
be taken into consideration. The construction or development of one of
these facilities is likely to have an adverse effect on an area, which in turn
can trigger the domino effect of loss of rents followed by a decline in maintenance, which in the long run causes greater loss of rents and the fast loss
of overall value. Only when new economic conversion can be brought to
such an area will the values rise.

The factors that cause a decline in a neighborhood are usually slow in
coming, and thus may not be as obvious as one might think. For example,
the subtle effect of the introduction or increase of crime in an area could
be the side effect of a nearby neighborhood spilling over into adjoining
areas, ultimately causing the decline of what previously was a part of the
community on the upswing.

Even a major impact such as the development of a new airport will cause
some property to go up in value at the same time it reduces the value of
other land. Clearly the investor should study the history of other communities in which airports or other major public works were built or expanded.

## Adverse Effects
## of Infrastructure Change

As communities grow and the infrastructure of that community is
increased, there can be major adverse effects on property values within the
community. The impact of an airport, as already mentioned, will present
both positive and negative results of some property values. The adverse
effects of some infrastructure are relatively obvious and are very predictable. Existing and already developed residential property that is under
the glide path of aircraft landing at airports should decline in value.
However, undeveloped land at the same location, which prior to the airport
was zoned for single-family homes, may be changed (if the governing bodies allow it to happen) to permit use that is more compatible with the location, such as industrial or commercial use in support of the airport. When
this rezoning occurs the value of some property can actually increase.

The irony of infrastructure change is that due to the actual construction of what may provide for long-term increases in value, there can be a sudden, though temporary, decline in the value of a property. This kind of value decline offers the investor a great opportunity to acquire an investment at a reduced price when the long-term effect is likely a rise in value.

New road construction offers many such opportunities. It is not uncommon for a major highway or intersection to take a year or more to be constructed. During that time traffic might be diverted to other roads, severely limiting access to existing commercial enterprises along the roadway under construction. Even if the access is only moderately limited, the noise and dirt caused by the construction can cause a great loss of patronage to the affected businesses.

Some property owners cannot hold out long when their highly leveraged investment begins to experience sudden vacancies, and even though they know (or at least hope) that business will return when construction is completed, the reality is that once a customer starts going elsewhere they may be slow in returning.

## Governmental Controls and Regulatory Changes

Bureaucracy has invaded virtually every aspect of the real estate industry, so much so in fact, that the cost to obtain permits to do many small remodeling projects far exceeds the actual project itself. Governing agencies abound, and each seems determined to exert more control than the other.

The following are just a few of the types of governmental controls or regulations with which property owners must contend:

- Building codes
  Type of construction to be approved
  Setbacks
  Approvals and inspections by department
  Bathroom sizes
  Licensed and approved contractors
  Fees

- Zoning ordinances
  Site plan approval
  Uses allowed or not allowed
  Green area
  Parking codes

- Health department controls
  Materials used
  Ground to be tested

Well water and septic tank approvals
Restaurant and food service inspections
Fees

- Fire department regulations
Plan approval
Fire protection provided
Maximum persons allowed
Inspections

- Setbacks
Site plan approval
Possible building height regulations
Possible establishment of green area

- Environmental controls
Tests and studies to disclose possible environmental problems with the site
Approvals required prior to building permit
Fees

- Army Corps of Engineers
Approval prior to building permit if they are involved

- Department of Transportation
Possible involvement of city, county, and state DOTs
Regulation of road access
Possible major impact fees

- School, hospital, or parks departments
Possible impact fees

A change in any existing rule or regulation that governs any of the above can throw the real estate development industry into a grinding halt. Building moratoriums occur even when a study is underway about a possible change in a rule or regulation.

An investor who purchases any real estate today based on yesterday's rules and regulations may wake up tomorrow to discover that the property will no longer meet the investor's needs. This factor has changed investor thinking about raw land and long-term speculation, requiring far more detailed study than in the past when any opportunity along the path of progress was a good and profitable investment. With even short delays in starting a project, the high cost of holding onto property can eliminate the economic benefits the investor anticipated.

Some communities make it known that they are "antidevelopment." This is a political stand often well supported by the residents of an area. In such locations there is usually a trend whereby building rules and regulations are constantly tightened to the extent that new development becomes next to impossible. The changes can be very subtle and do not appear to have the effect they do. For example, Lauderdale-by-the-Sea, a beachfront resort community in Florida, has reduced the building height allowed over the years from ten floors (for apartment buildings and hotels) to only three floors. At the same time the parking codes have been changed so that commercial buildings cannot count the public parking areas provided by the city in front of those buildings as a part of their allocated parking. The end result is such that virtually every existing commercial building does not meet present-day codes. While the current use is "grandfathered in," any thought of remodeling the structure would require the property to meet the current (and increasingly tougher) codes.

All governmental controls are made in the "name" of public betterment, and to be sure the vast majority of such controls are effective in maintaining a high standard of development with public safety keenly in mind. Nonetheless, investors should pay close attention to the local trend. A visit to the local building department will be the first step in determining whether the city encourages new development or redevelopment. The local planning council meetings and building department workshops are also prime places to find out how easy it will be to make economic conversions of property within that community.

### Economic Obsolescence

Everything from design to the equipment contained within a building may reach a point in time in which it is no longer economically viable for that property. Constant repair and maintenance can add many years of life to each part of a building, so much so in fact that the style or charm of the item actually adds to its economic value. However, the cost to keep up an old elevator or maintain out-of-date plumbing may well exceed the relative cost of replacement with modern fixtures.

When a property is not properly maintained and the equipment fast approaches economic obsolescence, the value of the property is reduced by the cost to replace these out-of-date items. Many investors fail to consider the age of many of the parts of a building that will eventually need to be replaced. They subsequently overpay based on the current income and expense figures without taking into account the future cost of replacement.

The following items of any property should be reviewed prior to acquisition. The probable number of years left before replacement and the likely cost of replacement should be analyzed.

- Air conditioning and heating equipment
- Air filters
- Driveway surface
- Electrical wiring

- Elevators or escalators
- Fire control
- Hot water heaters and boilers
- Light fixtures
- Paint
- Plumbing
- Roof structure

The proper way to review these items would be to ascertain the "like new" lifetime of each item, the current age of the item, and the likely cost to replace that item at the end of that term. This would be done for each item listed above and the "seller's portion" of the ultimate replacement cost then deducted from an **as-new** value of the building. For example, if a new roof normally lasts 20 years, and a replacement for the existing roof, which is now 10 years old, would be $20,000, then a 20-year sinking fund (an annual contribution earning interest that would equal the estimated cost of replacement at the end of 20 years) should be set up. As the investor will be required to install a new roof more or less at the 20th anniversary of the roof, a deduction in the value of the building equal to the amount of the sinking fund at the date of acquisition would be reasonable. In Chap. 16 the actual method of calculating a sinking fund will be reviewed. At this point in time, the reader need only remember that the **sinking fund** is based on annual (or monthly) payments into a bank account that is earning interest. For this example the annual cost would be less than $1,000.

> At a steady 8 percent interest rate earned in a bank, an annual payment of $437.04 would build up to the required $20,000 at the end of 20 years.

To calculate the "missing" amount of the sinking fund at the time the property is acquired, simply multiply the annual payment by the compound interest rate for the age of the item. In this example, the roof is 10 years old and the rate of 8 percent is used, so the annual contribution of $437.04 would be earning interest. Table 16-1 on p. 202 shows 14.48656247 at 8 percent for 10 years. The investor can deduct from the as-new value of the property 14.48656247 × $437.04 = $6,331.21 as the seller's contribution to the future roof.

If the as-new value of the building is $250,000 and the only sinking fund deduction to be made is the roof calculation of $6,331.21, then the adjusted as-new value is $243,668.79. If the actual price being paid by the investor is more than that amount, the investor should have good reasons to justify the possible overpayment.

## Supply and Demand

This is a two-edged sword that can cause increases in value as well as drive prices right into the ground. On paper the supply and demand theory of a market is rather simple and easy to adjust to. If the product in question were donuts, a bakery could adjust to the kinds of donuts that are in demand on a daily basis. The method of determining the demand is to look at the remaining stock at the end of the day and keep track of what sold out first and the number of requests for the types of sold-out donuts. The next day the situation is corrected, and new adjustments are made based on the demands for that day.

Products that take longer to plan and fabricate require more analysis in marketing and design that will satisfy the demands of the future market-place. Fashion clothing is one of the most difficult products for supply and demand planning, and often the manufacturer must *create* the demand through extensive advertising and promotion.

Real estate is fixed and cannot be moved from where it is not in vogue to another part of town or the country where it would be in demand. Donuts and clothing, after all, can be moved from one place to another to adjust to market differences. This notion of permanent location, coupled with the magnitude of the investment, causes long recovery periods when the law of supply and demand drives property values down.

The following are two major factors of supply and demand that cause real estate values to go down, or at best remain at the same level.

*Overbuilt:* The term **overbuilt** says it all. There is more of the item or product on the market than current demand can absorb in a reasonable time. The difficulty here is defining a reasonable time. In the "hot" days of the California real estate market, it was not unusual for an entire subdivision of several hundred homes to sell out in a matter of a few weeks. In a moderate market several hundred homes may take several months to sell.

*Tight money:* Tight money comes from the following causes: recession and depression, expensive or unavailable financing, and lack of confidence in the market. If this occurs when the real estate market is also overbuilt, the market can decrease quickly and stay down for a long time. Because tight money has the effect of bringing *new construction* to a halt, the overbuilt situation will be corrected before the market shows any real move upward.

The availability of long-term financing from lenders is the absolute key to real estate development. Institutional lending is structured with three major control points imposed by the lender: (1) the restrictions on the type of loan, (2) the interest charged, and (3) the term of the payback of the loan. The restrictions that certain banks and other institutional lenders set may actually prohibit loans on some kinds of real estate: no loans on hotels, for example, or high-rent apartment complexes. Other restrictions may establish low loan-to-value ratios that require the builder or developer to invest greater equity than they either have or want to invest. Lenders can simply impose more restrictions than can be reasonably met by the builder.

The interest charged is a function of the current market to some degree. As most lenders are using funds from outside sources (depositors, Federal Reserve, investors, etc.) they will lend at rates sufficiently above what they must pay to ensure a profit. However, the interest rate charged is not the primary dilemma in tight money markets: the term of the pay-back is.

When the lender can *sell* the loan to a secondary market, such as the Federal Home Loan Association, the lender is able to offer long-term financing at a moderately low rate because the secondary market accepts the long-term payback at that rate. However, commercial and other loans that are not bought by any secondary market must be held by the lender within its own portfolio of loans made. When lenders are reluctant to commit to long-term rates for loans they must hold, they require short-term payback of the principal. A development loan for a shopping center with a five-year payback does not offer the developer any margin for error. In the face of short-term payback, development slows down to a halt.

## Lack of Proper Maintenance

A run-down home in a nice neighborhood is an obvious example of what poor maintenance can do to the value of that property. Worse, it can also affect the values of properties that adjoin it or are across the street from it. Worse still is the fact that this may be a trend that, if left unchecked, could result in the decline of a whole neighborhood.

The gems of real estate investing are the single-family properties that are no longer adequately being taken care of. This happens for many different reasons, some of which are as follows:

- Absentee owner
- Owner has other, more pressing priorities
- Poor management
- Owner cannot afford the cost
- Tenant overlooking his obligations
- Ownership dispute

In each of these situations, the end result can be the same: a deteriorating property. If an investor is able to find a property that is going downhill for one of the above reasons, that property may represent a sound investment that could be *turned around* relatively inexpensively.

## Urgency to Sell

Unlike a block of IBM stock, most real estate cannot be sold at a moment's notice. It is well known that the instant a person *must sell* is the very moment when the *wolves arrive at the door.*

Real estate investors look for situations where the seller is highly motivated. The greater the motivation to sell, the better the deal the investor is likely to get. This is so important that when there is a hint of urgency, there can be great excitement, which is directed at getting a bargain deal. What should not be overlooked is that if the seller knows and understands how to use this urgency to his or her advantage, the end result desired, which is the *sale of the property,* can be accomplished.

Bargain sales are often a compromise between the price and terms of the transaction. A highly motivated seller may reduce the price but get all cash, or get the price by offering easy terms or taking another property as all or part exchange in the deal. Each of these terms is an alternative that sellers will have to sort out and decide which will move them closer to their goals.

Smart investors watch for property owners who must sell when the seller's motivation is strongest to make a deal. All investors try to avoid ever reaching the moment when they are forced to sell quickly.

Complete the following:

1. What are the three factors over which an investor has control that can cause property to go up in value?

    _____    _____    _____

2. What are the three factors that an investor looks for in property that has gone down in value that the investor may be able to quickly reverse?

    _____    _____    _____

3. Mark true or false to the following statements.
    a. If property values dropped in Houston, Texas, Jacksonville, Florida, and Portland, Maine, this is a sure sign that property values would drop in any possible comfort zone. ❑ T    ❑ F
    b. A land lease can be a good investment tool for both the buyer and the seller. ❑ T    ❑ F
    c. Whenever there is a major improvement in the infrastructure of a community, all property values go up. ❑ T    ❑ F
    d. Government controls can help property values go up. ❑ T    ❑ F
    e. A sinking fund is a form of accounting no longer used or effective in real estate investing. ❑ T    ❑ F
4. Turn to The Real Estate Investor's VIP List and complete the following:

(16)  City fire chief
(17)  City police chief
(18)  Head of the city water department
(19)  Head of the city sewage department
(24)  City council meetings
(25)  Planning and zoning meetings

*Tip:* One call to the city hall (1) should provide the phone numbers or extensions to sources to each of the above.

# 8

# Why *Location* Is Not the Whole Story

## Chapter Goals

The cliché that the three most important aspects of real estate are "location, location, and location" is only partially true. The real key and primary goal of this chapter is to illustrate that the *importance of a location* is what is critical. This chapter will show the reader how to distinguish good locations from poor ones. But this is only the start: what is most important is the discovery of the subtle differences between a good location and an *important* one.

When buying real estate, obtaining insight as to which location will possibly increase or decrease in value is an obvious advantage. The reader should note that the value of a property ultimately is affected by the following three factors.

## The Three Factors That Affect Values of Every Site

1. Location

2. Importance of that location

3. Use allowable at that location

Each of these factors are relative to any given need. A vacant commercial lot, for example, will have different economic value for different users *even though they may have the same type of use for the property*. This means that one hotel chain may be able or willing to pay more for a site due to the nature or clientele of the intended hotel in comparison to what another hotel chain could or would pay. Each hotel company, as would any prospective buyer for that property, would evaluate the geographic location on the basis of its own use and would examine how the location and use are important.

## Key Terms

- Access (visual and actual)
- Corners
- Crime statistics
- Demographics
- Impact fees required
- Master plan
- Traffic count
- Population shift

Each of these terms plays a role in the ultimate determination of the importance of any given site or location as it relates to the specific investor's need and use. Review each in detail.

### Access (Visual and Actual)

Wars have been fought over access rights to oceans, lakes, and rivers. When it comes to most real estate, and in particular, commercial real estate, poor access, either visual or actual, can mean the difference between a great location and a very poor one.

The question of access goes beyond the site itself because the kind of access may vary depending on the actual use. For example, the values of homes within a subdivision may vary greatly on the type of access to the subdivision. If the roads leading into the subdivision are private, well landscaped, and at the same time not traffic ways leading through the subdivision to some other area, then the property values are almost sure to be higher than an adjoining subdivision that has access off a major highway crossing the area.

Some commercial properties have excellent visual access, such as frontage on main highways or turnpikes, but by the time prospective patrons of businesses find an exit from the highway and locate those businesses, the advantage of visual access may be negated. At best, a possible user or tenant for such a location would have to weigh which of the two accesses of that site, visual or actual, was the most important.

### Corners

In every commercial site at current or future intersections, there are two types of corners: the **near corner** and the **far corner**.

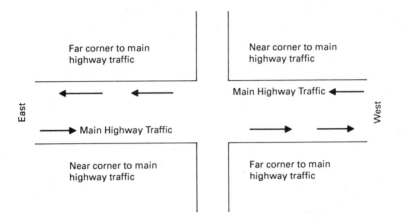

If all corners of an intersection are the same size and there is no unreasonable limitation to road access, the far corner will have the greatest value. This is because as traffic approaches an intersection, the farthest corner on the right is the most visible. This visibility gives the driver a second or two longer to anticipate turning into that corner. This is important to drive-in restaurants and gas stations, for example, because when all four corners are developed, the far corners will have that extra second or two of advertising pull. One disadvantage that can occur with any corner is that the governing DOT may limit or prohibit a **curb cut** from the road to the site. This limitation or restriction results from a possible traffic hazard caused by people trying to turn from a fast-moving traffic lane into the site. If the site has enough frontage on the highway and the DOT allows a **right-turn storage lane** to be constructed, the investor could build a separate lane along the right-hand right-of-way of the highway. This storage lane would allow high-speed traffic to make the turn to the right with time to decelerate first. While this may appear complex, several factors are important. First, if the property does not have enough frontage on the highway, then the actual access could be greatly restricted. Second, even if there were enough frontage, the road right-of-way may not allow sufficient width to construct the turn storage lane. Third, the cost of such construction with possible deduction from the site itself to contain the lane could be more than the use would warrant. An investor who has immediate use for a site should obtain the necessary approvals for the needed turn storage lane or permits for curb cuts and ascertain that the cost for the required work is acceptable *prior to the closing on the purchase of the site.*

## Crime Statistics

There should be no doubt in anyone's mind that high crime areas will greatly reduce the value of a property. An afternoon at the local police department with the person in charge of crime statistics in the area will provide data as to what is going on in a particular part of town. Very few businesses willingly locate in high crime areas, and when a "good" neighborhood goes "bad," values go down fast. Because this is a proven factor, it is important to look at the trend in the area. For example, a site might be 100 percent perfect in every aspect, and the area may even have a moderately low crime rate; however, this area adjoins a declining, expanding neighborhood.

One factor that can cause a sudden rise in crime rate is a dramatic change of traffic patterns. While new roads can turn a property into a gold mine, those same roadworks can cut off a part of town that was on the upward move. Access becomes difficult and in some cases the area is even isolated from other parts of town that are "okay." Overnight this "good" area shifts into a declining neighborhood.

When new roads, bridges, overpasses, changes in intersections, etc., are in the planning stages for areas near property being considered for investment, the investor should carefully review all potential changes that can occur.

## Demographics

Demographics are elements that pertain to the characteristics of the people who live in any given area, and includes race, sex, age, number of people per household, density, wage-earning strength, employment statistics, density per square mile, percentage of white- and blue-collar workers, and percentage of unemployed. Most of this information is available through various local planning offices or within the development departments of local utility companies. Many county tax assessor offices track this data and make it available to anyone interested. A real estate investor will look at the area that surrounds any comfort zone or possible investment location to see the pattern in that location. Statistical information is most useful when it is reviewed over a period of time. By plotting several years of demographic change, a **trend** may emerge, which will be like a crystal ball in foretelling the future of any location.

## Impact Fees Required

Some communities have discovered a new way to "tax" property owners without calling it a tax. They call it an **impact fee**. These fees are charged to investors or property owners generally prior to development of a specific property. However, some communities assess these impact fees on a less predictable basis. Generally, the impact fee is levied because the development of a property causes an adverse impact on the rest of the infrastructure of the community. This "impact" may be an increase in traffic on roads not designed to carry the number of cars currently traveling on them, or the creation of more demands on utilities or other public services than can be met.

A very strong case can be made that any such investment by the community should be shared by all property owners in an area and not specifically charged to a single property owner. Nonetheless, until a high court decides this issue most property owners pay the impact fee because they do not have the time or the finances to fight it out with local authorities.

The importance of these impact fees is that often the investors may not be aware that a major hidden cost could await them before being able to develop the "ideal" site they were lucky to find. These fees can be very high and could make the property no longer "ideal."

As would normally be sufficient to discover a concurrency problem, investors should check with building departments in the local community for any outstanding or pending impact fees. If there are, the investor would need to anticipate the amount of this added cost and determine if the site is still cost effective for the intended use with the added expense.

## Master Plan

Master plans exist in almost every community in the industrialized world. These plans may be comprehensive in that they are compiled from each of many different segments of infrastructure within the community, such as roads, water systems, sewer systems, fire protection, police protection, parks, hospitals, and schools. More often, the master plan is not so comprehensive, and the investor may find during a review that the individual master plans for each of the above-mentioned segments conflict with each other. For example, a new park may be planned where a new road is proposed, or a school is planned to be established in an area where another master plan shows future industrial zoning. This kind of confusion in community planning occurs periodically, and when the investor comes across this kind of conflicting data in the area being considered, the investor should make an effort to determine which information is correct.

## Traffic Count

Traffic counts are the study of the number of cars that pass a location or intersection during a 24-hour period. Usually the counts are done over a period of a week or month, and the average number of cars per day determined. The direction in which the cars travel can be very important to determine which of the far corners would be best for a user who needs maximum exposure and easy access to traffic. Many different governmental departments take traffic counts. By contacting the different DOTs within an area, an investor could find out if there has been a recent traffic count for any specific area. Usually the best information is obtained through a study of traffic counts around the area and not just a review of one count right in front of the prospective location.

Again, the key to value is through the trends that occur. If a review of two years of quarterly traffic counts show a continual growth of traffic moving in the direction of the prospective site, this trend clearly suggests increasing values for the area. However, investors should be cautious of temporary reasons for such trends, such as a detour from a closed major traffic artery undergoing long-term repairs.

### Population Shift

Population shifts for many different reasons. Some communities have seen a move from the cities to the suburbs and a change back to the inner city. Some population shifts can be anticipated, and investors can plan future investments based on a clear understanding of what causes population to shift. The reader has already been introduced to many of the reasons for population shifts. In a very simplistic look at population shifts, people tend to move toward a less complicated way of life and away from problems, such as a move from the cities to the suburbs.

## How to Determine the Importance of Location

The importance of any property to a specific investor, at any given point in time, is controlled by the following circumstances.

- Purpose for the investment
- Cost versus income produced
- Contributing factors that affect value

A review of each of these three factors illustrates the steps an investor can take to determine the importance of any prospective location from their point of view.

### Purpose for the Investment

There are two basic real estate investment strategies.

1. Buy what you need when you need it.
2. Speculate on long-term value increases.

Each of these two strategies has many followers. The real estate developer can be either or both depending on the development, but many commercial investors whose properties include but are not limited to fast food restaurants, gas stations, and franchises of any product or size fall into the immediate user investor category and rarely speculate on the outcome of sites they acquire.

If the investment is for immediate use, the investor has the least chance of making a mistake if proper due diligence is undertaken. The property's value now is far more accurately determined than what it might be ten years from now. The long-term effect of future roads and master plans, just to name two potential steering forces, are very critical to both methods of investing. Despite the importance of such effects, most immediate users who buy what they need now often overlook the review of these longer-term trends and discover (too late) that had they looked under a few more stones, they would have found that the "ideal" location was actually in a trend of decline.

Flexibility becomes the critical factor for the speculator who buys a tract of land in anticipation of future needs. These needs may not be predetermined, or the purpose may be solely directed towards a profit in a future sale. The best long-term plan for any site is to anticipate more than one possible use for the property. As economic trends change, other factors develop that can turn the "future factory site" into a golf course community. The greater the flexibility, the less the risk in any long-term land acquisition.

### Cost versus Income Produced

In every investment the desired return on the investment must be considered. In the case of the immediate user the economics are relatively easy to calculate because the investor is dealing with a current situation. The capital investment needed to buy the property and, if required, to construct buildings or other improvements can be estimated and income and expenses determined through recent experience. As long as there are no hidden impact fees or moratoriums on construction, the cost versus income produced can be accurately anticipated. A comparison of available properties can be made that could lead the investor to the best property to buy.

*Example:* The Burger Magic fast food restaurant franchise company knows the gross income one of its restaurants should produce with a given set of criteria (such as traffic count, demographics of the area and of the traffic, trends for population growth for the area). Property selection would be a relatively simple matter of adding all known costs for the construction of the facility to the acquisition cost of the site:

|  | Site A | Site B |
|---|---|---|
| NOI anticipated due to review of criteria | $ 180,000 | $160,000 |
| Cost to build facility | 400,000 | 400,000 |
| Cost to acquire land | 600,000 | 400,000 |
| Total Cost | $1,000,000 | $800,000 |
| Yield on Investment | 18% | 20% |

NOTE: Yield on investment is calculated without debt service. Yield = NOI ÷ Total cost

In the above review site B would be the better investment if all factors were more or less the same. An improving trend for B would make it a great buy.

**Do Not Rely on Long-Term Projections.**   Short time spans in projections is important because too many unknown factors can affect the property over a long term. Smart investors like to get a 20-year picture of what "seems" to be happening from growth and development trends, but the range of future projections and pro forma plans on which one would make a decision should be limited to no more than five years from the day the operation or use would begin.

**Speculator Risks Increases and Change.**   The real estate speculator who buys land or improved property anticipating an increase in value must spend the greatest time at due diligence. The total cost to hold onto a property includes more than the initial capital spent to acquire the property. These holding costs include financing cost, impact fees, tax increases, and additional capital investments to maintain a "temporary" improvement. While the speculator takes the greatest risk when acquiring a property that may take 10 years or more to reach the level of value the investor wants, with prudent planning some or even all of the holding cost can be covered by the property itself.

## Contributing Factors That Affect Value

There are a multitude of factors, which range from zoning and rezoning to density changes, traffic counts, trends in the area and surrounding neighborhoods, and master plans for future development. These factors are most difficult for the investor to compile, but all information necessary to ascertain the likely trends for the area is available.

When speculation is the investment purpose, the investor should study the trends that are developing in any given area without a specific use in mind, looking instead at a number of possible future uses. The immediate user compiles the same data, but applies the study to a specific use and makes investment decisions based primarily on the cost versus income viewpoint. Important locations from the speculation point of view must be based on the growth trend that is currently evident as well as the historic patterns of growth for the area. Some communities seem to grow naturally in one or two directions. This growth may be divided between residential and commercial use.

In long-range investing the investor must look at neighboring cities to see which of the two divisions of use is moving toward the intended investment. It is not uncommon for one community to be expanding with residential use toward another town that has industrial growth closing the gap. This can occur because the major job market is this industrial sector and the neighboring city the residential source for workers. When these two growth sectors collide, the residential area could be affected adversely.

### Case Study

Review the following and complete:

1. There is an intersection of two major roads. The road that travels north and south has the greatest traffic. Which of the following two corners would be best for a gas station and convience store?

   _____

   *a.* NE corner and the NW corner
   *b.* NE corner and the SW corner
   *c.* NW corner and the SE corner
   *d.* None of the above

2. In the above situation a road count check shows that the traffic count is greatest moving north in the morning, and south in the late afternoon. Which *one* corner would be the best location for a gas station and convenience store?_____

   *a.* NE corner
   *b.* SE corner
   *c.* NW corner
   *d.* SW corner

3. Why would this be likely? _____

   _____
   _____

4. Turn to The Real Estate Investor's VIP List and complete the following:
   (29)  Court house
   (30)  County commissioners names
   (31)  Commissioner
   (32)  Commissioner
   (33)  Commissioner
   (34)  Commissioner
   (37)  Director or head of county building department
   (38)  Director or head of county health department
   (39)  Head of county zoning department
   (40)  Head of county planning department ·
   (41)  Clerk of the circuit court
   (42)  Head of the county Department of Transportation

# 9

# Why Zoning Is Important and How to Change It to Increase Property Values

## Chapter Goals

This chapter introduces the reader to the importance of local zoning rules and regulations and illustrates how these rules and regulations affect the value of real estate. The primary goal of this chapter is to show the reader how to interpret zoning ordinances, use them, and change them to the investor's advantage. An equally important result of this goal is to provide the reader with insight on when to "move on" to another property if the zoning is too restrictive or the local government is not sympathetic to the needed zoning changes.

## Key Terms

- City manager's role
- Density
- Grandfather provisions

- Planning and zoning board
- Spot zoning

Review each of these seven items.

## City Manager's Role

The city manager, or county administrator, depending on the level of government, runs the day-to-day business of the city or county government. He or she answers to the city council or county commission but is a nonelected official who has specific training and experience in dealing with the business end of government as well as the finesse needed to act as an intermediary between the elected officials and the people they are supposed to represent. In normal circumstances this administrative position survives the elected officials, and it is not uncommon for the manager or administrator to be in the same position for an entire career. Sometimes these officials move on (up or down the ladder, depending on your point of view) and go into politics and run for elected offices. These administrators are very influential within their sphere of reference.

The reader should appreciate that developing a good relationship with the city and county administrator can be very helpful in many aspects of real estate investing. When it comes to "getting things done," the administrator can quickly cut through red tape and move a problem from endless frustration to a point of final determination.

In zoning matters the city or county administrator can assist the investor by providing direction to the elected officials who may be sympathetic to the investor's plight or needs. This information, coupled with advice on how to achieve maximum results, can be valuable to the investor in getting the most flexibility out of existing zoning rules or when going before the zoning board for the first step in obtaining a change in zoning.

## Density

Every zoning provision has some regulation that establishes the maximum density of development for any given property. In the case of residential property, the density may be stated in terms of the number of "families" that can live per acre on a tract of land. In rural areas this limitation may be set as so many families per number of acres, such as "one residence per five acres." In the case of multifamily property the density can be established with a set number not to be exceeded—such as 12 units (family units) per acre, or through a more complex square footage allocation per number of bathrooms or bedrooms constructed. The square footage allocation is a more restrictive form of density, as it can greatly limit the number of units that can be placed on a property depending on the size (number of bathrooms or bedrooms) contemplated. For example, a property that consists of 1 acre (43,560 sq ft of land area) is in a zoning that allows the following:

> One-bedroom apartments for each 4000 sq ft of land, two-bedroom apartments for each 5000 sq ft of land, three-bedroom apartments for each 6000 sq ft of land. In each case, for more than one bathroom add 356 sq ft to the square footage requirement. For more than three bedrooms add 500 sq ft to the square footage requirement.

To calculate the number of units that can be placed on a property without consideration to any other rule or regulation, the investor would be required to calculate the allocation per size of apartment desired.

This zoning density would allow the following. Up to:

- Ten one-bedroom two-bath units (4356 sq ft each of land area—found by taking the 4000 sq ft allocated for a one-bedroom apartment plus the extra bathroom requiring 356 ft of land area). Divide the total allocated 4356 sq ft into the total square footage of the property, which is 1 acre or 43,560 sq ft. The result is 10 apartments of this size.

- Eight two-bedroom two-bath units (5356 sq ft each of land area). *Note:* when this square footage is divided into the land area of 43,560 the result is 8.13, but when rounded to the lowest whole number the allowable number would be 8.

- Six three-bedroom three-bath units (6712 sq ft each of land area).

Combinations of the above can be used to provide a mix of different sizes of units provided that the total number of units does not exceed the allocated square footage of land area.

Critical to density calculations are some other rules within the zoning ordinances, such as setback rules, height restrictions, parking requirements, and minimum square footage allowed per bedroom unit. These restrictions may make the actual construction of the number of units desired impossible. For example, if in the above case the investor wanted to build six very large three-bedroom three-bath units of 4000 sq ft per apartment (to include enclosed garage and an enclosed screened porch), the developer may discover that setbacks, off-street parking, and landscaping area requirements could (in this case) restrict the building so that no more than 40 percent footage of actual land area could be used for the "footprint" (the outline the building makes on the lot) of the building. This would mean that 40 percent of 43,560 sq ft or 17,424 sq ft (43,560 × 40% = 17,424 sq ft) would be the maximum footage that could be covered by the building. To build six units of 4000 sq ft each would mean a total of 24,000 sq ft of floor area. To build these units on this property under the zoning as described would require at least two floors of construction. If the zoning allowed two floors of construction (which it may not), this added cost may be excessive in view of the income intended or needed to make the project economically feasible, and the investor would be faced with the following options:

1. To build part of the structure in two floors so that the footprint does not exceed 17,424 sq ft.

2. To adjust the total square footage of the units so that the desired six-apartment structure could be built on one level.

3. To change the nature of units so that the land area requirements are reduced—for example, by building four three-bedroom units and three one-bedroom units, the developer would actually get seven apartments overall but would still have to adjust the square footage to stay within the 17,424 sq ft available for the building footprint.

4. To apply for a variance to allow a change in the setbacks or other restrictive rules that have limited the percentage of land area for the footprint. Suppose the 40 percent limitation was due to the off-street parking requirement and the developer feels he or she can demonstrate that by having enclosed garages within the building, the added off-street parking requirements could be reduced. A possible outcome is a variance that would allow the developer to build even though strict code enforcement would not permit construction.

5. To apply for a change of zoning to a greater density use. The developer may decide that economically the best approach would be to build ten three-bedroom three-bath apartments on the site, but to do that would require a change to a less restrictive zoning.

6. To move on to another site.

## Grandfather Provisions

These are allowed violations to current zoning ordinances or building codes due to the fact that the existing structure was built prior to the existing rules and regulations. These provisions present hidden hazards for investors because while they may be allowed now, a needed change in the building (desired expansion or repair or rebuilding due to a fire or other casualty) may require that the entire structure now meet the current rules and regulations. In some cases the change can be as simple as the change of use, say, from an office building to retail stores. The only protection an investor has to ensure against these hidden hazards is to follow these three steps.

### The Three Steps to Deal with Grandfathered Provisions

1. In writing, ask the listing agent (and expect an answer in writing) if he or she is aware of any conditions which are "grandfathered in" that would otherwise be building code or zoning ordinance violations.

2. In the offer to purchase insert a provision that the seller warrants there are no conditions that are grandfathered in which would otherwise be building code or zoning ordinance violations.

3. Request an inspection from the local governing building department for them to attest in writing that no zoning or building code violations exist, grandfathered in or not.

## Planning and Zoning Board

This board comprises citizens of the community who have been appointed by the city council or county commission (depending on the level of the local authorities in question) who review planning and zoning matters and who give their recommendations to the city council or county commission for further disposition. When the investor initiates a petition to change the zoning of a specific property, this board is usually the first step. The procedure before the planning and zoning board may vary between different local communities, but in general the stages are the following.

### The Four Stages of a Rezoning Petition

1. A petition or application for zoning change is filed with the city clerk or county clerk (depending on the governing body). A fee is paid to start this process. A checklist accompanies the petition that indicates the required information. Usual material includes the following:

- Legal description
- Owner's name and address
- Recent survey
- Existing zoning
- Zoning requested
- Reason for the change requested

2. The petition is placed on a future agenda and is properly advertised according to the state laws for such events. It is customary that these rules require a 30-day advance public announcement and written notification of property owners within a certain distance from the property.

3. On the day the petition is presented to the planning and zoning board, the petitioner has the right to make a personal appearance (or have professionals do this with or for him or her), to present his or her case. The public, having been notified of the petition, can come to the meeting and speak out for or against the petition. It is not unusual for the audience to be predominantly against the petition.

4. Depending on the local rules, the petition can be deferred to another meeting, sent to workshop meetings to iron out problems, approved with or

without conditions, or not approved but passed on to the council or commission without the approval of the planning and zoning board. The final approval must come from the elected officials within the city council or county commission.

### Spot Zoning

**Spot zoning** occurs when one lot or a very small section within a subdivision has a zoning different from that around it. This occurs very often in normal planning but generally relates to special uses such as golf courses, parks, recreational use, churches, schools, and special commercial uses, e.g., gas stations and funeral homes.

Master plans attempt to have a natural flow of zoning so that commercial uses are delegated to highways and other high traffic roadways, with multi-family zoning often a buffer between the commercial uses and single-family residential use. When a developer or investor attempts to enhance the economic potential of a property by making a zoning change, he or she should note that the greatest resistance from the planning and zoning boards and the council or commission in reviewing petitions is from attempts to create spot zoning.

A petition that will result in spot zoning is therefore much more difficult to obtain. When the investor is faced with this likelihood, one way around this problem is to contact other property owners in the immediate area to see if enough would agree to a rezoning petition that would include their property as well so that the area to be rezoned would no longer fall into a spot zoning category.

## How to Use Zoning Changes to Increase Values and Limit Risk at the Same Time

While zoning establishes the basic use for any given location, there is generally some flexibility within the zoning ordinances or the investor can seek to create flexibility, giving added investment potential. If the flexibility in the actual zoning still will not permit the desired construction or use, the investor may want to attempt to change the zoning of the property to a classification that would allow the desired construction or use.

### Some Communities Encourage Development

Some communities encourage real estate development and tend to have a good "let's work it out" attitude within the building and zoning departments. When an investor encounters this kind of cooperation, variances or zoning changes are easier to accomplish than with a community that is against any and all changes. An investor should quickly discover which of these two attitudes prevail. It is possible that one community can be closed to all changes while a neighboring town can be open to reasonable changes that will bring growth and employment.

## Reduce Risk by Obtaining a More Flexible Zoning

The name of the game is to increase value while at the same time to reduce risk. Because a zoning change is likely to ensure an increase in value, if an investor can tie up a property knowing the value will go up when the zoning is changed, then the investment will have very little risk. However, the risk will not be zero because of the cost and time involved and because not every petition for rezoning is successful. The key to obtaining required changes is to know and understand the local political attitude about granting variances and zoning changes and to have an in-depth working knowledge of the zoning ordinances.

## The Six Steps to Obtain a Zoning Change

| | |
|---|---|
| The property | Have an "out" in the contract |
| Preliminary homework | File the rezoning petition |
| Tie up the property | Close on the contract |

**The Property.** Find a property in which a slight increase in zoning category will produce a profit. The type of property is determined by the market and availability.

**Preliminary Homework.** Sit down with the city manager and/or one of the city council members you know and discuss the proposal. Explain the intended use for the property and what must be changed to permit that use. The first meeting may provide clues about what these people feel their city really needs. If the original plan does not fit within those needs, the investor may wish to shift the plan so it has a better chance of being approved. Working with the flow can be more productive than fighting city hall.

**Tie Up the Property.** Contracts to purchase with contingencies that give the buyer an out or use an option can work well in allowing the investor to have control over the property without having to actually buy it until the zoning has been altered to the investor's best interests. The investor should have a firm agreement in hand before proceeding with any rezoning petitions. Once the process has started the property value can increase simply because the idea becomes public knowledge.

**Have an "Out" in the Contract.**   If the final decision to buy into or walk away from the deal depends on a zoning change or variance, it is essential that the investor has some kind of out or escape clause in the agreement that will give the investor the option to close on the transaction or not. To do this the investor must make the contract contingent on the investor obtaining a zoning change. One such provision is shown below:

> *Conditioned on rezoning:* The buyer, at his expense, will promptly file a petition with the proper governing authorities to change the current zoning from R-3 to R-4. This contract is conditioned on the buyer obtaining this rezoning without conditions, or if conditions are imposed as a part of the rezoning, the buyer must be in agreement with such conditions to the rezoning. The buyer has a period of 180 days in which to obtain this rezoning after which, if not successful as aforementioned, the buyer may elect to withdraw from this agreement and have any and all deposits refunded, or the buyer may elect to proceed to close under the terms of this agreement as though the zoning conditions have been met.

**File the Rezoning Petition.**   The investor should now proceed to effect the changes required by way of a variance or zoning change. A variance, when it will work, is often easier to get than a full zoning change. However, this will depend on the situation and the kind of cooperation available from the planning and zoning department and the city or county commission.

**Close on the Contract.**   Close according to the contract once the petition for change is granted and approved by all the required governing bodies. This action gives the investor a vested interest in the property that will make a sudden shift by the local governing bodies to rezone the property very difficult.

## How to Deal with
## the Zoning Process

Unlike flying an airplane, there is no actual school that teaches the process for obtaining rezoning. This book illustrates the importance of this procedure and gives the reader the necessary fundamentals, but each local community is so different that some "on the job" training is not only essential but critical. Because getting to know the workings of the local bureaucratic process is a necessary task for successful real estate investors, the reader will find that attending both planning and zoning board meetings and city and county council or commission meetings will provide "lessons" that can be later copied by the petitioners when their own rezoning petition is filed.

A check with the clerk at city hall will generally provide a schedule for all public meetings held by the city and county departments. Agendas of these meetings are not always printed in advance, but the clerk usually can provide the information over the phone a day or so in advance of the meeting. If matters concerning variances and rezoning are to be presented, the meeting should be attended.

At the meeting, the investor should make a list of each of the board or council members. The city lawyer is usually present, as will be other officials who tend to the tasks of recording the session, handling paperwork, dealing with security of the session, and so on. At times department heads or their assistants from different sections of the local government are present when their input is required to provide insight about an item on the agenda.

The investor will be able to get background information on each of these members from the city or county clerk. This background information may give clues about topics of mutual interest that will aid that investor's approach in making personal contact with members who may later be influential or helpful in giving advice on a zoning problem, or voting on the rezoning petition soon to be presented.

## Six Lessons to Be Learned from Attending Rezoning Hearings

Learn how the pros do it

Discover how the decision makers react

Find out where possible objections can come from

How to make the presentation like the pros do—only better

What if the majority of the zoning board votes no?

See how concessions and compromises work for both parties

Review each in detail.

**Learn How the Pros Do It.**   Important or difficult rezoning matters are often presented to boards and councils by professionals experienced in such matters. These professionals often are lawyers who are attended by the battery of needed experts such as engineers, architects, traffic experts, and environmental specialists. The methods these professionals use can be mimicked if the investor wishes to make his or her own presentation, or an investor will be able to make a qualified selection of one of these professionals, having seen them in action.

**Discover How the Decision Makers React.**    How the board and council members react to variances and rezoning matters, and how they interact among themselves, the professionals making presentations, and the general public in attendance at the meeting can be a critical lesson of learning *what not to do.*

There is no guarantee that any member of any board or council will be knowledgeable in the matter to be presented before it, so some of the less astute members may need to be carefully "taught" about the proposition and why it will be good for the area. Other members will simply follow their standard way of voting, while others will grasp the situation right from the start. When there are obvious "slow learners" on the board or council, the petitioner can accelerate the process and have a better chance of winning by sitting down with the "slow learner" and going over the proposition several days (or weeks) prior to the hearing. By taking a slow and positive approach the petitioner can keep a supporter on his or her side, or win over someone who might vote against the petition solely because the person did not fully grasp the impact or benefit of the project or change requested.

**Find out Where Possible Objections Can Come From.**    At most rezoning hearings there will be objections no matter how beneficial to the community the proposal may be. The dissenters may be professionals hired by others to voice these objections, or the objections can come from heads of homeowner's associations or other private or nonprofit groups in the community. When objections can be anticipated from certain groups, the presentation should be planned to answer objections *before they are raised.*

**How to Make the Presentation Like the Pros Do—Only Better.**    When the petition is not very complicated, a well-documented presentation by the property owner can have as much of a chance for success as the pros, in fact, even more. This is because the decision makers often respond better and more positively to the actual owner than to a high-priced team trying to "make up their mind" for them. Time and experience gathered by attending rezoning hearings will allow the investor to see how other property owners do. The key is to learn what works and where the decision makers' hot buttons are.

**What If the Majority of the Zoning Board Votes No?**    Even if the planning and zoning board says "no" to a petition, this is usually not the end of the world. The petition is then sent to the city council or county commission *without the zoning board's approval.* The petitioner will then present his or her case to the council or commission for actual approval or denial. As there will be some time between the "no" vote from the zoning board and the council or commission meeting, the petitioner can attempt to overcome some or all of the zoning board's objections or counter them in an effective way by concessions or changes. The final word comes from the council or commission.

**See How Concessions and Compromises Work for Both Parties.** Concessions are the name of the game. Savvy developers know this and know just how far they can go to win the rezoning by making concessions by following past rezoning petitions. At workshop sessions generally the compromises and concessions each party can live with are discussed. When the attitude is pro-development the problems seem to melt away, and each party goes away from the table satisfied.

Review the following section of a multifamily zoning ordinance.

---

### SECTION 47-13.1.0. "R-4-C" DISTRICT*

**Sec. 47-13.10.1. Purpose of district.**

The R-4-C district is a planned high rise, high density hotel and tourist residential district. It is intended for locations, such as parts of the beach, where it is desirable to encourage hotels and motels and other tourist-related facilities because of the importance of the tourist industry to the city and also to preserve and enhance the appearance and image of the city. Because of the relationship of such areas to non-tourist residential areas, traffic and transportation facilities, beaches and parks, and other community facilities, special provisions are required to allow such areas to be utilized for high intensity tourist facilities and insure a development consistent with a high quality tourist resort area. Those provisions depend on the details of site and building design and include the use, appearance, height, bulk and location of principal and accessory buildings, and the location and design of landscaping, open space land and water areas, recreation areas, parking areas and other features. Therefore, review and approval of a development plan are required to insure such provisions will be provided. (Ord. No. C-77-166, § 1, 1-3-78)

**Sec. 47-13.10.2. Uses permitted.**

No building or structure, or part thereof, shall be erected, altered or used, or land or water used, in whole or in part, for other than any use hereinafter set out:

(a) Any use permitted in R-4, if approved by the planning and zoning board, except hospitals and nursing homes.

*Editor's note—Ord. No. C-77-166, § 1, enacted Jan. 3, 1978, repealed former Section 47-13.10, §§ 47-13.10.1—47-13.10.10, relative to the R-4-C district, derived from Ord. No. C-74-73, § 1, adopted July 2, 1974, and enacted in lieu thereof a new Section 47-13.10, §§ 47-13.10.1—47-13.10.10, pertaining to the same subject matter.

---

*(Continued)*

(b) Accessory buildings for use as convention facilities, restaurants, bars, nightclubs, and recreation facilities located on the same site as a hotel or motel of one hundred (100) or more guest rooms, when approved by the planning and zoning board. Prior to approving such use, the board shall make a finding that such use is consistent with a high quality resort area and that the location will not be detrimental to nearby properties.

(c) Commercial or private recreation facilities such as pitch and putt courses, tennis courts, shuffleboard courts, boating and similar, provided the planning and zoning board finds that they are consistent with high quality tourist residential use of nearby property.

(d) Museum or cultural facility, including commercial art galleries, studios, and similar. (Ord. No. C-77-166, § 1, 1-3-78)

**Sec. 47-13.10.3. Special accessory uses.**

(a) Hotels, apartment hotels and motels having fifty (50) or more units may have restaurants, night clubs, dining rooms, or bars which are of such design and size as to cater primarily to the guests of the main use, subject to the provisions of all ordinances of the City of Fort Lauderdale and subject to limitation of subparagraph (c) of this section. Patio bars and food service areas shall also be permitted, subject to the foregoing limitations and subject to the prior approval of the planning and zoning board, which shall consider the following factors:

(1) The location of the proposed use on the property;

(2) The impact of the proposed use on the abutting properties;

(3) The adequacy of the parking for the proposed use; and

(4) The compatibility of the proposed use with existing land uses in the surrounding neighborhood.

The planning and zoning board shall either grant, deny, or grant with specified conditions, the application for the proposed outdoor use.

Turn to The Real Estate Investor's VIP List and complete the following:

(47) County tax assessor
(48) Head property appraiser
(49) County commission meetings
(50) County planning and zoning meetings

*Tip:* One call to the county court house (29) should give you numbers or extensions to the source of the above.

(61)  State Department of Transportation

(62)  State health department

(68)  Army Corps of Engineers

*Tip:* One call to the nearest state offices should provide numbers or extensions to the source of the above.

(103)  Architects

(104)  Architects

(121)  Real estate lawyer

(122)  Rezoning lawyer

*Tip:* Attend several county commission or city zoning hearings and names for the above will come up. Or, check with friends and local realtors for referrals.

# 10

# How to Reduce Investment Risk When Dealing with Building Codes and Restrictions

## Chapter Goals

Building codes and restrictions can have a profound impact on real estate values. The primary goal of this chapter is to show how these codes and restrictions affect the current and future values of property and to discover how to deal with the local building department. The basis for this is to illustrate how to avoid and overcome problems that occur due to possible violations of building codes. Building codes and restrictions as do zoning ordinances tend to become more restrictive over time. Changes in local building restrictions may cause older properties to be in violation of the new codes. This can create a "time bomb" of expense when the unsuspecting investor acquires a property that must now be improved to meet these codes.

## Key Terms

- Building department
- Building heights
- Encroachments

- Fire codes
- Green area and landscaping
- Building permits
- Property setbacks
- Deed restrictions
- Site plan approval
- Survey
- Utility and access easements

Review each of the items in detail.

## Building Department

Virtually every community has a building department of their own or shares one with a neighboring city. The building department reviews building plans and issues building permits for construction. They also maintain records of past construction when permits were issued. Because the permit may indicate the estimated cost of the improvement or construction, it is possible for investors to double-check statements given about the cost of such improvements. The building department also inspects construction to ensure that the work continues per code and as the submitted plans indicate.

During construction periodic inspections are made and until the work has been approved, that affected portion of the construction cannot continue.

As a reference center, the building department is very valuable to real estate investors. Often, it is impossible to find building plans on older structures except from the records at the building department. From these records an investor can ascertain if any work or construction was done without a permit. Construction occurs without permits all the time, so investors should be aware that sometimes unlicensed contractors or part-time carpenters do work that may violate the building codes. The building department has the authority to impose very expensive fines for such work with the possible result that the property owner be required to remove the construction made without permits.

## Building Heights

Many communities have height restrictions as a part of their zoning ordinances. However, building codes can also restrict height in the following two ways: economic and interpretation of code restrictions.

**Economic restrictions** occur when the cost to build higher floors becomes disproportionate to the income potential from the added structure. Elevators, interior fire stairwells, types of construction, sprinkler systems for fire protection, and the like become more expensive the higher the elevation. This added cost may not be offset by added income from the extra space constructed.

Building codes can limit building height through **interpretation of elements of the code**. For example, some communities have a shadow law that is part of the building code restrictions. This provision may prohibit any building from casting a shadow during certain hours of the day on adjoining or nearby property. If the investor desiring to construct a high-rise building owns enough property to contain the shadow, the restriction of height would not apply. Some fire codes limit the height of buildings for certain uses.

### Encroachments

When a building or other structure extends past a property line onto, over, or under the adjoining property, an **encroachment** occurs. Some encroachments are obvious and appear on the survey. Sometimes encroachments are less obvious, such as a septic tank drain field that crosses a property line but is underground and not visible until the neighbor digs it up while installing a swimming pool.

### The Five Reasons Encroachments Occur

1. *Improper survey:* An error is made with the location of property boundary and construction is later completed in the wrong place.

2. *Miscalculation in construction:* Measurements in plans are misread, property lines incorrectly drawn, etc.

3. *Division of property after structures are in place:* A property owner cuts up a farm and one or more of the buildings encroach over the new property lines.

4. *By design:* A building extends across a boundary on purpose to serve the needs of each property owner or for some other reason. This may have been okay at the time the encroachment was created, but a problem can exist for new owners unless there was an easement granted for the encroachment.

5. *By nature:* If a property line is a natural boundary such as a river, a change in the river can create an encroachment.

When an encroachment occurs without the property owner's permission, legal proceedings may be initiated by the owner of the property being trespassed. All investors need to be sure that when they buy a property there are no encroachments onto other property. Encroachments that do not involve property lines are the least obvious of all. They occur when a building is built into easements, within setback lines, and into the air rights of others. The most common of these is when a setback ordinance has been changed after a building has been built, creating a grandfathered provision for the existing building. A future edition or rebuilding in the event of a casualty (fire, for example), may not be approved unless the building codes can be relaxed (obtained through a variance).

## Fire Codes

In many communities building plans are reviewed carefully for compliance to fire protection codes. Because fire protection has improved due to new technology and more stringent fire codes, most structures over 10 years old may not meet the current regulations. Unlike other building codes that may allow the structure to be grandfathered "as is" without the requirement to upgrade to current standards, most fire codes become absolute requirements, and many unsuspecting investors have discovered, after the closing, that the state requires their newly purchased building to have fire sprinklers installed in every enclosed space within the building. It may not be just the cost to bring the building to current standards that hurts . . . this kind of construction can require the closing of the building for a period of time, which may mean the loss of income from rents when the new investor needs it the most. Worse still, the building may take some time to recover the possible loss of tenants.

Normally when there is a major change in a fire code that would require an existing building to install fire sprinklers, the owners are given several years in which to comply. A property owner who has not complied in hopes of selling the property to save a $50,000 cost, for example, may be a highly motivated seller. If this is the reason, and the investor *knows* of the fire code regulations, then the investor need only take the future cost into consideration when negotiating for the building.

## Green Area and Landscaping Requirements

There is a growing trend for more open space and landscaping around buildings. Green area is the amount of land area that cannot be used for anything except landscaping or sometimes water retention (ponds or lakes). This is often stated in the form of a percentage of the property, for example, "25 percent of the land must be green area." In some circumstances it may be possible to use this green area or to design it to be functional, such as gardens that separate buildings, tennis courts, putting greens, and other public areas for apartment buildings. Sometimes green area is a calculation based on several factors, such as the square footage of the building and/or its use. Landscaping requirements can be very detailed, even to the exclusion of certain kinds of plants or the requirement for specific plants to be used. Because many communities are trying to improve the aesthetic nature of some commercial areas, in particular vast parking lots, it is possible that an investor may suddenly discover a city requirement to plant trees and other landscape areas around a parking lot that serves the just-acquired shopping center. This is another "time bomb" expense that is easy to check in advance.

## Building Permits

Obtaining a building permit can be a very sobering experience to the novice builder and investor. Frustrations are bound to occur if the process is rushed. So "slow and easy" is the only way to contemplate getting a building permit. The best way to obtain a building permit is to let the builder or general contractor do it. However, it is a good idea for all real estate investors to know how the process works. The people within the building department are very helpful and usually have a checklist that can be followed. (See illustrations on pages 133–135.)

## Property Setbacks

Not every property has a required setback, but when they occur they are very important. Setbacks are the distances structures must be situated from a property line. These distances are generally shown within the zoning ordinances for each specific kind of zoning and may vary for front, rear, and side boundaries. Corners are usually treated as two front setback lines.

Generally the only structures that can be constructed within the setback lines would be walls and fences of limited height, driveways, utility lines, landscaping structures, and walkways. Each of these items must be constructed according to code. Encroachments into setback lines can create a building code or zoning violation and potential title problems later on, so every new construction should be watched carefully so that it does not violate these setback or boundary lines.

A hidden hazard with any restriction that seems to occur most with setback requirements is the **deed restriction** setback. Many residential developers formulate their own list of building restrictions within newly formed subdivisions. These restrictions are always more restrictive than the actual city codes or restrictions. For example, the city code may provide for a setback minimum of 5 ft on side lot lines, whereas the developer may create a setback minimum of 10 ft.

## Deed Restrictions

Other restrictions can be added to the deed that limit building design, prohibit "for sale" signs, prohibit animals over a certain size, require white roofs, limit or prohibit the sale of tobacco on the property, and so on—

there may be no logic to a deed restriction. Usually these restrictions are designed by the developer of the subdivision or the seller of any property to enhance the area by creating stricter standards than the local zoning or building codes establish. The problem with deed restrictions is that they may not be evident, despite the fact that to be valid they must have been properly recorded and would therefore have become a part of every deed unless limited by state statute or by the restriction itself. A deed may contain a clause that references deed restrictions that were recorded on a past date, without actually listing the deed restrictions. Failure to check those deed restrictions can become another hidden "time bomb" investors may face.

---

### DISPLAY THIS CARD ON FRONT OF JOB

# CITY OF FORT LAUDERDALE
# BUILDING PERMIT

PERMIT No.-F.L. *92-7063*                    ZONE *R-1*

OWNER *J. W. Cummings*                    DATE *5/19/92*

CONTRACTOR *EDWARD HOBEL*

PURPOSE *REROOF, FLAT*

LOT *12*                    BLOCK *"M"*

SUBDIVISION *Ocean Ridge*

ADDRESS *911 West Lake Drive*

---

CERTIFICATE OF OCCUPANCY MUST BE SECURED BEFORE THIS
BUILDING CAN BE USED FOR ANY PURPOSE

**DO NOT REMOVE THIS CARD BEFORE COMPLETION**

### For Inspection Call 761-5191

FORM AB —243 Rev. 2/91

# NO INSPECTION WILL BE MADE UNLESS PERMIT CARD DISPLAYED AND APPROVED PLANS ARE READILY AVAILABLE

# INSPECTION RECORD

### ZONING

| | INSPECTOR | DATE |
|---|---|---|
| Set Back | | |
| Height | | |
| Parking | | |
| Overhang | | |
| Rock | | |
| Occupancy | | |
| | | |
| Landscape | | |
| | | |
| FINAL | | |

### MECHANICAL

| | INSPECTOR | DATE |
|---|---|---|
| Slab | | |
| Duct | | |
| Pipes | | |
| Hood | | |
| W/Cooler | | |
| Notes | | |
| | | |
| | | |
| FINAL | | |

### BUILDING    PLUMBING    ELECTRICAL

+ ATTACH HERE +     +ATTACH HERE↓

| | INSPECTOR | DATE | | INSPECTOR | DATE | | INSPECTOR | DATE |
|---|---|---|---|---|---|---|---|---|
| Soil Treat. | | | Rough | | | Temp. Pole | | |
| Soil Comp. | | | Top Out | | | Slab | | |
| Foundation | | | Fire Spr. | | | Rough | | |
| Slab | | | Swim Pool | | | Service | | |
| Spot Survey | | | Storm Dra. | | | Pool | | |
| Columns | | | Gas | | | Meter Room | | |
| Tie Beam | | | Water Ser. | | | | | |
| Truss | | | Sewer | | | | | |
| Framing | | | Grease Tr. | | | | | |
| Insulation | | | Septic Tk. | | | | | |
| Wire Lath | | | Notes: | | | Notes | | |
| Dry Wall | | | | | | | | |
| Roof Sheat. | | | | | | | | |
| Wall Sheat. | | | | | | | | |
| Tin Cap | | | | | | | | |
| Pool Steel | | | | | | | | |
| Deck | | | | | | | | |
| Handicap | | | | | | | | |
| | | | | | | | | |
| Fire Prot. | | | | | | | | |
| | | | | | | | | |
| FINAL | | | FINAL | | | FINAL | | |

REQUIRES APPROVAL OF ELECTRICAL, PLUMBING, MECHANICAL BEFORE FRAMING

WARNING TO OWNER: YOUR FAILURE TO RECORD A NOTICE OF COMMENCE-MENT MAY RESULT IN YOUR PAYING TWICE FOR IMPROVEMENTS TO YOUR PROPERTY. IF YOU INTEND TO OBTAIN FINANCING, CONSULT WITH YOUR LENDER OR AN ATTORNEY BEFORE RECORDING YOUR NOTICE OF COMMENCEMENT.

CERTIFICATE OF OCCUPANCY MUST BE SECURED BEFORE THIS BUILDING CAN BE USED FOR ANY PURPOSE

## DO NOT REMOVE THIS CARD BEFORE COMPLETION

### For Inspection Call 761-5191

FORM AB —243 Rev. 2/91

**THIS PERMIT CARD MUST BE DISPLAYED
ON THE FRONT OF THE JOB BY ONE OF THE
FOLLOWING METHODS**

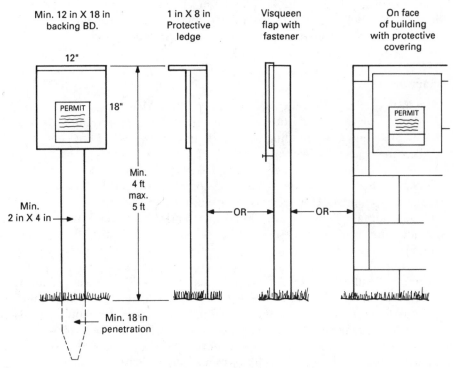

FASTEN TO BACKING AS INDICATED ON CARD

Deed restrictions require someone to enforce them for them to be effective over a long term. In the beginning, the developer, still selling within a subdivision, is the truant officer watching for violations. Later, long after the developer is gone, the trend is to ease away from the deed restrictions, but another property owner can—and sometimes will—insist on strict adherence to a deed restriction. Any seller can place a deed restriction when transferring a property; therefore it is necessary to check all transfers within the time that a state may establish that deed restrictions automatically become invalid.

## Site Plan Approval

In many instances, usually with commercial and multifamily development, prior to a building permit being issued the developer must present a site plan for approval by a reviewing board. The site plan is an architectural drawing showing the footprint of the building, sometimes the elevation views so that the idea of what the building will look like can be seen, with all roadways, traffic flow, parking spaces, utilities, fire protection, and landscaping indicated. Once the site plan has been approved the working drawings for the building can be completed and presented for the building department to review prior to approval of the building permit.

## Survey

The survey is the actual drawing of the property that has been completed by a licensed surveyor within the area. This survey becomes the initial layout for all plans and most building permits require surveyors to locate and verify that the corners of structures and all subsoil work (plumbing, electrical, septic tanks, drains, etc.) have been placed in the proper location with respect to the survey. When this is done correctly, there are never any current encroachments. However, in modern times many surveys are made with the surveyor taking his starting point from a marker or survey monument at an adjoining property. These markers are often pipes in the ground surrounded by cement and may not be permanent and may have been set in the wrong place from the beginning. A survey that has an incorrect "point of beginning" will have incorrect boundaries and will be likely to cause future encroachments. Fortunately, survey errors are not very evident and while they are likely more widespread than realized, the errors are usually so small that real problems rarely surface. Investors should get into the habit of having new surveys made for all property purchased. Once the survey is completed it should be compared with old surveys to make sure everything has remained the same. Any encroachment should show up on a survey. This is very important because most title insurance companies will not cover any loss or defend any action that would have been disclosed in a recent survey.

## Utility and Access Easements

An easement is the right granted by a property owner to one or more parties for the use of a portion of a property. Utility lines, such as water, sewer, phone, gas, and electric, all pass through, over, or under property. Sometimes there is a utility easement that runs across part of a property. This easement was granted at some time in the past by the owner of the property at that time. It might have been a requirement to get a building permit, to plat the property, or to give a concession to the utility companies to ensure service to the property. Access easements often are a roadway or pathway that when in use are clearly visible. These easements are often granted by a previous property owner to him or herself before selling off a portion of a property that would otherwise block entrance or access to the remainder.

Property in recreational areas that have beach, lake, or river frontage may have public or private easements that cross the property.

All easements should show on a recent survey, and the actual document showing the grant of the easement should be recorded in the county records. However, unless the surveyor has done a good job in checking the recorded documents at the local property records archives or if the survey occurs prior to the recording of the easement, the survey can be in error.

# Five Steps to Reduce Investment Risk in Dealing with Building Codes and Restrictions Before Making an Investment

1. Discover potential problems.

2. Review the worst-case scenario.

3. Discuss solutions with local officials.

4. Get estimates of the correction cost.

5. Plan your investment strategy.

Review each in detail.

### Discover Potential Problems

At the end of this chapter there is a "Hidden time bomb" checklist that all investors should follow. It lists the most frequent building and zoning problems in most communities. But only a clear understanding of the zoning ordinances and building codes of a *specific area* can make the list be complete.

Including catchall phrases within the contract and getting disclosures from the broker in a deal may give the investor legal recourse against the seller or broker if a "time bomb" problem shows up later that was not discovered before the investment. However, legal recourse may not be very satisfying and can take a long time and be costly for little or no net gain.

> *The idea is to avoid problems whenever possible, not to just have a solution to deal with them when they show up.*

Every contract that will end up with ownership rights (even a long-term lease should be treated this way) should contain a clause that puts the burden on the seller or gives the buyer an escape provision should a problem be discovered prior to the closing of the transaction. When the broker or lawyer is drawing the offer to purchase (or option or lease), make sure building and zoning "time bombs" are covered. For example:

> *Condition:* The seller herein warrants that to the best of his or her knowledge, no local building or zoning violations or property encroachments exist, and that the most recent survey of which a copy is attached and made a part of this agreement is correct and shows all easements and right-of-ways across or abutting the property, and all building locations and improvements are in their correct and legal location and that no building is in violation of any setback restriction or ordinance. Should any violation be discovered to exist, this contract is contingent on the seller correcting the violation within 30 days and closing will be delayed by that period of time. If the violation cannot be corrected within that time for any reason, the buyer at his or her option may elect to withdraw from this agreement, which would thereinafter be considered null and void, and the buyer would have all deposits promptly refunded, or the buyer may proceed to close of the subject property.

If the investor is prudent and uses care and good judgment, a worst-case scenario will never occur. However, there are some very obvious steps that most property owners overlook. The simple "look and see if what it is supposed to be is correct" approach will uncover most potential problems. Prior to every contract review the checklist at the end of this chapter.

## Review the Worst-Case Scenario

What if? Once violations are discovered, a decision has to be made to proceed despite them or not, so try to get the seller to correct them or deal with them yourself. Sometimes the violation is the *very reason* the seller wants to dispose of the property. If this is the case, does the seller know just how bad the situation really is? In this situation, the seller would avoid a clause in the contract that would require the seller to make any and all corrections to the problem prior to closing. Just because the seller is motivated due to a violation that needs to be corrected is *not* a reason to avoid buying that property. An investor who has the time and money to deal with the problem may have found the ideal property situation: a property the buyer likes at a price and with terms that are ideal because the seller is highly motivated.

## Discuss Solutions
## with Local Officials

When the agreement to buy has been executed, *before* any estimates for correction have been obtained, the next step would be a conference with the local building officials. It is very possible that some flexibility in the codes will allow modifications to be made that would be less expensive than a full compliance to the code. Flexibility within building departments will vary due to the local attitude about the problem at hand and the investor's ability to deal with the situation. A calm and easy approach showing the problem and a sincere request for help from the department is the best method to use. The investor should not overlook the possibility that if use of the property is changed there may not be a violation. The existing zoning may allow such a change, or the investor may seek a variance or a change in zoning.

*The key to solving any problem is to know what the options are. Continue to ask the question: "What else could I do?"*

## Get Estimates of the Correction Cost

Construction estimates usually can be obtained without any advance cost from general contractors. When getting estimates for any construction work the investor should insist that the price include all necessary permits and that it be in writing. Included in the price estimate should be the estimated time to complete the job. Always get at least two estimates from two different contractors. If there is a major difference in the prices quoted, question each as to the reason for the difference. It is possible that each has made an error and new estimates need be made, and a third contractor should then be brought into the picture to get another estimate. Once the prices are obtained another conference with the building department could be held in another attempt to gain additional flexibility and reduce the cost. At this point the contractor with the most local influence could appear at the meeting with the building department to see what can be done to bring the costs down.

## Plan Your Investment Strategy

Every cost must have a balance or trade-off in the investment plan. If costs get out of hand or far exceed estimates, then the investment plan must be re-adjusted in an attempt to bring the plan back into balance. The best way to plan for unexpected expenses is to allow for them, in essence, plan for extra expenses that could not have been anticipated. Some investors plan for this by showing a **vacancy factor** in rental income. A five to seven percent of gross income deducted from a pro forma or budget for the investment may give this safety factor for unexpected expenses as well as unexpected income loss.

*When construction starts, avoid making any changes at all unless necessary—changes can be very expensive.*

## Review the Precontract Checklist

All investors who have already gone to contract on a property should use the following checklist prior to closing on that property. *Review this list prior to every offer made to acquire a property.* If there are items on the checklist that should be made a **contingent** part of the agreement, that is to say, any aspect in the contract of which the buyer would want to approve prior to being committed to the agreement, then the contract should contain an "out" provision that would enable the investor to void the agreement unless that factor was approved.

> *Remember—the reason a seller may be motivated is because he or she knows something the investor should.*

## The Precontract Checklist

1. Is it the same as was represented?
   *a.* Improvements.
      (1) Was construction done according to code, or with proper permits?
      (2) Check date of improvements.
      (3) Building plans should match actual improvements.
   *b.* Property boundaries.
      (1) Walk them off according to the new survey.
      (2) Compare them to old survey.
   *c.* Encroachments.
      (1) Do any appear on the recent survey?
      (2) What has been done about the old encroachments?
2. Review possible or current building or zoning violations.
   *a.* Check for existing violations.
   *b.* Check for pending or future violations due to changes and deadlines for upgrades.
   *c.* Be sure to check long-term required changes:
      (1) Fire code changes.
      (2) Landscape changes or additions.
      (3) Sign changes.
      (4) Road access changes.
      (5) Traffic changes.
3. Review property assessments—unpaid or not yet assessed.
   *a.* Check for existing property assessments not yet paid.
   *b.* Obtain knowledge of future assessments to come but not sent out to property owners.

c. Look into impact fees or replatting costs required before any future improvements are made.

4. Review deed and association for any restrictions.
   a. Are current deed restrictions in violation?
   b. What are the deed restrictions?
   c. Is this property part of any association?
   d. Are there any association rules violations?
   e. What are the association restrictions?

5. Have the title examined by competent advisors.
   a. Is the title clear of any liens?
   b. Is there previous title insurance (get a copy of the policy to review exclusions)?
   c. Have all previous clouds on title been cleared and are there any clouds evident now?
   d. Do the *legal description and dimensions* match what was represented as well as the *title?*

6. Have the building inspected by competent advisors.
   a. Roof—check for repairs and problems.
   b. Structure—check for cracks and code violations.
   c. Electrical—check for code violations and problems.
   d. Appliances—check for function.
   e. Gas lines or tanks—check for code violations and problems.
   f. Termite damage or presence.
   g. Plumbing—full and comprehensive inspection.
   h. Pumps and sprinkler systems—check for function.
   i. Zoning and code compliance.
   j. Compare property lines to survey.
   k. Other (as per local conditions and codes).

7. Review all documents under which the buyer becomes obligated or that still have an effect on the property.
   a. Mortgages and notes.
   b. Insurance policies.
   c. Leases.
   d. Warranties.
   e. Deeds and deed restrictions.
   f. Employment contracts.
   g. Service agreements.
   h. Work orders.
   i. Other.

Turn to The Real Estate Investor's VIP List and complete the following:

   (84) Surveyor
   (85) General contractor

*Tip:* Check with one of the architects (103) for referral.

(105)  Local newspaper

(106)  Local newspaper

*Tip:* Check the Yellow Pages.

(108)  Local legal newspaper or legal announcement publication

*Tip:* Check with one of the lawyer's offices (121) for the number for the source of the legal publication in the area.

# 11

# How to Get the Most out of Economic Conversions

## Chapter Goals

The most dramatic way to success in real estate investing is through **economic conversion**. The goal of this chapter is to introduce the reader to this concept and to illustrate its use.

Economic conversion takes place when the investor acquires a property that has one use (or no use at all) and converts it to something else. When done properly this change increases the economic potential of the property, thereby increasing the property value. Several examples are changing a motel to an office complex, developing a vacant lot into a U-Pick-It Strawberry Patch, altering an apartment complex into a time-share resort, upgrading a restaurant into a nightclub, and converting a five-unit apartment into a seven-unit complex. Sometimes the change is very subtle, such as the change of a general office building to an all-medical practice, but the end result is always increased income potential.

## Key Terms

- Escape clause
- Property expert

- Leverage
- Option
- Risk

Review each in detail.

## Escape Clause

A provision or clause in a contract that gives one or both parties the option of canceling the transaction during a certain period of time is called an **escape clause** or often just an "**out**." Investors like to use these clauses because the provision enables the investor to accomplish the following two important things at the same time without being legally bound to the contract:

1. To ascertain the best terms in a transaction without being committed to close.
2. To tie up the property for a period of time while other factors can be determined, reviewed, or obtained.

The investor attempting to accomplish either or both of the above must make sure that the escape clause is one-sided and works only for the buyer. If both parties could walk away from the deal without liability, the property would not be tied up and the escape provision would not be effective. Keep in mind that it is possible that there may be other provisions in the same contract that give both parties an out for a limited period of time. In exchange agreements, for example, each party may have the right to inspect and approve the property they are to get, and other agreements may allow a limited time period to review documents or check inventory or some other aspect of the property. Once the approvals have been obtained, those provisions can no longer be used as escape clauses.

Sellers also use escape provisions; the best use of one is shown below:

> *Credit check:* Inasmuch as the seller is to hold a purchase money second mortgage from the buyer, the seller has a period of ten working days in which to do a credit check, at his or her own expense, on the buyer. To facilitate this the buyer is to return as soon as possible the attached personal history form which is requested by the Credit Bureau. The ten working days begin the first working day following the day this form has been returned to the seller. If the seller rejects the credit of the buyer for any reason, then at the seller's option this contract shall be null and void and each party therein after released from any further obligation to the other.

When the buyer is contemplating an economic conversion, the provision will enable him or her to ascertain if the conversion can be completed and obtain cost estimates and building permits if needed *prior to closing.* By doing this the investor is removing the risk of buying a property and later discovering problems that cannot be solved. An example of an escape clause a buyer may use is given below:

> *Buyer's option:* In that it is the buyer's intention to convert the subject property from a four-unit apartment complex to a six-unit apartment complex, this contract is conditioned on the buyer obtaining, at his or her own expense, all necessary approvals required from all governing agencies or departments to allow this conversion. These approvals will include but not be limited to the following:
>
> 1. A letter from the building and zoning departments of the city and county in which the property is located stating that the property is correctly zoned for this conversion, that there are no building or utility moratoriums that would prevent this intended conversion, and that no special assessments other than usual building permits are required.
> 2. Approval and the issue of a building permit for the actual construction contemplated.
>
> The buyer has a period of six weeks to obtain the above information and should there be a delay caused by one or more of the governing bodies or should the buyer need to take the conversion in question to a zoning board or the city or county commission for a variance or zoning change, then this period will be extended for the period of time needed to meet those requirements, but under no circumstances shall this extension time exceed 120 days. At the end of that time the buyer must either proceed to close by making an additional deposit of $15,000 to the escrow agent, which together with other deposits made by the buyer would be forfeited by the buyer in the event he or she was later in default, or the buyer must elect to withdraw from this agreement and have all deposits made promptly refunded to him or her, after which each party will be released from any further obligation to the other.

With a provision similar to that above the buyer would have the property fully locked up all the way through the building permit stage up to a maximum of 162 days (six weeks, then if rezoning or variance is needed, another 120 days).

## Property Expert

Real estate is very local in nature and statistics. This point was made earlier, and all real estate investors should continually be reminded that real estate investing is unlike any other kind of commodity or market investment. There are no two identical pieces of property. When there are very similar properties their values will rise and fall in a very close relationship.

> *Everyone can become the property expert in their area.*

Becoming an expert in real estate is very easy. Every reader of this book can become a local property expert within their community if they apply the principles contained herein. The length of this process would vary, of course, but even a modest effort would be successful within six months. There are very few categories of investing where the novice can become an expert in such a short period of time.

## Leverage

Leverage in financing terms is the result when money is borrowed at a cost that is less then the yield the property generates. Under some circumstances an investor can borrow 100 percent of the funds needed to build or buy a property. In this case if the property will pay the debt service, then that investment is leveraged 100 percent.

## Option

An option is an investment technique that creates a **unilateral contract**. This is a contract or agreement that is one-sided. When the investor has an option to buy or lease at a set price, the owner has no control over the decision making and must go through with the deal if the investor decides to exercise his option. Options can be part of an escape clause or out and can become an important contract tool that investors use. Options are widely used as part of overall investment strategy.

## Risk

Risk is relative to each person and each transaction. When investors have done their homework and recognize an opportunity, then risk is greatly reduced. Most investors get into trouble not because they take risks that are too great, but because they make mistakes in their investment plans. If the investor overestimates the income potential and/or underestimates the operating expenses, then the deal is headed for problems and, in retrospect, the transaction was filled with risk. The whole idea about investing in real estate is to reduce risk by learning everything possible and important about every investment.

# When to Use Economic Conversion to Create Value

Economic conversion is used in one or a combination of the following situations:

1. A specific use is in mind and the investor looks for a property that will meet those needs. Some businesses look for fast food operations that have gone out of business because they have discovered that a conversion of that kind of location best suits their completely different business. One developer is successful in converting large old homes into corporate offices. Another investor has found conversions of well-located apartment buildings into seasonal furnished rentals to be highly lucrative. Land developers prosper because they know how to turn vacant acreage into housing developments and commercial ventures.

2. An opportunity is found in which a property will automatically increase in value if the investor causes a change in use. This often just means changing the zoning from one use to another to broaden the market appeal. Many investors specialize in taking a vacant tract of land, working through all the governmental paperwork to get approvals for a change of use, and then selling the property to developers who would rather pay a profit to the first investor because they can now move ahead into a ready-to-go property.

3. When there is a change in market demands and reduced value of an existing property, the owner should look for a new use or change in the existing use that will increase the value of the property. For example, when a neighborhood declines, rents fall and property loses value. Property owners can become *stuck* in this kind of market condition and be unable to sell their property. It can be very frustrating to watch property values erode nearly overnight, and most property owners feel there is little they can do except drop the price further. Continually dropping prices establish a trend that can be very hard to stop, and the already declining neighborhood may decline even further. What the property owner should do is make a positive effort to find a use that stabilizes the decline. When this is done the trend will be reversed and property values start going up. In severe situations this change may take a collective approach with a block of property owners to find out what change would make a turnaround possible. Sometimes a rezoning will help.

4. Community changes of any kind can create the need for different use and greater economic return because of it. New roads, bridges, airports, schools, hospitals, etc., all can have a profound effect on the neighborhoods in the area (both positive and negative effects). The same increase in community infrastructure can cause some property values to go up and oth-

ers to go down. A change in zoning may be the right step to bring things back to where they were. Because most infrastructure changes take a long time to occur, the investor who is savvy with future planning of the community can be ready to take advantage of opportunities long before they are visible to the general public.

## Seven Steps to Maximize the Effect of Economic Conversions

1. Find out what the local market needs.
2. Find out the amount that can be financed.
3. Determine whether the local government is receptive to "changes."
4. Look for the right property and "tie it up."
5. Insert reasonable outs or options into the contract.
6. Review the steps needed to make the required change.
7. Close at the last reasonable moment.

Review each in detail.

**Find Out What the Local Market Needs.**   There are more ways to generate potential for profit than by building another shopping center in a community filled with shopping centers with lots of unrented space. The best way to know what the market needs is to know the community very well. To accomplish this, a determined review of rents in the area will give a good picture of the market trend for rental property. Many vacant buildings or very low rents do not support a strong market.

**Find Out the Amount that Can Be Financed.**   Another approach to this problem is to talk to lenders. What they feel the market needs will also tell you what can be financed. Even if the investor does not need outside financing, it is a good idea to find out what the lenders think of the community. If ten different lenders in town give the same information, for example, they like commercial hotels, day care centers, and franchise hot-dog stands, then those items should be checked out before looking into a more pragmatic idea that each of the lenders discourage.

**Determine Whether the Local Government Is Receptive to "Changes."**
The importance of the local government needs to be stressed. Some communities are so restrictive that the only change that takes place is when an official dies and is replaced by another. These communities embrace the philosophy that "we got here first and by God what we want is what we get." Several of these places exist and actually thrive because they attract the kind

of people who want the same thing as those who got there first. But for the real estate investor, other communities also thrive and are more attractive for investment criteria.

**Look for the Right Property and "Tie It Up."**  Syndicators have learned their lessons well. You never invite an investor to "buy" into your project until you have it locked up 100 percent. The reason is that until the syndicator has an absolute "lock" on the property, there is nothing tangible to offer any investor. The concept of "I'm thinking of buying this or that" is not as persuasive as, "I've just acquired this property and if you are interested in joining me you can buy up to 20 percent for . . . ."

Finding the right property to suit the transaction does not depend on a syndication. Every investor should realize that the key to profitable investing is a question of finding the right property at the right price with the right terms that make the whole deal come together. This combination is not so easily found. Few investors can afford to contract to buy anything without some contingencies. Many of the deals that look *so* good that buyers are enticed to pay cash and close quickly with no contingencies usually turn out to be bad investments.

**Insert Reasonable Outs or Options into the Contract.**  The use of an escape clause will give the investor time to ascertain every aspect of the possible economic conversion. These clauses can be simple or very complex. When the seller understands the reason for the escape clause and is cooperative, a simple "option" that gives the buyer the required time to do what is necessary is ideal. Sometimes the seller is uneasy about the project or feels that the buyer is simply trying to tie up the property and then do nothing about the economic conversion. When this happens, the seller needs to be sold on the plan and the buyer's ability to follow through.

Once the investor has found a reasonable deal and tied it up with an escape clause or option, then the investor can spend the time and money necessary to make sure that the situation is as was presented.

If lengthy governmental processes are required to effect the economic conversion, the contract should contain provisions that take this time into consideration. Platting or zoning changes can take months, and it is not unlikely that there will be situations that can take up to a year or longer to work through all the necessary government departments before obtaining a satisfactory conclusion.

Red tape has its own slow timetable, and often all the influence and pressure can do nothing to speed it up.

**Review the Steps Needed to Make the Required Change.**  Once the property has been tied up, the investor can compile the necessary data to estimate the time and expense that will be needed to bring about the economic conversion. If the cost in time and money is worthy of the estimated return from the economic conversion, then the investor can proceed with the closing.

**Close at the Last Reasonable Moment.**   When the investor is going to implement an economic change, it is usually in the buyer's favor to delay the closing of title as long as possible, providing the buyer needs the time to lead up to the actual conversion. Even when the provisions governed by the escape clause have been satisfied, there may still be things that need to be done. For example, the investor includes a provision that he or she can void the contract unless the city will allow the four existing units with the garage in the back to be converted into six apartments. Once satisfied that this conversion can take place, the buyer will need plans, a building permit, and the work to be actually completed before income starts coming in. If the buyer could delay the closing right up to the day construction starts, the buyer would be closer to that income than if he or she closed and *then* took four months to get the needed permits.

## How to Avoid
## Two Common Problems
## with Economic Conversion

*Problem: What do you do when the seller wants a contract that has no outs?*
*Tip:*   Educate the seller about the problems that beset your investment plan. Many property owners are unaware of the problems that confront a real estate developer or investor. Sometimes it is not the seller that has a problem with "outs," but the seller's advisors who create the roadblocks.

*Problem: How do you tie up a property for a year or longer and still have an out?*
*Tip:*   The key is to let the seller have access to what is going on. In the case of rezoning for economic conversion, the buyer would want to include the seller as much as possible. After all, the seller is motivated for the buyer to get what he or she wants as a condition to the contract. There is a problem with this, however, if the process is drawn out and takes longer than anyone thought. Sellers have a tendency to get the feeling that they are being "used" in these situations. Having established a good rapport with the seller will help reduce this problem.

## Making Economic
## Conversions Work

The key to making an economic conversion work is to know what kind of property is convertible and what to convert it to. At times, the answer is simply the addition of more rental units to the property. For example, if the property is doing well as a rental apartment building and the rental vacancies in the area are low, it would be logical that the property could increase in value by adding several more units. However, the additional income to be earned must give a desired return to the investor. A downward turn in the overall yield after the addition of units because of the added expense and the capital cost to make the improvements would strongly indicate that this is the wrong choice to make.

If the addition of rental units can be done in such a way that the yield goes up, this would clearly be a good choice, but this still may not be the only route to pursue.

What else could be done? This is the question that each investor must continually ask. The answer will be found in several different places. Start with the current zoning and go from there.

- What uses does the current zoning allow for that location?
- Are there any restrictions from any source that would prohibit such a use?
- Of the uses allowed, how could improvements be made both to the in-an-as-is condition as well as with major modifications?
- Would a change to another zoning or obtaining a zoning variance offer another use that would produce greater income from the site or the improvements?

The investor will quickly get a good picture of the different uses allowed for any specific property. If the investor is reviewing several different properties and can only commit to one of them, the first choice would be the property that could be economically converted with an increased yield and the least possible problems. This becomes the base upon which the investor can rely even if he or she attempts to go through a rezoning in order to obtain another use that *might* produce even greater income.

Turn to The Real Estate Investor's VIP List and complete the following:

    (69)  Commercial banks
    (72)  Savings and loans institutions
    (75)  Mortgage banker and brokers

*Tip:* Check with your realtor (123) for recommendations or get a copy of their mortgage sheet the Board of Realtors may distribute to them containing the above-noted sources and more.

    (115)  Accountants and CPAs

*Tip:* Check with the local Board of Realtors to see if accountants lecture or give courses at Board meetings. Ask your lawyer for a referral.

Make plans to attend the next county zoning hearing.

# BROWARD COUNTY
# PUBLIC NOTICE

The Broward County Board of Commissioners, pursuant to Chapter 380.06(19) Florida statutes, will consider a public hearing on July 1, 1992 at 10:00 A.M., in the County Commission Chambers, 115 South Andrews Avenue, Fort Lauderdale, Florida, 33301, for consideration of proposed changes to the previously approved Indian Trace (Weston) Development of Regional Impact and to render a substantial deviation determination. The location of the Development of Regional Impact is shown in the map in this advertisement.

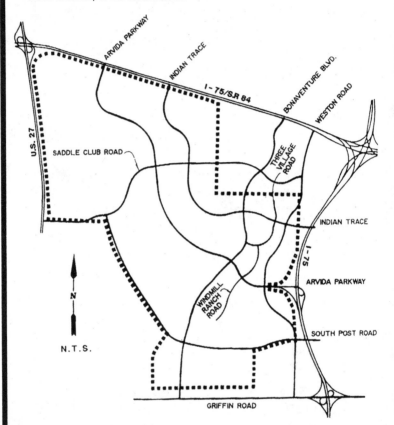

Information and reports for the proposed changes may be inspected at the Broward County Office of Planning, 115 South Andrews Avenue, Fort Lauderdale, Florida 33301. Any interested parties may appear at this meeting and be heard regarding the proposed changes.

Pursuant to Chapter 286, Florida Statutes, Section 286.0105, any person who decides to appeal any action made by the County Commission with respect to any matter considered at this hearing will need a record of the proceedings and, for such purpose, may need to ensure that a verbatim record of the proceedings is made, which record includes the testimony and evidence upon which the appeal is to be based.

# 12

# Quick and Inexpensive Ways to Increase Property Value

## Chapter Goals

The goal of this chapter is to illustrate five quick and inexpensive ways an investor can increase the value of real estate. In every instance, by using creative purchasing techniques, the investor can actually implement the necessary steps to increase the value *before* the purchase is closed and paid for. Because the seller pays the carrying cost for a property up until the date of closing, by using the "seller's time" the investor can often save the cost of the improvement.

## Key Terms

- Landscape enhancement
- *R*-factor insulation
- Municipal trash pickup
- Wholesale buying power
- Local cleanup codes

Review each in detail.

## Landscape Enhancement

Many investors view landscaping as a long-term investment that takes years to pay big dividends. While this is true, there are circumstances in which, with good planning, a change (addition or subtraction) to the existing landscaping can provide dramatic and valuable changes to the property almost overnight. It is important to remember that landscape enhancement does not mean just plants . . . it can also mean rocks, mulch, cutting and removing plants, change of location of existing plants, cleaning up trash of the property to be purchased, as well as neighboring properties. All of these can create nearly instant value. The cost can be little more than a couple of weekends of work.

Many communities have landscape codes that regulate the kinds of plants that are preferred or even required for new landscaping projects. While these codes may not affect a redesigned landscape, it is a good idea to check with the local authorities to ensure that no building codes are violated. In addition, these same officials can provide valuable information about the kinds of plants that will grow best in certain areas of town. Each state and most counties have agricultural departments that offer free or very inexpensive tests of soil, information on plant illnesses, and so on. In some areas there are reforestation projects in which a land owner can get free plants if the owner agrees to plant them according to the rules of the department. While this may be clearly a long-range project, the very fact that this step has been taken *now* may attract a long-term investor who will view this as a positive way to increase the value of the property.

An older property may have excess landscaping that hides the natural beauty of the property and/or that makes it dark and unattractive inside. Because some mature landscaping can be very expensive, it may be possible to swap the mature and undesirable plant material for new landscaping and landscape material from a retail landscape company. In some instances the sale of the old material will produce a *cash* surplus.

## *R*-Factor Insulation

Insulation within a building can have a dramatic effect on air-conditioning and heating costs. If a sudden change of expense has a beneficial effect on the "bottom line," then the value of the property can jump by a multiple of 10 times or more the savings. For example, if insulation can cause a monthly savings of as little as $75 per month, the annual savings would be $900. An increase in the annual cash flow of $900 would be a 10 percent return on a value of $9000. It is likely that the actual investment to install the insulation would cost only a fraction of this added value. In addition, many local power companies offer refunds to property owners for adding insulation. This incentive allows the investor to receive a refund from the utility company for a portion of the cost of the insulation. If the investor has included certain "fixup costs" as part of the initial investment, the seller will actually be paying to increase the value of the buyer's new investment. An example of this would be a purchase agreement that showed a total down payment of 20 percent of the total purchase price; however, $5000 of that amount would be spent by the buyer for improvements to the property. The provision may have been negotiated into the agreement after the buyer's first offer of 15 percent down with the seller holding the balance in the form of a purchase money mortgage. This offer was rejected by the seller because he or she felt the buyer should have a greater equity in the property when the seller would be holding part of the purchase price in the form of a mortgage. Because the buyer anticipates spending money on the property right away, adding this $5000 to the down payment is no hardship to the buyer. At the same time, the seller sees the buyer's added investment in the property. While the seller does not get the extra $5000, it is added security to the mortgage the seller is to hold.

## Municipal Trash Pickup

Many communities have "bulk" trash pickup. This kind of trash pickup may require a phone call to the proper authority to get the service, or it may be on a monthly or other long-term schedule. Because this service is usually a part of the existing utility charge, scheduling a cleanup of a property so that this "free" service can be utilized can save in private trash hauling charges. A call to the city or county trash pickup department will provide the necessary details on this kind of service. If there is no "free" bulk pickup, there may be a "for hire" municipal service that is inexpensive.

## Wholesale Buying Power

Wholesale vendors, which would likely include landscape nurseries, generally do not sell directly to the public, but then, as a real estate developer and investor, the situation changes. All it may take to have access to the wholesale marketplace (not just landscaping but all building materials as well as interior decorations, etc.) may be a city occupational license and a state sales tax number. The usual requirement to get a city occupational license is to have a business address (in a zoning that permits business locations), and to meet the other requirements for the type of license requested. Prior to showing up at the city occupational license office, it would be a good idea to check the requirements for different "building type licenses." Usually there are no special requirements, such as state tests or other educational qualifications, for occupational licenses for the following: interior decorators, remodeling counselors, landscape decorations, painting services, and the like.

The state sales tax number is obtained through the local state sales tax office (check with state revenue department) for the requirements. Once a state sales tax number is obtained, periodic reports may need to be filed, but this number will allow the holder to buy wholesale and not to pay the state tax (depending on state rules on certain items or services), for "pass through items" that are going to be resold. Even if the investor decides or elects to pay the state tax, many wholesale operations use this state sales tax number to distinguish qualified buyers from people looking to usurp the normal retail channels.

## Local Cleanup Codes

When the neighborhood is in a run-down condition it is not unusual for junk to pile up in yards, cars to be left abandoned or junked, and so on. If no one complains the local authorities may not be aware of the situation and therefore not enforce local ordinances that would either require the property owners to clean up the place or provide automatic municipal service to remove the debris and junk. The only way to determine what ordinances apply would be to call the local code enforcement departments of the appropriate city, county, and state involved. Each may have a separate department that would control different aspects of the situation. For example, the state health department may have control and power to clean up a potential health hazard (rotting garbage, rats, vagrants living in unsanitary conditions, etc.) while the county may have control over abandoned cars and the city control over excessive growth to vacant property. It is the right of every property owner to seek local help in maintaining the values of the neighborhood.

# Five Steps to Quick and Inexpensive Value Boosts

1. Upgrade the land.
2. Clean up the exterior of the improvements.
3. Give TLC to the interiors.
4. Demonstrate pride of ownership.
5. Establish your own new value and publish it.

## Upgrade the Land

Start with the basics. Review the following ideas that can give vacant land a sudden boost of value.

**Get a Temporary Use for It.**   As long as the use is not detrimental to the property, the sudden new look that a vacant property has when it is put to use attracts new interest, which can reflect in increased value. With rural land a temporary use could be to turn the plot into a U-Pick-It Strawberry Patch. If the investor is not agriculturally inclined, a drive around the area may turn up a farmer who would love to enter into a joint venture for a season or two of strawberries. One solid benefit to the land owner may be that the property becomes cleared of unwanted shrubs and growth that would be costly to remove (if not impossible due to landscaping regulations that may not apply to farmers). In the end, the farmer may leave the property freshly planted with thousands of "free" timber seedlings obtained from the state agricultural department.

A temporary use can turn into a permanent use once the user discovers that the site proves to be economically viable for their purposes. An example of this is when the buyer of a commercial site lets a local new car dealer turn the vacant site into a parking lot for excess inventory or for used car sales, and the car dealer later wants to make the site a permanent one.

**Clean Up the Junk around It.**   Obviously, this is the first step if the property needs it. As has already been mentioned the investor should go the extra step and get neighborhood property cleaned up too.

**Plant Trees on It.**   If the state agricultural department will not help out with free or inexpensive trees, there still may be a way to get the job done cheaply. Is there mature landscaping that can be traded to a retail landscaper for smaller items that can grow in size and value? When planting trees some attention should be given to where the trees would go. This is not complicated, and the question "Where would I landscape around a building that might be constructed here?" would be the first place to start. It is relatively easy to mark off setbacks and to put the bulk of planting in these areas, usually closer to the property lines than the future building area. Some trees are easier to transplant than others, so plant those easiest to transplant in areas where you are unsure if they would need to be moved.

**File for a Rezoning.**   Yes, this step may be both simple and inexpensive. Not all rezoning requires months and expensive efforts. Check with the local authorities first, make sure the land is tied up in a long-term contract as a safety factor, and then "go for it." Because the contract is not closed until some time in the future, the normal carrying cost of the land, i.e., taxes and insurance, will remain the obligation of the existing owner and may go a long way to pay for the rezoning cost.

## Clean Up the Exterior
## of the Improvements

The first impression a prospective buyer gets of the property may mean the difference between a sale with a profit or no sale at all. The landscaping around the improvements can ultimately be the best long-term element to be considered, with some positive and immediate results as well. The actual improvements can usually be given a sudden *new look* with a three-step process:

- Clean

- Fix

- Paint

Investors who are handy with one or more of these three tasks will find the actual cost to spruce up the exterior of a property is more a matter of time than money.

A redesign of the entrance to a property can also make a major difference in the appearance, and that single factor can increase the value of a property overnight. A new walkway, a new front door (or a door repainted to look new), etc., can turn a dull, drab property into a fresh vibrant one that seems to beckon new buyers.

The word **fix** is an important factor to consider from two points of view. Novice investors should shy away from property that needs a lot of fixing up, unless there is ample capital to handle the hidden problems and the investor needs to expand his abilities and is willing to pay for the lesson (if mistakes are made).

---

*Small items that need to be fixed should be completely repaired with quality material.*

---

Most important, however, is that small items that need to be fixed should be completely and properly fixed. Broken toilet seats, doors that stick, cabinets that will not open or close, plumbing that drips, and so on, are all minor things that investors will find in any property . . . and they can be fixed without much cost.

When fixing little items it pays to do it right and to use quality material. One of the very best single expenditures is the "front door appearance." New door hardware, a new brass mailbox, and a new brass door knocker around a freshly painted or new door can be all it takes to give an overall impression of quality throughout.

## Give TLC to the Interiors

Tender loving care is usually what the previous owner did not do, which is why the price is so low and the investment a sound one. Turning around a property that has not been cared for can take a little more than just cleaning, fixing, and painting. It may also take time.

There are some quick and easy things that can be done to give the interiors of any property a fresh and more valued look. The idea is to look for the "hidden gems" that are the treasures found within some properties. These make fixup and the return of tender loving care quick and easy.

**Look under the Carpet.**   Do you find hardwood floors, tile, or marble? These may be much easier to bring back to their natural state than to recarpet. These are gems, but watch out—under old carpets can also be rotten floorboards, termite damage, and worst of all, asbestos. The key is to know what you are dealing with in all eventualities. If the gem is there, then that is your bonus. If a problem is encountered, then get an estimate on what it will cost to deal with it, or walk away from the deal by using one of the outs in the purchase contract.

**Check under the Paint.**   Solid brass that has been painted over a thousand times does not look very nice until all the paint is removed. Doorplates, hardware, railings, and countless other brass items can be found in older properties that cannot be replaced today for less than a fortune.

**Tap Doors and Walls with a Plastic Hammer.**   Solid building material has an "expensive" sound to it, and solid wood doors in good shape can be restored. "Solid"-sounding walls might indicate block or heavy plaster, which are more costly than cheap wallboard or other more modern but not as good building products.

## Demonstrate Pride of Ownership

Pride of ownership is evident when the owner makes an effort to maintain a property in top condition and shape. This means all property owned, not just the property that has been purchased for a fast turnover. When an investor is working within a small community the way that investor maintains his property becomes public knowledge in a short period of time. In a large city this fact may take a bit longer to be known to the general public, but within real estate circles it still gets around quickly.

Taking good care of everything owned, from the shoes on the investor's feet to the car the investor drives, becomes a matter of pride in appearance as well as respect for the items owned. Investors who let property run down generally show a total lack of tender loving care in their whole lifestyle.

Pride of ownership need not be extravagant or lavish; all it takes is to be clean and neat, with good taste for the occasion, and to show that everything owned is well maintained.

### Establish Your Own New Value and Publish It

There is nothing subtle about this approach, as it is bold and direct and generally works. Once the property is on the way to being cleaned, fixed, and painted, and the TLC starts to show, then a well-prepared sales brochure with the new price can let everyone know what you think about the present value of the property. Neighbors, by the way, may be the first to agree with you if that new price makes their property look good too.

The best way to find out how to make a great looking property brochure is to look at some that professionals have already made up. A check with several realtors in the area should turn up several such examples.

## Tips in Dealing with Old House Smells

*Problem: Dog or other animal smell. Unfortunately many property owners who have an old animal or several animals do not seem to even notice the smell. But this smell will turn off a buyer quickly and must be dealt with immediately and with positive 100 percent results demanded. A half-way solution just is not enough.*

*Solution:*   The first step usually is to get rid of what is "holding" the smell. This can be the carpets on the floor, an old sofa that was the dog's bed, or drapes that have soaked up the animal smell over a long time. Once the fabric that contained the smell is removed, then the whole place needs to be cleaned with a strong cleaning solution—but one that does not introduce smells that are equally difficult to remove. Trisodium phosphate (TSP) is one of the strongest cleaning agents available, and when purchased in a five-pound box at a hardware store will last a long time because it is very concentrated and a little dissolved in warm water goes a long way. Best of all, it has no lasting smell at all.

There are several acceptable, if not desirable, smells that can be introduced into a building that will help overcome any kind of old smell. Paint is one, but be careful, this does not apply to all paint. Some paints are noxious; others produce vapors that will even kill you (or make you very sick). Safest generally are latex water-based paints, but ask your qualified paint expert (not the clerk from the nails department who is assigned to the paint department for the day) which paint has the nicest "freshly painted" smell. Another wonderful smell is leather. One new piece of leather furniture can give a whole room a great smell.

*Problem: The damp mildew smell seems to last no matter what you do. How can it be removed?*

*Solution:* Removing mildew smells is not as difficult as it once was, thanks to several different cleaning materials that kill mildew. The real problem is not the existing mildew, because with proper treatment it can be eliminated; the problem is to keep it from returning. Mildew is a plantlike material that grows best in a dark, warm, and moist environment where there is poor air circulation. The enemy of mildew then is circulating air, sunlight, and a dry environment. Roof and plumbing leaks can leave the insides of walls just damp enough to become ideal mildew hideouts, but not so sopping wet that the actual leak is noticed. Mildew inside walls may not be seen for a long time, but the smell is very evident to any newcomer to the property. The owners may have gradually grown accustomed to the smell so that they no longer even noticed it. The key then is to stop the leak in order to eliminate the mildew.

Fans to circulate air in the area will help, and together with some of the antimildew sprays that are available in any good hardware store, mildew can be beaten.

In hot, humid areas it is a good idea to keep air circulating in a closed-up house to keep mildew from getting a foothold.

The introductory smell, that is, the first smell a person notices when they enter a home, can be very important in the potential sale of the property. Dog and animal smells, mentioned earlier, are definite "turnoffs" and should be eliminated. Mildew and other problem smells are more subtle, annoying smells that also must be dealt with as soon as possible.

In addition to the general cleaning, painting, and touches such as leather furniture already mentioned, there are several "memory" smells that can produce a good aroma within a home. These smells can evoke a past memory that was pleasant and can become a type of subliminal sales tool. These smells may have different levels of appeal to different people, but in general none of the following smells will produce a negative reaction from a prospective buyer. Each of these smells can be "made" within the house, and each has a relatively short duration.

- Freshly baked bread and/or cookies.
- Fresh hot cocoa.
- Fresh coffee being brewed.
- Freshly made popcorn.
- A boiling pot of spices (cloves, cinnamon, vanilla).
- Fresh roses or orange blossoms (very few).
- An apple or peach pie being baked (or reheated).
- Cooking chocolate or peanut butter fudge.
- Burning a citrus-scented candle.

## Pitfalls in the "Cleaning— Fixing—Painting" Routine

There are two major pitfalls when it comes to cleaning, fixing, and painting: *time* and *money*.

Even working on the simplest looking job can suddenly drag into six weekends in a row. Other demands on your time or a change in the weather that sends the workers home should be anticipated. The old saying, "make hay while the sun shines" works here. When the weather is good, clean, fix, and paint the outside; the inside can be done anytime.

The cost for extra labor and materials can easily exceed original estimates, and it is not unusual for a simple remodeling project to become a major reconstruction project. Taking it slow and easy at first is one way to keep out of trouble and limit overruns of the time you have to give to the project and the money available to pay for it.

Never plan for any remodeling that requires the removal of any structure or built-in fixture (walls, windows, plumbing, cabinets) until the structure has been examined. This may require that a section of a wall be opened up to see if the removal will be as simple as it may appear. Once a side has been take off, there may be elements now visible that should not be there—such as a roof support or plumbing or electrical lines. Checking before the architect has run up a big bill is safest.

Turn to The Real Estate Investor's VIP List and complete the following:

(79)  Appliance repairs

*Tip:* Check the Yellow Pages for a repairperson close to you, and get one that makes house calls and can repair every type of kitchen appliance and window air conditioner.

(81)  Carpet sales

(87)  Hardware store

(89)  Local large hardware and housewares store

(91)  Lumberyard

*Tip:* Check the Yellow Pages for the stores closest to you.

(109)  Printing service

*Tip:* Check with one of the realtors who showed you a nice brochure of a property they represent. Ask who did the printing and contact that printer.

(117)  Landscapers

*Tip:* Check the Yellow Pages under *Wholesale Landscape Material.*

# PART 3
# How to Find the Right Property to Buy

# 13

# The Five Different Kinds of Property in Which to Invest

## Chapter Goals

This chapter segments real estate investments into one of five categories. Each category is then reviewed to show the usual advantages and disadvantages each category presents. The primary goal of this chapter is to acquaint the reader with the various kinds of property in which one can invest and to show how each property can serve different goals, depending on the method of acquisition and holding period of the investor.

## Key Terms

- Downside risk
- Pattern of growth
- Single-purpose use
- Multipurpose use
- "Cranking" cash
- Alligator

Review each in detail.

## Downside Risk

Every investment has what can be estimated to be the downside risk: the worst-case scenario under slightly exaggerated negative circumstances. If an investor is looking at vacant land as a growth investment, the downside risk might be that the value of the land does not reach the level the investor would like. However, even if the property is never more than "farmland," it should have a value. If the value of farmland is above the price paid for the site, then the downside risk is not great. If the investment is income property, an acceptable downside risk may be a break-even point—that is, the point at which income matches total expenses, including debt service. Each investor must decide for themselves what is an acceptable downside risk to balance the upside potential.

## Pattern of Growth

The trends of growth in any given area develop collectively into what is called a **pattern of growth**. The word **pattern** is appropriate because real estate development occurs in set growth areas and is not distributed from a center equally in all directions. Instead, development follows new roadways, surrounds lakes, moves around parks, and so on. Industrial areas often are blocked together, whereas expensive single-family home projects may sprawl out around golf courses. When a community is viewed from the air, these patterns are often more obvious than when seen from the ground. Investors need to study the pattern of growth for any area they intend to invest in to ensure that the property being acquired fits into the current and pending pattern.

## Single-Purpose Use

Any property that has only one likely use is a **single-purpose use** property. The key here is: What makes that property single-purpose use? It might be zoning, which determines that the land under the home is zoned for "single-family homes," or it could be that the building design is clearly for a fast food operation, and so on. Obviously no property is really single purpose, because with the right amount of money and time, any building can be altered to accommodate another use. Even in very restrictive zoning such as "single-family residential zoning" other uses are usually possible, for example, churches, schools, and parks. In general terms, single-purpose use refers to the reasonable use of the property as zoned and built.

## Multipurpose Use

This use is clearly flexible due to the zoning and/or the building design. When this flexibility is very obvious there is never any problem in seeing the multipurpose nature of a property. What is important is that all real estate investors need to sharpen their vision of property to "see" what is not so obvious. Economic conversion depends on the investor being able to take a property with one use now, and a price based on that use, and turn it into a property with a greater income potential at a cost that makes the investment successful. An example of this is a single-family home situated on a lot zoned to permit professional offices. The obvious fact is that the home is just a home and nothing more. However, if the investor knew about the flexibility in the zoning, knew that there would be a demand for office space in the area, say as a private medical office, lawyer's office, or insurance firm, and knew the office space rents attainable to be much greater than the rent of a single-family home, then the multipurpose capability of that single-family home makes it a potentially good investment.

## "Cranking" Cash

This is an insider term: To **crank cash** means that a mortgage can be put on the property that can have the potential of returning to the acquiring investor cash that may be needed for the investment or just to generate cash for some other purpose. For example, an investor found a single-family home free of debt that had a multipurpose potential. One possible use to which it could be converted was a medical office building. The price of the property is $100,000. The investor enters into a purchase agreement that provides for the existing owner to take $25,000 in cash, $25,000 in equity the investor has in a vacant lot as a part exchange, and $50,000 in a first mortgage on another property owned by the investor.

| Seller to get | Value |
|---|---|
| Cash to seller at closing | $ 25,000 |
| Vacant lot in exchange | 25,000 |
| First mortgage on another property | 50,000 |
| Total value of deal | $100,000 |

The investor knows it will cost $35,000 for the necessary remodeling to the home to convert it into the medical offices. The investor either does not have the cash for this work or wants to maximize the investment by pulling as much or all of the needed cash out of the deal itself (**cranking cash**).

The investor needs $35,000 for remodeling and also $25,000 for the seller, a total of $60,000. If the property was truly worth $100,000 or more in the first place, it would be reasonable to expect that after remodeling the property would be worth even more. It is likely that in such an economic conversion from a single-family home to a medical office building that the value may well double. In any event, the downside risk, from a lender's point of view, would suggest that a $100,000 value on which to base a loan would be very conservative. The needed $60,000 then should be easy to crank in this deal. At the closing of the transaction, the investor would not put any of his or her own cash into the deal.

### Alligator

This is not one of those green-gray animals that Tarzan was always fighting underwater, but a property that just lays there and eats. By definition, all non-income-producing property can be labeled as an **alligator** unless the investor is getting some other benefit from the property that counterbalances the cost to hold the property. When the value increases considerably more than the cost to "feed the alligator," the negative cash situation can be tolerated for a while, at least, until the ability to feed the alligator stops.

## The Five Categories of Real Estate Investments

1. Land speculation
2. Single-family homes
3. Multifamily properties
4. Commercial and industrial properties
5. Retail shops and shopping centers

Review each in detail.

### Land Speculation

Land speculation is the investment in land with the hope that it will go up in value sufficient to (a) cover the cost to hold or (b) provide a desired return over and above the total invested capital.

Land speculation requires much due diligence. Investors must determine the pattern of growth in the community and tie that together with the future infrastructure planned by the community. When the investor sees that new roads and other planned projects (local, state, private, public, etc.) will have a beneficial effect on an area that is slightly beyond and in the path of an established growth pattern, then investing in land in that area should be considered. If the long-term cost to hold onto the property could be financed by an arrangement with the seller at below market rates, or with soft terms the investment would have greater appeal to the investor. For example, Able determines that land anywhere from 5 to 10 miles west of the edge of current development around town should see great value increases because of a new interstate road network that is going to run along the western edge of town 10 miles away with one direct link into town. The property is wooded pine lands, with pulp wood possibilities in three or four years. The land is priced accordingly and only slightly lower than what cleared farmland would bring.

Able ties up a 300-acre tract of property with a contract contingent on his getting approval to get rezoning to allow single-family development. The seller agrees to an attractive price and gives Able a full 12 months to get the approvals Able wants. Once Able closes, the down payment will be $50,000 with another $130,000 owed. Able is to pay interest at the rate of 8 percent, which is $10,400 per year. Prior to development Able must pay off the total principal owned.

Able knows that if he gets the rezoning, the value of this land, even before the interstate road network is completed, will increase. He also knows that his downside risk is not very great because within a year he could, if needed, sell off the timber a little earlier than would be ideal to produce most if not all the $50,000 cash down. With the land cleared it is worth even more than he paid as farmland.

**Advantages of Land Speculation.**   The economic advantage is that the greatest increase of value in real estate comes from taking vacant land that has the lowest basic value along the chain of real values, and turning it into a pyramid of values that includes everything from commercial sites to parks. When circumstances are favorable to land investment there can be little risk if the investors have the time and carrying ability. The key to land speculation is the ability to assess properly the growth patterns of the community, and to get a good picture of future development in the works or on the planning boards.

**Disadvantages of Land Speculation.**   It is not uncommon for local governments to have a 180 degree switch in their ability to follow through with future plans. The plans themselves can be changed as well; for example, moving that interstate road a few miles to the east can put that 300-acre tract on the wrong side of the highway, or worse, relocating the road network to the other side of town or canceling the project altogether can shift attention away from the area so much that even farmland goes down in value in that part of the county.

Long-term investing in land is much more difficult and can be far more expensive than investors think. Liberal estimates in carrying costs must be taken into consideration because costs go up. Taxes can increase substantially to the point where they double or triple above the estimated increases. Local governments can impose building restrictions or moratoriums that can limit if not prohibit reasonable development until utilities are brought to the site—utilities that may be charged against the property owner.

In the above-noted example, Able has little to risk during the first 12-month period of time except the time and money it might take to process the desired single-family zoning. If things were to work out successfully by the end of the first 12 months, Able may "flip" his contract (resell prior to closing) and walk away from the deal with a nice profit, having done no more than foretell what was about to happen. On the other hand, if, at the end of the 12 months, the rezoning had not been approved then he might just walk away from the deal.

### Single-Family Homes

Many real estate investors swear by this kind of property. Buying single-family homes as an investment generally fits into three different investment strategies:

1. Buy, fix up, and sell.

2. Buy and rent (with or without fix up).

3. Buy, live in, slowly improve, and then sell.

There is no "best" of the above three, as each method will have a different appeal depending on the goal of the investor. Some investors may apply more than one of these methods at the same time. They may buy one home to live in while slowly improving it and others to fix up and sell, while still others are rented out while the market improves. The term "buy" used above is meant to include other techniques of acquisition that give the investor the same or similar position to sell even though the investor may never actually take title to the subject property. An example of this would be if Frances obtained an "option" to buy a property that she leased in the meantime. During the lease Frances improves the property and then sells her option to Bob, who takes title to the property. In a later chapter the technique of using options is explained in detail.

**How to Buy Single-Family Homes.** The key with buying single-family homes is to cover the carrying cost. Once the investor knows that there will be no cost to hold onto the property, time generally will ensure appreciation of value and an ultimate profit. This will, of course, depend on the investor's due diligence having been carefully accomplished to ensure that the area is not in a decline and that there are no pending public or private works that can adversely affect the property in any way. Downside risk in single-family homes then will depend on the terms of the purchase and the cost to carry the property (taxes, mortgage payment, property maintenance, insurance, property improvement). If the home has the flexibility of a future economic conversion to some other use, then that can be an added bonus to what may already be a good investment.

**Advantages of Single-Family Home Investments.**  There are many advantages to buying single-family homes, but the best is the fact that single-family sellers are often the most motivated of all sellers. This is because of the many different reasons people *need* to sell a home. Below is a list of some of the predominant reasons that people sell a home.

*The Ten Most Important Reasons Why People Sell Their Homes*
1. Are transferred to another work location.
2. Need a larger home due to family growth.
3. Need a smaller home due to
    *a.* Reduced family.
    *b.* The present home can no longer be afforded.
    *c.* Divorce.
    *d.* Death of a family member(s).
4. Have economic problems, either current or future ones, and cannot afford to keep the property anymore.
5. Are undergoing a foreclosure, either pending or in action.
6. Have a mortgage due.
7. Have bought another home already.
8. Need to raise cash to take advantage of another investment.
9. Can no longer (or no longer wants to) maintain the property.
10. Wish to dispose of an unwanted gift or inheritance.

In each of these situations there is a motivated seller.

Investors quickly learn that the seller who puts his or her property on the market with the motive "anything is for sale if I can make a buck" is not the best kind of seller to work with, unless that seller is not telling the truth and the real reason is being hidden. If the real reason is something like *termites* or *a structural failure,* then the motivation may be real but the property not worthwhile.

Downside risk can be slight when investing in single-family homes.

**Disadvantages of Single-Family Home Investments.**  The potential profit may not be all that great if the investor is looking for quick growth. If the investor wants to build an income stream by buying and then renting out the homes, the investor will discover quickly that the property maintenance problems that come with owning several single-family homes may not warrant the purchase of this kind of rental property. There will be exceptions to this of course, but in general, the best reason for buying a single-family home and renting it is to "buy time" and let the market improve while the property can be slowly enhanced and upgraded, using, whenever possible, the tenant's rent money to accomplish those goals.

## Multifamily Properties

Any property that has more than one family unit is considered a multifamily property. The smallest would be a duplex (when this word is used to mean two units, often side by side or one on top of the other). From this point on, the size ranges to large rental complexes that consist of hundreds of apartments.

**How to Buy Multifamily Properties.**    All income-producing properties have the advantage of being able to support debt from the income they produce. This factor leads investors to the principal other people's money (OPM). The significance of the introduction of OPM into the picture gives the investor an edge in the ultimate financing of the investment. Unlike the situation with vacant property and single-family home financing in which the investor's financial strength is the most important element lenders consider, all income properties are viewed from the point of view of the property first, the investor second. If the property is represented fairly to the lender and the income and expenses shown are accurate, then the lender will evaluate the property based on this income stream. The current trend for lenders is to establish a conservative value on the property and to lend a much lower loan-to-value ratio than was prevalent in the 1980s. Higher loan-to-value ratios can be obtained by stronger borrowers.

The key to buying any income property is the ability to establish a sound financing package on the property that does not place excessive burdens on the property or the investor. To achieve this it may be necessary for the seller to work with the investor to create a composite of financing that gives this end result.

All rental apartments thrive or die because of the OPM scenario. When there is a shortage of apartments for a particular market, then the vacancy factors approach zero, and the property owners can be more selective about the type of tenant they rent to. This last factor, the type of tenant in the building, is very important because it will establish the ultimate direction of the building or complex. When a rental market shifts to the point where there is a shortage of tenants, then owners can no longer be as selective about tenants because they are dependent on OPM to meet their debt service and other obligations to keep the property.

Fortunately, multifamily property investors will quickly discover that one of the easiest trends to spot within any community is the rental market. All that is necessary is to drive around the community, make a list of all rental properties that have vacancies, and ascertain rental prices and how selective property managers are in acquiring tenants.

If the investor sees that selection is tight and rents are on the increase, then this is a good sign that there is a shortage of rental units in any given market and that opportunities may exist in that sector of real estate.

An element of economic conversion that can be nicely applied to multi-family units is the upgrade from one level of rent to another. This occurs when former property owners have let the property run down to the point where rents had to be decreased to keep the units filled. This factor can snowball, and the situation deteriorates progressively to the point that even reduced rents cannot maintain high occupancy.

If these properties are in a good area of town or in an area that is returning to a former higher quality, then the remodeling of a rundown apartment complex can be a profitable venture. The important element that must be determined carefully is, how run down is it? As stated before, major fixing up is not for the novice investor because of the many problems that can lurk behind the surface crack that the investor thinks needs only to be filled, for example.

**Advantages of All Income-Producing Property Investments.** The most obvious is the investor will grow wealthy in the long run simply by holding onto the property and letting the OPM pay off the debt—even if there is no immediate cash flow.

To understand this, take a look at the following example. Spencer has bought a 50-unit apartment complex at a fair price of $2,000,000. This is $40,000 per unit, and the value is warranted because the apartments have a rent roll of slightly over $360,000 per year. This occurs because the average monthly rent is $600 per apartment or $7200 per year per apartment.

Lenders in the community know that expenses for this kind of apartment complex should not exceed 40 percent of the total rent roll, so Spencer should have a net operating income of 60 percent the total rent roll.

| | |
|---|---|
| Gross rents collected: | $360,000 |
| Less 40 percent expenses: | 144,000 |
| Net operating income (60 percent): | $210,000 |

If Spencer or the lender anticipated a 10 percent return on capital invested to be a good return, then the NOI of $210,000 would represent a 10 percent return on $2,100,000.

If Spencer was able to borrow a total of $1,600,000 on this property with a 20-year payback to the lender of $160,000 per year (principal and interest included), the OPM from the rents will ultimately pay off the $1,600,000, leaving the property free of debt. If Spencer maintains the property in good condition, normal inflation and cost of living would suggest that the rents will increase substantially over the same 20 years and that the debt-free property will be worth considerably more than the original purchase price of $2,000,000.

Multifamily properties serve a basic need, which limits the downside risk. They provide shelter to those who cannot afford or who do not choose to buy. In any given marketplace there are members of the community who are moving to and from property ownership. This causes a chain of events in which some people are upgrading their living accommodations, while others are moving into more modest and less expensive quarters. When the labor market is strong and there is a low percentage of unemployed workers, the rental market is at its strongest.

**Disadvantages of Multifamily Property Investments.**   The disadvantages center mostly around the management problems that come in dealing with tenants. Apartments can be very management intensive, although not as great as hotels and other "business" forms of accommodation rentals. On a small scale the key to minimal management problems is in the selection of tenants and in keeping the rent at slightly under the going market. The rent lost by not staying just above the going market, which is a tactic a well-managed facility may choose to follow, can be offset by the increased occupancy and reduced management problems.

## Commercial and Industrial Properties

These income-producing properties range from office buildings to warehouse complexes and everything in between. If the property is a building that is not used for habitation it is most likely a commercial or industrial kind of property.

Commercial and industrial properties fall into two basic categories: single use and multiuse. If IBM, for example, occupies an entire building or complex, it is clearly a single tenant, but the use could be multiple to the extent that the building is flexible in that it could house offices, repair facilities, a medical clinic, etc. Note the difference between single tenant and single purpose as in the case of a fast food restaurant. This too is a single tenant, but the use is greatly limited, and without major remodeling it is a single-use hamburger restaurant.

Multiuse buildings are more often also multitenant buildings, which spread the obligation of the rent over several or many different tenants. When the single tenant is very strong and has a top credit rating, the single-tenant building can be more attractive than multitenant buildings. However, when the single-tenant building is vacant, the vacancy is 100 percent until a new tenant can be found.

**Advantages of Commercial and/or Industrial Property Investments.** The tenant is often a net or triple net tenant: when rent is quoted as **net** or

**triple net,** the owner of the building usually passes on other expenses and cost to the tenant over and above the actual rent. Because the terms net and triple net are not universal in their meaning, a prospective tenant or new investor should obtain an exact definition of other obligations tenants are to pay. One cannot assume that triple net means that the tenant pays everything . . . even though this is exactly the case in some leases.

When the tenant pays rent, plus building maintenance, taxes, insurance (the common basis for triple net), plus all other costs that may be assessed against a property, the cost to the tenant is established *as though the tenant actually owned the property.* This type of rental situation is highly sought after by many investors because the investments require very little management. Only a straight **land lease**, where tenants lease the land and then construct their own building, requires less management.

**Advantages of Commercial and Industrial Investments.**   Advantages are the ease of operation and often favorable acceptance to institutional lenders. As with all income properties, the income stream of the property will be a major factor in the ultimate value of the property and the basis for financing. When an investor can take over a property that can be improved or converted to a higher income stream, then great profits could be generated.

**Disadvantages of Commercial and/or Industrial Property Investments.** Some disadvantages are often the result of the lag time that occurs in the development of this kind of property. Shortages of office space or commercial buildings encourage investors to build more. As the time from initial idea to finished building may be several years, the shortage may suddenly become a glut on the market and a slow rental market a result. If some other economic decline happens during this same period, the end result can be a major decline in commercial rents in a wide area, and real estate values can fall very quickly.

The downside risk in commercial and industrial buildings is the strength of the tenant. This factor has become even more critical as some of the "best risk" tenants have seen some very hard times and even the giants of industry are no longer thought of as risk-free tenants.

## Retail Shops and Shopping Centers

Retail shops and shopping centers seem to be everywhere, and even in bad economic times new shops are being built, even when whole shopping centers are less than half filled. There are some very good reasons for this, which makes this kind of investing very profitable if the circumstances are right and the investor sees the opportunities in time to take advantage of them.

This category of property differs from the preceding category in that the majority of rentals in a multitenant situation will be retail and service-oriented shops rather than office space. Some shopping centers and retail shop areas also have offices for rent, but in strictly defined commercial projects, such as office parks and office buildings, the only retail shops found will generally be limited to restaurants, sundry shops, print shops, and the like designed to serve the needs of the workers and businesses in the offices rather than outside customers.

A typical business district in almost any town in the world is apt to have individual shops lining the main streets for several blocks. In older cities it is not uncommon for many differently designed buildings to adjoin each other, giving cities a "quilt" look. To counter this look, many cities now have design codes that must be strictly followed to prevent this hodgepodge appearance and to bring about a more homogeneous look to the commercial areas. One such town, Boca Raton, Florida, has a code that insists that buildings have a colonial Spanish look along the lines of certain existing buildings. Cities in many areas of California have similar design codes.

Finding retail shops and shopping centers is relatively easy. First, the areas are limited, usually along main streets that make it easy to check out through deed records in the court house or deed searches by members of the real estate industry. Many of these buildings may be for sale even though there is no sign out front announcing that fact. Why? Most property owners do not want their tenants to know the property is for sale. This means that the pickings will go to the investor who digs up the information and acts on it.

**Advantages of Retail Shop and/or Shopping Center Investments.** In established areas it is relatively easy to see the trends and flow of traffic. It does not take long to tell which area is improving and why, and which area is losing ground and why. Of these trends that investors look for, there are two that are significant and can open the door to profitable investing if both the trend can be spotted and a deal can be made.

*Two Trends to Look for When Investing in Retail Shops or Centers*

1. A Decline in rents with increases in vacancy factors due to a temporary situation.

2. A Moderate to strong rental market area that is about to experience an event that will have a strong, positive impact on rental space.

Each of these two trends will lead to a stronger rental market in the relatively near future. The investor who gets in on the "ground floor" of these trends will have the first chance to acquire the better locations that may be offered for sale. Selecting the property to buy will depend greatly on the ability of the investor to deal with the complexity of renting out retail shop or shopping center space. Buying large retail space is not for the novice investor unless there is sufficient capital to hire managers with that kind of experience. However, small strip stores or small buildings with several shops can be a good way to get into this category of investing relatively safely. Because these buildings often are in need of repairs and can lend themselves to remodeling to upgrade the look and hopefully the rent, there can be substantial room to improve the income generated from some of these investments.

The biggest advantage in this kind of investment is that it serves a general need of the community, and if the investor has chosen the location well, it is doubtful that there will be a high vacancy factor.

### Disadvantages of Retail Shop and/or Shopping Center Investments.

The main disadvantage is in dealing with the tenants. It is important to be as selective as possible to continually upgrade the status of the building. It can be tempting to fill a vacant space with a tenant that is less than ideal, yet the investor should set a goal to maintain a certain status of the building or the street. One slip from this goal, by introducing the wrong kind of tenant into the area, can start a downhill slide that will eventually cause other vacancies.

Take an inexpensive city map of an area that you know well. It may even be the area around your ultimate comfort zone. Go over the map and mark off the different areas with which you are familiar into each of the five categories described in this chapter.

*Tips:* All vacant land should be marked as V for vacant, but should be further categorized based on the zoning that would determine its ultimate use. A large vacant tract that was zoned for apartments would then be labeled V-MF (MF = multifamily). Use these following abbreviations and symbols:

V    =    Vacant land

SF    =    Single-family homes

MF    =    Apartments and hotels and/or motels (multifamily use)

C    =    Offices and commercial space

I    =    Industrial areas

S    =    Shops and shopping centers

When you pick an area to be developed as a **comfort zone**, it is important to ascertain how the different categories of property evolved. What was the trend that resulted in the present situation, and how are the different property types faring at present? This pattern is essential to discover to begin to remove risk from your investments.

# 14

# How to Build an Investment Comfort Zone

## Chapter Goals

All real estate investors should focus their time and effort to a narrow market area. This focus should ultimately be directed to the exact kind of real estate the investor wants to buy. In the beginning, the investor may not have decided which category of property to concentrate on, so he or she should form an investment comfort zone in a part of town that meets the guidelines of this chapter and begin working in that area until a specific property begins to be more interesting than others. The primary goal of this chapter is to illustrate the steps that any investor can take to establish his or her own comfort zone and to show how that zone will be critical to the investor's success in real estate investing.

## Key Terms

- Goal orientation
- Priority of time
- Sphere of reference

Review each in detail.

## Goal Orientation

A major factor for attaining success in anything is the strength of a person's focus on his or her goals. As important as focus is, the reader should understand that without a well-defined goal success will continually slip away.

Proper goal orientation requires work and practice, and continual fine-tuning must take place along the way. In real estate investing the adjustments occur as investors learn about their own aspirations, future desires, and abilities and expand on each. In each situation the individual will discover that it will be confining to set goals within the current reach of those abilities. Every goal process *must* include the improvement of abilities, so that greater and more challenging goals can be set, attempted, and achieved. Some of the most successful people in any form of endeavor are continually learning, and they take pride in this process. People who think they know it all already know all they will ever learn. In contrast, the person seeking success should make an effort to learn something meaningful every day, then apply that new bit of knowledge as soon as possible.

---

*Wonderful phrases to success: "I didn't know that, will you teach it to me?" "I need to learn how to do that? What would you suggest I do?" "Boy, you make that look so easy, would you show me how you do it?"*

*When you don't know something, admit it; then ask how to learn it. People will respect your desire to learn.*

---

This is the formula for happiness as well as success.

## Priority of Time

When the goal is clearly in sight, and the steps to get from start to finish are well planned, the proper use of time becomes a critical step in the attainment of those goals. If time is not valued, goals may take too long to attain, and frustration and disappointment can become stronger than the desire to attain the original goal. A common error is to overbudget the use of time or to underestimate the time it will take to attain a certain intermediate step. For example, one of the elements of a comfort zone is to become an expert of the property and events that are going on within that zone. This is not an overnight process, and in fact, it is something that continues for the entire time of evolvement within that investment zone. However, the process must start somewhere, and a certain, definite time must be set aside for the process to occur. That time should build rather slowly to allow the investor to adapt to the new and growing sphere of reference.

### Sphere of Reference

As the comfort zone develops investors will see and feel the growth of the sphere of reference around them. If the reader has been faithfully completing the assignments to The Real Estate Investor's VIP List, this sphere of reference is a thousand percent greater than the day this book was opened.

Step by step this sphere grows. The **sphere of reference** is the envelope of everything that goes on around investors over which they have some control, or if not control, direct contact. The process is not automatic, however, as to gain benefit from the natural process, investors must follow up on the growing contacts around them. Keep this firmly in mind when the line "Secretary _____" is completed in the Investor's VIP list. Mostly everything is accomplished through the VIP's secretary.

## The Four Key Steps to Building a Workable Comfort Zone

1. Establish a geographic territory.

2. Become the expert of that territory.

3. Build the investment techniques required.

4. Act on opportunities.

Review each in detail.

### Establish a Geographic Territory

The first step is to decide *where* the investment zone will be. The best place to begin with will be a geographic area that is convenient to where the investor currently lives or works. However, it is important that the zone meet the following minimum criteria.

### The Four Minimum Criteria for an Investment Comfort Zone

1. Should not be a deteriorating neighborhood.

2. Should contain affordable properties.

3. Should have between 600 and 1000 property owners.

4. Should be within one community.

Study each in detail.

A **deteriorating neighborhood** is usually obvious, but there may be plans in the works not yet publicized that are about to shake up a stable neighborhood. One such event might be the closing of the only major employment in the community, or a new superhighway that is going to slice through the neighborhood, cutting it in half and making it either unaccessible or undesirable. Whatever the situation, the investor should avoid spending any time in a deteriorating neighborhood. In fact, if you live in one, my suggestion would be to *get out* as soon as possible. Where you live can have a profound effect on your mental outlook. Living in a negative area of town will affect you negatively. You will be surprised to learn that if you look hard, and even use some "sweat equity," you can move to an improving neighborhood easier than you think. Live and work in positive surroundings.

**Affordable properties** do not mean properties that investors think they can afford at this moment. By the time this course has been completed, investors will have discovered it is possible to buy properties and profit from them even though they may seem out of reach, pricewise, at this moment in time. *Affordable* means property that is priced from the middle of the specific market for the area to the lower end of that same market. If the price range is from $150,000 to $250,000, then the affordable range is from $150,000 to $200,000. That is the area in which there can still be improvement in value, and it may present an opportunity to investors.

At the start, each comfort zone should have between **600 and 1000 property owners**. The basic reason for this is to give investors a wide choice of properties from which to select, while at the same time limiting the size of the zone with which investors start. This will enable investors to focus attention on a narrow part of town.

*All these properties should be within one community,* because in the beginning investors need to concentrate their efforts on one governmental process. Different communities, even though they neighbor each other, often have different procedures, rules, ordinances, and possibly worse, a different attitude about real estate developments. Investors must concentrate on one closed area, getting to know it like the back of their hands before moving to another. If there are two different possible comfort zones and all the criteria are similar except for the governmental attitude toward real estate development, then select the community that works with rather than against property owners and real estate investors.

## Become the Expert of that Territory

The fortunate part of real estate investment is that nearly everything of importance occurs locally. This localized nature makes it possible for any determined investor to become an expert in any given area in a short period of time. Even though becoming an expert is very simple and basic, most property owners have never taken these steps.

This chapter and the rest of Part 3 detail the different steps that can be taken to develop the investment comfort zone and how to get the most out of it. The steps are simple, and all that is needed is well-planned use of what limited time is available. The following is a list of the information investment experts strive to obtain about their comfort zone. Keep in mind that many of these factors change from time to time and thus a constant review of the current circumstances is required.

### Twenty Facts Experts Know about Their Investment Comfort Zone

1. Geographic layout
2. Street names
3. Subdivision names
4. Zoning rules and regulations
5. Local ordinances that affect real estate
6. Price ranges by subdivision and/or by streets
7. Rental market data and rents charged
8. Future road plans
9. Future utility plans
10. Future developments in planning stages
11. Local employment statistics
12. Employment trends
13. Major impacts that will affect employment trends
14. The "how" and "who" of local government
15. "What," "how," and "who" of the local building department
16. School districts and how to get into other schools
17. Bus and other local transportation routes
18. "What," "how," and "who" of public records
19. Names of prominent business leaders in the community
20. Sources for local financing

And where does this data come from? The sources have already been discussed. There are just a few, and the most bountiful of all is the deed search that would be accomplished by a realtor or at the tax assessor's office. Every item mentioned above is part of the public data that is available. It is up to devoted investors to utilize the information sources already disclosed in this book to extract the data that can provide the path to their own "King Solomon's mine."

## Build the Investment Techniques Required

Part 4 of this book, How to Buy and Sell Real Estate for a Profit, will help the investor build the techniques that will become the tools for building an investment portfolio. As with any tool, practice will hone the edge and will give the investor confidence in both the technique and the investor's ability to use it.

Just as no single tool can be used for every purpose, so it is with real estate investing techniques. By now the reader has been introduced to various techniques that investors use through the examples in this book. By the time the reader has finished this course, how and when to apply these techniques to best attain the desired results will begin to be evident. However, continued study beyond this course is recommended because the real estate environment is constantly changing. Tax laws that affect real estate depreciation or tax consequences in the event of a sale or other disposition of the property go through frequent changes by the Internal Revenue Service, and adjustments in investment plans may be needed to keep abreast of the current events.

## Act on Opportunities

As investors begin to get the feel for the comfort zone, there will be a sudden shift in what investors actually see. It is almost like looking at a forest and not recognizing one species of tree from another. They are all green, and while some may stand out as pines, the rest may look more or less the same. Finding that sugar maple may be an impossible task . . . until one learns what the sugar maple looks like. The same perception happens in the investment comfort zone.

Opportunities in real estate are rarely so obvious that they have a sign out front that announces them as "the opportunity of the day." Frequently it is the subtle, usually not so obvious potential for economic conversion that guarantees a profit.

When investors know the geographic territory like the backs of their hands and have a firm grasp of the 20 facts mentioned earlier in this chapter, opportunities will stand out like sugar maples growing among pines.

## Pitfalls to Avoid in Building a Comfort Zone

1. Don't look for shortcuts.

2. Let failure work for you, not against you.

3. Don't let anyone tell you that you can't succeed.

When it comes to running into brick walls, real estate investors have their share of hard lumps that come from such walls. The key is to keep working at the process, and to continue to build this very important sphere of reference mentioned earlier in this chapter. But as stressed before, building a sphere of reference only works if the particular reference gets to know and remember you. This requires follow up and more follow up on *your part*. If you are looking for shortcuts, you will find many, but they are all pathways to some other destination, and not the *goal* you so strongly seek.

**Failure** is what I call the "French word," kind of soft and alluring if you say it slowly while at the same time thinking of Casablanca . . . there is nothing harsh or sinister about the way the word sounds. Then why is everyone so frightened of it? Fail is what people, even successful people, do a lot of the time. In fact, failure that occurs just a little bit less than half the time can indicate huge success. People who are not successful in working their comfort zone attain a lack of success because they do not take chances. It is usually not that they shirk responsibility and hard work . . . quite the opposite; they often work harder trying to avoid a confrontation with another person where they may (heaven forbid) actually *fail* at something.

Think of everything as small bits and pieces that guide you to success. If your goal is to *buy a small income property*, then look at the elements that can lead to that goal:

1. Get to know the area.

2. Look at everything on the market.

3. Find a realtor that is compatible with this goal.

4. Make offers.

5. Make offers.

6. Work with cooperative sellers to **close a deal**.

These steps contain intermediary steps that have to be accomplished, but each is a move in a positive direction. Frequently the drive toward the goal loses momentum at items 4 and 5. Somebody steps in the way—a broker, a lawyer, a negative seller—who actually says "no" to your offer. None of these people are roadblocks; they represent road signs to make you stop for a while and see if something can be done to work out the deal or to move on to another property and another seller. There will always be another seller.

The unfortunate aspect of life is that there are more negative people than positive people. The nice part of life is that positive people generally attract more positive people around them. It is simple mathematics, if you think about it. Because there are more negative people, and because positive people attract more positive people, then make the shift and get in on another simple fact of life:

> *Positive people enjoy their success while negative people never believe they have attained enough of it.*

## Study and Review

Obtain a copy of the plat of a subdivision in your target comfort zone, or any area of the local community where you reside or work. Pick one block of residential property and either ask a realtor contact to run a deed search (long form) for that entire block, from which you would get the names and addresses of present and past owners, legal descriptions, property assessments, taxes, prices paid in the past, and much more data.

Or, and best of all, go to the local tax assessor's office and tell the clerk you want to do a deed search for the entire subdivision where you live (or work, or want to live or work). Make sure you have a subdivision in mind prior to asking this question. Once you have the computer printout, ask the clerk to go over a sample listing to explain each of the codes and abbreviations in the search.

# 15

# How to Get the Inside Track to Real Estate Values and Trends

## Chapter Goals

The primary goal of this chapter is to introduce the reader to the main sources of "trend" information and other real estate data that will help the investor keep track of the local real estate market. In addition, this chapter provides hints on how to use that data to discover potential investment opportunities.

There are many private and governmental organizations that spend millions of dollars collectively on research and studies that can be of great benefit to the local real estate investor. In addition to this data, there is a vast wealth of "public" information about real estate that will give the investor a full and complete history of virtually every real estate transaction that has taken place within recent times. This data is usually so complete that it is easy for investors to discover prices paid, payoff dates of mortgages, cost of improvements, names of current and past owners, and much more. All this information is generally available to the investor willing to ask for it.

## Key Terms

- Deed search
- Legal description
- Tax assessment

Review each in detail.

## Deed Search

Every real estate transaction is recorded in the official records of the county in which that property is located. This information is very comprehensive and usually includes the following data:

Previous owner

Current owner

Current owner's address (often different than the property address)

Property address

Legal description of the property

Tax folio (number used by tax assessor)

Assessed value (for both improvements and vacant land)

Square footage of land area

Tax assessment

Data on improvements

Square footage of improvements

Date constructed

Price of last transfer(s)

## Legal Description

This is the description given to every property that distinguishes it from another property. In subdivided property this description is written as **lot, block and subdivision**.

Lot 5 of Block 20 of West Highlands Subdivision, in East Ridge County, Texas.

Rural property may be described in **metes and bounds**, which is a descriptive form that gives actual measurements from a known starting point.

From Marker 107 on State Road 17 West 270 degrees a distance of 82.4 feet to a point of beginning, thence Northerly and parallel to the right-of-way of State Road 17 a distance of 200 feet, thence West 270 degrees a distance of 1200 feet, thence South 180 degrees a distance of 200 feet, thence East 90 degrees 1200 feet to the point of beginning.

The above metes and bounds describes a tract of land that has 200 ft of frontage on State Road 17 and is a rectangle that is 200 ft by 1200 ft.

**Section, township, and range** descriptions are common for large tracts of land. The entire United States is divided into township and range lines. Each crossing forms a grid that encloses 36 sections. A section consists of a square that is approximately one mile on each side (there will be very slight adjustments in these sizes due to the curvature of the earth). Each section is divided into quarters, each quarter further divided into quarters or halves. A section of land consists of 640 acres.

The following legal description is for a tract of land that is 40 acres in size.

> The North East quarter of the South West quarter of Section 36, Township 49 South, Range 41 West.

## Tax Assessment

The tax assessment is the amount of money charged by the local taxing authority against the property. This sum generally includes several items that are lumped together from the different taxing authorities within the county. These may include school board, hospital district, city taxes, county taxes, and special assessments. Most of these amounts are based on a percentage called **millage**, which is then multiplied by the assessed value. The underlying assessed value is an evaluation that may not actually reflect the real value or the market value of the property. It has been customary in many parts of the country for the assessed value to take into consideration age (therefore depreciation) and other factors with the end result that a property built today may have an assessed value greater than an identical one built 20 years earlier. All property owners can challenge the assessed value if they have reason to support what they feel is an excess evaluation. When property assessments are generally less than the market value, property owners usually do not contest the evaluation. After all, as tax assessors are quick to point out, you wouldn't sell the property for the tax assessed value, would you? However, because property assessed values rarely equal the market value, the relative assessment of one property should be in balance to all other properties of similar criteria in the area. The owner of any property assessed more than the average value of similar properties would have a very good reason to contest the higher tax evaluation.

To contest a tax assessed value properly, the property owner should gather as much information about the assessed values for all property within the general area of the subject property and isolate properties most similar in size (lot size and property square footage). The subject property should have an assessed value in line with these other properties, despite the possibility that none of the assessed values may match real or market values. Investors should acquaint themselves with the procedures to contest tax assessed values, as most tax assessment departments have an annual deadline for any tax dispute.

## Sources of Real Estate Trend Information

Airport, sea, river, or lake port authorities

Banks and savings and loan institutions

Building and zoning departments

Cable television companies

Chamber of Commerce

County recorded documents

Government planning offices

Industrial development board

When reviewing each of these sources every investor will want to know the answer to the following four questions.

### Four Important Questions when Compiling Trend Information

1. Where can this source be found?

2. What data can be obtained?

3. Who is the best source?

4. How can the information be used?

Review each of the above sources with particular attention to the answers to these four questions. Use The Real Estate Investor's VIP List as a primary source of information.

Once the investor is in touch with the appropriate person, ask specific questions about what information is available and how to obtain the information. Each locality may vary greatly in how information is disseminated to the public. In general, the following list of questions will serve as the starting point for each of the sources:

### Source Checklist

1. Name of source.

2. Address, phone number, and fax number.

3. Names of persons in charge of future planning and agendas.

4. Names of persons in charge of complaints.

5. Are there any meetings open to the public?

6. If so, what is the schedule?

7. What are the office hours?

8. What information is available that would be helpful to real estate investors?

9. Is there a charge for the data? If so, how much?

10. Can other information sources be recommended that would be helpful to real estate investors?

11. Can you be put on a mailing list?


## Airport, Sea, River, or Lake Port Authorities

**Where Can This Source Be Found?**    Local airports, sea, river, or lake ports may not be found in every community, or there may be several within easy commuting distance. If there is one or more within a drive time radius of 1½ hours, the investor should make contact with the appropriate management offices of each to ascertain who is in charge of future planning for the facility.

**What Data Can Be Obtained?**    Growth and business trends for airports and water ports are very important because they can give long-range signals that are important to real estate growth or decline. Because the expansion of this type of facility often involves very long-range planning and government funding, the data often is very comprehensive and extends well beyond the actual port facilities themselves. For example, to substantiate a multimillion dollar federal loan or grant request, the data submitted may contain statistics on every aspect of the local community including new business patterns, population growth, long-range travel patterns, and much more. Expansions of any kind of port may also require other infrastructure to be developed, such as railways, and new or expanded road systems, hotels, rental car facilities, local transportation, and other service businesses. In a growth pattern everything tends to give cause for some other business to grow. In a decline, the sudden disappearance of business rarely will come as a surprise to the investor who has been following the information closely.

**Who Is the Best Source?**    Start at the top. In most cases port facilities are under some sort of local government control: generally a county commissioner is appointed or elected to oversee the operations, or a professional manager is hired to run the day-to-day operations of the facility. If there is a commissioner (elected or appointed), that is the person to contact first. If there is a subsequent manager below the commissioner the investor would ask the commissioner (or the commissioner's secretary) to introduce the investor to that manager. This may be accomplished over the phone.

**How Can the Information Be Used?**   In the beginning all data collected may have no direct bearing on what investors are doing. The long-range goal is to make the initial contact and find out the details of the situation. As investors begin to collect information from different sources a pattern will begin to evolve. The most important part of this evolution will be the growing confidence investors have in themselves by virtue of becoming experts of the area.

Some information may be instantly useable. Learning of a new expansion or major cutback would obviously give the investor a lead in the market place.

## Banks and Savings and Loan Institutions

**Where Can This Source Be Found?**   Pick the biggest three in the comfort zone or nearest to it and start there. The major lenders are a good start. Later on, the investor may be introduced to other lenders from different sources. This building of contacts is an excellent way to establish a position in the community as a real estate investor.

**What Data Can Be Obtained?**   The first data to obtain from lenders is the kind of property they make loans on. Other useful information would be

- Is the institution expanding or cutting back?
- What parts of town are lenders expanding to?
- Who is in charge of their REO (real estate owned) department?
- Who is their best loan officer?
- What are their lending rates and loan charges (points and other out-of-pocket expenses)?

**How Can the Information Be Used?**   Again the major goal is the contact. However, it is very important for the investor to know what properties lenders *will lend on* before the investor spends a lot of time looking in the wrong direction for properties on which lenders will not make favorable loans. When it is time to apply for a loan the contacts made within the lending side of real estate will be very valuable. Every potential loan should be "shopped" between at least two or three lenders, and an investor who has spent the time to meet with and develop some rapport with loan officers at different lending institutions will have a much easier time getting the loan officer to "go that extra mile" to get the best loan amount and terms possible.

## Building and Zoning Departments

**Where Can This Source Be Found?**   This source is found both within
the county and the city where the property is located. These departments
have already been discussed in previous chapters, and the following is a
review of the source and the information available.

Every local community has a building department that may or may not be
combined with the zoning department. Investors need to become acquainted
with both the city and the county offices, as each may have some control over
the use of property within their boundaries.

**What Data Can Be Obtained?**   Building restrictions and codes and zoning ordinances affect or control what can be built and how property can be
used. In addition, these sources become primary data banks for future
growth and development as virtually every major project (and many minor
ones) goes through the process of **site plan approval**, which may occur
months before the ground breaking occurs.

**Who Is the Best Source?**   The actual person to contact may depend on
how the departments are organized. In general there are four people with
whom the investor would want to establish rapport.

1. Chief building inspector
2. Head of planning department
3. Head of zoning department
4. City clerk

In small communities all the above responsibilities may be delegated to one
or two people.

**How Can the Information Be Used?**   This is part of this continual building process of getting to know the "who," "what," and "why" of real estate. The
obvious advantage is that the investor can learn of future projects that can
give advance lead time to tie up other properties in the path or just beyond
the path of progress. Investors should never assume that just because this
information is available, the general public will know about it. The truth is
that the general public rarely hears about future projects until they actually
break ground. Even when a proposed project is reported in a newspaper, several years may pass without further mention, and whatever the public learned
is forgotten. Savvy investors know this and take advantage of it.

## Cable Television Companies

As with all utility companies, cable television companies continually
expand. They try to expand in areas of solid growth potential. Using

their planning research may corroborate and add to other information obtained from other sources.

**Where Can This Source Be Found?**   Often there will be more than one cable television company in any county. Each company will serve its own franchise or licensed area and will naturally be interested in keeping a close watch on their own area. Check the Yellow Pages or a local television guide book for the weekly programs for information on how to contact each company.

**What Data Can Be Obtained?**   Growth potential, areas of heaviest cable use, areas in which most collection problems occur, and areas in which the cable company is spending money are important data to collect.

**How Can the Information Be Used?**   This is good backup data that can verify other information obtained. The cable TV companies have a lot of political clout in any community because they spend a lot of money in the community and are often major employment centers. Because they also are a media and have their own programming, they can be a good contact to know and cultivate.

## Chamber of Commerce

**Where Can This Source Be Found?**   Virtually every community in the United States has a Chamber of Commerce that functions to promote the influx of new commercial development as well as the exploitation of existing businesses. A private but associated organization, the Junior Chamber of Commerce, consists of local businesspeople interested in accomplishing the same goals. Each of these organizations become good starting places for the investor to build lists of important people and information sources. In addition, the investor can become a member of the Chamber of Commerce as well as the Junior Chamber of Commerce and participate in their frequent functions, which are excellent places to meet the local VIPs on their home turf.

**What Data Can Be Obtained?**   Statistical data on employment, employers, local government, tax data, investment incentives, future development, and population demographics are just some of the useful information available from the Chamber of Commerce. Promotional material about the community can be very useful in putting together a brochure or marketing program to sell a property in the investment portfolio.

**Who Is the Best Source?**   As usual, start at the top, and work down to those who actually do the work in the areas of interest. Because the Chamber of Commerce is a good meeting place of important people, the best sources of information may come from the contacts made there rather than the Chamber itself.

**How Can the Information Be Used?**   The Chamber of Commerce is a sphere-building organization in addition to being a good source for growth trends. Contacts made within this and other such organizations will provide good references as well as become an excellent source of referrals.

## County Recorded Documents

**Where Can This Source Be Found?**   Public recording of documents is one facet of the detailed record keeping that is a part of most modern societies. In the United States as elsewhere, the usual authority for record keeping falls to the local county offices. All transactions required to be recorded that have taken place within that county would be on record at those offices.

**What Data Can Be Obtained?**   The magnitude of the different kinds of records that must be or are recorded is monumental. A partial list of such documents is shown below:

*Adverse Possession.*   A person or other entity claims title to a property by virtue of having taken possession of the property according to the provisions of state law.

*Affidavits.*   Statements legally attested to as being truthful.

*Deed Transfers.*   All real estate deed transfers should be recorded to protect the rights of the new owner.

*Divorce Actions.*   Generally are recorded to show change of marital status and legal obligations thereof.

*Leases.*   May be recorded.

*Liens.*   Several different kinds. The most usual are tax liens, mechanics liens, and legal judgements.

*Lis Pendens.*   A form of lien against the property.

*Mortgages.*   Both the note and the mortgage are recorded to ensure proper notice to any subsequent lender that there is already a loan made with the property pledged as security.

*Satisfactions.*   When any lien or mortgage has been paid in full, a satisfaction of lien will show that the property owner has been released from the obligation.

It is easy to see that, from the different items mentioned above, there is a great deal of potential leads for the real estate investor. The most useful data is the deed transaction records which, along with other "property records," is assimilated by the local tax assessor and can be viewed in one composite set of records in the **deed search** mentioned earlier in this chapter. The deed search, however, will not have the full details that would be visible in the copy of the recorded deed or other document that can be found within the county records.

**Who Is the Best Source?**　　Most county records departments have one or more people who assist the public in finding information. Because the information may be spread among different departments, the investor should anticipate spending a few hours to learn where and how the information is retrieved. Most modern records offices have data on microfilm or microfiche, which is updated frequently to ensure that the latest recorded documents are included. Because making microfilm and microfiche takes time the data available is *never* current. In searching for very important documents it would be helpful to know how many days it usually takes between recording and the microfilm or microfiche being available for that specific system.

**How Can the Information Be Used?**　　The use of the information depends on the data obtained. Deed searches are used most because the information applies directly to the investor's goals. Find out who owns the property, what that owner paid for the property, and what improvements have been made. Discovering details on the property such as size, square footage, tax assessments, and the like are all part of the learning process to become an expert of the comfort zone. Death notices suggest possible properties for sale, birth notices suggest the need for a larger home and the sale or other disposition of the existing one. Mortgage satisfactions indicate that the mortgagor no longer has an obligation to meet and may now be ready to move up and take on more debt, and of great importance, the mortgagee may have received cash ahead of time, which could be spent on something else. Divorce data opens up other doors that are both buy and sell possibilities.

## Government Planning Offices

**Where Can This Source Be Found?**　　Government is almost everywhere until you try to find the right person to help you with your problem. With real estate investing, several different government planning offices or departments are very helpful. These offices may be duplicated within an investor's comfort zone because of adjoining city, county, or state offices that may have some control or effect within cities. The investor should start with the city offices and departments and expand from that point. The question "What other office or governmental department has control or affects real estate?" should become a habit when ever dealing with any governmental department. Often, unless this question is asked, the needed information is not volunteered.

### Important Government Planning Offices or Departments

| | |
|---|---|
| Department of Transportation | Health Department |
| Department of planning | Building rules review |
| Utilities (water and sewer) | Parks and public works |
| Schools | Hospitals |

The investor should be aware that the titles for these offices or departments may vary, and that each office or department may have several divisions. The Department of Transportation, for example, may have a bus division, roadway division, metro division, and so on.

Usually every court house or city hall will have a directory that can be purchased (rarely free). If the book is expensive, it may be possible to photocopy it or copy by hand the important data. This book or a published listing will provide the locations of the different offices, and often the names of the officials within those departments who are in charge. Keep in mind that unless the book is of recent publication, the names of officials may be out of date so the investor calling on any office may want to update the "names" portion of the list annually.

**What Data Can Be Obtained?**    There is a vast amount of data that flows through these offices and departments, and in general the investor should divide the data into two types: (1) control and (2) changes to the status quo.

Data on **control** would be any information that shows or indicates where the government exerts control over real estate either directly or indirectly. A direct control would be the building codes or city ordinances that limit or restrict what can be done on or to a property. Indirect controls are less obvious and generally occur in administrative procedures that must be met prior to building or obtaining permits. An example would be the requirement for the *community itself* to meet state or county standards before any new building can occur. In this situation the individual may be prevented from doing something and may have no direct remedy until the city meets the standards set by higher authority.

Data on **changes to the status quo** is very important because the proposed changes may have a major impact on the property values in any area—either positive or negative.

**Who Is the Best Source?**    Start with the head of any government department.

**How Can the Information Be Used?**    Investors increase their sphere of reference by building their contacts within the governmental offices that control or affect real estate. The contacts themselves can become more important than any single bit of information, unless that bit leads you directly to the bargain property that is turned into a gold mine. The investor will look for any data that points to a change in the status quo because this is the kind of information that hastens opportunities.

## Industrial Development Board

**Where Can This Source Be Found?**    This organization, when present within a community, functions for the sole purpose of bringing new commercial development to the community. This body often has the power to assist in financing by the issuance of industrial bonds, which are usually a *tax-free* investment for the purchaser of the bond, guaranteed by the local community. The funds are then lent to companies to pay for new construction, training of employees, plant investment, and other start-up costs for new enterprises coming to the area. These loans are usually issued on a long-term payback at a modest interest rate lower than the usual bank rates available from institutional lenders.

**What Data Can Be Obtained?**   The usual information that would be helpful to a real estate investor would be growth in the business or industrial sectors. This office or department also may provide lists for new companies interested in locating in the area. These new companies may become tenants for investors who have existing properties to rent or in future buildings to be built. A major employer who comes to the community can have a major impact on real estate values, so land and other property may go up or down in value depending on the nature of the employer (or up in one place and down in another). The sooner the investor knows where that employer is going to locate (even if that investor has nothing to do with the relocation), the better the investment opportunity.

**Who Is the Best Source?**   The chairperson of the board is usually an appointed member but may be an elected official who has been given this added authority.

## Study and Review

A good habit for any real estate investor is to read the daily review of local public announcements published in local newspapers. These announcements occur in both the classified section of the newspaper and in normal display format, which may have no specific location in the paper. These announcements may be required by law and may provide information on anything from sheriff sales to foreclosures on properties. Divorces, marriages, deaths, public meetings, zoning changes, proposed public works, etc., are all part of the usual public announcements, courtesy of the local newspaper.

Over the next several days, look for any public announcement such as those described above. Many can be seen as relatively large display advertising, often showing a sketch or drawing of community boundaries; others are in classified form and are frequently found at the beginning of the classified advertising section. Find and read several different ones but most importantly these three:

1. A foreclosure notice of sale
2. Deed transfer
3. Mortgage satisfaction

*Tip:* If the local newspaper does not carry each of these three legal notices, then find out if there is a "legal newspaper" published in your area. The local library as well as most lawyers' offices would have a copy and you can always subscribe to it later.

# DEEDS & MORTGAGES

The following real estate transactions record sales of $60,000 and above. Included, are the names of the buyers, sellers, address and a description of the property. When available, the sale price, previous sale price, financing, taxes and the assessed value.

The O.R. (Official Record) Book and Page Number and the folio numbers are included.

Data provided by Laser-Scan Systems Inc.

**Business Data**

New Deeds and Mortgages are now available on computer printouts or diskettes.

For more information on rates and formats, please call Noël Decker at 347-6620 (Miami) or 1-800-777-7300

**OR BOOK 19484 to 19490**

**HOLLYWOOD**
**Residential**

ADDRESS .... 5120 POLK ST
                    33024
PRICE ................. $137,000
LAST SALE ....... $133,000 10/87
BUYER ....... JOSEPH ANTHONY &
                    ANN M GAITA
SELLER ......... JOSE & OLGA BELLO
SQ. FEET ................ 2848
ASSESSED ............. $121,760
FINANCING $84,400 w/BARNETT
                    BANK BROWARD CO
                    19486
SUBDIV ...... HOLLYWOOD HILLS 6-
                    22 B
TAXES ............. $2,466.89
ORB/PAGE ..... 19486-0472
FOLIO ......... 5142 07 07 128 0


ADDRESS .... 2110 N 50 AVE
                    33021
PRICE ................. $110,000
LAST SALE ....... $23,700 3/68
BUYER ...... GIUSEPPE & ROSA
                    COLOCA
SELLER ...... J E & SHIRLEY
                    BONETTI
SQ. FEET ................ 2206
ASSESSED ............. $80,910
FINANCING $50,000 w/
                    JEFFERSON NATIONAL
                    BANK 19487
SUBDIV ...... HOLLYWOOD HILLS
                    AMEN PLAT 6-31 B
TAXES ............. $1,425.41
ORB/PAGE ...... 19487-0726
FOLIO ......... 5142 07 08 254 0

# FORECLOSURE SALES

**NOTICE OF SALE**
**Pursuant to Chapter 45**
IN THE CIRCUIT COURT OF THE 17 JUDICIAL CIRCUIT IN AND FOR BROWARD COUNTY, FLORIDA
CASE NO: 92-03787-05
LINCOLN SERVICE CORPORATION,
Plaintiff,
vs.
MARILYN STANGE, et al.
Defendants.
NOTICE IS HEREBY GIVEN pursuant to an Order or Summary and Default Final Judgment of foreclosure dated June 10, 1992 and entered in Case 92-03787-05 Division 95 of the Circuit Court of the 17th Judicial Circuit in and for Broward County, Florida, wherein LINCOLN SERVICE CORPORATION is Plaintiff, and MARILYN STANGE, SANDRA STANGE, F/K/A _____, UNKNOWN TENANT IN POSSESSION OF SUBJECT PROPERTY, JACK L. WILSON, JOAN M. WILSON and UNITED STATES are Defendants, I will sell to the highest and best bidder for cash in the lobby of the Broward County Courthouse in Fort Lauderdale, Broward County, Florida at 11:00 o'clock a.m. on the 25 day of August, 1992, the following-described property as set forth in said Order or Summary and Default Final Judgment, to-wit:
Lot 14, Block 5 of "LINWOOD GARDENS NO. 2" according to the Plat thereof, as recorded in Plat Book 51 at Page 37 of the Public Records of Broward County, Florida.
Dated at Fort Lauderdale, Florida this 10 day of June, 1992.
ROBERT E. LOCKWOOD
As Clerk, Circuit Court
Broward County, Florida
A TRUE COPY
Circuit Court Seal
BY: THOMAS WILLIAMS
As Deputy Clerk
Edmund O. Loos, III, Esquire
FRIED, SLACHTER &
FISHMAN, P.A.
Attorneys for Plaintiff
7700 N. KENDALL DRIVE,
Third Floor
MIAMI, FLORIDA 33156
(305) 598-1900
6/15-22

**NOTICE OF SALE**
**PURSUANT TO CHAPTER 45**
IN THE CIRCUIT COURT OF FLORIDA IN AND FOR BROWARD COUNTY
CASE NO. 92-05697 CA 01
FIRST NATIONWIDE BANK, a Federal Savings Bank, f/k/a FIRST NATIONWIDE SAVINGS, a Federal Savings and Loan Association,
Plaintiff,
vs.
Catalino Colon and Alma S. Colon,
Defendant(s).
NOTICE IS HEREBY GIVEN pursuant to a Summary Final Judgment in Foreclosure dated June 10, 1992, and entered in Case No. 92-05697 CA of the Circuit Court of the Seventeenth Judicial Circuit in and for Broward County, Florida wherein FIRST NATIONWIDE BANK, a Federal Savings Bank, f/k/a FIRST NATIONWIDE SAVINGS, a Federal Savings and Loan Association is plaintiff, and Catalino Colon and Alma S. Colon are defendants, I will sell to the highest and best bidder for cash at the lobby of the Broward County Courthouse in Fort Lauderdale, Broward County, Florida at 11:00 o'clock a.m. on August 24, 1992, the following described property as set forth in said Summary Final Judgment in Foreclosure, to-wit:
Lot 3, Block 41, LAKE FOREST SECTION FOUR, according to the Plat thereof, recorded in Plat Book 38, Page 4, of the Public Records of Broward County, Florida a/k/a 3021 SW 34th Avenue, Hollywood, Florida 33023.
DATED at Fort Lauderdale, Florida this June 10, 1992.
ROBERT E. LOCKWOOD
As Clerk, Circuit Court
A TRUE COPY
Circuit Court Seal
BY THOMAS WILLIAMS
As Deputy Clerk
Attorney for Plaintiff
Gary R. Siegel, Esquire
Miami Center, Suite 880
201 S. Biscayne Boulevard
Miami, Florida 33131

**NOTICE OF SALE**
IN THE CIRCUIT COURT OF THE 17TH JUDICIAL CIRCUIT, IN AND FOR BROWARD COUNTY, FLORIDA
CASE NO.. 91-26419 10
CALIFORNIA FEDERAL BANK, A FEDERAL SAVINGS BANK F/K/A CALIFORNIA FEDERAL SAVINGS AND LOAN ASSOCIATION,
Plaintiff,
vs.
RICHARD A. FAULKNER, et. al.,
Defendants.
NOTICE IS HEREBY GIVEN pursuant to a Final Judgment of Foreclosure dated June 10, 1992 and entered in Case No. 91-26419 of the Circuit Court of the 17th Judicial Circuit in and for Broward County, Florida wherein RICHARD A. FAULKNER, et. al., are defendants, I will sell to the highest and best bidder for cash in the lobby of the Broward County Courthouse, 201 S.E. 6th Street, Fort Lauderdale, Broward County, Florida at 11:00 o'clock A.M. on the 24 day of August, 1992, the following described property as set forth in said Final Judgment, to-wit:
The North One-half (½) of Lot 17, Block 3, VICTORIA ISLES, as recorded in Plat Book 15, Page 67, of the Public Records of Broward County, Florida.
Dated at Fort Lauderdale, Florida this 10 day of June, 1992.
ROBERT E. LOCKWOOD
As Clerk, Circuit Court
Broward County, Florida
A TRUE COPY
Circuit Court Seal
By: THOMAS WILLIAMS
As Deputy Clerk
JOHN A. WATSON, ESQUIRE
WATSON, CLARK & PURDY, P.A.
Post Office Box 11959
Fort Lauderdale, Florida 33339
Attorneys for Plaintiff
Phone (305) 776-3800
FLORIDA BAR NO. 340197
6/15-22            B92-F-061517

# 16

# How to Evaluate a Property Before You Buy It

## Chapter Goals

The primary goal of this chapter is to show the reader several simple methods of ascertaining the value of a property. The best way to ensure future profit is to make sure that the purchase price paid does not exceed the current value.

## Key Terms

- Cash flow
- Desired return
- Net operating income calculations
- Sinking fund

Review each in detail.

## Cash Flow

**Cash flow** is the actual cash, or money in the bank, that is left at the end of any period after all expenses and debt service (except depreciation and income taxes) are deducted from the income from the property. For example, Paula owns eight one-bedroom apartments that are rented at an average of $500.00 per month. She has a first mortgage on the property of

$210,000 with monthly payments for the next 24 years of $1583.34 per month (principal and interest). Paula feels this property is worth $362,000. After subtracting the amount of the first mortgage from this price, Paula has an equity of $152,000. Paula rationalizes that if a buyer paid $152,000 for the property there would be a 10 percent cash return on the investment, based on Paula's calculations of income and expense.

### Paula's Eight-Unit Apartment Complex

|                          | An average month | Annual   |
|--------------------------|------------------|----------|
| Gross rents:             | $4,000.00        | $48,000  |
| Less operating expenses: | 1,150.00         | 13,800   |
| Less mortgage payments:  | 1,583.34         | 19,000   |
| Cash flow:               | $1,266.66        | $15,200  |

If the buyer pays $152,000 and assumes the mortgage, the buyer will make 10 percent cash flow on the invested capital.

## Desired Return

The yield or return investors hope to make from their invested capital is the **desired return**. If Paula had invested $76,000 in the eight-unit apartment complex along with the money obtained in the first mortgage ($210,000), she would realize a return of 20 percent based on the cash flow shown above of $15,200 per year. Most apartment properties are valued at a real return of 7 to 12 percent of the cash invested.

## Net Operating Income Calculations

Arriving at the NOI is important because this is much the same as cash flow, except that the debt service is not deducted from the income. In the case of Paula's eight units shown earlier in this chapter, the net operating income would be as follows:

| Annual                   |          |
|--------------------------|----------|
| Gross income:            | $48,000  |
| Less operating expenses: | 13,800   |
| Net operating income:    | $34,200  |

Because this is an eight-unit apartment building, a prospective buyer would see that this property is producing $4275 of NOI per apartment. If there was another property being reviewed of more or less apartments, a comparison of the price per unit and the NOI per unit may indicate which of the two properties was a better buy. This concept will be examined in more detail later in this chapter.

## Sinking Fund

**Sinking fund** accounting is a method of *setting aside* funds, usually in a bank account, that are used to pay for anticipated future expenses or capital replacements. For example, the following are lists of items that will need repair or replacement at some time in the future. Replacement: roof, carpets, furniture, air conditioning and heating equipment, appliances and other electrical or mechanical equipment, wood docks and decks, etc. Repair or upkeep items: repaint interiors and exteriors of buildings, resurface driveways and pool surfaces, etc.

In a review of the actual income and expenses of any property, the investor would first look to see if the income and expense statement included either a sinking fund or if any of these major expenses occurred during the year for which the income and expenses are reported. If there was a sinking fund or major nonreoccurring expenses included in the expenses, the investor would need to satisfy him- or herself that the sinking fund was sufficient or that the nonreoccurring expenses took care of the problem and were not simply a cosmetic cover-up of the problem.

When no sinking fund is present and nonreoccurring expenses are not shown, the investor would need to *include* a separate deduction from the reported net operating income to adjust for future expense. For example, when reviewing Paula's eight-unit apartment complex mentioned earlier, consider that any reasonable study of the property would indicate that an investor could expect the following major expenses to occur within the time frame shown below.

### Sinking Fund Checklist

| Item | Years to go | Estimated cost |
| --- | --- | --- |
| New roof | 10 | $6000 |
| Paint exteriors | 4 | 1800 |
| Replace compressors | 8 | 2800 |
| Resurface parking | 10 | 1500 |

A prospective investor would anticipate an annual deduction from the current NOI as reported by Paula to take care of these expenses when they occur.

Because the sinking fund is calculated with the assumption that money is being set aside in a bank account that would earn interest, the investor cannot simply divide the years to go into the estimated cost; also, it is difficult to estimate future costs. By using Table 16-1, an annuity buildup table, the investor can ascertain an annual sum that can be used in these calculations. This table assumes investors can earn 8 percent on their invested capital. If the actual interest to be earned is different than this, the investor would need to use a calculator that would accurately calculate annuities or a more detailed annuity table.

To find the annual sum needed to build up to meet the estimated expense (at 8 percent interest earned), divide the expense by the appropriate factor for the number of years remaining. The reroofing expense estimated to be $6000 in 10 years would result in the following calculation.

$$\$6000 \div 14.48656247 = \$414.18 \text{ (rounded up)}$$

The completed sinking fund annuity checklist is shown in Table 16-2.

## Two Basic Methods of Property Evaluation

- Income approach
- Market value approach

All income properties should be valued using both methods, and it is not critical which of the two is completed first. Normally the **market value**

**Table 16-1.** Annuity Table for 8 Percent Annual Compound Interest

| Number of years | Factor |
|---|---|
| 1 | 1.00000000 |
| 2 | 2.08000000 |
| 3 | 3.24640000 |
| 4 | 4.50611200 |
| 5 | 5.86660096 |
| 6 | 7.33592904 |
| 7 | 8.92280336 |
| 8 | 10.63662763 |
| 9 | 12.48755784 |
| 10 | 14.48656247 |
| 11 | 16.64548746 |
| 12 | 18.97712646 |
| 13 | 21.49529658 |
| 14 | 24.21492030 |
| 15 | 27.15211393 |
| 16 | 30.32428304 |
| 17 | 33.75022569 |
| 18 | 37.45024374 |
| 19 | 41.44626324 |
| 20 | 45.76196430 |

**Table 16-2.** The Completed Sinking Fund Annuity Checklist

| Item | Years to Go | Estimate Cost | Annuity |
|---|---|---|---|
| New roof | 10 | $6000 | $ 414.18 |
| Paint exteriors | 4 | 1800 | 399.46 |
| Replace compressors | 8 | 2800 | 263.24 |
| Resurface parking | 10 | 1500 | 103.54 |
| Total annual sinking fund | | | $1180.42 |

approach will show a greater value than the **income value** once the prospective buyer has made adjustments to the data supplied by the seller.

Review each approach in detail.

## Income Approach to Property Evaluation

Prior to attempting any evaluation the investor or appraiser would require certain information to enable the evaluation to be as accurate as possible. Table 16-3, the preevaluation checklist, can be used for rental apartment buildings; similar checklists can be made up by the investor for other types of properties following the same pattern as that for apartments.

Given the data on Paula's eight-unit apartment complex, a prospective investor, Frank, would analyze the property as in Table 16-4.

**Frank's Income Evaluation Approach of Paula's Eight-Unit Apartments.**
Based on the information provided by Paula, and prior to any review or adjustment to Paula's figures, Frank's initial evaluation of this property would be $285,000. Frank determined this by dividing the NOI by the desired return of 12 percent ($34,200 ÷ 0.12—remember when you divide or multiply by a percentage the decimal must be moved two places to the left).

In essence, Frank has determined that $34,200 is 12 percent of $285,000. If Frank wants to earn a minimum of 12 percent on his investment, then the maximum he could pay (under the already stated income and expenses) would be $285,000. Note carefully that the 12 percent figure is what Frank wants and is not an amount *fixed in stone*. Another investor may be very happy with as low as a 9 percent return. At a 9 percent return the purchase price would be $380,000 ($34,200 ÷ 0.09 = $380,000). A slight change in the desired return rate has a major impact on the purchase price a buyer would be willing to pay.

At this point the debt service is not considered, even though the actual debt service may have a negative effect on the desired yield. The reason for this is that Frank is attempting to find a value for the property based solely on the income and operating expenses. Once that value has been found, additional study of the property and the terms of purchase will be pertinent.

**Table 16-3.** Preevaluation Checklist for Rental Apartments

Name of Apartments: _____

Address: _____

Owner/Broker: _____

Phone number of Owner/Broker: _____ / _____

Number of units: ____

Studios: ____   1 Bdrm: ____   2 Bdrm: ____   3 Bdrm: ____

Asking price: _____   **Evaluation:** _____

Mortgage: _____

Monthly debt service: _____

| Item on checklist | Standard to the market | As presented by owner | As adjusted |
|---|---|---|---|
| Average rent per apt. | | | |
| Price per unit | | | |
| RE tax per unit | | | |
| RE tax per % gross rent | | | |
| Oper. exp. per % gross rent | | | |
| Oper. exp. per unit | | | |
| Vacancy per % gross rent | | | |
| Amt. of repairs per unit (inc. sinking fund) | | | |
| Management expense | | | |
| Sinking fund per unit | | | |
| NOI per unit | | | |
| Total NOI | | | |
|   Less debt service | | | |
|   Cash flow | | | |
| Desired return or return available | | | |
| Evaluation based on NOI | | | |
|   Cash flow | | | |

**Review of Income and Expenses.** Any analysis of an income property should be reviewed in comparison to the local "standards" of operating expenses. Often the local tax assessor's office publishes these norms. It is important to follow the local standards of operating expenses because textbook rules of thumb are not accurate and can lead an investor into economic disaster. In addition, most sellers view their property optimistically and often show less expenses than really exist.

This standard may show, in the case of Paula's eight apartment units, that the operating expenses for a rental with a rent of $450 to $550 per one bed-

**Table 16-4.** Preevaluation Checklist for Rental Apartments

Name of Apartments: <u>Paula's 8 unit apartment complex</u>
Address: <u>1087 West Marine Drive, Chicago, Ill.</u>
Owner/Broker: <u>Paula / The Prudential of Chicago</u>
Phone number of Owner/Broker: _____ / <u>761-44552</u>
Number of units: <u>8</u>
Studios: <u>n/a</u>  1 Bdrm: <u>8</u>  2 Bdrm: <u>n/a</u>  3 Bdrm: <u>n/a</u>
Asking price: <u>$362,000</u>  **Evaluation:** _____
Mortgage: <u>(1st) $210,000 / with potential second from Paula</u>
Monthly debt service: <u>(1st) $1,583.34 per month (P&I)</u>

| Item on checklist | Standard to the market | As presented by owner | As adjusted |
|---|---|---|---|
| Average rent per apt. | $500/525 | $500 | $500 |
| Price per unit | $38,000 | $45,250 | |
| RE tax per unit | $760 | $750 | $750 |
| RE tax per % gross rent | 12.66% | 12.5% | 12.66% |
| Oper. exp. per % gross rent | 26 to 35% | 28.75% | 30% |
| Oper. exp. per unit | $1560 to $2205 | $1725 | $1,995 (after vacancy) |
| Vacancy per % gross rent | 5% | 0 | 5% |
| Amt. of repairs per unit (inc. sinking fund) | $265 | $100 | $265 |
| Management expense | 4% | 0 | 4% |
| Sinking fund per unit | $147.55 | | $147.55 |
| NOI per unit | | $4,275 | $3,842.45 |
| Total NOI | | 34,200 | 30,739.60 |
| Less debt service | | 19,000 | 19,000.00 |
| Cash flow | | 15,200 | 11,739.60 |
| Desired return or return available | 9% to 12% | 10% | 12% |
| Evaluation based on NOI | | $342,000 | $256,163 |
| Cash flow | | 362,000 | 307,830 |

room unit per month would be between 26 and 35 percent of the actual collected income. If the income actually collected was $48,000 this would mean that the expenses could run between $12,480 and $16,800 per year. In his review of Paula's figures, Frank feels Paula has understated the **repairs** situation by failing to take into account future nonreoccurring expenses either with a sinking fund or by showing actual capital expenses for major replacements or repairs. By including the sinking fund in the calculation, Frank decided that 30 percent for operating expenses would be sufficient.

*Adjusted Income and Expenses of Paula's Apartment Units*

| | | |
|---|---|---|
| Gross rents possible: | $48,000.00 | |
| Less vacancy factor (5%): | −2,400.00 | |
| Collectable rents: | $45,600.00 | |
| | Less operating expenses and sinking fund | |
| 30% of collectable rents: | $13,680.00 | $1,710 per unit |
| Sinking fund: | −1,180.40 | 147.55 per unit |
| Net operating income: | $30,739.60 | $3,842.45 per unit |
| Less debt service: | −19,000.00 | |
| Cash flow: | $11,739.60 | |

Based on the above cash flow, Frank determines that a cash investment of $97,830 would give him the desired 12 percent return.

If Frank invests $97,830.00 and assumes the existing debt, he gets a real $11,739.60 return that will equal 12 percent on his invested capital. This is found by dividing the cash flow of $11,739.60 by 0.12, which equals $97,830.00. Adding the principal amount of the mortgage to this equity, per Frank's calculations to earn his desired rate, would place an evaluation on the property of $307,830 (the mortgage principal owed of $210,000 plus the equity of $97,830 equals $307,830). In hopes of buying the property at this amount Frank may offer Paula less to give himself a safety factor in case the calculations are optimistic and to leave some room for negotiations with Paula.

If Frank decides to reduce his desired return to 10 percent, the equity picture would change dramatically and he would be able to pay more for the property. For example, at a 10 percent return, the cash flow of $11,739.60 would reflect an equity of $117,396 or an overall price of $327,396 ($210,000 + $117,396 = $327,396).

**Positive leverage** is present in this situation, as is evident from the increase of evaluation between the NOI and cash flow calculations. In this example, the annual mortgage debt payments are at a lower *constant rate* than the desired return. The constant rate is the combination of interest plus principal paid on the loan and is found by dividing the annual payment by the total amount of principal due at the start of that specific period. In the case of Paula's mortgage of $210,000 with a total annual payment of $19,000, the constant rate is 9.0476 percent ($19,000 ÷ $210,000 = 0.090476, which is then converted to a percentage by moving the decimal two places to the right: 9.0476 percent). The effect of the positive leverage increases the amount an investor could pay for the property and still earn the desired return over the NOI-based evaluation.

In this example Frank has examined all the pertinent details and has taken a conservative approach to the evaluation of the property. In view of this it would be reasonable to expect that he would also look to a more realistic return, which according to the current marketplace, could well be in the area of 9 to 10 percent.

Whatever Frank's final determination based on the income and expense approach, Frank would still want to follow up with the second evaluation process: the market value approach.

## Market Value Approach to Property Evaluation

The market value approach to property evaluation does not consider current income and expenses in the evaluation process. Instead, this approach is a comparative analysis of one property against all others that (a) have recently been sold and (b) are still on the market.

In many respects this approach to value becomes the *fine-tuning* of the income and expense approach when the property in question is being valued for its income production. However, when the property has value above its current income, as would be the case for vacant land, or when income-producing real estate of which the land value alone would exceed that of the current income produced, then the market approach may be the only realistic method of determining the relative value of the property.

The best way to determine the market value is to have a real estate broker friend review the **current listings** and **sold listings** from the local board of realtors or, when available, the **deed transfer** information from the local courthouse property records.

This kind of data source is very valuable to real estate investors because it enables the investor to view entire subdivisions at a glance and see every real estate transfer that has taken place.

By breaking down these transactions, real estate investors can find out the exact price other investors paid for similar properties.

The key to obtaining accurate information from a market approach is to look at data of **similar properties**. By this, the investor should not look at broad-based data. It is important to draw a conclusion from the specific market area only. This narrows the amount of data necessary and will produce a more accurate result. The question arises: How narrow an area determines the **market area**? The answer is found by asking several realtors how broad an area *they* review when making a **listing presentation** to arrive at a market value. The answer generally is a very narrow approach into three or four subdivisions or areas of town where similar property attributes are found. In some communities it is possible that a property is in a truly unique setting and that very few similar properties can be found. This type of property presents a major difficulty in obtaining a market value and thus is not for the novice investor.

The information checklist will give the investor the basic information to follow. The price per unit, average rent per unit, and NOI per unit are the three criteria that will help the investor narrow comparisons to similar properties.

In general, unless there has been a dramatic drop in property values, sold properties will indicate a lower per unit price than the unsold property information. The investor must look at all available information about the geographic area to determine if there is a trend that indicates that property values are going down or that a poor seller's market has reached its bottom and therefore property values are about to rise. The actual market approach may not disclose this fact until the turn has already happened. A far better guide to such trends is the fact that there is a sudden decrease of property on the market. This phenomenon occurs whenever there is a shift of the market in favor of the seller because casual sellers (sellers who say anything is for sale at a price) are the first to withdraw their property from the market when activity heats up.

Comparisons to market conditions should be made on the smallest increment of a property. Income per unit, price per unit, NOI per unit, and so on, enable the investor to compare accurately different sized apartment complexes, different square footage shopping centers, etc.

## The Five Key Steps in Accurate Property Evaluations

There are five key steps in accurate property evaluations:

1. Inspect property weekly.
2. Keep good inspection records.
3. Track property history.
4. Maintain good property and investment files.
5. Review records before and after inspections.

Review each in detail.

### Inspect Property Weekly

Personal inspection and then a review of those inspections are essential to building knowledge about what is going on in the market. Every investor should set up a series of files designed to aid in making future evaluations.

## Keep Good Inspection Records

The basic file would be called the **inspected property file**. Along with listing brochures and other sales material available on that property, the investor should have an inspection checklist (see the end of this chapter) with personal notes indicating the investor's opinions of the property at the time of inspection. The property should be filed by address or legal description, with a note made in an **inspection log** that would show the exact date the inspection was made (along with phone numbers of owners or agents for fast reference).

## Track Property History

A **property sold** file would allow the investor to know where the comfort zone is moving and at what price. This information can include or be cross-referenced to the inspection file, so that the investor begins to get a feel for values. When several properties have been inspected that later sell for different prices, the total picture of value and why a buyer will pay more for one property over another begins to take firm shape.

## Maintain Good Property and Investment Files

Three other files are very valuable to the real estate investor. These are **property listed**, **offers made**, and **property acquired**. The property listed file would contain a list of every property on the market in the comfort zone. Ultimately all of these properties should be inspected or reviewed (some may be vacant land or rental properties). When one of these properties is sold the data would simply be moved over to the property sold file.

An investor's personal offers to acquire another property should be kept regardless of what happens to the offer. I know many investors who discard their old and unsuccessful offers. This is a mistake, despite the number of files you fill up, because when working in a comfort zone, there may be a future opportunity to acquire that same property.

## Review Records Before and After Inspections

This might sound obvious but should be stressed. Constant reminders of what is going on is never a bad habit when it comes to real estate investing.

---

**PROPERTY INSPECTION CHECKLIST FOR HOMES**

Date of inspection: _____

Property address: _____

Legal address: _____

Description of property: _____

Owner: _____

Owner's address: _____

Owner's phone: _____

Reason for selling: _____

Broker: _____     Phone: _____

Property size: _____

Year building was constructed: _____

Building data:  Bedrooms _____ ;  Bathrooms _____ ;

Family room _____ ;  Den _____ ;  Basement _____ ;

Eat-in kitchen _____ ;  Living room size _____ ;

Dining room _____ ;  Dining area _____ ;  Pool _____

Other features: _____

_____

Notes: _____

_____

_____

_____

_____

---

## Study and Review

1. Make several copies of the property inspection checklist provided in this chapter.
2. Make appointments to inspect at least two homes on the market. *Tip:* On weekends realtors often hold open houses for such

inspections. Call about any "for sale" sign and ask when the realtor's office is holding open houses or if can you make a private appointment to see the property.

3. Fill in as much of the information as possible during the inspection. As soon as you leave the property continue to add personal notes that will enable you to remember this property. If the property is listed by a broker be sure to attach a copy of the information sheet the broker may have on that property.

# PART 4

# How to Buy and Sell Real Estate for a Profit

# 17

# Four Basic Buying Techniques and How to Use Them Effectively

## Chapter Goals

The primary goal of this chapter is to introduce four basic real estate investment techniques that can help the reader begin a real estate investment career without large sums of capital. Although these techniques are basic and simple to use and understand, they are often a part of major real estate transactions. Simplicity often works best.

## Key Terms

- The "G" syndrome
- The "greener grass" phenomenon

Review each in detail.

## The "G" Syndrome

There is a bit of **greed** in most people, and smart real estate investors know how to use this in negotiations to acquire or sell property. Through the subtle use of purchase terms and conditions or other techniques, the seller can get exactly what he or she wants, while at the same time the buyer gives exactly what he or she wants to pay. There is a phrase that most real estate investors are acquainted with: "I'll pay your price if you accept my terms." This summarizes exactly the way in which the "G" syndrome functions. After all, most real estate sellers want to get the *most* they can when they sell their property. The fact that there may be more important motivations than the large sum of money can often be overlooked in the heat of negotiations.

---

*The key is to look for a focal point of each acquisition.*

---

A seller fixed on selling for no less than $100,000 may have a hard time in a market in which the highest offer to date has been $85,000. However, a buyer who understands the real problem (a stubborn seller unwilling to accept the reality of the market) may offer to pay the seller $100,000 as follows: $50,000 down and five separate promissory notes, each of which pays off at $10,000, and each of which is due one year later than the other for a total of five years. This totals the $100,000 the seller requested, and the offer may be accepted. Of course, if these notes were discounted at 9 percent the present value would total around $85,000. In this situation the focal point is the $100,000.

Sometimes *time* is the focal point as time can make the difference and the buyer who definitely is going to buy can use this option very effectively as a prime tool when the "G" syndrome is present.

### The "Greener Grass" Phenomenon

When it comes to greener grass on the other side of the fence, people are no different than the horse that sticks its neck through the fence to eat what is on the other side. The problem is the property we are closest to is often more valuable than that "grass," which only seems greener.

In the use of secondary financing, it is often far easier to get a seller to hold a second mortgage on another property (see how green it looks) than on the property being sold. For the same reason it is almost always possible to get a seller to accept, in exchange, some small item or property as a part of a larger transaction. The reader will find several examples of the greener grass phenomenon in the balance of this book.

## Four Creative Investment Tools and How to Use Them

1. The option
2. Sweat equity

3. Lease/purchase

4. Secondary seller-held financing

Review each in detail.

## The Option

The option is a highly flexible technique that almost always gives the buyer an edge in the transaction, but when properly used, the option works on the seller's "G" syndrome and produces signed transactions that may ultimately work for both parties. Several examples of the use of options follow.

> *Example 1:* Frank has looked at Paula's eight apartment units (see Chap. 16). Frank is almost convinced that if he could convert the eight apartments into executive offices, he could increase the rent from $500 per month per apartment to over $700 per month. However, to do this conversion Frank must request and be granted a change in zoning from the city in which the property is located. Frank enters into a contract with Paula to buy the property only if Frank is successful in obtaining the rezoning. Paula will get her full price (enter the "G" syndrome), and in turn Frank is given a period of five months (the option) to attempt to get the zoning and to be satisfied with the conditions the city may impose on Frank. Anytime along the way, Frank can elect to proceed to close on the purchase regardless of the outcome of the zoning procedures. Frank puts up a $5000 deposit that would be applied toward the purchase price at closing or be refunded to Frank if the zoning matter is not acceptable to Frank. The deposit is to be held in an interest-earning account with interest credited to Frank.

In the above example the term *option* is never used. Even in the contract there would be no need to use the term, yet this is a classic use of the option. Frank has a five-month **option** to acquire the property. Frank can elect to buy without ever getting the zoning, and even if he gets the zoning, he can decide he doesn't like the conditions the city imposes and he can bow out of the deal. Frank is in the driver's seat in this transaction, and if he ultimately buys the property, the deposit of $5000 is applied against the purchase price. He has obtained five months of time at no appreciable cost.

> *Example 2:* Jack wants to buy Ann's golf course lot for the purpose of holding it for a future home site. She is asking $59,000 for the site, but Jack doesn't want to pay more than $49,000. Jack offers to buy the lot for $55,000 and agrees to give her a nonrefundable "option payment" of $10,000 if she will give him time to have the soil tested, to have plans drawn, and to have a building permit issued. He wants 24 months to do this and will close within 30 days after the building permit has been issued or at the end of 24 months, whichever is the longer. The option money will apply against the purchase price.

Obviously, if Jack does not close on the deal Ann keeps the $10,000 ("G" syndrome works again) and still has her lot. If he does close, she has had the money to spend now, and gets close to her price. Jack can, if he wants, actually start to make some improvements to the site providing he doesn't put any mortgages on the lot, and can plan some landscaping, etc. In this situation Jack knows he is going to buy the lot and is simply letting Ann hold onto the land a bit longer to let the value go up before he has to close. She pays for the 24 months of carrying cost to own this lot.

> *Example 3:* Often an option is part of another transaction. For example, Alex has purchased an apartment complex from Gary, and as a part of the deal Alex asks for a 12-month option to buy the adjoining property also owned by Gary. The price and terms for this second deal are included in the terms of the option, but Alex does not pay anything more for the "option" other than the acquisition of the first apartment complex. Gary, not knowing if Alex will take the first complex without the option, agrees.

**Why sellers accept options** is relative to *what* is offered and how that offer helps the seller move closer to his or her goals. Some sellers try to compare what is offered with what they want, which can often be a very unrealistic approach. The reason this can be unrealistic is there may *never be a buyer who will offer what the seller wants.* In the heat of negotiation and because the option allows the buyer to gain an advantage, the buyer may give up something to the seller such as a cash payment or an increased purchase price, or the buyer may spend time and money in an attempt to buy the property.

When it is a buyer's market, some properties are very difficult to sell. Vacant tracts may require rezoning before they are usable. Improved properties may need to be remodeled to attract a tenant. All these factors take *time* to resolve and time is on the side of the buyer. The seller may need to become aggressive and find a prospective builder or investor to take a free option on the land to work out the rezoning or to obtain permits for the remodeling to the point that the property is worth that builder's investment.

**Dangers in using options** occur because the buyer may not have good intentions. Buyers need to demonstrate good intentions and sellers need to examine them carefully. Sellers need to ask for references, and buyers need to be ready to give something of value as good faith. The stronger the good faith given to the seller, the less effort the seller needs to spend checking on past references of the buyer.

### Four Ideal Times to Use Options

1. *When the investor has no immediate use for the property.* The option can "buy" time. This time may be **investment maturity**, which is the time needed to let the value go up or to let other events the investor knows about occur that will ensure future profit or make the property usable.

2. *When the investor is not sure about the investment and wants to tie up the property.* For example, a rezoning may be necessary, soil tests may be required, or a building permit must be granted; otherwise the investor has no use for the property.

3. *As a negotiating tool when buying other property.* The investor asks for an option as part of a contract on some other property, either to give the seller something to negotiate out of the offer or to tie up the property in the event of a property value increase due to some future event (caused by the investor or others).

4. *As part of a lease that would give the investor time to get to know the property or time to hold on to the property at a reduced cost prior to buying it.*

### Sweat Equity

Sweat equity transactions enable a buyer to enter into a transaction to acquire a property that can be a "win-win" situation for both the buyer and the seller. This is a form of option in which the buyer gives the value of his or her **sweat** as equity to "buy" the option.

### Two Examples of Sweat Equity

*Example 1:* Frank goes to Paula and convinces her that if the eight apartment units were painted inside and out and the yard given a major upgrade with new plants, brick walkways, wood decks, and flower arrangements, the rents could be increased to a minimum of $600 per month. Frank says that if Paula will give him a 12-month option to buy the property, Frank will, on his own time and effort, do all these things.

Paula agrees to all that Frank has said and even adds extra remodeling items to the package that she will pay for if Frank installs them using his labor. These items include new kitchen countertops, sinks, door hardware, a partial fence, a gas grill for the back yard, new mailboxes, and some other minor repairs Paula knows need to be done. The price is set, and Frank starts the work.

Paula has little to lose except time, but as no one has been knocking her door down to buy the apartments, the chance to get a lot of the required work done appeals to her "G" syndrome. Moreover, an important part of the deal is that Frank will refinance the apartments with a second mortgage to help pay Paula off. The only way Frank can do this is for the property to have increased rents reflecting a higher value. The incentive is very strong for Frank to do good work because he is improving what he hopes will become his own property.

*Example 2:* Ted has found a beautiful home he would like to buy but he doesn't have a down payment of $5000 to close the deal. In doing his homework about his comfort zone, Ted has discovered that the owner of the home also has some commercial property. Ted offers to do considerable painting and other needed work to the commercial property as his down payment. The seller agrees to the deal on the condition that Ted complete the work before the closing on the home.

In each of these situations the outcome is that the prospective buyer ends up building equity to be used as a down payment on the desired property. While sweat equity is best when the work improves the value of the property being acquired, which occurred when Frank agreed to do the work at Paula's apartment complex, it is not essential, as in Ted's case, in which the work or sweat equity was done on another property in exchange for the down payment.

**Sweat Equity Pitfalls to Watch For.**   The prospective buyer in any kind of future closing should have some control over the property for any situation that may extend past the closing date. For example, Frank would want to have the right to approve any leases that Paula might execute that would lock in a tenant past the closing date when Frank would become the owner. This would ensure that Paula would not rent the apartments for less than the amount Frank feels would be warranted. As Frank wants to show a greater income potential to refinance the debt, leases that were less than the needed rent would be counterproductive. Without firm and written protection in the contract between Frank and Paula, Frank may discover that Paula would "fall in love" with his newly remodeled eight-unit apartment complex and start looking for ways to keep Frank from being able to close on the deal.

## Lease/Purchase

The long-term lease with an option to purchase is a good way to tie up a property for a long enough period during which major improvements can be made to the property that will greatly increase the value and ensure a profit for the tenant/buyer. The advantage to the tenant/buyer is that the amount of cash or equity needed to initiate this transaction is often much less than a straight purchase. Because the landlord/seller retains title to the property and all the benefits of ownership during the lease, there is often greater incentive for the landlord to enter into a lease with an option if an ultimate sale is what the landlord wants. If the immediate benefits are strong enough, the landlord may agree to the option to buy with the ideal that the prospective buyer may not actually *be in a position to buy when the option period ends.* This is the "G" syndrome appearing again.

The following are several examples of lease/purchase agreements.

1. Alice offers to lease one side of David's duplex apartment. At the moment David's parents live in the other side, but he expects that within a few years they will be moving out of state to live with David's sister. So

when Alice first agrees to do some needed repairs to the building as her *sweat equity* for the first and last two months security on the lease, David agrees. But Alice also asks for an option to buy the duplex within 90 days following the date David's parents vacate the property.

David does not want to be tied down quite that much, but does agree to give her the *first right of refusal.* This is spelled out in the agreement they sign to indicate that anytime David wants to sell the property and there is a valid offer (an offer in writing with deposit and no contingencies other than mortgage assumption), Alice has a period of 30 days to match the offer. Alice accepts this because she knows it is better than no option at all, and often the 30 day tie-up scares away prospective buyers.

2. Jim wants to build an office building to move to in several years. He is in no real hurry, as his current lease where his business is located is not up for six years. But he does want to tie up a good site at today's prices if he can.

Jim locates a vacant lot that would be ideal for his new location, and instead of buying it he offers a lease arrangement to the owner. In the lease Jim includes a purchase option that can be exercised anytime within the next six years for a price established in the agreement. Jim also includes a provision stating that half the rent paid will apply against the purchase.

The numbers of this deal look like this:

*a.* The property is on the market for $200,000.

*b.* $150,000 would be a very good buy for Jim.

*c.* Jim offers to pay a $10,000 per year lease and a purchase option for $180,000 anytime within six years. Half the rent will apply to the purchase price.

*d.* The property owner accepts the deal because he can use the $10,000 rent money now and will bet ("G" syndrome) that Jim will not exercise the option.

*e.* At the end of five years Jim buys the property. He gets credit for $25,000 already paid in rent, so he comes up with $155,000 for the purchase price. Jim has not had to pay taxes on the land for five years, nor did he have to pay interest on the unpaid purchase price during this time. The land is now worth over $250,000 so he is very happy.

## Secondary Seller-Held Financing

Any mortgage included in a real estate transaction that is not a first mortgage on the property being acquired is called **secondary financing**. The best secondary financing is when the seller holds paper for part of the deal, for example, an investor buys property and the seller holds a second mortgage as a part of the transaction. This second mortgage is called a **purchase money second mortgage**. The term *purchase money* is used whenever the seller is holding a mortgage that is secured by the property being sold. If, as part of the purchase price, the buyer gives the seller a mortgage from another property, then this is not a purchase money mortgage and is referred to simply as a second mortgage.

In many situations the best financing terms that can be obtained are through seller-held secondary financing. The fundamental reason for this is that the seller is often very motivated to sell the property in question, and holding some paper or taking back a mortgage on another property is often the way to achieve that goal.

The green grass phenomenon works well with several secondary financing techniques that involve debt secured by other property. In fact, when the circumstances are right, it is possible for an investor to acquire two different properties using secondary financing from each to acquire the other.

In this highly creative form of pyramiding, an investor will tie up two or more different properties using one of the option techniques. For example, Roberta enters into a sweat equity purchase agreement for property A, which is a small apartment building in desperate need of painting and other repairs. A period of 12 months is set for Roberta to accomplish the needed work, at the end of which she agrees to buy the property, giving the seller of property A $20,000 cash, paying off the existing first mortgage of $55,000, and giving the seller an additional $25,000 second mortgage on property B that she is about to start remodeling in a few weeks. This amounts to a $100,000 total purchase price. Roberta shows the sketches on how property B is going to look (greener grass), and explains that it will have a new first mortgage of $95,000 and should be worth an easy $150,000, so the $25,000 second mortgage would be secure. Roberta plans to fix up property A and has estimated that when she is finished with her work in about six months, the property should be worth $155,000. She plans to borrow $90,000, which will be used to pay off the existing first mortgage, and give the seller $20,000 cash, and the remaining $15,000 will replace her cash spent for repairs and to cover closing costs.

At the same time Roberta is negotiating with the owner of property B. She enters into a similar transaction with that owner, giving as part of the transaction a second mortgage on property A as part of the down payment. Because the greener grass phenomenon works also in this direction, each seller ends up with a second mortgage on another property as a part of the deal.

Roberta may run into a situation in which the seller balks at holding a second mortgage on any property. This objection is not unusual and can sometimes be overcome by offering a first mortgage on another property instead of a second mortgage. Roberta may have a free and clear property, a vacant lot, for example, that she can pledge as security for the required $25,000 part of the transaction. If the property has good value, the very fact that the mortgage offered is a first mortgage can be sufficient to persuade a seller to accept the offer.

**The Advantages of Using Secondary Financing.** Possible buyers look to seller-held financing because they can avoid the problems and cost of obtaining an institutional loan. Sellers are often far more motivated to make a deal whereas banks and other lenders are less motivated to part with their money unless they can be convinced they are in a very secure position. In today's difficult times, the rules and regulations that lenders impose on their borrowers can make the investment less attractive.

Most lenders shy away from commercial ventures or at least ask for (and generally get) terms of payback that can be very hard on investors if conditions falter and high vacancy factors result. Short-term loans, nonassumable loans, and adjustable interest rates can make long-term projections impossible or dangerous. Therefore most sellers of commercial or investment properties are open to some form of secondary financing.

**What to Look for When Using Seller-Held Financing.** When the seller is asked to hold a purchase money second (or first or third) mortgage, the contract should be very specific as to the exact terms of the mortgage, and should contain details as to the form of note and mortgage to be used, the property that will be security to the mortgage, and other data that the investor may feel is essential or that the seller insists on including.

**Important Questions about Seller-Held Mortgages**
- What is the interest rate?
- How is the interest rate charged?
- What is the method of determining amortization or principal payments?
- What are the dates of payments?
- What are the terms of payback?
- What is the date the final payment is due?
- What is the amount of final payment (assuming no prepayments)?
- What is the balloon payment date and amount (if any)?
- Is there a grace period for late payments?
- What is the penalty for late payments (if any)?
- What is the penalty for prepayment of principal (if any)?
- What is the form of note and mortgage?
- Who prepares the note and mortgage?
- Can the mortgagor (buyer) substitute other property as security on the note and mortgage? If so, how?
- Is there any subordination (present or future) of the mortgage to what would normally be a lesser position mortgage?

One way to ensure that there is no misunderstanding between the buyer and the seller is for the contract to purchase to include a copy of the note and mortgage that will be used, properly drawn to show all the terms and conditions of the loan.

## Study and Review

One of the keys to using the techniques mentioned in this chapter is to recognize which property can be improved in value. If there is a property and a way to improve it, then this is worthy of your offer. The important element is to tie up the property with *time* on your side.

*Assignment:* Look for a property that is run down, in a very good neighborhood. Make sure that the "sold" properties from the deed search indicate that the asking price is well below the market.

Now, offer less, subject to one or more of the following:

1. A rezoning at your expense to a higher income potential zoning.
2. Your sweat equity to improve the property and obtain higher-rent-paying tenants.
3. You have a period of eight months to accomplish a worklist that will improve the property for the present owner, if he or she will agree to your purchase terms.

Make sure you have the escape provision that *unless you obtain approvals or tenants of whom you approve* then the deal is null and void.

You risk nothing, but gain a world of experience.

# 18

# How to Use Exchanges to Buy and Sell Real Estate

## Chapter Goals

The goal of this chapter is to present to the reader one of the best tools the real estate investor has at his or her disposal. This tool is **exchanging**.

There are many different reasons why exchanging is important, and this chapter is designed to explore the fundamentals of exchanging ranging from the "tax-free" exchange as provided by Internal Revenue Service Sec. 1031 to the most basic of all exchanges, barter.

## Key Terms

- Boot
- Equity balance
- "Havers" and "takers"
- Legs
- Like-kind property
- Property basis

Review each of these in detail.

## Boot

The term **boot** refers to any cash or other items of the exchange that would not qualify as a part of the "tax-free" characteristics of the Internal Revenue Service Sec. 1031 exchange. There are many benefits of using an IRS Sec. 1031 tax-free exchange, but the reader should be aware that the vast majority of real estate exchanges is not made with tax savings in mind.

## Equity Balance

This procedure balances the equity between the two or more parties entering into an exchange. The equity balance of a simple two-party exchange is shown in Table 18-1.

To illustrate the use of this balance board, consider the following exchange.

Mike wants to exchange acquire Anna's four-unit apartment building. The apartments are on the market for $160,000 and there is an assumable first mortgage for $100,000.

Mike has a vacant lot in Naples, Florida, which he has priced at $42,000 and is free and clear of any debt. He wants to offer this lot to Anna and can balance the equity with a purchase money second mortgage of $18,000 to be held by Anna. Review the balance board in Table 18-2 (notice that unnecessary items have been removed from the board).

Assume that Anna rejects this exchange because she does not want to hold a second mortgage on her own property. She does agree, however,

**Table 18-1.** A Two-Party Exchange—Balance Board

| Two-party balance | First party | Second party |
|---|---|---|
| Owner value | | |
| Less existing mortgage | | |
| Equity | | |
| Balance mortgage | | |
| Equity to transfer | | |
|   Pays cash | | |
|   Gives paper | | |
|   Gives boot | | |
|   Gives other | | |
| Total to transfer | | |
|   Gets cash | | |
|   Gets paper | | |
|   Gets boot | | |
|   Gets other | | |
| Balance of equity | | |

**Table 18-2.** Mike and Anna's Equity Balance Board

| Two-party balance | Mike | Anna |
|---|---|---|
| Owner value | $ 42,000 | $160,000 |
| Less existing mortgage | 0 | −100,000 |
| Equity | 42,000 | 60,000 |
| Less balance mortgage (new second mortgage) | | −18,000 |
| Equity to transfer | $ 42,000 | $42,000 |

to accept $5500 cash at closing, take a car from Mike worth $6000, and balance off with a first mortgage of $6500 on another property Mike owns. The adjustments to the balance board are shown in Table 18-3.

In using the balance board, the reader must distinguish between the balance mortgage and the "gives" and "gets" paper. When the balance mortgage is used to balance the equity, this mortgage is secured by one of the properties in the exchange. In the two-party balance board the mortgage becomes a purchase money mortgage and is held by the party giving up that property. Paper, on the other hand, is never secured by one of the properties of the exchange and need not even be a mortgage. Because this is not a purchase money mortgage, it would not qualify for tax-deferred treatment under either the IRS Sec. 1031 or the installment sale provisions paper and therefore would be treated as a form of **boot**.

**Table 18-3.** Mike and Anna's Equity Balance Board, Adjusted

| Two-party balance | Mike | Anna |
|---|---|---|
| Owner value | $ 42,000 | $160,000 |
| Less existing mortgage | 0 | −100,000 |
| Equity | $ 42,000 | $ 60,000 |
| Less balance mortgage | | 0 |
| Equity to transfer | $ 42,000 (A) | $ 60,000 (B) |
| Pays cash | 5,500 | |
| Gives paper (1st mgt.) | 6,500 | |
| Gives boot | | |
| Gives other (car) | 6,000 | |
| Total to transfer | $ 60,000 | $ 60,000 |
| Gets cash | | (5,500) |
| Gets paper | | (6,500) |
| Gets boot | | |
| Gets other | (60,000) (B) | (6,000) (car) |
| | | (42,000) (A) |
| Balance of equity | 0 | 0 |

Remember that the balance should be zero at the bottom of the board and that everything the party gets becomes a deduction from the Total to transfer.

### "Havers" and "Takers"

These important terms are used by real estate exchangers when putting together a multiple exchange. "Havers" refer to property owners who *have* what another investor or broker is looking for. A "taker" is anyone who would *take* a property being offered. It is not unusual for several parties to work together to effect an exchange. Party A gives his property to party B, who gives her property to party C, who gives his property to party A. To start the process, exchangers are interested in learning who has what they need, regardless of what they want in exchange, and who will take what they have, regardless of what they have to offer in the exchange. Often the taker has other properties that may appeal to a haver, and a three-way deal is possible.

The reader should make an attempt to become associated with a real estate exchange club, either by joining (if possible) or by getting to know several active members in a local club.

### Legs

**Legs** is the term for the stages in multiple transactions. Sometimes a deal that starts out as a two-party exchange develops beyond the ability of the two parties to match up acceptable equity. When this occurs one side may accept the exchange provided another property can be found within a reasonable time. An example of this may have occurred in the exchange shown between Mike and Anna (see Table 18-3 balance board). Anna might have told Mike that everything was fine, except that instead of the $6000 car that Mike offered in the second go-round, she would accept a time-share week in an Orlando resort of the same value. Mike would now need to acquire one of these weeks (or make another proposal to Anna). If Mike attempts to find a haver that owns one or more of the needed time-share weeks, then Mike is attempting to bring a **leg** into his transaction with Anna. If Mike found a haver who would take the $6000 car for the time-share week, the three-way exchange has been *perfected,* and the deal can proceed to close.

### Like-Kind Property

This term describes the kind of property that qualifies for the IRS Sec. 1031 "tax-free" exchange. This exchange is also called the **like-kind** exchange.

The definition seems to confuse many people, and it is not unusual to find accountants and lawyers who will tell you that *like kind* means an office building in exchange for an office building or a farm for a farm. *This is not what like kind means. Like kind* is directed to the *category of property* and not the specific nature of the property. For the purpose of this discussion and its relative use to real estate, there are two categories of property: *the legal residence of the investor and investment property owned by the investor.* The provisions of IRS Sec. 1031 exclude the exchange of the legal residence for another legal residence (provisions for this kind of exchange are found in IRS Sec. 1034, which leaves investment property as the real estate that is covered under IRS Sec. 1031.

It is important to note, however, that the intent of ownership is what establishes investment property. This can be any kind of real estate as long as it is intended to be an investment. This can include a property that was once the legal residence of the owner. If a property is owned as an investment, is not "inventory" (as would be vacant lots a land developer is selling), is not the investor's personal residence (qualifies under Sec. 1034 and not Sec. 1031), and is not located in a foreign country, then the property can qualify for the full tax-free benefits of the IRS Sec. 1031 provisions.

## Property Basis

Every asset purchased, including real estate, has a book value or basis that can change over time during which the property is owned. **Basis** is an important figure as it establishes two possible tax consequences. The first is the income tax on the **capital gain** at the time of a sale or nonqualified tax-deferred transaction. The second is a sale or exchange with a **mortgage over basis**, which occurs when a mortgage is placed on a property and the amount of money borrowed exceeds the basis of the property. Because money borrowed is not taxed as income, any amount of a mortgage that is in excess of the property basis at the time of a transfer will be treated as though the seller received *cash* as a part of the transaction.

Basis is a function of the price paid for the real estate plus any additions to it during the time it is owned, less any depreciation taken or improvements removed. Not included in the calculation is any personal property, inventory, or other items that are leased and not owned unless there is a value to those items (lease purchase agreement).

Most property owners do not properly maintain their basis records, and it is recommended that every property owner use the following Property Basis Adjustment Checklist to do an annual update of the basis of their real estate. The best time to accomplish this is during preparation for the year-end IRS reporting.

---

### PROPERTY BASIS ADJUSTMENT CHECKLIST

1. Basis at beginning of year                    $_____

2. *Plus* improvements made

   _____

   _____

   _____

   _____                $_____
   
                   Subtotal                       $_____

3. Less depreciation taken                        $ –_____

4. Less improvements removed                      $ –_____

5. New basis at the end of the year               $_____

---

## The Four Reasons Why Real Estate Exchanges Work

1. Tax-free benefits.

2. A move closer to your goals.

3. A "face-saving" prospect.

4. An accommodation move.

Review each in detail.

### Tax-Free Benefits

In a tax-free exchange (IRS Sec. 1031), the IRS provisions permit parties to move their basis from the property owned to the property they will acquire, with several adjustments to be taken into account. Review the following example.

> Charlie has a large vacant tract of land that he purchased 20 years ear-lier for $50,000. No buildings are on the property, and it has a small mortgage of $15,000 that Charlie took out two years ago. The current value of the land is $700,000. Charlie wants to offer this tract to Don as a *down payment* on a hotel Don owns. The hotel is valued at $3,000,000 and has a first mortgage of $1,800,000. Charlie offers to balance the equity with a purchase money second mortgage that Don will hold (see Table 18-4).

The first step is to ascertain whether Charlie will have a tax savings in this exchange and if so, how much. To accomplish this Charlie would anticipate

**Table 18-4.** Charlie and Don's Equity Balance Board

| Two-party balance | Charlie | Don |
|---|---|---|
| Owner value | $700,000 | $3,000,000 |
| Less existing mortgage | −15,000 | −1,800,000 |
| Equity | $685,000 | $1,200,000 |
| Less balance mortgage (new second mortgage) | | −515,000 |
| Equity to transfer | $685,000 | $ 685,000 |

the tax on the capital gains he would pay in the event of a sale. To be realistic he assumes he will have a commission to pay. His tax calculations are shown below:

*Charlie's Tax Calculations*

| | |
|---|---|
| Sales price | $700,000 |
| Less commission and cost of sale | −80,000 |
| Subtotal | $620,000 |
| Less his basis (no mortgage over basis) | −50,000 |
| Capital gain | $570,000 |
| Calculate Charlie's tax at 28% of the capital gain $570,000 × 0.28 = tax | −$159,000 |
| Balance of sale to reinvest: $620,000 less the tax of $159,000 = | $461,000 |

By effecting an IRS Sec. 1031 exchange Charlie is able to save on tax, as calculated above, and will get full reinvestment potential from the increased value of his vacant land.

> *Any exchange that moves you closer to your goal is a good exchange.*

## A Move Closer to Your Goals

This is the second most important aspect of exchanges. When everything else fails, a transaction that involves an exchange may solve problems and help you move closer to your goals. This kind of strategy is best suited to investors who have gotten themselves into a problem. The problem may be complicated further due to a poor seller's market, the impossibility of refinancing, and balloon mortgages coming due. When things turn against the investor, the whole market can dry up. Money is not available, buyers are not interested in what you have to offer at any reasonable price, and investment confidence disappears. Until that situation turns around, sellers should become aggressive buyers if they want to sell or exchange their own real estate. It is a logical step because when it is a poor seller's market it is a very strong buyer's market.

---

*Solve someone else's problem and you may solve your own.*

---

This approach may require a reassessment of investment goals. The question to ask is "Do I need to change my direction in light of the current economic circumstances?" Take a hard look at what is going on around you. Are there opportunities that can open up new directions to follow? Are you hanging onto bad investments that are getting worse? The best time to do real estate exchanges is when the real estate market shifts in favor of the buyer. Why? Motivated sellers will often do anything to solve their problem—even take a property they would not buy.

Sometimes the best of plans goes sour. In real estate terms that usually means "debt heavy," and if there is greater debt service than income, something has to be done to change that situation. Sometimes the best approach is to get rid of the debt by selling or exchanging the property. Review the following example to see how Sylvia adjusted her plan to achieve her original goals.

Sylvia has a town home she has been trying to sell for nearly two years. She has dropped the price several times and is now asking $125,000. She has a first mortgage in the amount of $70,000. She plans on moving to Atlanta as soon as she can sell her property.

She has recently learned about real estate exchanges and suggests to the listing broker that they encourage a prospective buyer to offer something in partial exchange as part or all of the down payment. Sylvia is going to make it easy for someone to buy her town home by holding a purchase money second mortgage for the balance of the price.

Armed with this information her broker attends one of the local exchange clubs and presents the town home. The broker explains that Sylvia wants to move to Atlanta. There are several "minioffers" given to the broker by members of the club. These minioffers are informal proposals discussed among members that often result in a more formalized offer. One member suggests the broker call an exchange club in Atlanta. After a few calls an offer is formalized. Sylvia is offered $15,000 of prepaid rent in an apartment complex in Atlanta as a down payment on the town home. A friend of Sylvia in Atlanta inspects the complex, and based on what she is told Sylvia accepts the contract based on her holding an additional second mortgage for the balance of $40,000 payable over six years at 9 percent per annum interest. Sylvia conditions the contract on her own personal inspection of the apartments available in Atlanta and the terms and conditions of the lease. She wisely has the agreement fully executed prior to spending the time and money to make the quick trip to Atlanta.

## A "Face-Saving" Prospect

For many sellers the need to maintain "face" is very important. After all, no one likes the prospect of buying high and selling low. Worse, no one wants to be in a position where they have to sell their property at a loss. One way around this humiliating experience is to agree to accept something in exchange for all or part of the deal.

There are many different reasons why sellers will accept something in exchange for a part of a deal. The more motivated the sellers are, and the closer they can be moved toward their goals through the exchange, the better the chance of making the transaction work for all parties. Review the following exchange.

Bobby has a five-acre tract of land in a rural area of Maine. He has had it for over 15 years and always thought he would build a summer home there. He paid $2500 for the tract and knows of similar property that has sold recently for $30,000. This land is free and clear of any debt.

Phyllis has a summer home about 20 miles away, worth $80,000 with a first mortgage of $50,000. Phyllis needs to sell because the taxes and mortgage payments, which total $7000 per year, are more than she can handle. She has not even had time to use the home more than a couple of weeks in the past three years. Phyllis has the home on the market but has had no offers over $65,000.

An exchange between Bobby and Phyllis could be very attractive for both parties. Under the right circumstances Bobby would qualify for the IRS Sec. 1031 tax-free provisions and have no capital gains tax to pay, and taking a free and clear tract of land solves Phyllis's problem. Both parties can reach their ultimate goals in one exchange. Best of all, Phyllis "saves face" by getting her price.

## An Accommodation Move

The **accommodation move** is the most common of all real estate exchanges. In this situation one party will accept something in exchange solely because it is a part of the offer even though the property or item taken in exchange does not have any real or apparent benefit. Often the item taken in exchange amounts to less than 20 percent of the total value of the property given up and may be something other than real estate, as shown in the following example.

Donna has a marina that she has not been able to sell. Its current price is $7,500,000, lower than the original $10,000,000 price two years earlier. The existing mortgage totals $5,000,000 and Donna is very motivated.

Along comes Bill, who has been looking for a boat repair yard. He sees Donna's marina and instantly realizes that in addition to the existing marina business, Bill can add his boat repair facilities, taking over one of the two dry storage buildings that are not even being used by Donna. Instead of operating at 50 percent (as Donna is now) Bill will have 100 percent use for the facility. However, Bill doesn't want to come up with all the cash Donna is asking for.

Instead, Bill offers Donna $800,000 equity in a $1,000,000 waterfront site in Miami. This site was an old boat repair yard that Bill's family owned and operated for many years. Rising values of waterfront land in Miami has made the site triple in value as a future condominium site. To balance the equity Bill will give Donna a purchase money third mortgage secured by Donna's marina for $1,700,000.

Review the balance board in Table 18-5.

While the site in Miami does not have any obvious benefit to Donna, it becomes a way out of the marina she has been trying to sell. Bill would have a possible tax-free exchange.

The key to getting Donna to accept this exchange is by showing her that her problem has been solved.

Virtually every large transaction can absorb some small portion of exchange. If investors have dividable items in their inventories, those parcels can be "moved out" as investors become buyers of other property. The reader should remember that these items need not be real estate and can include services or personal property. The maximum use of any investor's assets is realized every time one acquisition can convert an idle asset into a new investment.

## Making the Offer to Exchange

Printed forms for real estate exchange offers may be available at local business supply stores or the local board of realtors offices. If no forms are available, investors can ask their lawyers or local title insurance company to draft one. The following is the author's standard two-party exchange agreement. This agreement is stored on a computer disk and can be filled in and modified for each of the author's offers. The following offer form should not be used as presented, but may help a lawyer draw one appropriate for the specific state in which the investor resides.

**Table 18-5.** Bill and Donna's Equity Balance Board

| Two-party balance | Bill | Donna |
|---|---|---|
| Owner value | $1,000,000 | $7,500,000 |
| Less existing mortgage | −200,000 | −5,000,000 |
| Equity | $ 800,000 | $2,500,000 |
| Balance mortgage | | −1,700,000 |
| Equity to transfer | $ 800,000 | $ 800,000 |

## TWO-PARTY EXCHANGE OFFER

Date of Offer: _____    Date Closed:_____

### AGREEMENT TO EXCHANGE

**First Party**: The undersigned, _____
and/or his assigns and hereinafter called First Party, does agree to
exchange to the Second Party the following property:

**Description of property given by the First Party:**

_____
_____
_____

**Said property is subject to the following debt, which will be assumed
by the Second Party:**

_____
_____

In addition to the above property, the First Party agrees to pay to the
Second Party, at the closing, the following:

_____

**Second Party**: The undersigned, _____
and/or his or her assigns and hereinafter called Second Party, does
agree to exchange to the First Party the following property:

**Description of property given by the Second Party:**

_____
_____
_____

**Said property is subject to the following debt, which will be assumed
by the First Party:**

_____
_____

In addition to the above property, the Second Party agrees to pay to
the First Party, at the closing, the following:

_____

### TERMS AND CONDITIONS OF THIS EXCHANGE

1. **IRS Section 1031 Exchange**—It is the intention of the First Party
that this agreement meet the requirements of the United States Internal
Revenue Section 1031 exchange and both parties agree to cooperate

*(Continued)*

with any documentation required at or prior to the closing to substantiate this intent.

2. **Standards of Real Estate Transactions**—Attached to this agreement are Standards that are common to real estate closings in this area. In that these standards refer to "buyer" and "seller," these terms shall apply in that each party shall be treated as a "buyer" of that property received and as a "seller" of that property given up. These terms do not alter the provisions shown in Paragraph 1 of these terms and conditions with respect to the fact that as an exchange, this agreement is not to be considered a buy and sell contract.

3. **Inspections of the Property to Be Received**—The First Party has a period of _____ calendar days following the acceptance of this agreement by the Second Party to review and inspect the property and the following documentation: Recent land survey showing all improvements and possible encroachments, all leases, tenant agreements, advance rents and rent rolls, copies of service agreements, employment contracts, mortgage notes and mortgages to which the property is security, copies of any liens or unpaid assessments against the property, and to make any other inspection provided for in the Standards attached, which may include but not be limited to structural, electrical, plumbing, roof, termite, and mechanical and to **approve said reviews and inspections without qualification, no later than noon of the deadline stated herein, unless extended by mutual agreement or as a function of Paragraph 4 below.** In the event the First Party fails to approve in writing said reviews and inspections for any reason, this agreement shall be considered null and void, and each party is hereinafter released from further obligation to the other. The Second Party may likewise inspect that property to be received in this exchange **prior** to execution of this agreement to exchange and the First Party agrees to cooperate fully with said inspection. According to the number of days provided for the inspection, the deadline for the notice in writing from the First Party is (date) _____.

4. **Delay of Inspections or Reviews**—If at no cause of the First Party, the inspections by that party cannot be made due to inability of the Second Party to provide access to the property or to deliver the required documents as mentioned above, then the time period called for in Paragraph 3 above for the First Party to make said inspections and reviews shall automatically be extended by the delay, providing that both parties make reasonable attempt to reschedule inspections. In the event some or all requested documentation cannot be made available to the First

Party, the Second Party shall give notice of this fact, and the First Party shall have an additional period equal to the calendar days indicated in Paragraph 3 from the date the Second Party has given notice that certain documents are not available as requested, to give notice to approval or disapproval of the subject property without the requested documentation.

5. **Closing**—The closing of title for this exchange shall take place at the offices of a closing agent to be selected by the First Party. Said offices to be within the same county as that property given up by the First Party or any other location mutually agreeable between the parties. Said location to be given to the Second Party at the same time written notice of approval of the inspections and reviews is made. The closing shall occur on or before the _____ day following delivery of the approval of the inspections and reviews.

6. **Brokers and Broker Commissions**—The First Party is a registered Real Estate Broker/Associate within the State of Florida and is doing business for his own account. As his own agent the First Party shall not owe to any other person, broker, principal, or agent a fee or commission as a result of this exchange except where evidenced by a signed agreement from the First Party to that effect. The Second Party agrees to pay any fee or commission to the following:

_____

as per separate agreement not made a part of this contract and the Second Party agrees to indemnify the First Party against any claim from others to collect a fee or commission from the First Party as a result of this exchange.

7. **Recording of This Agreement**—Both parties agree that this agreement shall not be recorded.

8. **Valid Contract**—Unless this agreement is fully executed by both parties on or before noon of _____, then the agreement is withdrawn and shall become null and void and all deposits, if any, shall be promptly returned to the First Party.

9. **Other Terms and Conditions**
   A. Standards as attached, consist of _____ pages and are initialed by the First Party in the lower right-hand corner.
   B. Exhibits attached to this agreement are:

   _____

   _____

   _____

*(Continued)*

*C.* Other terms and conditions are shown below:

_____

_____

_____

_____

_____

_____

AS TO FIRST PARTY                    **Date Signed**: _____
Witness hereto

_____        _____
                                                        FIRST PARTY

AS TO SECOND PARTY                   Date Signed: _____
Witness hereto

_____        _____
                                                        SECOND PARTY

To illustrate how the above standard form could be used and modified, review its use in the following exchange.

> John Parker offers on March 5, 1993, to exchange a four-unit apartment building for a small office building owned by Sid Goldman. The details of the exchange are shown in the following agreement. Each of the two parties has their respective property listed with real estate agents and are bound by commission agreements as shown in the offer.

The reader should study the Parker–Goldman exchange offer from Goldman's point of view. At every aspect of the terms and conditions of the exchange, readers should ask themselves the question: How could Goldman make the deal better without risking the transaction? In turn, the offer could also be reviewed from Parker's point of view with these two questions: Should Parker include something more that Goldman can "play with" or take out? Should Parker "tighten up" (include more conditions favorable to Parker) the offer even more than it is?

All real estate investors know that in most deals there is some give and take between the two parties. If the market is a very strong seller's market, then outright exchange may not be possible since buyers would be numerous. But sellers with a tax problem and the opportunity to qualify for an IRS Sec. 1031 exchange are well advised to revise a buyer's offer to turn the "sale" into a delayed exchange so they can reinvest the proceeds from the sale without having to pay any capital gains tax.

This procedure is possible but must be accomplished with all the IRS rules carefully followed. Any seller of an investment property (if it isn't the

## TWO-PARTY EXCHANGE OFFER

Date of Offer: <u>March 5, 1993</u>   Date Closed: _____

### AGREEMENT TO EXCHANGE

**First Party**: The undersigned, <u>John Parker</u> and/or his assigns and hereinafter called First Party, does agree to exchange to the Second Party the following property:

**Description of property given by the First Party**:

A 4-unit apartment complex located at 2134 West Hillmont Avenue, Savannah, Ga. also known as LOT 7 OF BLOCK D OF WEST HILLMONT SUBDIVISION UNIT A OF SAVANNAH, GEORGIA. Together with all furniture and fixtures as is shown on the attached inventory list.

**Said property is subject to the following debt, which will be assumed by the Second Party**:

A first mortgage held by First Union of Savannah, in the amount of $75,000. Payable over a remaining 15 years at 8 percent per annum.

In addition to the above property, the FIRST PARTY agrees to pay to the SECOND PARTY, at the closing, the following:

A cash payment of $20,000.

**Second Party**: The undersigned, <u>Sid Goldman</u> and/or his assigns and hereinafter called Second Party, does agree to exchange to the First Party the following property:

**Description of property given by the Second Party**:

An office building located at 91 South River Drive, Savannah, Georgia. Also known as LOT 20 OF BLOCK 8 OF SAVANNAH COMMERCIAL PARK, SAVANNAH, GEORGIA.

**Said property is subject to the following debt, which will be assumed by the First Party**:

A first mortgage held by North Carolina National Bank of Savannah, in the amount of $310,000 payable over a remaining 11 years at 9.5 percent interest per annum. And a purchase money second mortgage to be held by Sid Goldman in the amount of $55,000. Said mortgage to be payable interest only at 8 percent per annum, annual installments, with a balloon of remaining principal due at the end of the 10th anniversary of the closing

*(Continued)*

of this exchange. Said note and mortgage to be as is standard to Savannah real estate closings and a blank note and mortgage are attached. Said mortgage will provide for a 30 day grace period on all payments and no penalty for prepayments of principal. The sole security to be the office building at 91 South River Drive as described above.

## TERMS AND CONDITIONS OF THIS EXCHANGE

1. **IRS Section 1031 Exchange**—It is the intention of the First Party that this agreement meet the requirements of the United States Internal Revenue Section 1031 exchange and both parties agree to cooperate with any documentation required at or prior to the closing to substantiate this intent.

2. **Standards of Real Estate Transactions**—Attached to this agreement are Standards that are common to real estate closings in this area. In that these standards refer to "buyer" and "seller," these terms shall apply in that each party shall be treated as a "buyer" of that property received and as a "seller" of that property given up. These terms do not alter the provisions shown in Paragraph 1 of these terms and conditions with respect to the fact that as an exchange, this agreement is not to be considered a buy and sell contract.

3. **Inspections of the Property to Be Received**—The First Party has a period of 15 week days following the acceptance of this agreement by the Second Party to review and inspect the property and the following documentation: Recent land survey showing all improvements and possible encroachments, all leases, tenant agreements, advance rents and rent rolls, copies of service agreements, employment contracts, mortgage notes and mortgages to which the property is security, copies of any liens or unpaid assessments against the property, and to make any other inspection provided for in the Standards attached, which may include but not be limited to structural, electrical, plumbing, roof, termite, and mechanical and to **approve said reviews and inspections without qualification, no later than noon of the deadline stated herein, unless extended by mutual agreement or as a function of Paragraph 4 below.** In the event the First Party fails to approve in writing said reviews and inspections for any reason, this agreement shall be considered null and void and each party is hereinafter released from further obligation to the other. The Second Party may likewise inspect that property to be received in this exchange **prior** to execution of this agreement to exchange and the First Party agrees to cooperate fully with said inspection. According to the number of days provided for the inspection, the deadline for the notice

in writing from the First Party is (date)_____. (to be filled in when the last signing party executes this agreement)

4. **Delay of Inspections or Reviews**—If at no cause of the First Party, the inspections by that party cannot be made due to inability for the Second Party to provide access to the property or to deliver the required documents as mentioned above, then the time period called for in Paragraph 3 above for the First Party to make said inspections and reviews shall automatically be extended by the delay, providing that both parties make reasonable attempt to reschedule inspections. In the event some or all requested documentation cannot be made available to the First Party, the Second Party shall give notice of this fact, and the First Party shall have an additional period equal to the calendar days indicated in Paragraph 3 to give notice to approval or disapproval of the subject property without the requested documentation.

5. **Closing**—The closing of title for this exchange shall take place at the offices of THE SAVANNAH BRANCH OF THE NORTH CAROLINA NATIONAL BANK, at 125 South River Drive, Savannah, Georgia.

6. **Brokers and Broker Commissions**—Each party has listed their respective property with different real estate agents and each party shall be responsible to pay their own agent a fee as per their listing agreement. Attached to this agreement is a signed statement from each of the respective agents attesting to the sum due them as fee or commission. The First Party will deposit with the closing agent a sum equal to the fee due his agent, and at the closing a sum equal to that due the Second Party's agent will be deducted from the cash portion of what is due the Second Party.

7. **Recording of This Agreement**—Both parties agree that this agreement shall not be recorded.

8. **Valid Contract**—Unless this agreement is fully executed by both parties on or before noon of March 15, 1993, then the agreement is withdrawn and shall become null and void and all deposits, if any, shall be promptly returned to the First Party.

9. **Other Terms and Conditions**
   A. Standards as attached, consist of 3 pages and are initialed by the First Party in the lower right-hand corner.
   B. Exhibits attached to this agreement are:

   AN INVENTORY LIST

   TWO SIGNED COMMISSION AGREEMENTS

   BLANK COPY OF NOTE AND MORTGAGE TO BE USED

*(Continued)*

| AS TO FIRST PARTY<br>Witness hereto | Date Signed: <u>March 5, 1993</u> |
|---|---|
| _____ | _____<br>John Parker<br>FIRST PARTY |
| AS TO SECOND PARTY<br>Witness hereto | Date Signed: _____ |
| _____ | _____<br>Sid Goldman<br>SECOND PARTY |

house or apartment where you live, and it is not inventory that you buy and sell, it is *investment real estate*) may qualify. If there is a large capital gain and you are not sure if you will qualify, ask an accountant or tax lawyer *who is knowledgeable about the IRS Code 1031 provisions.*

## Barter and Other Trades

Several examples of exchanges in this chapter have illustrated items that were not real estate; some did not involve ownership of real estate. Barter is a major business practice around the world. Many real estate transactions are made solely because of some product or service that is included as part of the transaction. It should be obvious that most "sweat equity" transactions involve barter of labor or other services.

Barter will be used more and more once it becomes a part of the investor's "tool bag." As long as the barter is valued fairly and the investor taking the produce or service can use it or exchange it again, then making the larger deal can be worthwhile.

Investors looking to sell or exchange property in difficult times can use barter to make it easy for the "buyer" to acquire the property. One way to actually find such buyers is to discover "lost" products or services that the investor can use or has a specific use for and that can be used in exchange (all or part). The following is a short list of some of these "lost" items; each is a service, product, or event that is tied to time that once past has been lost forever.

Advertising time and space

Airline tickets

Hotel rooms

Professional services (when the professional is not using his or her facilities at 100 percent capability all the time)

Restaurant meals

Tickets to sporting events or theaters

Vacancy in apartment and office buildings, etc.

The list can become much longer once you begin to examine all the different kinds of services that rarely function at 100-percent levels.

One way to become better acquainted with barter and its benefits is to find one or more barter clubs (barter and exchange, trading companies, swap clubs, etc.) and find out how they work and what kind of membership requirements they have. Never join until you check several clubs and call several members to ask them how they like the organization. If the club has a frequent "club or auction night" attend before joining to get a feel for what is going on.

## Study and Review

Turn to the Real Estate Investor's VIP List and complete the following:

(129) Real estate exchange club

*Tip:* Call the local board of realtors and ask them for the local real estate exchange organization. If they do not know, then ask for the name of one or more of their members who specializes in exchanges. Those members would know if there is a local exchange club.

(130) Barter company

(131) Barter company

*Tip:* Use the local Yellow Pages or ask the same source for the real estate exchange club.

# 19

# Making Offers and How to Overcome Objections to Them

## Chapter Goals

This chapter dissects one of the most critical stages in the buying and selling process: **the offer**. This chapter's primary goal is to divide the offer process into three stages: (1) doing homework before the offer, (2) structuring the offer, and (3) negotiating the offer and counteroffers. Each of these stages has its own unique problems with which the investor must deal and overcome. This chapter is designed to help the investor negotiate to attain satisfactory results whenever possible.

## Key Terms

- Assumable mortgages
- Buyer's broker
- Earnest money deposit
- Letter of intent

Review each in detail.

## Assumable Mortgages

When a mortgage is created, the property owner goes to the lender and gives that lender a document (the mortgage) that shows the property being used to secure (collateralize) the loan. In addition to the mortgage is a **promissory note**, which is evidence of the sum of money lent, the terms of the payback, and the person responsible for paying back the money. If there is **no personal liability** on the loan, the property pledged is the only asset at risk in the event of a default. If there is personal liability, then the signing party as well as any cosigners is liable for the amount borrowed even if the asset pledged no longer has value to secure the loan. The person who borrows is the mortgagor and the lender is the mortgagee. When the lender agrees to allow another person to step into the shoes of the original mortgagor, the lender then allows this mortgage to be assumed. Because most institutional lenders structure their loans so that they can be packaged and sold to other investors (insurance companies, mortgage backed funds, and others), a standard set of rules and regulations has been developed to provide certain limitations on the flexibility of the mortgagee in relationship to the mortgagor. The most critical regulation for the borrower concerns the assumability of the mortgages. The lender inserts wording in the mortgage document which states that in the event of a sale, exchange, or long-term lease, the mortgagee is under no obligation to allow the mortgage to be assumed by the new owner and that if the lender does not agree to such assumption then the loan must be repaid. Many private loans do not have these provisions, and when an investor is able to negotiate a loan that will allow a loan to be assumed, the investor has *won* a major point that could mean the difference between a future sale or a property that cannot be sold. A pitfall in such mortgages is that it may appear to be assumable but in reality is not. This occurs when some lenders put a positive statement in their mortgage such as follows: "This mortgage may be assumed without penalty. (see procedure for Loan Assumption Application on page 16 of the master mortgage document)." On page 16 (if you are lucky enough to find page 16) the explanation of the loan assumption process gives the lender the right to reject an applicant for a wide range of criteria, such as poor or inadequate credit, bad past loan history, and poor net worth. In addition, the lender can collect a fee for loan application, change the terms of the loan, and require the borrower to do all that would be necessary to obtain a new loan: in short, pay off the old loan by getting a new one. This kind of mortgage is not an assumable mortgage.

## Buyer's Broker

Unless the broker or agent has entered into an agreement with the *buyer* to act for that buyer as a **buyer's broker**, both the real estate salespeople and the broker actually represent the *seller.* That means that they owe their loyalty to the seller and not the buyer. Most buyers get the impression that the agent represents them, but without specific understanding to the contrary this is not the case. This simple fact limits the service that the buyer can receive. As a buyer's broker the agent can act in such a way to use all his or her tools and information available to help the buyer obtain the lowest purchase price with the best terms. The buyer's broker must in turn notify any prospective seller or seller's agent that the agent is acting as a buyer's broker. The buyer's broker is paid by the buyer, and the fee is taken into account when the buyer makes his offer to buy.

### Earnest Money Deposit

All real estate salespeople are taught to make sure that the offer they draw up has an earnest money deposit, which generally is equal to or greater than the commission that would be due. There is no law that says every buyer should make an earnest money deposit nor should every seller expect one.

However, as a seller, you would want to make sure that if a long time will pass between signing the contract and closing, the prospective buyer should have something at risk to compensate you for taking your property off the market pending the closing.

Some sellers feel the buyer should have some money placed in deposit to show their "good intentions." While it is true that money does talk, money isn't the only thing that can be put up as a deposit. Creative investors and real estate exchangers know that the following options work.

1. *The Promissory Note:* This is an unsecured note or promise to pay in the event certain conditions or circumstances are met. A prospective buyer could use such a note as an earnest money deposit. A standard note could not be used, however, as the note must detail the exact terms and conditions to those terms for payment. Later in this chapter an example of such a promissory note is provided.

2. *Collateral:* This is a very simple way to secure any contract. The buyer gives an item of value to a third party to hold as an intention of the buyer's serious intent to follow through with the contract. The item of value can be anything: a ring, a watch, a title to a car, a third-party promissory note (one made payable to the buyer from another party), gemstones, and so on. The contract would simply give reference to the item as the deposit, and it would be treated as though it were *cash.*

3. *Promise to exchange other property or services:* This occurs in most exchange agreements. The first party agrees to give to the second party one item in exchange for the other. By execution of this kind of agreement each party has created an obligation to deliver what they have for something else. It is rare in an exchange agreement to have additional deposits of funds or

earnest money deposits because each party would then have a potential legal action on the other party for specific performance that would force the party to act according to the contract's terms and conditions.

## Letter of Intent

A **letter of intent** is a form of agreement that may not be legally binding depending on the wording of the letter but can be used to start negotiations. Because the letter of intent may not be a valid contract, it often has less impact than a formal agreement that details property at risk. However, since some formal contracts are cumbersome and expensive to draft, the more informal letter of intent is frequently used. Sometimes the very fact that the letter of intent is not legally binding allows the parties to come to terms on the basics without having to deal with all the legal language that the formal contract will contain. In complicated agreements that require a lot of "good faith acts" between the parties, the letter of intent can be a very good starting point. Another name for this kind of preliminary negotiation is the **agreement in principle**.

Great care needs to be taken to keep the letter of intent or the agreement in principle from becoming a legal contract. This is necessary because this initial probe rarely has all the details and fine-tuning that would be necessary in a formal purchase or exchange agreement. On the following page is an example of how the author would use a letter of intent and is not meant to be a pattern you should follow. As with any potential legal contracts, seek legal advice.

As the reader can see, the letter of intent is meant to be a simple, straightforward expression of the buyer's interest and intent to enter into an agreement with the seller.

If the situation is best served by a formal offer right from the very start, then the buyer should have no objection to making a formal offer provided there is no excessive legal cost to do so.

# The Three Stages to the Offer

1. Doing homework before the offer.
2. Structuring the offer.
3. Negotiating the offer and counteroffers.

## Doing Homework Before the Offer

When the buyer has a good idea of the seller's motivation, it is much easier to draft an initial offer that will be directed toward the most important

## AUTHOR'S LETTER OF INTENT

To:   Harvey Winninghold
From:   Jack Cummings
Hand Delivered by Alex Bresnan, Realtor

Dear Mr. Winninghold,

The purpose of this letter is to express my intent to enter into an agreement with you to acquire an office building you own that is located at the corner of Broadway and East 22 Street, in New York City, commonly known as Broadway Towers.

If the terms and conditions of this acquisition as will be outlined in this letter are acceptable to you, or if you care to make some refinements to these terms and they are acceptable to me, I will need a period of 10 working days from the date we have a meeting of the minds as to mutually acceptable terms for my legal staff to draft the formal agreement for your review. It is fully understood that neither this letter nor any other correspondence we have between each other in this letter of intent format shall constitute a legally binding agreement, but serve simply to bring us together to a meeting of the minds. Only the signing of a formal contract presented to both parties for review and approval would constitute a legal and binding agreement between us. The following are the terms that the formal contract would contain:

Price—$1,450,000.

Subject to buyer's assumption of an existing first mortgage in the amount of $850,000 at terms that must be renegotiated with the mortgagee to reflect the total remaining years following the closing of title, at an interest rate that can be adjustable but not to exceed 10 percent and will begin 2 percent above prime, said mortgage to self-amortize.

Seller to hold a $150,000 purchase money second mortgage, for a term of 15 years payable interest only for the first five years at 8 percent per annum, and then interest at 9 percent on unpaid balance plus annual reductions of $15,000 until amortized. No penalty for prepayment in all or part for either the first or second mortgages.

Seller to take in exchange a vacant tract of land in San Francisco, California, known as Cummings Tract A, of which there is a copy of the legal description attached. Said land is free and clear of debt and is valued at $250,000. The balance will be paid in cash at the closing of title.

The purchase agreement would provide that the buyer would have a period of 30 days to make and approve of inspections of the building, rental records, leases, contracts of employment, service records on mechanical and electrical apparatuses within or that serve the building, and other such inspections that may be required of the building as is normal in this kind of transaction. Naturally, your cooperation would be required to gain access within reasonable hours with reasonable notice.

The closing of title will occur no more than 60 days following confirmation that the mortgagee of the first mortgage has agreed to the required changes in the terms of that mortgage.

Unless there is a reply from you no later than noon of the last day of this month, I will presume that none of these terms is of interest and that you do not care to respond further.

However, I hope that we can move ahead on this matter as soon as possible. Please communicate directly with my broker who will be delivering this letter to you.

Sincerely,

Jack Cummings

problem the seller wants to solve. All buyers should embrace the concept that *if you can help solve the other party's problem, you can help solve your own.*

The problem with trying to learn about the other party is that no absolute source of information can be 100 percent reliable. In fact, some of what is learned from any source needs to be discounted, except when the facts, which can be easily checked out, are obvious, such as divorce, death, job transfer, serious illness, job promotion, and so on.

Both parties to an agreement may purposely mislead the brokers or other parties to the transaction. In addition, agents often create reasons or motivations for their clients that the other agents think "sound good" but have little or no connection to reality.

Often the best way to learn about the other party is to meet them in their home (their workplace might have to do if you cannot get access to their home). The key to the learning process is not to attempt to negotiate anything at that time but simply be interested in anything they have to say. Getting anyone to talk about themselves is relatively easy and only requires that you ask simple questions about the person, such as "How did you ever get started in real estate?" and then be a good listener. Observing the "home turf" surroundings can be an important unbiased source of 100 percent accurate information, too. Look around and ask questions that are not offensive and seem innocent in nature. Many people open up nicely to that approach. If things are going well in such a confrontation there is one really effective question that can be asked: What can you do to help me to acquire your property?

## Structuring the Offer

### Four Key Factors When Structuring the Offer

- Do not burden the investment with excess debt.

- When new debt is created, attempt to make it assumable.

- Future profit or loss can be a direct result of the terms and conditions of the acquisition.

- Remember that all parties to a transaction want to come away feeling that they have won something.

**How Much Do You Offer?**   All buyers should determine the maximum values that can be paid for the subject property. These maximum values are viewed for each of the following: price, down payment, monthly payment on debt, and minimum term of debt. Review the following case history.

> Rachel has decided that to buy a property she is looking at, a price of $200,000 cash would be the maximum she could pay for the property. If she would convert the transaction to a more conventional deal, however, the price could be changed. Rachel realizes that if she puts a maximum of $25,000 down and has a monthly debt service not to exceed $1,387.50, she can increase the maximum purchase price to $215,000.
>
> If Rachel was able to exchange, as part of the deal, a vacant lot she has in Arizona at a $30,000 value, her motivation may increase even more, allowing her to pay as much as $225,000 overall.

Once investors have a clear understanding of the highest values they can pay in certain circumstances, then the initial offer can be presented, reflecting a reduction from these maximum values to provide room to negotiate and to allow the buyer to see how good a "buy" can be obtained.

**How Little Should the Buyer Offer?**   There is no set rule. The practical approach is to find out how low an offer can be made with some rational justification. If the listing agent or the investor him- or herself has some solid facts to back up the "reason" or "rationale" for the offer, then obtaining a counteroffer is easier. It may be that the low offer made is far more realistic than the asking price, but the difference a sudden shock to the seller. Buyers must be very careful that the "sudden shock" is not interpreted as an insult.

*As a seller you should never be "insulted" when someone makes an offer— just think of all those people who don't even like the property enough to make an offer.*

The real estate agent can be helpful in providing information on other similar property in the same area that has sold recently. This will give statistics to substantiate the "low" offer. However, a good listing agent should have already made this kind of data available to the seller (in an attempt to adjust the price to the market value).

If the market is in favor of the seller, a buyer will ultimately pay the seller's price or very close to it. A highly motivated seller may have already reduced the price sufficiently to attract a buyer.

## Negotiating the Offer and the Counteroffer

For most real estate investors the offer and (later) counteroffer procedure is as follows:

The buyer and the buyer's broker meet with the listing agent to review the property. The buyer's broker has done his or her homework well, as the property shown was exactly what the buyer wanted. Thus the buyer and the buyer's broker draw up an offer.

The buyer's broker later phones the listing agent and says, "I am expecting an offer on the listing we just saw, can we get an appointment with the seller for later this afternoon? How about 4:30?"

Keep in mind that even if the buyer's broker is looking at the offer he or she will not tell the listing agent that the offer was already completed nor would he or she give any details as to what the "pending" offer would be.

The two agents would then meet with the seller, and depending on the situation the buyer's broker would do most of the talking. Care would be taken to point out all the factors of the offer that "seem" to solve the seller's problems (avoiding the use of the word *problem,* of course) and that help the seller attain his or her goals.

When there is reluctance from the seller to give positive signals, the agents may go back over the terms and conditions of the contract to see if the seller has understood the entire nature of the agreement. The buyer's broker would look for elements of acceptance, because even the smallest factor can be used to build on: the closing date, for example. Does the seller agree to close within 30 days as the buyer is asking? This can be a positive factor, as a fast closing may appeal to the seller. On the other hand, if the seller needs 90 days to move into another place, the buyer's broker would test the seller by making a statement such as "If the buyer would agree to a 90 to 100 day closing, do we have a deal?" If the seller said he or she would need at least 90 days but still will not give the "OK" for the agreement, then the buyer's broker will test other items of the proposal, such as the down payment, terms of a second mortgage, and so on, looking for agreement item by item.

Once modification of the offer has been discussed and physical changes have been made to the offer (if this is possible) in pen and ink, the agents would then ask the seller to sign the counteroffer with initials at each point of change.

The counteroffer is taken to the buyer where the process is much the same. The listing agent (if present) would look for points of agreement and places where the gaps of differences could be changed.

## Pitfalls in Offer and Counteroffer Negotiations

### The Three Most Common Problems

1. Insulted sellers

2. Sellers who will not counter

3. Objections to seller-held mortgages

When the process fails to produce conditions and terms that each party can agree to, the contract becomes a dead issue. Experienced investors know that once this happens it may be very hard to bring a deal back to life, so it is important for both the buyer and seller to work hard to keep the door open and the flow of negotiations moving back and forth.

There are a number of common problems which arise that can be anticipated and often dealt with easily some of the time. Review three problems below.

**Insulted Sellers.**    It may not matter why the seller is insulted. It could be the low price, the low down payment, the terms, the exchange, or the fact that the buyer insists on changing the color of the carpets (which the seller thinks are beautiful). When dealing with insulted sellers or in the event of an insulted buyer at the counteroffer stage, all investors must realize that if they are going to get insulted at any kind of offer that is made, regardless of its terms or conditions, how are investors going to feel about people who *don't even think enough of the property to make an offer?*

This is an attitude problem; it can also be some acting for the benefit of playing mind games with the presenting broker or agents. When this happens, it is up to the agents to step in and make the deal less stressful. The buyer's broker would smooth the way by letting the seller know how much the buyer likes the property and that the broker is confident that the buyer wants to work out a deal. Then, without mentioning the buyer working out a deal again, the buyer's broker would go back over the offer, this time showing the reasoning for the different elements. This would be the time for the broker's homework to pay off, showing the prices paid for similar properties in the area and other information that can be used to attempt to bring reason and logic into this often very emotional stage.

**Sellers Who Will Not Counter.** It should be obvious that if the seller will not counter at all, the buyer who is reviewing several other properties may simply move on to another to see if a more cooperative seller can be found. All investors look for two things in an investment: a property that will serve to move them closer to their goals, and a seller who will cooperate to help that happen. Keep this firmly in mind, as roles change and the buyer later may become a seller of the same property. Sellers should help buyers acquire the property that will help them achieve their goals. It is worth repeating that *to solve your problems and attain your goals, help others do the same.*

**Objections to Seller-Held Mortgages.** Objections are frequent when the buyer asks the seller to hold a second or third mortgage. To overcome these objections, the person presenting the offer should be aware of the tax advantages to an installment sale. It could be that the seller would profit by spreading some of the gain from a sale over a few years. This could be a "win-win" situation in which the seller actually gets more, in the long run, by accepting the paper. Other solutions could be to add security to the mortgage by pledging other collateral to secure the loan or by shifting the purchase money mortgage to another property altogether. The interest rate in the second mortgage would likely be higher than the interest the seller could earn at a savings bank, which is another plus for the seller. Sometimes it may be necessary to shorten the term of the mortgage if the seller sees an upcoming need for ready cash.

## Study and Review

Read the following offer which has been made on a standard form used by realtors in the south Florida area. Similar forms common in your area of the country will most likely vary from this one, but many of the same terms and concepts will be used.

Get a copy of a standard form used by the local realtors in your area and compare it to this one.

**DEPOSIT RECEIPT AND CONTRACT FOR SALE AND PURCHASE**
(IF FHA, VA OR CONDOMINIUM CONTRACT, RIDER REQUIRED.)

BUYER _____

of _____ (Tel: (___) _____ and

SELLER _____

of _____ (Tel: (___) _____

hereby agree that the Seller shall sell and the Buyer shall buy the following described property together with existing improvements thereon, UPON THE TERMS AND CONDITIONS HEREINAFTER SET FORTH.

1. LEGAL DESCRIPTION of real estate located in _____ County, Florida.  Tax Folio # _____

COMPLETE PROPERTY ADDRESS: _____
                               (Address)                (City)              (Zip)

PERSONAL PROPERTY INCLUDED: All fixed equipment, all window screens, treatments and hardware, all attached floor coverings and attached lighting fixtures as now installed on said property.  Also included are the checked major appliances: range _____, refrigerator _____, dishwasher _____, disposal _____, microwave oven _____, trash compactor _____, washer _____, dryer _____, owned pool equipment _____, ceiling fans _____.

ADDITIONAL PERSONAL PROPERTY INCLUDED: _____
_____

PERSONAL PROPERTY NOT INCLUDED: _____

LEASED EQUIPMENT: _____

Seller represents that the property can be used for the following purposes: _____

CONCURRENCY: No representation is made regarding the ability to change the current use of, or improve, the subject property under the Local Government Comprehensive Planning and Land Development Regulation Act (Chapter 163 et seq., Florida Statutes) or any comprehensive plan or other similar ordinance promulgated by local governmental authorities in accordance with the Act.

2. PURCHASE PRICE IS: (In U.S. funds). . . . . . . . . . . . . . . . . . . . . . . . . . . . . . . . . . . . . . . . $_____

METHOD OF PAYMENT:

(a) Deposit herewith . . . . . . . . . . . . . . . . . . . . . . . . . . . . . . . . . . . . . . . . . . . . . . . . . $_____
(b) Additional deposit due within _____ United States
     banking days after date of acceptance. Time is of the
     essence as to additional deposit. . . . . . . . . . . . . . . . . . . . . . . . . . . . . . . . . . . $_____
     ALL DEPOSITS TO BE HELD BY: _____
(c) Amount of new note and mortgage to be executed by the Buyer. . . . . . . . . . . . $_____
     to any lender other than the Seller.
     TYPE OF MORTGAGE:
     (CHECK ONE) Conventional ( ), FHA ( ), VA ( )    (If FHA or VA see Rider)
     (CHECK ONE) Fixed Rate ( ), Variable ( )
     Interest Rate _____%, with initial Monthly Payment of $_____.
     Other terms:_____
(d) Existing mortgage balance encumbering the property
     to be ASSUMED by the Buyer approximately . . . . . . . . . . . . . . . . . . . . . . . . . . $_____
     Name of the mortgagee _____
     Loan No. _____
     At an interest rate which may be changeable to the rate of
     interest at time of closing not to exceed the rate _____%
     per annum. (CHECK ONE) Fixed rate ( ) or Adjustable rate ( )
     with a maximum ceiling of _____%.
     Buyer is assuming a balloon mortgage.   YES _____    NO _____.
     Balloon due date _____.
     Other terms:_____
(e) Purchase money note and mortgage, first ( ) second ( ), to Seller. . . . . . . . . . . $_____
     bearing interest at the rate of _____% per annum and payable
     $_____ principal and interest per _____ based upon
     an amortization period of _____ years. If balloon mortgage, final
     maturity date (balloon payment) shall be _____ years from closing.
(f) OTHER CONSIDERATION: _____ . . . $_____
(g) Balance of funds due from Buyer in the form of U.S. currency, cashier's check or
     equivalent drawn on a Broward County financial institution, on closing and delivery of deed
     (or such greater or lesser amount a may be necessary to complete payment of purchase
     price after credits, adjustments and prorations).  Said funds may be held in escrow pursuant
     to provisions of Paragraph U of this Contract  (If FHA or VA see Rider). . . . . . . . . . $_____

     TOTAL PURCHASE PRICE . . . . . . . . . . . . . . . . . . . . . . . . . . . . . . . . . . . . . . . $_____

3. FHA, VA or Condominium Contracts: See required rider attached hereto and made a part hereof which shall control.

4. SPECIAL CLAUSES: See Page _____ or Addendum, if any.

5. ACCEPTANCE DATE: This offer shall be null and void unless accepted, in writing, and a signed copy received by _____ _____ on or before _____ day of _____, 19____ by _____ AM/PM.

6. CLOSING DATE: This Contract shall be closed and the deed and possession shall be delivered on or before the _____ day of _____, 19_____, unless extended by other provisions of this Contract or separate agreement.

## STANDARDS FOR REAL ESTATE TRANSACTIONS

A. EVIDENCE OF TITLE: The Seller shall, within _______ banking days (ten(10) banking days if this blank is not filled in), order for Buyer a complete abstract of title prepared by a reputable abstract firm purporting to be an accurate synopsis of the instruments affecting the title to real property recorded in the Public Records of that county to the date of this Contract or alternate title information acceptable to Buyer's closing agent, in his sole discretion, showing in Seller a marketable title in accordance with title standards adopted from time to time by the Florida Bar subject only to liens, encumbrances, exceptions or qualification set forth in this Contract, and those which shall be discharged by Seller at or before closing. The abstract shall be delivered at least fifteen (15) days prior to closing. Buyer shall have fifteen (15) days from the date of receiving said abstract of title to examine same. Seller shall use best efforts to obtain releases of canal reservations, if any. In the event there are oil, gas and/or mineral reservations, Seller shall use best efforts to obtain releases of same. Failure to release reservations or right of entry for oil, mineral and gas reservations shall constitute a title defect. If title is found to be defective, Buyer shall, within said period, notify the Seller in writing, specifying the defects. If the said defects render the title unmarketable, the Seller shall have ninety (90) days from receipt of such notice to cure the defects, and if after said period, Seller shall not have cured the defects, Buyer shall have the option of (1) accepting title as it then is, or (2) demanding a refund of all monies paid hereunder which shall forthwith be returned to the Buyer, and thereupon, the Buyer and Seller shall be released of all further obligations to each other under this Contract.

B. CONVEYANCE: Seller shall convey title to the subject property to Buyer by statutory warranty deed or fiduciary special warranty deed, if applicable, subject to: (1) zoning and/or restrictions and prohibitions imposed by governmental authority; (2) restrictions, easements and other matters appearing on the plat and/or common to the subdivision; (3) taxes for the year of closing; and (4) other matter specified in this Contract, if any.

C. EXISTING MORTGAGES: The Seller shall obtain and furnish a statement from the mortgagee setting forth the principal balance, method of payment, interest rate, and whether the mortgage is in good standing. If there is a charge for the change of ownership, including charges for an assumption fee, it shall be borne by the Buyer unless the total charges exceed one percent (1%) of the unpaid balance of the mortgage. In the event the total cost of the above-referred to items exceed one percent (1%) of the unpaid balance of the mortgage to be assumed, then either party shall have the option of paying any amount in excess so that the entire cost is paid, and this Contract shall remain in full force and effect. However, if neither party agrees to pay the additional amount, then, at the Buyer's or Seller's option, this Contract may be cancelled by delivery of written notice to the other party or his agent, the deposit shall be returned to the Buyer and all parties shall be released from all further obligations hereunder.

Buyer shall make application for assumption of the existing mortgage within ____ banking days (five (5) banking days if this blank is not filled in) from the date of this Contract. Buyer agrees to make a good faith, diligent effort to assume the existing mortgage and agrees to execute all documents required by the mortgagee for the assumption of said mortgage. In the event the mortgagee does not give written consent to permit the Buyer to assume the existing mortgage at the rate and terms of payment previously specified, within ____ banking days (twenty (20) banking days from the date of this Contract if this blank is not filled in) then, either party may terminate this Contract by delivery of written notice to the other party or his agent, the deposit shall be returned to the Buyer and all parties shall be released from all further obligations hereunder. This right of termination shall cease upon the Buyer obtaining written approval for assumption of the mortgage prior to the delivery of the notice of termination.

Any variance in the amount of a mortgage to be assumed and the amount stated in the Contract shall be added or deducted from the cash payment. In the event the mortgage balance is more that three percent (3%) less than the amount indicated in the Contract, Seller shall have the option of adjusting the purchase price to an amount where the differential is no more than the three percent (3%) allowed, and if he declines to do so, then either party may terminate this Contract by delivery of written notice to the other party or his agent, the deposit shall be returned to the Buyer and all parties shall be released from all further obligations hereunder. The notice must be given no less than five (5) days prior to the closing.

D. NEW MORTGAGES: Except as specifically hereinafter provided, any purchase money note and mortgage to Seller shall follow a form with terms generally accepted and used by institutional lenders doing business in the county where the property is located. A purchase money mortgage shall provide for an annual proof of payment of taxes and insurance against loss by fire with extended coverage in an amount not less than the full insurable value of the improvements. A first mortgage and note shall provide for acceleration, at the option of the holder, after thirty (30) days default, and a junior mortgage shall have a ten (10) day default clause. The note shall provide for a late charge of five percent (5%) of the payment due if payment is received by the mortgagee more than ten (10) days after the due date and mortgagee has not elected to accelerate. Junior mortgages shall require the owner of the property encumbered to keep all prior liens and encumbrances in good standing and shall forbid the owner from accepting modifications or future advances under any prior mortgages. Any prepayment shall apply against principal amounts last maturing. In the event Buyer executes a mortgage to one other than the Seller, all costs and charges incidental thereto shall be paid by the Buyer. If this Contract provides for Buyer to obtain a new mortgage, then Buyer's performance under this Contract shall be contingent upon Buyer's obtaining said mortgage financing upon the terms stated, or if none are stated, then upon the terms generally prevailing at such time in the county where the property is located. The Buyer agrees to apply within _____ banking days (five (5) banking days if this blank is not filled in) and to make a good faith, diligent effort to obtain the mortgage financing. In the event a commitment for said financing is not obtained within ______ banking days (thirty (30) banking days if this blank is not filled in) from the date of this Contract, then either party may terminate this Contract by delivery of written notice to the other party or his agent, the deposit shall be returned to the Buyer and all parties shall be released from all further obligations hereunder. This right of termination shall cease upon the Buyer obtaining a written commitment letter for mortgage financing at the rate and terms of payment previously specified herein prior to the delivery of the notice of termination.

E. ASSIGNMENT: This Contract is not assignable without the specific written consent of the Seller if new mortgage financing or an assumption of an existing mortgage is a contingency.

F. SURVEY: The Buyer, within the time allowed for delivery of evidence of title and examination thereof, may have the property surveyed at his expense. If the survey shows any encroachment on said property or shows the improvements located on the subject property in fact encroach on adjoining property, or violate any of the covenants herein, the same shall be treated as a title defect.

G. INSPECTIONS: The Buyer shall have the right to have the following inspections at Buyer's expense, subject to the provisions of paragraphs 1-5 below. Seller agrees to provide access and utilities for inspection upon reasonable notice. Seller's agent has the right to be present at inspection and should be given reasonable notice of the date and time of inspections. All inspections shall be completed and written reports submitted to Seller upon completions but not later than _______ days prior to the closing (ten (10) days if blank not filled in). However, the Buyer is entitled to a walk through inspection immediately prior to closing to check the items below to ensure no major functional defects have occurred subsequent to the professional inspections and compliance with subparagraphs below.

1. Termite: The Buyer shall have the right to have the property inspected by a licensed exterminating company to determine whether there is any active termite or wood-destroying organism present in any improvements on said property or any damage from prior termite or wood destroying organism to said improvements. If there is any such infestation or damage, the Seller shall pay all costs of treatment and repairing and/or replacing all portions of said improvements which are infested or have been damaged subject to paragraph 5 below.

2. General: The Buyer shall have the right to have roof, seawall, pool, electric, plumbing, appliance, machinery, structural and environmental inspections made by persons or companies qualified and licensed to perform such services. If such inspections reveal functional defects (as differentiated from aesthetic defects), Seller shall pay all costs of repairing said defects subject to paragraph 5 below.

3. Escrow for Repairs: If treatment, replacement or repair called for in subparagraphs 1 and 2 hereof are not completed prior to closing, sufficient funds shall be escrowed at time of closing to effect same.

4. Reinspection: In the event the Seller disagrees with Buyer's inspection reports, Seller shall have the right to have inspections made at his cost. In the event Buyer's and Seller's inspection reports do not agree, as submitted to all parties, the parties shall agree on a third inspector, whose report shall be binding upon the parties. The cost of the third inspector shall be borne equally between the Buyer and Seller.

5. Limitation and Option Clause: Seller shall be responsible for all costs of the above treatment, replacement or repairs up to $_______________ (or 2% of the purchase price if this blank is not filled in). In the event the total costs of items to be accomplished under subparagraphs 1, 2 and 3 exceed this amount, then either party shall have the option of paying any amount in excess and this Contract shall then remain in full force and effect. However, if neither party agrees to pay the additional amount above the dollar or applicable percentage of the purchase price, then, at the Seller's or Buyer's option, this Contract shall be cancelled by delivery of written notice to the other party or his agent, and the deposit shall be returned to Buyer.

H. ENVIRONMENTAL CONDITION: Seller is not aware of any prior or existing environmental condition, situation or incident on, at, or concerning the subject property or any adjacent property that may give rise as against Seller or the subject property to an action or to liability under any law, rule, ordinance or common law theory. This representation shall survive the closing.

I. RADON GAS: Radon is a naturally occurring radioactive gas that, when it has accumulated in a building in sufficient quantities, may present health risks to persons who are exposed to it over time. Levels of radon that exceed federal and state guidelines have been found in buildings in Florida. Additional information regarding radon and radon testing may be obtained from your county public health unit.

J. INSURANCE: The premium on any hazard or flood insurance policy in force covering improvements on the subject property, shall be prorated between the parties, or the policy may be cancelled as the Buyer may elect. If insurance is to be prorated, the Seller shall, on or before the closing date, furnish to the Buyer all insurance policies or copies thereof. The Buyer has the option of accepting or rejecting any continuation of service contract if accepted, the charge thereof shall be prorated providing the service contract is assignable to Buyer. Any transfer fee shall be borne by the Buyer.

K. LEASES: The Seller shall, ten (10) days prior to closing, furnish to Buyer copies of all written leases and estoppel letters from each tenant specifying the nature and duration of said tenant's occupancy, rental rate, advance rents or security deposits paid by tenant. In the event Seller is unable to obtain estoppel letters from tenants, the same information may be furnished by Seller to Buyer in the form of a seller's affidavit. Unless indicated under special clauses, at closing there shall be no lease or right of occupancy encumbering the property.

L. SELLER'S AFFIDAVIT: Seller shall furnish to Buyer at time of closing an affidavit attesting to the absence of any claims of lien or potential lienors known to Seller. If the property has been improved within ninety (90) days prior to closing, Seller shall deliver to Buyer an affidavit setting forth names and addresses of all contractors, subcontractors, suppliers and materialmen and stating that all bills for work on subject property have been paid, and Buyer may require releases of all such potential liens. Furthermore, the affidavit shall state that there are no matters pending against the affiant that could give rise to a lien that would attach to the property between the disbursing of the closing funds and the recording of the instrument of conveyance, and that Seller has not, and will not, execute any instrument that could adversely affect the title to the property.

M. PLACE OF CLOSING: Closing shall be held at the office of the Buyer's closing agent, if located within the county where the property is located, and if not, then at the office of Seller's agent, if located within the county where the property is located, and if not, then at such place as mutually agreed upon.

N. DOCUMENTS FOR CLOSING: Seller shall prepare and provide deed, purchase money mortgage, mortgage note, bill of sale, Seller's affidavits regarding liens, FIRPTA affidavit, survey or affidavit regarding coastal construction control line, F.S. 161.57, if applicable, and any corrective instruments that may be required in connection with perfecting the title. Buyer's closing agent shall prepare closing statement.

O. EXPENSES: Abstracting prior to closing, state documentary stamps which are required to be affixed to the instrument of conveyance and the cost of recording any corrective instruments, shall be paid by the Seller. Intangible personal property taxes and documentary stamps to be affixed to the purchase money mortgage, if any, or required on any mortgage modification, the cost of recording the deed and purchase money mortgage and documentary stamps and recording costs assessed in connection with assumption of any existing mortgage shall be paid by the Buyer.

P. PRORATION OF TAXES (REAL AND PERSONAL): Taxes shall be prorated on the current year's tax, if known. If the closing occurs at a date when the current year's taxes are not fixed, and the current year's assessment is available, taxes will be prorated based upon such assessment and the prior year's millage. If the current year's assessment is not available, then taxes will be prorated on the prior year's tax; provided, however, if there are completed improvements on the subject premises by January 1st of the year of closing, which improvements were not in existence on January 1st of the prior year, then the taxes shall be prorated to the date of closing based upon the prior year's millage and at an equitable assessment to be agreed upon between the parties, failing which, requests will be made to the county tax assessor for an informal assessment taking into consideration homestead exemption, if any. However, any tax proration based on an estimate may, at the request of either party to the transaction, be subsequently readjusted upon receipt of tax bill, and this agreement shall survive the closing. All such prorations whether based on actual tax or estimated tax will make appropriate allowance for the maximum allowable discount and for homestead or other exemptions if allowed for the current year.

Q. PRORATIONS AND ESCROW BALANCE: Taxes, insurance, assumed interest, utilities, rents, and other expenses and revenue of said property shall be prorated through the day prior to closing. In the event that Buyer assumes mortgage, Seller shall receive as credit at closing an amount equal to the escrow funds held by the mortgagee, which funds shall thereupon be transferred to the Buyer.

R. SPECIAL ASSESSMENT LIENS: Certified, confirmed and ratified special assessment liens through the day prior to closing (and not as of the date of this Contract) are to be paid by the Seller. Pending liens as of the date of closing shall be assumed by the Buyer.

S. RISK OF LOSS: If the improvements are damaged by fire or other casualty before delivery of the deed and can be restored to substantially the same condition as now existing within a period of sixty (60) days thereafter, Seller may restore the improvements and the closing date and date of delivery of possession herein before provided shall be extended accordingly. If Seller fails to do so, the Buyer shall have the option of (1) taking the property as is together with insurance proceeds, if any, or (2) cancelling the Contract and all deposits will be forthwith returned to the Buyer and the parties released of any further liability hereunder.

T. MAINTENANCE: Between the date of the Contract and the date of closing, the property, including lawn, shrubbery and pool, if any, shall be maintained by the Seller in the condition as it existed as of the date of the Contract, ordinary wear and tear excepted.

U. ESCROW OF PROCEEDS OF SALE AND CLOSING PROCEDURE: The deed shall be recorded and evidence of the title continued at Buyer's expense, to show title in Buyer, without any encumbrances or changes which would render Seller's title unmarketable, from the date of the last evidence and the cash proceeds of sale may be held in escrow by Seller's attorney or by such other escrow agent as may be mutually agreed upon for a period of not longer than ten (10) days. If Seller's title is rendered unmarketable, Buyer's closing agent shall, within said ten (10) day period, notify Seller or Seller's attorney in writing of the defect, and Seller shall have thirty (30) days from date of receipt of such notice to cure said defect and shall use best efforts to do so. In the event Seller fails to timely cure said defect, all monies paid hereunder by Buyer shall, upon written demand therefor, and within five (5) days thereafter, be returned to Buyer and, simultaneously with such repayment, Buyer shall vacate the premises and reconvey the property in question to the Seller by special warranty deed. In the event Buyer fails to make timely demand for refund, he shall take title as is, waiving all rights against Seller as to such intervening defect except such rights as may be available to Buyer by virtue of warranties contained in deed. Possession and occupancy will be delivered to Buyer at time of closing. The broker's professional service fee shall be disbursed simultaneously with disbursement of Seller's closing proceeds. At the option of the closing agent, the professional service fee may be disbursed; 1) directly from the deposit held by the escrow agent; or 2) through the closing agent. Payment shall be made in the form of U.S. currency, local cashier's check, local certified check, unless in the event a portion of the purchase price is to be derived from institutional financing or refinancing, the requirements of the lending institution as to place, time and procedures for closing and for disbursement of mortgage proceeds shall control, anything in this Contract to the contrary notwithstanding.

The foregoing notwithstanding, if title insurance is available, at standard rates insuring Buyer as to any title defects arising between the effective date of title binder and recording of Buyer's deed, proceeds of sales shall be disbursed to the Seller at closing.

V. ESCROW: The party receiving the deposit agrees by the acceptance thereof to hold same in escrow and to disburse it in accordance with the terms and conditions of this Contract. Provided, however, that in the event a dispute shall arise between any of the parties to this Contract as to the proper disbursement of the deposit, the party holding the deposit may, at his option: (1) take no action and hold all funds (and documents, if any) until agreement is reached between the disputing parties, or until a judgement has been entered by a court of competent jurisdiction and the appeal period has expired thereon, or if appealed then until the matter has been finally concluded, and then to act in accordance with such final judgement; or (2) institute an action for declaratory judgement, interpleader or otherwise joining all affected parties and thereafter complying with the ultimate judgement of the court with regard to the disbursement of the deposit and disposition of documents, if any. In the event of any suit between Buyer and Seller wherein the escrow agent is made a party by virtue of acting as such escrow agent hereunder, or in the event of any suit wherein escrow agent interpleads the subject matter of this escrow, the escrow agent shall be entitled to recover all attorney's fees and costs incurred, including costs and attorney's fees for appellate proceeding, if any, said fees and costs are to be charged and assessed as court costs against the losing party or parties, jointly and severally. The party receiving the deposit shall be entitled to the foregoing interpleader relief and award of attorney's fees and costs regardless of whether said party is also claiming a portion of the deposit monies as real estate commission and whether or not suit is first filed by one or both Buyer and Seller in a suit involving the escrow holder and whether or not any party, Buyer or Seller, has an independent action against the escrow holder and whether or not the escrow holder has instituted the interpleader action for his own protection.

W. ATTORNEY FEES AND COSTS: In connection with any arbitration or litigation arising out of this Contract, the prevailing party, whether Buyer, Seller or brokers, shall be entitled to recover all costs incurred including attorney's fees and legal assistant fees for services rendered in connection therewith, including appellate proceedings and postjudgement proceedings.

X. DEFAULT: In the event of default of either party, the rights of the non-defaulting party and the broker shall be as provided herein and such rights shall be deemed to be the sole and exclusive rights in such event; (a) If Buyer fails to perform any of the covenants of this Contract, all money paid or deposited pursuant to this Contract by the Buyer shall be retained by or for the account of the Seller as consideration for the execution of this Contract as agreed and liquidated damages and in full settlement of any claims for damages and specific performance by the Seller against the Buyer. (b) If Seller fails to perform any of the covenants of this Contract, all money paid or deposited pursuant to this Contract by the Buyer shall be returned to the Buyer upon demand, or the Buyer shall have the right of specific performance. In addition, Seller shall pay forthwith to broker the full professional service fee provided for in this Contract. Any controversy or claim between Buyer and Seller arising out of or relating to this Contract, or a breach thereof, may, at the election of the parties, be settled by mediation or by arbitration or by litigation. Any of the above proceedings shall be brought in the county where the Real Property is located and shall be conducted pursuant to Florida Statutes relating to mediation, arbitration or litigation.

Y. CONTRACT NOT RECORDABLE AND PERSONS BOUND: The benefits and obligations of the covenants herein shall inure to and bind the respective heirs, representatives, successors and assigns (when assignment permitted) of the parties hereto. Whenever used, the singular number shall include the plural, the plural the singular, and the use of any gender shall include all genders. Neither this contract nor any notice shall be recorded in any public records.

Z. SURVIVAL OF COVENANTS AND SPECIAL COVENANTS: Seller covenants and warrants that there is ingress and egress to subject property over public or private roads or easements, which covenants shall survive delivery of deed. No other provision, covenant or warranty of this Contract shall survive the delivery of the deed except as expressly provided herein.

FINAL AGREEMENT: This Contract represents the final agreement of the parties and no agreements or representations, unless incorporated into this Contract, shall be binding on any of the parties. Typewritten provisions shall supersede printed provisions and handwritten provisions shall supercede typewritten and/or printed provisions. Such handwritten or typewritten provisions as are appropriate may be inserted on this form or attached hereto as an addendum. The date of this Contract shall be the day upon which it becomes fully executed by all parties.

SPECIAL CLAUSES:

All parties are advised that the I.R.S. code requires the Buyer to withhold ten (10%) of the sales price for tax on sales by certain foreigners. The tax will be withheld unless affidavits of compliance with the I.R.S.code or an I.R.S. qualifying statement are provided to Buyer at closing.

Executed by Buyer

on _____, 19____ Time: _____

BUYER _____ (SEAL)

Social Security or Tax I.D. # _____

BUYER _____ (SEAL)

Social Security or Tax I.D. # _____

Deposit received on _____, 19____ to be held subject to this Contract; if check, subject to clearance.

By: _____ By: _____

Escrow Agent

ACCEPTANCE OF CONTRACT & PROFESSIONAL SERVICE FEE: The Seller hereby approves and accepts the offer contained herein and recognizes _____

Address: _____ Phone No. _____

AND _____

Address: _____ Phone No. _____

as Broker(s) in this transaction.

(CHECK and COMPLETE THE ONE APPLICABLE)

( ) IF A WRITTEN LISTING AGREEMENT IS CURRENTLY IN EFFECT:
Seller agrees to pay the Broker named above including cooperating sub-agents named, according to the terms of an existing, separate written agreement;
OR
( ) IF NO WRITTEN LISTING AGREEMENT IS CURRENTLY IN EFFECT:
Seller shall pay the Broker(s) named above, at the time of closing, from the disbursements of the proceeds of the sale, compensation in the amount of (COMPLETE ONLY ONE) _____% of gross purchase price OR $_____, for Broker(s) services in effecting the sale by finding the Buyer ready willing and able to purchase pursuant to the foregoing Contract.

If Buyer fails to perform and deposit(s) is retained, 50% thereof, but not exceeding the Broker's fee above provided, shall be paid Broker, as full consideration for Broker's services including costs expended by Broker, and the balance shall be paid to Seller.

Executed by Seller

on _____, 19____ Time: _____

SELLER _____ (SEAL)

Social Security or Tax I.D. # _____

SELLER _____ (SEAL)

Social Security or Tax I.D. # _____

BE ADVISED: When this agreement has been completely executed, it becomes a legally binding instrument. The form of this "Deposit Receipt and Contract for Sale and Purchase" has been approved by the Broward County Bar Association and the Fort Lauderdale Area Association of REALTORS®, Inc.

PAGE 4 OF 4

REVISED 12/90

# 20

# How to Obtain the Best Financing Possible

## Chapter Goals

This chapter introduces the reader to the seven key steps to obtain the best financing possible for each specific investment. The primary goal of this chapter is to increase the knowledge of how to use these techniques. Financing is an important factor in real estate investing.

## Key Terms

- Adjustable rate mortgage
- Amortization
- Balloon payment
- Blanket mortgage
- Wraparound mortgage

Review each in detail.

### Adjustable Rate Mortgage

This is a very common mortgage, offered by many lending institutions. Often referred to as an ARM, this mortgage allows the lender to have periodic adjustments of the interest rate. This rate can go up as well as down and is usually several interest points above a **standard rate**. This standard rate may be the interest earned on Treasury Bonds, an average prime rate from the major commercial banks, or any other rate the lender wants to use as a benchmark for their loans. The advantage of these loans is that they usually offer the lowest initial rate when compared to a "fixed rate" for long-term loans. The reason for this is that the lender is not locked into a low rate if market conditions cause interest rates to rise. These rates can be good for investors when the standard goes down or at least remains fairly stable. The provisions of any ARM can be used by any lender, even private loans between individuals. Most institutional loans have a cap or a maximum rate to which the ARM could adjust over the life of the loan.

## Amortization

The term **amortization** simply means to reduce periodically. In finance terms a mortgage amortization schedule will show periodic payments, usually divided between interest and principal with the outstanding principal resulting.

There are four basic types of payment schedules that can be used separately or in combination with each other. Each has an impact on the payment schedule and the principal owed.

### The Four Different Payment Schedules for Mortgages

1. Equal installments
2. Equal principal payments plus interest
3. Interest-only payments
4. Deficit payments

Review each in detail.

*Equal installments (of interest and principal combined)* are the most common form of amortization; for example, a $100,000 mortgage payable over 240 months (10 years) at 8 percent interest repaid with equal installments of $836.42 per month would have the following monthly amortization (first four months shown).

| Month | Payment | Interest | Principal | Principal remaining |
|-------|---------|----------|-----------|---------------------|
| 0 | | | | $100,000.00 |
| 1 | $836.42 | $666.67 | $169.75 | 99,830.25 |
| 2 | 836.42 | 665.53 | 170.89 | 99,659.36 |
| 3 | 836.42 | 664.39 | 172.03 | 99,487.33 |
| 4 | 836.42 | 663.24 | 173.18 | 99,314.15 |

The monthly payment remains the same for the entire 240 months. As small portions of the principal are paid against the principal owed, the interest, which is calculated each month on the remaining balance owed, grows slightly smaller each month. As the total payment does not change, the principal paid each month grows and the amortization or the reduction of the principal accelerates slowly. By the end of the 15th year there will be a principal still owed of $44,541.76 and the monthly payments will still be $836.42.

*Equal principal payments plus interest* might seem similar to the first method, but this type of amortization provides an equal principal payment that is found by dividing the number of payments into the principal owed. A $100,000 loan payable over 20 years would have a principal payment each month of $416.66 ($100,000 ÷ 240 months = $416.66). To this amount would be added interest on the principal owed at the start of each month. The schedule below shows several months of this type of schedule at 8 percent interest.

| Month | Payment | Interest | Principal | Principal remaining |
|-------|---------|----------|-----------|---------------------|
| 0 | | | | $100,000.00 |
| 1 | $1,083.32 | $666.66 | $416.66 | 99,583.34 |
| 2 | 1,080.48 | 663.82 | 416.66 | 99,166.68 |
| 3 | 1,077.76 | 661.10 | 416.66 | 98,750.02 |
| 4 | 1,074.99 | 658.33 | 416.66 | 98,333.36 |

The change in the wording in a contract can dramatically change the monthly payment. In the equal installment example, the monthly installment was $836.42 while in this mortgage the payment begins at $1,083.32 and declines. An investor who may need every penny of cash flow a property is producing may find that this mortgage will make the venture impossible. On the other hand, an investor who has other income coming in now and wants to channel that extra cash into debt reduction may be inclined to take the equal principal payment plus interest form of amortization. While this is an interesting form of mortgage, the better choice would be the equal installment example but with the provision that the borrower can make *prepayment in all or part anytime without penalty* to allow principal reduction along the way if extra cash is available.

*Interest-only payments* are technically not a form of amortization, as there is no principal paid off. However, it is included here because many mortgages incorporate this provision as a part of an amortization schedule. The terms of the mortgage may read as follows:

> . . . Principal owed of $100,000 shall be paid interest only at 8 percent per annum in 24 monthly installments and then beginning on the 25th month and continuing through to the 240th month change to equal installments of interest and principal combined.

| Month | Payment | Interest | Principal | Principal remaining |
|-------|---------|----------|-----------|---------------------|
| 0 | | | | $100,000.00 |
| 1 | $666.66 | $666.67 | 0 | 100,000.00 |
| 24 | 666.66 | 666.67 | 0 | 100,000.00 |
| | The payment schedule changes | | | |
| 25 | 875.00 | 666.67 | $208.33 | 99,791.67 |
| 26 | 875.00 | 665.27 | 209.73 | 99,581.94 |

The interest-only payment for the first 24 months keeps the payment at the break-even point to carry the debt. Then amortization begins on the 25th month, which gives that mortgage 18 years of more normal amortization. Some mortgages use a schedule that reduces the early payments to a point lower than the actual interest charged.

*Deficit payment* mortgages are examples of a mortgage in which the principal owed actually *grows* each month because the payment is less than interest-only payments. With this mortgage the unpaid interest is added to the principal owed. This type of mortgage may be used in combination with an adjustable rate, which means that as the interest charged on the mortgage changes so does the level of deficit. Review the wording of this mortgage and a portion of the payment schedule.

> ... Principal of $100,000 with an ARM, which will begin at 8 percent and adjust annually to 2 points above prime, the annual payment shall not exceed $7500, with any unpaid interest adding to the principal. All adjusted principal shall be due and payable in a balloon payment on the 8th installment. (Assume the ARM adjusts as follows: Years 1, 2, and 3 remain at 8 percent; years 4, 5, and 6 are 10 percent; and years 7 and 8 are at 7 percent.)

| Year | Payment | Interest | Deficit | Principal remaining |
|------|---------|----------|---------|---------------------|
| 0 | | | | $100,000.00 |
| 1 | $7,500.00 | $8,000.00 | $500.00 | 100,500.00 |
| 2 | 7,500.00 | 8,040.00 | 540.00 | 101,040.00 |
| 3 | 7,500.00 | 8,083.20 | 583.00 | 101,623.00 |
| 4 | 7,500.00 | 10,162.30 | 2,662.30 | 104,285.00 |
| 5 | 7,500.00 | 10,428.50 | 2,928.50 | 107,213.50 |
| 6 | 7,500.00 | 10,721.35 | 3,221.35 | 110,434.85 |
| 7 | 7,500.00 | 7,730.44 | 230.44 | 110,665.29 |
| 8 | $118,411.86 | 7,746.57 | 0 | 0 |

During the life of this mortgage, unless the interest rate went considerably under 7.5 percent, the principal will grow until the mortgage is finally paid off.

## Balloon Payment

This is a prescheduled payment that can be all or part of the principal owed plus interest due, often a partial payment made during a term of a mortgage or a sudden payoff of the mortgage that has been set up on a longer amortization schedule than the actual repayment of principal. For example, in a mortgage of equal installments of a 20-year mortgage at 8 percent interest, with the provisions of the mortgage calling for a *payment in full* at the end of the 15th year, this payment is called a **balloon payment**. This payment is the principal that the amortization schedule would indicate is due plus one month (or period if greater than one month) of interest at 8 percent. Balloon payments are used quite often but have the disadvantage of sneaking up on the investor who fails to keep track of the due date.

## Blanket Mortgage

A blanket mortgage occurs when one loan is secured by more than one property. Blanket mortgages are quite common in real estate developments in which many residential lots or tract homes may be used as the security. Most blanket mortgages allow the mortgagor to release the security as the loan is paid. This enables the developer to sell individual lots or homes and to separate them from the blanket mortgage. Any mortgage can be a blanket mortgage and some lenders often request additional collateral to secure the loan.

## Wraparound Mortgage

The **wraparound mortgage** is one of the best tools to consolidate a payment schedule for a buyer or to give the seller positive leverage when taking back purchase money mortgages. Actually, the wraparound mortgage was used extensively in the late 1960s and early 1970s until institutional lenders started the practice of requiring the existing loans to be renegotiated or paid off in the event of a sale. The lenders realized that the sellers, taking back a purchase money second wraparound mortgage, were leaving the original lower interest rate first mortgage in place and leveraging their own return on the purchase money second mortgage at the same time. While this practice made for very good real estate investing and was good for both buyers and sellers, the lenders argued that they were being hurt because they were forced to stay with the deal at the low rate. There is no real logic in that argument, because if the seller could not or would not sell, then the lender was "forced" to do exactly what they contracted for when they made the loan.

Wraparound mortgages have their place in the investor's tool box because they can be and still are useful when the underlying loans do not require loan renegotiation or repayment.

When a seller holds a wraparound mortgage, the buyer makes *one* payment to the seller to cover *all the underlying debt,* including any seller-held purchase money mortgages. In a situation in which there are several mortgages in place plus a third mortgage position the seller is to hold, there is increased risk that the buyer may not be able to meet a heavy debt payment. The seller is not as secure as he or she would want to be because the buyer could let the mortgages go into default and actually get many months behind payments before the seller would ever know about it. Even though the underlying mortgagees "say" they will notify the holder of any inferior debt, because of the magnitude of business that the larger lenders do each day, with main offices handling debt collection often a thousand miles away, no investor can count on being notified of a late payment. The wraparound mortgage eliminates this problem and at the same time can give the buyer a steady debt service.

The seller and buyer agree to an independent collection agent or management firm that collects the single payment and then makes the corresponding payments to the previous and still existing debt. The seller gets the remainder, and when existing debt is paid off sooner than the terms of the wraparound mortgage, the seller receives more. Because the wraparound mortgage often has an interest rate slightly higher than either of the underlying mortgages (but not a requirement), the seller leverages over that sum. For example, if the wraparound mortgage was for $250,000 at 8.5 percent and the total existing debt was $200,000 at 7.5 percent, then the seller gets 8.5 percent on the seller's equity of the wraparound of $50,000, as well as *an additional* 1 percent on the existing $200,000. This can be very attractive because 1 percent of the additional $200,000 is the same as an additional 4 percent on the equity of $50,000. This would approximate a net return of 12.5 percent (the 8.5 percent plus the extra 4 percent); because there are other factors taken into account (the most important is the time at which the seller gets paid off), the actual yield is not so easily calculated. A moderately priced hand-held financial calculator can perform the exact calculations if the investor finds it critical to know those exact details.

## The Seven Key Steps to Getting the Best Financing Possible

1. Build contacts with lenders.

2. Know what the lenders like to loan on.

3. Demonstrate knowledge of the property.

4. Have a sound plan to increase the value.

5. Document placement of equity.

6. Prepare a property presentation.

7. Don't take "no" too quickly.

Review each in detail.

## Build Contacts with Lenders

Every real estate investor should develop good rapport with several lenders in the community. This is easy to do and requires only the time to make personal visits to the lenders or their representatives' offices. The best lenders to start with would be the local commercial banks and local branches of savings and loans or thrift institutions in the area.

There are several key factors that will maximize the future benefits that can be obtained from these contacts.

### The Six Key Steps to Follow When Contacting Lenders

- Start at the top of the organization. If the president is not the person with which ultimately to do business, let the president introduce you to that person.

- Keep the first meeting simple. The investor wants to build rapport, not get turned down for a loan.

- Present the best image possible. This means dress well, look prosperous, respect the contact's time, and do not be intimidated.

- Meet the real boss of the office—the boss' secretary.

- Follow up with all the important people you have met. A phone call may suffice to begin with, but don't let a lot of time go by without keeping in touch with follow-up correspondence.

- Once the contact has been made, proceed to the next step.

## Know What the Lenders
## Like to Loan on

Some lenders shy away from certain kinds of properties, while others specialize in exactly what others will not touch. The big lenders, which could be insurance companies or real estate investment trusts, usually reached through **mortgage brokers**, can vary greatly in the kinds of loans they will make and the terms they will charge. Once rapport with the lender or the lender's representative has begun, the investor would want to discover the kind of property most apt to attract the lender and to get the best terms for payback.

## Demonstrate Knowledge
## of the Property

When the loan is applied for, the investor should be very careful to have done his or her homework properly on the area in which the real estate is located and the specific property in question. A thick file containing a mountain of information that has been put together about the property will set the investor apart from the casual real estate "buyer" who doesn't really know what he or she is doing. The lender will want to be "sold" on the property and the borrower.

## Have a Sound Plan
## to Increase the Value

Asking for a loan is not just a question of taking out money to buy a property, but showing the lender what is planned to increase the value of that property above the initial purchase price. This concept will vary depending on the type of property in question, but every property can be improved. In income property, the improvements do not need to be great. A small increase here and there can make a major change in the value.

## Document Placement of Equity

Lenders look to the **loan-to-value ratio** as an important factor in negotiating loan terms. When the borrower can decrease the percentage of the loan in relation to the value, the lender often responds with "softer" terms. These terms can include a longer payback period, lower initial *points charged to the borrower,* and a lower interest rate.

Many borrowers overlook an important aspect of equity and inadvertently shortchange themselves in the loan-to-value ratio calculation. A substantial part of the evaluation of a property should include the borrower's **sweat equity**. Review, for example, the following situation.

Alexis plans to buy a four-unit apartment building for a price of $140,000. She has $50,000 to put down but wants to borrow an additional $100,000 to balance the purchase price and to give her another $10,000 for repairs and some remodeling she wants to do to the building. Alexis intends to convert a garage on the property into two additional units.

The additional income from the two added units will increase the value of the property, and as Alexis intends to do some of the work herself and to oversee the rest of the work, she would be entitled to show the *new value* of the property based on the additional work to be done. However, in addition to the $10,000 of actual materials and outside labor, Alexis is investing her time and effort into the property. This is a *real* value and should be included in the loan-to-value ratio.

If the lender simply looked at the purchase price of $140,000 a $100,000 loan would represent 71 percent of the value ($100,000 ÷ $140,000). However, if the real value of the property at the time the work is completed is $160,000 (the repairs, material, etc., including Alexis's time and effort), then the lender is looking at a 62 percent loan-to-value ratio ($100,000 ÷ $160,000). With this substantial reduction in the loan-to-value ratio, Alexis should have some bargaining power with this lender.

## Prepare a Property Presentation

The property presentation should answer all the lender's questions about the property and the borrower as well as show the *new value* of the property following the intended plan the borrower has for that property. Most lenders have a pattern for a property presentation, or **loan request**, that they would like borrowers to follow. However, the borrower should have additional information that can be added to the lender's format. This information should help the borrower express to the lender why the specific property has been selected by the investor and why the value is going up. In so doing, the added information shown will support the borrower's investment plan and demonstrate two of the important factors mentioned earlier—the borrower's knowledge of the property and the borrower's added equity. Adding some "sales approach" techniques to the presentation can help you get an approval. A nice color aerial photograph that shows the property could help. An artist's rendering of a new sign or new plans for landscaping could be another touch that keeps this presentation away from the rejection file.

## Don't Take "No" Too Quickly

When lenders reject a loan request they may be doing so because they do not have enough information about the property or the lender, or it may be that it is a property they would shy away from in any event. It is important for the borrower to find out exactly why the loan request was turned down. This is where the rapport developed with the lender's representative can pay off. Lenders often reconsider and grant loans that were rejected in the first go-round.

Knowing why a request is rejected may be a learning process that can be of benefit when another loan request is put together for presentation to another lender.

## Study and Review

1. Turn to The Real Estate Investor's VIP List and complete the following:

(75)  Mortgage banker and broker

(76)  Mortgage banker and broker

*Tip:* Check with one of the realtors on your list to find out the names of several mortgage bankers.

2. Turn to the mortgage calculation tables in the Appendix and review the section titled How to Use the Tables.

3. Make an appointment with a lender from one of the savings and loans institutions from your VIP list. Your sole goal is to *get to know several of the local lenders.* Because you are not asking for a loan, the loan officer will need to "sell" his institution to you.

*Tip:* Start with the lender that is farthest away from where you would invest, but still in the general area. Get some practice with the least likely lender that you would use in the future.

# The Real Estate Investor's VIP List

## Government

### City

(1) City hall

Phone number: _____

Address: _____

Business hours: _____

(2) City manager

Name: _____

Secretary's name: _____

Phone number: _____

Address: _____

(3) Mayor

Name: _____

Secretary's name: _____

Phone number: _____

Address: _____

(4) City council member

Name: _____

Secretary's name: _____

Phone number: _____

Address: _____

(5) City council member

Name: _____

Secretary's name: _____

Phone number: _____

Address: _____

(6) City council member

Name: _____

Secretary's name: _____

Phone number: _____

Address: _____

(7) City council member

Name: _____

Secretary's name: _____

Phone number: _____

Address: _____

(8) City council member

Name: _____

Secretary's name: _____

Phone number: _____

Address: _____

(9) City council member

Name: _____

Secretary's name: _____

Phone number: _____

Address: _____

(10) City council member

Name: _____

Secretary's name: _____

Phone number: _____

Address: _____

(11) Head of the city building department

Name: _____

Secretary's name: _____

Phone number: _____

Address: _____

(12) Head of the city zoning department

Name: _____

Secretary's name: _____

Phone number: _____

Address: _____

(13) Head of the city planning department

Name: _____

Secretary's name: _____

Phone number: _____

Address: _____

(14) City clerk

Name: _____

Secretary's name: _____

Phone number: _____

Address: _____

(15) Head of the city Department of Transportation

Name: _____

Secretary's name: _____

Phone number: _____

Address: _____

(16) City fire chief

Name: _____

Secretary's name: _____

Phone number: _____

Address: _____

(17) City police chief

Name: _____

Secretary's name: _____

Phone number: _____

Address: _____

(18) Head of the city water department

Name: _____

Secretary's name: _____

Phone number: _____

Address: _____

(19) Head of the city sewage department

Name: _____

Secretary's name: _____

Phone number: _____

Address: _____

(20)  Head of other city department

Name: _____

Department: _____

Secretary's name: _____

Phone number: _____

Address: _____

(21)  Head of other city department

Name: _____

Department: _____

Secretary's name: _____

Phone number: _____

Address: _____

(22)  Head of other city department

Name: _____

Department: _____

Secretary's name: _____

Phone number: _____

Address: _____

(23)  Head of other city department

Name: _____

Department: _____

Secretary's name: _____

Phone number: _____

Address: _____

(24)  City council meetings

Usual day of the month held: _____

Where held: _____

Address for agenda: _____

Phone number of contact: _____

Name of contact: _____

Notes: _____

(25)  Planning and zoning meetings

Usual day of the month held: _____

Where held: _____

Address for agenda: _____

Phone number of contact: _____

Name of contact: _____

Notes: _____

(26)  Other meetings

Type of meetings: _____

Usual day of the month held: _____

Where held: _____

Address for agenda: _____

Phone number of contact: _____

Name of contact: _____

Notes: _____

(27)  Other meetings

Type of meetings: _____

Usual day of the month held: _____

Where held: _____

Address for agenda: _____

Phone number of contact: _____

Name of contact: _____

Notes: _____

(28)  Other meetings

Type of meetings: _____

Usual day of the month held: _____

Where held: _____

Address for agenda: _____

Phone number of contact: _____

Name of contact: _____

Notes: _____

## County

(29)  Courthouse

Phone number: _____

Address: _____

Business hours: _____

(30)  County commissioner

Name: _____

Department: _____

Secretary's name: _____

Phone number: _____

Address: _____

(31) County commissioner

    Name: _____

    Department: _____

    Secretary's name: _____

    Phone number: _____

    Address: _____

(32) County commissioner

    Name: _____

    Department: _____

    Secretary's name: _____

    Phone number: _____

    Address: _____

(33) County commissioner

    Name: _____

    Department: _____

    Secretary's name: _____

    Phone number: _____

    Address: _____

(34) County commissioner

    Name: _____

    Department: _____

    Secretary's name: _____

    Phone number: _____

    Address: _____

(35) County commissioner

    Name: _____

    Department: _____

    Secretary's name: _____

    Phone number: _____

    Address: _____

(36) County commissioner

    Name: _____

    Department: _____

    Secretary's name: _____

    Phone number: _____

    Address: _____

(37)  Director of the county building department
   Name: _____
   Secretary's name: _____
   Phone number: _____
   Address: _____

(38)  Head of the county health department
   Name: _____
   Secretary's name: _____
   Phone number: _____
   Address: _____

(39)  Head of the county zoning department
   Name: _____
   Secretary's name: _____
   Phone number: _____
   Address: _____

(40)  Head of the county planning department
   Name: _____
   Secretary's name: _____
   Phone number: _____
   Address: _____

(41)  Clerk of the circuit court
   Name: _____
   Secretary's name: _____
   Phone number: _____
   Address: _____

(42)  Head of the county Department of Transportation
   Name: _____
   Secretary's name: _____
   Phone number: _____
   Address: _____

(43)  Fire marshal
   Name: _____
   Secretary's name: _____
   Phone number: _____
   Address: _____

(44) Sheriff

Name: _____

Secretary's name: _____

Phone number: _____

Address: _____

(45) Head of the county water department

Name: _____

Secretary's name: _____

Phone number: _____

Address: _____

(46) Head of the sewage department

Name: _____

Secretary's name: _____

Phone number: _____

Address: _____

(47) County tax assessor

Name: _____

Secretary's name: _____

Phone number: _____

Address: _____

(48) Head property appraiser

Name: _____

Secretary's name: _____

Phone number: _____

Address: _____

(49) County commission meetings

Usual day of the month held: _____

Where held: _____

Address for agenda: _____

Phone number of contact: _____

Name of contact: _____

Notes: _____

(50) County planning and zoning meetings

Usual day of the month held: _____

Where held: _____

Address for agenda: _____

Phone number of contact: _____

Name of contact: _____

Notes: _____

(51) Other county meetings

Type of meetings: _____

Usual day of the month held: _____

Where held: _____

Address for agenda: _____

Phone number of contact: _____

Name of contact: _____

Notes: _____

(52) Other county meetings

Type of meetings: _____

Usual day of the month held: _____

Where held: _____

Address for agenda: _____

Phone number of contact: _____

Name of contact: _____

Notes: _____

(53) Other county meetings

Type of meetings: _____

Usual day of the month held: _____

Where held: _____

Address for agenda: _____

Phone number of contact: _____

Name of contact: _____

Notes: _____

## State

(54) State legislature member from your area

Name: _____

Secretary's name: _____

Phone number: _____

Address: _____

(55) State legislature member from your area

Name: _____

Secretary's name: _____

Phone number: _____

Address: _____

(56) State legislature member from your area

Name: _____

Secretary's name: _____

Phone number: _____

Address: _____

(57) State legislature member from your area

Name: _____

Secretary's name: _____

Phone number: _____

Address: _____

(58) State legislature member from your area

Name: _____

Secretary's name: _____

Phone number: _____

Address: _____

(59) State legislature member from your area

Name: _____

Secretary's name: _____

Phone number: _____

Address: _____

(60) State sales tax collections

Name: _____

Secretary's name: _____

Phone number: _____

Address: _____

(61) State Department of Transportation

Name: _____

Secretary's name: _____

Phone number: _____

Address: _____

(62) Head of the state health department

Name: _____

Secretary's name: _____

Phone number: _____

Address: _____

## Federal

(63) Congress member from your area

Name: _____

Secretary's name: _____

Phone number: _____

Address: _____

(64) Congress member from your area

Name: _____

Secretary's name: _____

Phone number: _____

Address: _____

(65) Congress member from your area

Name: _____

Secretary's name: _____

Phone number: _____

Address: _____

(66) Congress member from your area

Name: _____

Secretary's name: _____

Phone number: _____

Address: _____

(67) Congress member from your area

Name: _____

Secretary's name: _____

Phone number: _____

Address: _____

(68) Head of the Army Corps of Engineers in your area

Name: _____

Secretary's name: _____

Phone number: _____

Address: _____

# Money Sources

(69) Commercial bank

Name of lender: _____
Name of president: _____
Secretary's name: _____
Phone number: _____
Address: _____
Head loan officer's name: _____

(70) Commercial bank

Name of lender: _____
Name of president: _____
Secretary's name: _____
Phone number: _____
Address: _____
Head loan officer's name: _____

(71) Commercial bank

Name of lender: _____
Name of president: _____
Secretary's name: _____
Phone number: _____
Address: _____
Head loan officer's name: _____

(72) Savings and loans institution

Name of lender: _____
Name of president: _____
Secretary's name: _____
Phone number: _____
Address: _____
Head loan officer's name: _____

(73) Savings and loans institution

Name of lender: _____
Name of president: _____
Secretary's name: _____
Phone number: _____
Address: _____
Head loan officer's name: _____

(74) Savings and loans institution

Name of lender: _____

Name of president: _____

Secretary's name: _____

Phone number: _____

Address: _____

Head loan officer's name: _____

(75) Mortgage banker and broker

Name of company: _____

Name of president: _____

Secretary's name: _____

Phone number: _____

Address: _____

Head loan officer's name: _____

(76) Mortgage banker and broker

Name of company: _____

Name of president: _____

Secretary's name: _____

Phone number: _____

Address: _____

Head loan officer's name: _____

(77) Other lender

Name of company: _____

Name of president: _____

Secretary's name: _____

Phone number: _____

Address: _____

Head loan officer's name: _____

(78) Other lender

Name of company: _____

Name of president: _____

Secretary's name: _____

Phone number: _____

Address: _____

Head loan officer's name: _____

# Construction

(79) Appliance repairs

Name of company: _____

Name of owner: _____

Secretary's name: _____

Phone number: _____

Address: _____

Notes: _____

(80) Appliance repairs

Name of company: _____

Name of owner: _____

Secretary's name: _____

Phone number: _____

Address: _____

Notes: _____

(81) Carpets

Name of company: _____

Name of owner: _____

Secretary's name: _____

Phone number: _____

Address: _____

Notes: _____

(82) Carpets

Name of company: _____

Name of owner: _____

Secretary's name: _____

Phone number: _____

Address: _____

Notes: _____

(83) Concrete sales

Name of company: _____

Name of president: _____

Secretary's name: _____

Phone number: _____

Address: _____

Notes: _____

(84) Surveyor

Name of company: _____

Name of owner: _____

Secretary's name: _____

Phone number: _____

Address: _____

Notes: _____

(85) General contractor

Name of company: _____

Name of president: _____

Secretary's name: _____

Phone number: _____

Address: _____

Notes: _____

(86) General contractor

Name of company: _____

Name of president: _____

Secretary's name: _____

Phone number: _____

Address: _____

Notes: _____

(87) Hardware store

Name of company: _____

Name of owner: _____

Secretary's name: _____

Phone number: _____

Address: _____

Notes: _____

(88) Hardware store

Name of company: _____

Name of president: _____

Secretary's name: _____

Phone number: _____

Address: _____

Notes: _____

(89) Large hardware and housewares store

　　　Name of company: _____
　　　Name of manager: _____
　　　Secretary's name: _____
　　　Phone number: _____
　　　Address: _____
　　　Notes: _____

(90) Large hardware and housewares store

　　　Name of company: _____
　　　Name of manager: _____
　　　Secretary's name: _____
　　　Phone number: _____
　　　Address: _____
　　　Notes: _____

(91) Lumberyard

　　　Name of company: _____
　　　Name of manager: _____
　　　Secretary's name: _____
　　　Phone number: _____
　　　Address: _____
　　　Notes: _____

(92) Lumberyard

　　　Name of company: _____
　　　Name of manager: _____
　　　Secretary's name: _____
　　　Phone number: _____
　　　Address: _____
　　　Notes: _____

(93) Painters

　　　Name of company: _____
　　　Name of owner: _____
　　　Secretary's name: _____
　　　Phone number: _____
　　　Address: _____
　　　Notes: _____

(94) Painter

Name of company: _____
Name of owner: _____
Secretary's name: _____
Phone number: _____
Address: _____
Notes: _____

(95) Plumber

Name of company: _____
Name of manager: _____
Secretary's name: _____
Phone number: _____
Address: _____
Notes: _____

(96) Plumber

Name of company: _____
Name of manager: _____
Secretary's name: _____
Phone number: _____
Address: _____
Notes: _____

(97) Roofer

Name of company: _____
Name of owner: _____
Secretary's name: _____
Phone number: _____
Address: _____
Notes: _____

(98) Roofer

Name of company: _____
Name of owner: _____
Secretary's name: _____
Phone number: _____
Address: _____
Notes: _____

(99) Sand and other fill

Name of company: _____

Name of supervisor: _____

Secretary's name: _____

Phone number: _____

Address: _____

Notes: _____

(100) Sand and other fill

Name of company: _____

Name of supervisor: _____

Secretary's name: _____

Phone number: _____

Address: _____

Notes: _____

(101) Other

Name of company: _____

Name of owner: _____

Secretary's name: _____

Phone number: _____

Address: _____

Notes: _____

(102) Other

Name of company: _____

Name of owner: _____

Secretary's name: _____

Phone number: _____

Address: _____

Notes: _____

(103) Plans, renderings, architects

Name of company: _____

Name of contact: _____

Secretary's name: _____

Phone number: _____

Address: _____

Notes: _____

(104)  Plans, renderings, architects

Name of company: _____

Name of contact: _____

Secretary's name: _____

Phone number: _____

Address: _____

Notes: _____

## Advertising

(105)  Local newspaper

Name of paper: _____

Time of delivery: _____

Type of newspaper: _____

Phone for classified advertising: _____

Phone for display advertising: _____

Address for billing: _____

Notes: _____

(106)  Local newspaper

Name of paper: _____

Time of delivery: _____

Type of newspaper: _____

Phone for classified advertising: _____

Phone for display advertising: _____

Address for billing: _____

Notes: _____

(107)  Local newspaper

Name of paper: _____

Time of delivery: _____

Type of newspaper: _____

Phone for classified advertising: _____

Phone for display advertising: _____

Address for billing: _____

Notes: _____

(108) Legal newspaper or local legal review

Name of paper: _____

Time of delivery: _____

Type of newspaper: _____

Phone for classified advertising: _____

Phone for display advertising: _____

Address for billing: _____

Notes: _____

(109) Printing service

Name of company: _____

Name of contact: _____

Secretary's name: _____

Phone number: _____

Address: _____

Notes: _____

(110) Printing service

Name of company: _____

Name of contact: _____

Secretary's name: _____

Phone number: _____

Address: _____

Notes: _____

(111) Express shipping service

Name of company: _____

Name of contact: _____

Secretary's name: _____

Phone number: _____

Address: _____

Notes: _____

(112) Express shipping service

Name of company: _____

Name of contact: _____

Secretary's name: _____

Phone number: _____

Address: _____

Notes: _____

(113)  Ad agency

    Name of company: _____

    Name of contact: _____

    Secretary's name: _____

    Phone number: _____

    Address: _____

    Notes: _____

(114)  Ad agency

    Name of company: _____

    Name of contact: _____

    Secretary's name: _____

    Phone number: _____

    Address: _____

    Notes: _____

## Advisors

(115)  Accountant and CPA

    Name of company: _____

    Name of contact: _____

    Secretary's name: _____

    Phone number: _____

    Address: _____

    Notes: _____

(116)  Accountant and CPA

    Name of company: _____

    Name of contact: _____

    Secretary's name: _____

    Phone number: _____

    Address: _____

    Notes: _____

(117)  Interior decorator

    Name of company: _____

    Name of contact: _____

    Secretary's name: _____

    Phone number: _____

    Address: _____

    Notes: _____

(118)  Interior decorator

Name of company: _____

Name of contact: _____

Secretary's name: _____

Phone number: _____

Address: _____

Notes: _____

(119)  Landscaper

Name of company: _____

Name of contact: _____

Secretary's name: _____

Phone number: _____

Address: _____

Notes: _____

(120)  Landscaper

Name of company: _____

Name of contact: _____

Secretary's name: _____

Phone number: _____

Address: _____

Notes: _____

(121)  Lawyer

Name of company: _____

Name of contact: _____

Secretary's name: _____

Phone number: _____

Address: _____

Notes: _____

(122)  Lawyer

Name of company: _____

Name of contact: _____

Secretary's name: _____

Phone number: _____

Address: _____

Notes: _____

(123)  Realtor

    Name of company: _____

    Name of contact: _____

    Secretary's name: _____

    Phone number: _____

    Address: _____

    Notes: _____

(124)  Realtor

    Name of company: _____

    Name of contact: _____

    Secretary's name: _____

    Phone number: _____

    Address: _____

    Notes: _____

## Investment Services

(125)  Property insurance company

    Name of company: _____

    Name of contact: _____

    Secretary's name: _____

    Phone number: _____

    Address: _____

    Notes: _____

(126)  Property insurance company

    Name of company: _____

    Name of contact: _____

    Secretary's name: _____

    Phone number: _____

    Address: _____

    Notes: _____

(127)  Title insurance company

    Name of company: _____

    Name of contact: _____

    Secretary's name: _____

    Phone number: _____

    Address: _____

    Notes: _____

(128)  Title insurance company

Name of company: _____

Name of contact: _____

Secretary's name: _____

Phone number: _____

Address: _____

Notes: _____

(129)  Miscellaneous

Name of company: _____

Name of contact: _____

Secretary's name: _____

Phone number: _____

Address: _____

Notes: _____

(130)  Miscellaneous

Name of company: _____

Name of contact: _____

Secretary's name: _____

Phone number: _____

Address: _____

Notes: _____

(131)  Miscellaneous

Name of company: _____

Name of contact: _____

Secretary's name: _____

Phone number: _____

Address: _____

Notes: _____

(132)  Miscellaneous

Name of company: _____

Name of contact: _____

Secretary's name: _____

Phone number: _____

Address: _____

Notes: _____

(133) Barter company

Phone number: _____

Address: _____

Business hours: _____

(134) Barter company

Phone number: _____

Address: _____

Business hours: _____

(135) Real estate exchange clubs

Phone number: _____

Address: _____

Business hours: _____

## Utilities

(136) Local power and light phone and address

Phone number: _____

Address: _____

Business hours: _____

(137) Local water and sewer phone and address

Phone number: _____

Address: _____

Business hours: _____

(138) City garbage pickup

Phone number: _____

Address: _____

Business hours: _____

Day of normal pickup: _____

Day of bulk pickup: _____

(139) Local telephone company number and address

Phone number: _____

Address: _____

Business hours: _____

Notes: _____

_____

# Chapter Review Answers

At the end of most chapters there is a study and review section of items that each reader should spend the extra time to accomplish. The most important part of these exercises is The Real Estate Investor's VIP List. This list will become a major source of information and contacts once the reader begins to *use* the knowledge gained from this book.

## Chapter 3

1. $28,800.

2. 
| | |
|---|---|
| Gross Income Possible: | $28,800 |
| Less vacancy factor: | −1,440 |
| Collectable income: | $27,360 |
| Less Operating Expenses: | −14,800 |
| Net operating income: | $12,560 |

3. To calculate the cash flow, remember to take into account both the first and the second mortgage. Use Table A-1 of the Appendix to locate the constant rate for the two mortgages. In the case of the first mortgage of $75,000 for 20 years at 8 percent the constant is 10.037 percent and the total annual payment of that mortgage $7,527.75 ($75,000 × 0.10037 = $7527.75). The second mortgage of $25,000 for 8 years at 8 percent interest has a total annual payment of $4,241.00 ($25,000 × the constant rate for that mortgage of 16.964 percent). The combined debt service is $11,768.75 shown below.

| | |
|---|---|
| Net operating income: | $12,560.00 |
| Less debt service: | −11,768.75 |
| Cash flow: | $    791.25 |

4. Calculate the new cash flow:

| | |
|---|---|
| Gross income possible: | $38,400.00 |
| Less vacancy factor: | −1,920.00 |
| Collectable income: | $36,480.00 |
| Less operating expenses: | −17,800.00 |

| Net operating income: | $18,680.00 |
|---|---|
| Less debt service: | −11,768.75 |
| Cash flow: | $  6,911.25 |

5. Remember the new debt service will be much less than in the previous
   question because the $25,000 held by the seller is at interest only or
   an annual total of $25,000 × 0.075 = $1875.00 which is added to the
   existing first mortgage of $7527.75 to give a total debt service of
   $9402.75, which is then deducted from the NOI to show the cash flow.
   *a.* New cash flow          $8,397.25
   *b.* Cash on cash yield        33.589 percent

### Cash on Cash Yield

| Cash down: | $20,000 |
|---|---|
| Remodeling expenses: | 5,000 |
| Total investment: | $25,000 |

$$\text{Cash on cash yield} = \frac{\$\,8,397.25}{25,000}$$

$$= \ 33.589 \text{ percent}$$

## Chapter 4

1. *d*
2. *d*

## Chapter 5

1. City council meeting

## Chapter 7

1. Voluntary change, increased bottom line, capital improvements.
2. Any of the following: absentee owner, professional who has other
   things on his or her mind, poor management, lack of capital, a poor
   tenant–landlord relationship, and squabble between owners.
3. True or false:
   *a.* F
   *b.* T
   *c.* F
   *d.* T
   *e.* T

## Chapter 8

1. *b*
2. *b*
3. Why? People are more likely to stop at a gas and convenience store
   on the way home than when they are pressed for time going to work.

# Real Estate Finance Tables

The author has included two **constant rate** tables that can be used in several different financial calculations involving mortgages. By using an inexpensive calculator and these tables, the reader will be able to accurately calculate the following:

1. Equal monthly payments of principal and interest combined, for mortgages at interest rates from 8 percent to 25 percent over periods from 6 months to 40 years: Use Table A-1.

2. Equal annual payments of principal and interest combined, for mortgages at interest rates from 6 percent to 10.25 percent over periods from 1 year to 40 years: Use Table A-2.

## How to Use the Tables

### Table A-1

This table is used to find the monthly payment of a mortgage of equal monthly payments of principal and interest combined, over periods from 6 months to 40 years.

**Step 1.** Make sure you have a calculator that is not rounding off to two or less decimal points. To check this, take the calculator and divide 6 by 12. The answer will be 0.50. Then clear the calculator and divide 6.25 by 12. The correct answer would be 0.520833 (and more 3s), just to carry this problem to 12 decimal points to the right. If your calculator gives you 0.5 or even 0.52, then you need to review the operating book of that calculator to see if you can adjust the calculator to give you a minimum of 6 numbers to the right of the decimal point. There are ways to "trick" the calculator to arrive at the right answer, but these methods add steps to the process that can be overlooked or misread and in reality are unnecessary if you simply check the calculator *before you buy it.*

**Step 2.** Review the problem. For example, find the monthly payment that will give 300 equal payments to amortize fully a $100,000 principal amount borrowed (25 years × 12 = 300 installments), at a **fixed rate** of 9 percent interest.

Look at Table A-1 and turn to the page that shows the years 24.5 to 28 years at the top. Move down the interest column and go to 9 percent interest, and then move right to the appropriate number under 25 years. The number you now see should be 10.070, which is the **constant annual percentage** for a mortgage of equal monthly installments (payments) of principal and interest combined at 9 percent interest for the term of 25 years.

This constant rate is an annual percent rate that automatically takes into account both principal and interest combined. This percentage is important because a borrower can quickly ascertain the total debt service for a year. The number found (10.070) would be ten point zero seven percent.

Multiply the principal amount of the loan by the constant rate to find the total annual debt service (based on monthly payments). Remember that when you multiply by a percentage, move the decimal point two spaces to the left. The math problem is shown below:

$100,000  (the amount of the loan)

× 0.1007  (the constant rate converted)

$10,070.00  (the total of 12 payments)

To now ascertain the monthly installment that would be in effect for the whole 300 payments, divide the annual sum by 12.

$10,070 ÷ 12 = $839.166666

Round this value up to a monthly payment of $839.67.

## Table A-2

Use Table A-2 to find the annual payment of a mortgage that had only one payment per year of principal and interest combined.

**Step 1.** If you have already done step 1 for Table A-1 and have been able to adjust your calculator to give the desired answer, then proceed to step 2 below.

**Step 2.** Review the problem. Find the annual payment that will give 25 equal annual payments to fully amortize a $100,000 principal amount borrowed (25 years × 1 payment per year = 25 installments), at a **fixed rate** of 9 percent interest.

Turn to Table A-2 and the constant rate that is in the 25-year column at 9 percent interest. That number is 10.181 and represents the ten point one eight one percent constant rate. Notice that the single annual payment for the same interest and term of years will be higher than the constant rate for twelve monthly payments per year. The reason for this is the principal amount of the amount borrowed is being reduced each and every month whereas with a single annual payment the interest rate charged for the year applies to the same principal owned for the whole year.

To find the single annual payment multiply the constant (converted to a mathematical number) by the amount of the loan:

$100,000        (the amount of the total loan)

× 0.10181       (the constant percent)

$10,181.00      (the single annual installment)

## Important Pitfalls

When using either Table A-1 or Table A-2 the reader should be aware that the answers found may vary slightly from other amortization schedules. This occurs due to the complexity of the numbers used (the extent of the numbers to the right of the decimal point). For example, look at Table A-1 and find 11 percent interest for 25.5 years. The constant rate shown is 11.718 and if the mortgage amount was $1,000,000 there would be a monthly payment of $9,765.00, whereas if the constant had been rounded off to 11.72 the monthly payment would show as $9,766.67.

This was found by first multiplying the loan amount of $1,000,000 by 0.11718 = $117,180, then dividing by 12 = $9,765.00, or

$$\$1,000,000 \times 0.1172 = \$117,200$$

$$\$117,200 \div 12 = \$9766.67$$

The greater the number of decimals used in a constant rate to the right of the decimal point, the more accurate (and lower) the payment will be. The tables given here provide a mathematical percentage that when used according to the instructions of this book is sufficient for approximate calculations. Exact amortization schedules should be obtained and then compared with the answer obtained using Table A-1 or A-2 (according to the type of mortgage used). If the tables of this book produce a lower payment, then the schedule ordered has used less numbers to the right of the decimal point.

**Table A-1.** Constant Annual Percents Expressing the Sum of 12 Equal Monthly Payments Needed to Amortize a Principal Amount for the Term of Years Shown

| % Interest | \multicolumn{8}{c}{Years} |
|---|---|---|---|---|---|---|---|---|
|  | 0.5 | 1 | 1.5 | 2 | 2.5 | 3 | 3.5 | 4 |
| 8 | 204.694 | 104.387 | 70.969 | 54.273 | 44.266 | 37.604 | 32.853 | 29.296 |
| 8.25 | 204.836 | 104.523 | 71.104 | 54.409 | 44.403 | 37.742 | 32.992 | 29.436 |
| 8.5 | 204.991 | 104.666 | 71.244 | 54.548 | 44.542 | 37.882 | 33.133 | 29.578 |
| 8.75 | 205.139 | 104.805 | 71.381 | 54.685 | 44.680 | 38.021 | 33.273 | 29.720 |
| 9 | 205.287 | 104.944 | 71.518 | 54.823 | 44.819 | 38.160 | 33.414 | 29.863 |
| 9.25 | 205.433 | 105.083 | 71.656 | 54.960 | 44.957 | 38.300 | 33.555 | 30.005 |
| 9.5 | 205.578 | 105.220 | 71.793 | 55.098 | 45.095 | 38.440 | 33.696 | 30.148 |
| 9.75 | 205.729 | 105.361 | 71.931 | 55.236 | 45.235 | 38.580 | 33.838 | 30.292 |
| 10 | 205.879 | 105.502 | 72.070 | 55.375 | 45.375 | 38.722 | 33.981 | 30.436 |
| 10.25 | 206.021 | 105.639 | 72.207 | 55.512 | 45.513 | 38.862 | 34.123 | 30.579 |
| 10.5 | 206.171 | 105.779 | 72.345 | 55.652 | 45.653 | 39.003 | 34.266 | 30.724 |
| 10.75 | 206.318 | 105.918 | 72.484 | 55.790 | 45.793 | 39.145 | 34.409 | 30.869 |
| 11 | 206.464 | 106.057 | 72.622 | 55.929 | 45.933 | 39.286 | 34.552 | 31.015 |
| 11.25 | 206.615 | 106.199 | 72.762 | 56.069 | 46.075 | 39.429 | 34.697 | 31.161 |
| 11.5 | 206.766 | 106.340 | 72.902 | 56.210 | 46.216 | 39.572 | 34.842 | 31.307 |
| 11.75 | 206.911 | 106.479 | 73.040 | 56.348 | 46.357 | 39.714 | 34.986 | 31.454 |
| 12 | 207.060 | 106.620 | 73.179 | 56.489 | 46.498 | 39.858 | 35.131 | 31.601 |
| 12.25 | 207.204 | 106.758 | 73.317 | 56.628 | 46.639 | 40.000 | 35.276 | 31.748 |
| 12.5 | 207.356 | 106.900 | 73.458 | 56.769 | 46.782 | 40.145 | 35.422 | 31.896 |
| 12.75 | 207.503 | 107.040 | 73.597 | 56.909 | 46.923 | 40.288 | 35.568 | 32.044 |
| 13 | 207.654 | 107.182 | 73.738 | 57.051 | 47.066 | 40.433 | 35.715 | 32.193 |
| 13.25 | 207.800 | 107.322 | 73.877 | 57.191 | 47.209 | 40.578 | 35.861 | 32.342 |
| 13.5 | 207.946 | 107.461 | 74.017 | 57.332 | 47.351 | 40.722 | 36.008 | 32.491 |
| 13.75 | 208.099 | 107.605 | 74.158 | 57.474 | 47.495 | 40.868 | 36.156 | 32.642 |
| 14 | 208.248 | 107.746 | 74.299 | 57.616 | 47.639 | 41.014 | 36.304 | 32.792 |
| 14.25 | 208.396 | 107.887 | 74.440 | 57.758 | 47.782 | 41.159 | 36.452 | 32.943 |
| 14.5 | 208.544 | 108.028 | 74.580 | 57.900 | 47.926 | 41.305 | 36.601 | 33.094 |
| 14.75 | 208.691 | 108.168 | 74.720 | 58.041 | 48.070 | 41.451 | 36.749 | 33.245 |
| 15 | 208.841 | 108.310 | 74.862 | 58.184 | 48.214 | 41.599 | 36.899 | 33.397 |
| 15.25 | 208.991 | 108.453 | 75.004 | 58.327 | 48.359 | 41.746 | 37.049 | 33.549 |
| 15.5 | 209.141 | 108.595 | 75.145 | 58.470 | 48.504 | 41.893 | 37.199 | 33.702 |
| 15.75 | 209.287 | 108.735 | 75.286 | 58.612 | 48.649 | 42.040 | 37.349 | 33.855 |
| 16 | 209.435 | 108.876 | 75.427 | 58.755 | 48.794 | 42.188 | 37.499 | 34.008 |
| 16.25 | 209.587 | 109.020 | 75.570 | 58.900 | 48.940 | 42.337 | 37.651 | 34.162 |
| 16.5 | 209.738 | 109.163 | 75.713 | 59.044 | 49.087 | 42.486 | 37.802 | 34.317 |
| 16.75 | 209.885 | 109.304 | 75.854 | 59.187 | 49.233 | 42.634 | 37.954 | 34.471 |
| 17 | 210.035 | 109.447 | 75.997 | 59.331 | 49.379 | 42.784 | 38.106 | 34.626 |
| 17.25 | 210.182 | 109.588 | 76.138 | 59.475 | 49.525 | 42.933 | 38.258 | 34.781 |
| 17.5 | 210.331 | 109.731 | 76.281 | 59.619 | 49.672 | 43.082 | 38.411 | 34.937 |
| 17.75 | 210.483 | 109.874 | 76.425 | 59.765 | 49.820 | 43.233 | 38.564 | 35.094 |
| 18 | 210.632 | 110.017 | 76.567 | 59.909 | 49.967 | 43.383 | 38.717 | 35.250 |
| 18.25 | 210.780 | 110.159 | 76.710 | 60.054 | 50.115 | 43.534 | 38.871 | 35.407 |
| 18.5 | 210.931 | 110.303 | 76.854 | 60.200 | 50.263 | 43.685 | 39.025 | 35.564 |

| % Interest | | | | Years | | | | |
|---|---|---|---|---|---|---|---|---|
| | 0.5 | 1 | 1.5 | 2 | 2.5 | 3 | 3.5 | 4 |
| 18.75 | 211.078 | 110.444 | 76.996 | 60.344 | 50.411 | 43.836 | 39.179 | 35.722 |
| 19 | 211.228 | 110.588 | 77.140 | 60.490 | 50.559 | 43.987 | 39.334 | 35.880 |
| 19.25 | 211.381 | 110.732 | 77.285 | 60.637 | 50.709 | 44.139 | 39.490 | 36.039 |
| 19.5 | 211.530 | 110.875 | 77.428 | 60.783 | 50.857 | 44.291 | 39.645 | 36.198 |
| 19.75 | 211.679 | 111.018 | 77.572 | 60.929 | 51.006 | 44.444 | 39.801 | 36.357 |
| 20 | 211.827 | 111.161 | 77.716 | 61.075 | 51.155 | 44.596 | 39.957 | 36.516 |
| 20.25 | 211.976 | 111.304 | 77.860 | 61.221 | 51.305 | 44.749 | 40.113 | 36.676 |
| 20.5 | 212.129 | 111.450 | 78.005 | 61.369 | 51.456 | 44.903 | 40.270 | 36.837 |
| 20.75 | 212.279 | 111.594 | 78.150 | 61.516 | 51.606 | 45.057 | 40.428 | 36.998 |
| 21 | 212.427 | 111.737 | 78.294 | 61.663 | 51.756 | 45.210 | 40.585 | 37.159 |
| 21.25 | 212.576 | 111.880 | 78.439 | 61.810 | 51.906 | 45.364 | 40.742 | 37.320 |
| 21.5 | 212.726 | 112.024 | 78.583 | 61.958 | 52.057 | 45.518 | 40.900 | 37.482 |
| 21.75 | 212.880 | 112.170 | 78.730 | 62.106 | 52.209 | 45.674 | 41.060 | 37.645 |
| 22 | 213.029 | 112.314 | 78.875 | 62.254 | 52.360 | 45.829 | 41.218 | 37.807 |
| 22.25 | 213.180 | 112.459 | 79.021 | 62.403 | 52.512 | 45.984 | 41.377 | 37.971 |
| 22.5 | 213.328 | 112.602 | 79.166 | 62.550 | 52.663 | 46.140 | 41.537 | 38.134 |
| 22.75 | 213.478 | 112.747 | 79.311 | 62.699 | 52.815 | 46.295 | 41.697 | 38.298 |
| 23 | 213.628 | 112.891 | 79.457 | 62.848 | 52.968 | 46.452 | 41.857 | 38.462 |
| 23.25 | 213.780 | 113.037 | 79.604 | 62.997 | 53.121 | 46.608 | 42.017 | 38.626 |
| 23.5 | 213.930 | 113.181 | 79.750 | 63.146 | 53.273 | 46.765 | 42.178 | 38.791 |
| 23.75 | 214.081 | 113.327 | 79.896 | 63.296 | 53.427 | 46.922 | 42.339 | 38.957 |
| 24 | 214.230 | 113.471 | 80.042 | 63.445 | 53.580 | 47.079 | 42.501 | 39.122 |
| 24.25 | 214.381 | 113.617 | 80.189 | 63.595 | 53.733 | 47.237 | 42.663 | 39.288 |
| 24.5 | 214.534 | 113.763 | 80.337 | 63.746 | 53.888 | 47.395 | 42.825 | 39.455 |
| 24.75 | 214.685 | 113.908 | 80.484 | 63.896 | 54.042 | 47.554 | 42.987 | 39.622 |
| 25 | 214.835 | 114.053 | 80.630 | 64.046 | 54.196 | 47.712 | 43.150 | 39.789 |

**302**

Appendix

**Table A-1.** Constant Annual Percents Expressing the Sum of 12
Equal Monthly Payments Needed to Amortize a Principal Amount
for the Term of Years Shown (*Continued*)

| % Interest | Years | | | | | | | |
|---|---|---|---|---|---|---|---|---|
| | 4.5 | 5 | 5.5 | 6 | 6.5 | 7 | 7.5 | 8 |
| 8 | 26.535 | 24.332 | 22.534 | 21.040 | 19.780 | 18.704 | 17.774 | 16.964 |
| 8.25 | 26.677 | 24.475 | 22.679 | 21.186 | 19.928 | 18.853 | 17.925 | 17.117 |
| 8.5 | 26.821 | 24.620 | 22.825 | 21.334 | 20.077 | 19.004 | 18.078 | 17.271 |
| 8.75 | 26.964 | 24.765 | 22.972 | 21.482 | 20.227 | 19.155 | 18.231 | 17.425 |
| 9 | 27.108 | 24.910 | 23.119 | 21.631 | 20.377 | 19.307 | 18.384 | 17.580 |
| 9.25 | 27.252 | 25.056 | 23.266 | 21.780 | 20.528 | 19.460 | 18.538 | 17.736 |
| 9.5 | 27.396 | 25.202 | 23.414 | 21.930 | 20.679 | 19.613 | 18.693 | 17.893 |
| 9.75 | 27.542 | 25.349 | 23.563 | 22.080 | 20.832 | 19.767 | 18.849 | 18.051 |
| 10 | 27.687 | 25.497 | 23.712 | 22.231 | 20.985 | 19.922 | 19.006 | 18.209 |
| 10.25 | 27.833 | 25.644 | 23.861 | 22.383 | 21.138 | 20.077 | 19.163 | 18.368 |
| 10.5 | 27.980 | 25.793 | 24.012 | 22.535 | 21.292 | 20.233 | 19.321 | 18.528 |
| 10.75 | 28.126 | 25.942 | 24.162 | 22.688 | 21.447 | 20.390 | 19.479 | 18.689 |
| 11 | 28.274 | 26.091 | 24.314 | 22.841 | 21.602 | 20.547 | 19.639 | 18.850 |
| 11.25 | 28.422 | 26.241 | 24.466 | 22.995 | 21.758 | 20.705 | 19.799 | 19.012 |
| 11.5 | 28.570 | 26.392 | 24.619 | 23.150 | 21.915 | 20.864 | 19.960 | 19.176 |
| 11.75 | 28.719 | 26.542 | 24.771 | 23.305 | 22.072 | 21.023 | 20.121 | 19.339 |
| 12 | 28.868 | 26.694 | 24.925 | 23.460 | 22.230 | 21.183 | 20.284 | 19.504 |
| 12.25 | 29.017 | 26.845 | 25.078 | 23.616 | 22.388 | 21.344 | 20.447 | 19.668 |
| 12.5 | 29.168 | 26.998 | 25.233 | 23.774 | 22.548 | 21.506 | 20.610 | 19.835 |
| 12.75 | 29.318 | 27.150 | 25.388 | 23.931 | 22.707 | 21.668 | 20.775 | 20.001 |
| 13 | 29.470 | 27.304 | 25.544 | 24.089 | 22.868 | 21.831 | 20.940 | 20.169 |
| 13.25 | 29.621 | 27.458 | 25.700 | 24.248 | 23.029 | 21.994 | 21.106 | 20.337 |
| 13.5 | 29.772 | 27.612 | 25.857 | 24.407 | 23.190 | 22.158 | 21.272 | 20.506 |
| 13.75 | 29.925 | 27.767 | 26.015 | 24.567 | 23.353 | 22.323 | 21.440 | 20.676 |
| 14 | 30.078 | 27.922 | 26.172 | 24.727 | 23.516 | 22.488 | 21.607 | 20.846 |
| 14.25 | 30.231 | 28.078 | 26.331 | 24.888 | 23.679 | 22.654 | 21.776 | 21.017 |
| 14.5 | 30.385 | 28.234 | 26.490 | 25.049 | 23.843 | 22.821 | 21.945 | 21.189 |
| 14.75 | 30.538 | 28.391 | 26.649 | 25.211 | 24.008 | 22.988 | 22.115 | 21.361 |
| 15 | 30.693 | 28.548 | 26.809 | 25.374 | 24.173 | 23.156 | 22.286 | 21.535 |
| 15.25 | 30.848 | 28.706 | 26.969 | 25.537 | 24.339 | 23.325 | 22.457 | 21.709 |
| 15.5 | 31.004 | 28.864 | 27.130 | 25.701 | 24.506 | 23.494 | 22.629 | 21.883 |
| 15.75 | 31.159 | 29.022 | 27.292 | 25.865 | 24.673 | 23.664 | 22.802 | 22.058 |
| 16 | 31.316 | 29.182 | 27.454 | 26.030 | 24.840 | 23.834 | 22.975 | 22.234 |
| 16.25 | 31.473 | 29.341 | 27.616 | 26.196 | 25.009 | 24.006 | 23.149 | 22.411 |
| 16.5 | 31.630 | 29.502 | 27.780 | 26.362 | 25.178 | 24.178 | 23.324 | 22.589 |
| 16.75 | 31.787 | 29.662 | 27.943 | 26.528 | 25.347 | 24.350 | 23.499 | 22.767 |
| 17 | 31.945 | 29.823 | 28.107 | 26.696 | 25.518 | 24.523 | 23.675 | 22.946 |
| 17.25 | 32.104 | 29.985 | 28.272 | 26.863 | 25.688 | 24.697 | 23.852 | 23.125 |
| 17.5 | 32.263 | 30.147 | 28.437 | 27.031 | 25.859 | 24.871 | 24.029 | 23.305 |
| 17.75 | 32.422 | 30.309 | 28.603 | 27.200 | 26.031 | 25.046 | 24.207 | 23.486 |
| 18 | 32.582 | 30.472 | 28.769 | 27.369 | 26.204 | 25.221 | 24.385 | 23.668 |
| 18.25 | 32.742 | 30.636 | 28.935 | 27.539 | 26.377 | 25.398 | 24.565 | 23.850 |

| %<br>Interest | Years | | | | | | | |
|---|---|---|---|---|---|---|---|---|
| | 4.5 | 5 | 5.5 | 6 | 6.5 | 7 | 7.5 | 8 |
| 18.5 | 32.903 | 30.800 | 29.103 | 27.710 | 26.550 | 25.574 | 24.744 | 24.033 |
| 18.75 | 33.063 | 30.964 | 29.270 | 27.881 | 26.724 | 25.752 | 24.925 | 24.216 |
| 19 | 33.225 | 31.129 | 29.438 | 28.052 | 26.899 | 25.930 | 25.106 | 24.401 |
| 19.25 | 33.387 | 31.294 | 29.607 | 28.224 | 27.075 | 26.108 | 25.288 | 24.586 |
| 19.5 | 33.549 | 31.460 | 29.776 | 28.397 | 27.251 | 26.287 | 25.470 | 24.771 |
| 19.75 | 33.712 | 31.626 | 29.946 | 28.570 | 27.427 | 26.467 | 25.653 | 24.957 |
| 20 | 33.875 | 31.793 | 30.116 | 28.743 | 27.604 | 26.647 | 25.837 | 25.144 |
| 20.25 | 34.039 | 31.960 | 30.287 | 28.917 | 27.781 | 26.828 | 26.021 | 25.331 |
| 20.5 | 34.203 | 32.128 | 30.458 | 29.092 | 27.960 | 27.010 | 26.206 | 25.519 |
| 20.75 | 34.367 | 32.296 | 30.630 | 29.268 | 28.139 | 27.192 | 26.391 | 25.708 |
| 21 | 34.532 | 32.464 | 30.802 | 29.443 | 28.318 | 27.375 | 26.577 | 25.897 |
| 21.25 | 34.697 | 32.633 | 30.974 | 29.619 | 28.497 | 27.558 | 26.764 | 26.087 |
| 21.5 | 34.863 | 32.802 | 31.147 | 29.796 | 28.678 | 27.742 | 26.951 | 26.278 |
| 21.75 | 35.029 | 32.973 | 31.321 | 29.974 | 28.859 | 27.926 | 27.139 | 26.469 |
| 22 | 35.196 | 33.143 | 31.495 | 30.151 | 29.040 | 28.111 | 27.327 | 26.661 |
| 22.25 | 35.363 | 33.314 | 31.670 | 30.330 | 29.222 | 28.297 | 27.516 | 26.853 |
| 22.5 | 35.530 | 33.485 | 31.845 | 30.509 | 29.405 | 28.483 | 27.706 | 27.046 |
| 22.75 | 35.698 | 33.656 | 32.020 | 30.688 | 29.588 | 28.669 | 27.896 | 27.239 |
| 23 | 35.866 | 33.828 | 32.197 | 30.868 | 29.771 | 28.857 | 28.087 | 27.433 |
| 23.25 | 36.035 | 34.001 | 32.373 | 31.048 | 29.955 | 29.044 | 28.278 | 27.628 |
| 23.5 | 36.203 | 34.174 | 32.550 | 31.229 | 30.140 | 29.233 | 28.470 | 27.823 |
| 23.75 | 36.373 | 34.348 | 32.728 | 31.410 | 30.325 | 29.422 | 28.662 | 28.019 |
| 24 | 36.543 | 34.521 | 32.905 | 31.592 | 30.511 | 29.611 | 28.855 | 28.216 |
| 24.25 | 36.713 | 34.696 | 33.084 | 31.775 | 30.697 | 29.801 | 29.049 | 28.413 |
| 24.5 | 36.884 | 34.871 | 33.263 | 31.958 | 30.884 | 29.992 | 29.243 | 28.610 |
| 24.75 | 37.055 | 35.046 | 33.442 | 32.141 | 31.071 | 30.182 | 29.438 | 28.809 |
| 25 | 37.226 | 35.222 | 33.622 | 32.325 | 31.259 | 30.374 | 29.633 | 29.007 |

**Table A-1.** Constant Annual Percents Expressing the Sum of 12 Equal Monthly Payments Needed to Amortize a Principal Amount for the Term of Years Shown (*Continued*)

| % Interest | \multicolumn{8}{c}{Years} |
|---|---|---|---|---|---|---|---|---|
| | 8.5 | 9 | 9.5 | 10 | 10.5 | 11 | 11.5 | 12 |
| 8 | 16.252 | 15.623 | 15.062 | 14.559 | 14.107 | 13.699 | 13.328 | 12.989 |
| 8.25 | 16.406 | 15.778 | 15.219 | 14.718 | 14.268 | 13.860 | 13.491 | 13.154 |
| 8.5 | 16.562 | 15.935 | 15.378 | 14.878 | 14.429 | 14.024 | 13.656 | 13.321 |
| 8.75 | 16.718 | 16.093 | 15.537 | 15.039 | 14.592 | 14.188 | 13.822 | 13.488 |
| 9 | 16.875 | 16.252 | 15.697 | 15.201 | 14.756 | 14.353 | 13.988 | 13.657 |
| 9.25 | 17.033 | 16.411 | 15.858 | 15.364 | 14.920 | 14.519 | 14.156 | 13.826 |
| 9.5 | 17.191 | 16.571 | 16.020 | 15.528 | 15.085 | 14.686 | 14.325 | 13.997 |
| 9.75 | 17.351 | 16.733 | 16.183 | 15.693 | 15.252 | 14.855 | 14.495 | 14.168 |
| 10 | 17.511 | 16.895 | 16.347 | 15.858 | 15.420 | 15.024 | 14.666 | 14.341 |
| 10.25 | 17.672 | 17.057 | 16.512 | 16.025 | 15.588 | 15.194 | 14.838 | 14.515 |
| 10.5 | 17.834 | 17.221 | 16.677 | 16.192 | 15.757 | 15.365 | 15.011 | 14.690 |
| 10.75 | 17.996 | 17.386 | 16.844 | 16.361 | 15.928 | 15.538 | 15.185 | 14.866 |
| 11 | 18.160 | 17.551 | 17.011 | 16.530 | 16.099 | 15.711 | 15.360 | 15.043 |
| 11.25 | 18.324 | 17.717 | 17.180 | 16.700 | 16.271 | 15.885 | 15.537 | 15.221 |
| 11.5 | 18.489 | 17.885 | 17.349 | 16.872 | 16.444 | 16.060 | 15.714 | 15.400 |
| 11.75 | 18.655 | 18.052 | 17.519 | 17.044 | 16.618 | 16.236 | 15.892 | 15.580 |
| 12 | 18.821 | 18.221 | 17.690 | 17.217 | 16.794 | 16.414 | 16.071 | 15.761 |
| 12.25 | 18.989 | 18.391 | 17.861 | 17.390 | 16.969 | 16.591 | 16.251 | 15.943 |
| 12.5 | 19.157 | 18.561 | 18.034 | 17.565 | 17.146 | 16.771 | 16.432 | 16.126 |
| 12.75 | 19.326 | 18.732 | 18.207 | 17.741 | 17.324 | 16.950 | 16.614 | 16.310 |
| 13 | 19.496 | 18.904 | 18.382 | 17.917 | 17.503 | 17.131 | 16.797 | 16.496 |
| 13.25 | 19.666 | 19.077 | 18.557 | 18.095 | 17.682 | 17.313 | 16.981 | 16.682 |
| 13.5 | 19.837 | 19.251 | 18.733 | 18.273 | 17.863 | 17.496 | 17.166 | 16.869 |
| 13.75 | 20.010 | 19.425 | 18.910 | 18.452 | 18.044 | 17.680 | 17.352 | 17.057 |
| 14 | 20.182 | 19.601 | 19.087 | 18.632 | 18.227 | 17.864 | 17.539 | 17.246 |
| 14.25 | 20.356 | 19.777 | 19.266 | 18.813 | 18.410 | 18.049 | 17.726 | 17.435 |
| 14.5 | 20.530 | 19.953 | 19.445 | 18.994 | 18.594 | 18.236 | 17.915 | 17.626 |
| 14.75 | 20.705 | 20.131 | 19.625 | 19.177 | 18.779 | 18.423 | 18.104 | 17.818 |
| 15 | 20.881 | 20.309 | 19.806 | 19.360 | 18.964 | 18.611 | 18.295 | 18.011 |
| 15.25 | 21.058 | 20.488 | 19.987 | 19.544 | 19.151 | 18.800 | 18.486 | 18.204 |
| 15.5 | 21.235 | 20.668 | 20.170 | 19.729 | 19.338 | 18.990 | 18.678 | 18.399 |
| 15.75 | 21.413 | 20.849 | 20.353 | 19.915 | 19.526 | 19.180 | 18.871 | 18.594 |
| 16 | 21.592 | 21.030 | 20.537 | 20.102 | 19.715 | 19.372 | 19.065 | 18.790 |
| 16.25 | 21.771 | 21.213 | 20.722 | 20.289 | 19.905 | 19.564 | 19.260 | 18.987 |
| 16.5 | 21.952 | 21.396 | 20.908 | 20.477 | 20.096 | 19.757 | 19.455 | 19.185 |
| 16.75 | 22.133 | 21.579 | 21.094 | 20.666 | 20.288 | 19.951 | 19.652 | 19.384 |
| 17 | 22.314 | 21.764 | 21.281 | 20.856 | 20.480 | 20.146 | 19.849 | 19.583 |
| 17.25 | 22.496 | 21.949 | 21.469 | 21.046 | 20.673 | 20.342 | 20.047 | 19.783 |
| 17.5 | 22.679 | 22.134 | 21.657 | 21.237 | 20.867 | 20.538 | 20.245 | 19.985 |
| 17.75 | 22.863 | 22.321 | 21.847 | 21.430 | 21.061 | 20.735 | 20.445 | 20.187 |
| 18 | 23.048 | 22.508 | 22.037 | 21.622 | 21.257 | 20.933 | 20.646 | 20.389 |
| 18.25 | 23.233 | 22.696 | 22.227 | 21.816 | 21.453 | 21.132 | 20.847 | 20.593 |

| % Interest | Years | | | | | | | |
|---|---|---|---|---|---|---|---|---|
| | 8.5 | 9 | 9.5 | 10 | 10.5 | 11 | 11.5 | 12 |
| 18.5 | 23.419 | 22.885 | 22.419 | 22.010 | 21.650 | 21.331 | 21.049 | 20.797 |
| 18.75 | 23.605 | 23.074 | 22.611 | 22.205 | 21.847 | 21.531 | 21.251 | 21.002 |
| 19 | 23.792 | 23.264 | 22.804 | 22.401 | 22.046 | 21.732 | 21.455 | 21.208 |
| 19.25 | 23.980 | 23.455 | 22.998 | 22.597 | 22.245 | 21.934 | 21.659 | 21.415 |
| 19.5 | 24.169 | 23.647 | 23.192 | 22.794 | 22.445 | 22.137 | 21.864 | 21.622 |
| 19.75 | 24.358 | 23.839 | 23.387 | 22.992 | 22.645 | 22.340 | 22.070 | 21.831 |
| 20 | 24.548 | 24.032 | 23.583 | 23.191 | 22.847 | 22.544 | 22.276 | 22.039 |
| 20.25 | 24.738 | 24.225 | 23.779 | 23.390 | 23.048 | 22.748 | 22.483 | 22.249 |
| 20.5 | 24.929 | 24.420 | 23.977 | 23.590 | 23.251 | 22.954 | 22.691 | 22.459 |
| 20.75 | 25.121 | 24.614 | 24.174 | 23.791 | 23.455 | 23.160 | 22.900 | 22.670 |
| 21 | 25.314 | 24.810 | 24.373 | 23.992 | 23.659 | 23.366 | 23.109 | 22.882 |
| 21.25 | 25.507 | 25.006 | 24.572 | 24.194 | 23.863 | 23.573 | 23.319 | 23.094 |
| 21.5 | 25.700 | 25.203 | 24.772 | 24.396 | 24.069 | 23.781 | 23.529 | 23.307 |
| 21.75 | 25.895 | 25.400 | 24.972 | 24.600 | 24.275 | 23.990 | 23.740 | 23.521 |
| 22 | 26.090 | 25.598 | 25.173 | 24.804 | 24.481 | 24.200 | 23.952 | 23.735 |
| 22.25 | 26.285 | 25.797 | 25.375 | 25.008 | 24.689 | 24.410 | 24.165 | 23.950 |
| 22.5 | 26.481 | 25.996 | 25.577 | 25.213 | 24.897 | 24.620 | 24.378 | 24.165 |
| 22.75 | 26.678 | 26.196 | 25.780 | 25.419 | 25.105 | 24.831 | 24.592 | 24.381 |
| 23 | 26.876 | 26.397 | 25.984 | 25.626 | 25.315 | 25.043 | 24.806 | 24.598 |
| 23.25 | 27.074 | 26.598 | 26.188 | 25.833 | 25.524 | 25.256 | 25.021 | 24.815 |
| 23.5 | 27.272 | 26.800 | 26.393 | 26.041 | 25.735 | 25.469 | 25.237 | 25.033 |
| 23.75 | 27.471 | 27.002 | 26.598 | 26.249 | 25.946 | 25.683 | 25.453 | 25.252 |
| 24 | 27.671 | 27.205 | 26.804 | 26.458 | 26.158 | 25.897 | 25.670 | 25.471 |
| 24.25 | 27.872 | 27.409 | 27.011 | 26.667 | 26.370 | 26.112 | 25.887 | 25.691 |
| 24.5 | 28.073 | 27.613 | 27.218 | 26.877 | 26.583 | 26.327 | 26.105 | 25.911 |
| 24.75 | 28.274 | 27.817 | 27.426 | 27.088 | 26.796 | 26.543 | 26.323 | 26.132 |
| 25 | 28.476 | 28.023 | 27.634 | 27.299 | 27.010 | 26.760 | 26.542 | 26.353 |

**Table A-1.** Constant Annual Percents Expressing the Sum of 12
Equal Monthly Payments Needed to Amortize a Principal Amount
for the Term of Years Shown (*Continued*)

| %<br>Interest | Years | | | | | | | |
|---|---|---|---|---|---|---|---|---|
| | 12.5 | 13 | 13.5 | 14 | 14.5 | 15 | 15.5 | 16 |
| 8 | 12.680 | 12.397 | 12.136 | 11.896 | 11.674 | 11.468 | 11.277 | 11.099 |
| 8.25 | 12.847 | 12.565 | 12.306 | 12.067 | 11.846 | 11.642 | 11.452 | 11.276 |
| 8.5 | 13.015 | 12.734 | 12.477 | 12.239 | 12.020 | 11.817 | 11.629 | 11.454 |
| 8.75 | 13.184 | 12.905 | 12.649 | 12.413 | 12.195 | 11.994 | 11.807 | 11.633 |
| 9 | 13.354 | 13.076 | 12.822 | 12.587 | 12.371 | 12.171 | 11.986 | 11.814 |
| 9.25 | 13.525 | 13.249 | 12.996 | 12.763 | 12.549 | 12.350 | 12.167 | 11.996 |
| 9.5 | 13.697 | 13.423 | 13.172 | 12.940 | 12.727 | 12.531 | 12.349 | 12.180 |
| 9.75 | 13.870 | 13.598 | 13.348 | 13.119 | 12.908 | 12.712 | 12.532 | 12.365 |
| 10 | 14.045 | 13.774 | 13.526 | 13.299 | 13.089 | 12.895 | 12.717 | 12.551 |
| 10.25 | 14.220 | 13.952 | 13.705 | 13.479 | 13.271 | 13.079 | 12.902 | 12.738 |
| 10.5 | 14.397 | 14.130 | 13.886 | 13.661 | 13.455 | 13.265 | 13.089 | 12.927 |
| 10.75 | 14.575 | 14.310 | 14.067 | 13.844 | 13.640 | 13.451 | 13.278 | 13.117 |
| 11 | 14.754 | 14.490 | 14.249 | 14.029 | 13.826 | 13.639 | 13.467 | 13.308 |
| 11.25 | 14.934 | 14.672 | 14.433 | 14.214 | 14.013 | 13.828 | 13.658 | 13.500 |
| 11.5 | 15.115 | 14.855 | 14.618 | 14.401 | 14.202 | 14.018 | 13.850 | 13.694 |
| 11.75 | 15.297 | 15.039 | 14.804 | 14.588 | 14.391 | 14.210 | 14.043 | 13.889 |
| 12 | 15.480 | 15.224 | 14.991 | 14.777 | 14.582 | 14.402 | 14.237 | 14.085 |
| 12.25 | 15.664 | 15.410 | 15.179 | 14.967 | 14.773 | 14.596 | 14.432 | 14.282 |
| 12.5 | 15.849 | 15.597 | 15.368 | 15.158 | 14.966 | 14.790 | 14.629 | 14.480 |
| 12.75 | 16.035 | 15.785 | 15.558 | 15.350 | 15.160 | 14.986 | 14.826 | 14.679 |
| 13 | 16.223 | 15.975 | 15.749 | 15.543 | 15.355 | 15.183 | 15.025 | 14.880 |
| 13.25 | 16.411 | 16.165 | 15.941 | 15.737 | 15.551 | 15.381 | 15.225 | 15.081 |
| 13.5 | 16.600 | 16.356 | 16.134 | 15.932 | 15.748 | 15.580 | 15.425 | 15.284 |
| 13.75 | 16.790 | 16.548 | 16.329 | 16.129 | 15.946 | 15.780 | 15.627 | 15.488 |
| 14 | 16.981 | 16.741 | 16.524 | 16.326 | 16.146 | 15.981 | 15.830 | 15.692 |
| 14.25 | 17.173 | 16.935 | 16.720 | 16.524 | 16.346 | 16.183 | 16.034 | 15.898 |
| 14.5 | 17.366 | 17.130 | 16.917 | 16.723 | 16.547 | 16.386 | 16.239 | 16.105 |
| 14.75 | 17.560 | 17.326 | 17.115 | 16.923 | 16.749 | 16.590 | 16.445 | 16.313 |
| 15 | 17.755 | 17.523 | 17.314 | 17.124 | 16.952 | 16.795 | 16.652 | 16.521 |
| 15.25 | 17.950 | 17.721 | 17.514 | 17.327 | 17.156 | 17.001 | 16.860 | 16.731 |
| 15.5 | 18.147 | 17.920 | 17.715 | 17.530 | 17.361 | 17.208 | 17.069 | 16.941 |
| 15.75 | 18.344 | 18.120 | 17.917 | 17.733 | 17.567 | 17.416 | 17.278 | 17.153 |
| 16 | 18.543 | 18.320 | 18.120 | 17.938 | 17.774 | 17.624 | 17.489 | 17.365 |
| 16.25 | 18.742 | 18.522 | 18.323 | 18.144 | 17.981 | 17.834 | 17.700 | 17.579 |
| 16.5 | 18.942 | 18.724 | 18.528 | 18.350 | 18.190 | 18.045 | 17.913 | 17.793 |
| 16.75 | 19.143 | 18.928 | 18.733 | 18.558 | 18.399 | 18.256 | 18.126 | 18.008 |
| 17 | 19.345 | 19.132 | 18.939 | 18.766 | 18.610 | 18.468 | 18.340 | 18.224 |
| 17.25 | 19.548 | 19.336 | 19.146 | 18.975 | 18.821 | 18.681 | 18.555 | 18.440 |
| 17.5 | 19.751 | 19.542 | 19.354 | 19.185 | 19.033 | 18.895 | 18.770 | 18.658 |
| 17.75 | 19.956 | 19.749 | 19.563 | 19.396 | 19.245 | 19.110 | 18.987 | 18.876 |
| 18 | 20.161 | 19.956 | 19.772 | 19.607 | 19.459 | 19.325 | 19.204 | 19.095 |
| 18.25 | 20.367 | 20.164 | 19.983 | 19.820 | 19.673 | 19.541 | 19.422 | 19.315 |

| %        |        |        |        | Years  |        |        |        |        |
|----------|--------|--------|--------|--------|--------|--------|--------|--------|
| Interest | 12.5   | 13     | 13.5   | 14     | 14.5   | 15     | 15.5   | 16     |
| 18.5     | 20.573 | 20.373 | 20.194 | 20.033 | 19.888 | 19.758 | 19.641 | 19.535 |
| 18.75    | 20.781 | 20.583 | 20.406 | 20.247 | 20.104 | 19.976 | 19.861 | 19.757 |
| 19       | 20.989 | 20.793 | 20.618 | 20.461 | 20.321 | 20.195 | 20.081 | 19.979 |
| 19.25    | 21.198 | 21.004 | 20.831 | 20.677 | 20.538 | 20.414 | 20.302 | 20.201 |
| 19.5     | 21.408 | 21.216 | 21.046 | 20.893 | 20.756 | 20.634 | 20.524 | 20.425 |
| 19.75    | 21.618 | 21.429 | 21.260 | 21.110 | 20.975 | 20.854 | 20.746 | 20.649 |
| 20       | 21.829 | 21.642 | 21.476 | 21.327 | 21.194 | 21.076 | 20.969 | 20.874 |
| 20.25    | 22.041 | 21.856 | 21.692 | 21.545 | 21.414 | 21.297 | 21.193 | 21.099 |
| 20.5     | 22.254 | 22.071 | 21.909 | 21.764 | 21.635 | 21.520 | 21.417 | 21.325 |
| 20.75    | 22.467 | 22.287 | 22.126 | 21.984 | 21.857 | 21.743 | 21.642 | 21.552 |
| 21       | 22.681 | 22.503 | 22.345 | 22.204 | 22.079 | 21.967 | 21.868 | 21.779 |
| 21.25    | 22.895 | 22.719 | 22.563 | 22.425 | 22.302 | 22.192 | 22.094 | 22.007 |
| 21.5     | 23.111 | 22.937 | 22.783 | 22.646 | 22.525 | 22.417 | 22.321 | 22.235 |
| 21.75    | 23.327 | 23.155 | 23.003 | 22.869 | 22.749 | 22.643 | 22.548 | 22.464 |
| 22       | 23.543 | 23.374 | 23.224 | 23.091 | 22.974 | 22.869 | 22.776 | 22.693 |
| 22.25    | 23.760 | 23.593 | 23.445 | 23.315 | 23.199 | 23.096 | 23.005 | 22.924 |
| 22.5     | 23.978 | 23.813 | 23.667 | 23.539 | 23.424 | 23.323 | 23.234 | 23.154 |
| 22.75    | 24.196 | 24.034 | 23.890 | 23.763 | 23.651 | 23.551 | 23.463 | 23.385 |
| 23       | 24.415 | 24.255 | 24.113 | 23.988 | 23.878 | 23.780 | 23.693 | 23.617 |
| 23.25    | 24.635 | 24.476 | 24.337 | 24.214 | 24.105 | 24.009 | 23.924 | 23.849 |
| 23.5     | 24.855 | 24.699 | 24.561 | 24.440 | 24.333 | 24.239 | 24.155 | 24.081 |
| 23.75    | 25.076 | 24.922 | 24.786 | 24.667 | 24.561 | 24.469 | 24.387 | 24.314 |
| 24       | 25.297 | 25.145 | 25.011 | 24.894 | 24.790 | 24.699 | 24.619 | 24.548 |
| 24.25    | 25.519 | 25.369 | 25.237 | 25.122 | 25.020 | 24.930 | 24.851 | 24.782 |
| 24.5     | 25.742 | 25.594 | 25.464 | 25.350 | 25.250 | 25.162 | 25.085 | 25.016 |
| 24.75    | 25.965 | 25.819 | 25.691 | 25.579 | 25.480 | 25.394 | 25.318 | 25.251 |
| 25       | 26.188 | 26.044 | 25.918 | 25.808 | 25.711 | 25.626 | 25.552 | 25.486 |

**Table A-1.** Constant Annual Percents Expressing the Sum of 12 Equal Monthly Payments Needed to Amortize a Principal Amount for the Term of Years Shown (*Continued*)

| %<br>Interest | Years | | | | | | | |
|---|---|---|---|---|---|---|---|---|
| | 16.5 | 17 | 17.5 | 18 | 18.5 | 19 | 19.5 | 20 |
| 8 | 10.934 | 10.779 | 10.635 | 10.500 | 10.373 | 10.254 | 10.142 | 10.037 |
| 8.25 | 11.112 | 10.958 | 10.815 | 10.682 | 10.556 | 10.439 | 10.328 | 10.225 |
| 8.5 | 11.291 | 11.140 | 10.998 | 10.866 | 10.742 | 10.625 | 10.516 | 10.414 |
| 8.75 | 11.472 | 11.322 | 11.182 | 11.051 | 10.928 | 10.813 | 10.706 | 10.605 |
| 9 | 11.655 | 11.506 | 11.367 | 11.237 | 11.116 | 11.003 | 10.897 | 10.797 |
| 9.25 | 11.838 | 11.691 | 11.554 | 11.426 | 11.306 | 11.194 | 11.089 | 10.990 |
| 9.5 | 12.023 | 11.877 | 11.742 | 11.615 | 11.497 | 11.386 | 11.283 | 11.186 |
| 9.75 | 12.210 | 12.065 | 11.931 | 11.806 | 11.689 | 11.580 | 11.478 | 11.382 |
| 10 | 12.397 | 12.255 | 12.122 | 11.998 | 11.883 | 11.775 | 11.675 | 11.580 |
| 10.25 | 12.586 | 12.445 | 12.314 | 12.192 | 12.078 | 11.972 | 11.872 | 11.780 |
| 10.5 | 12.777 | 12.637 | 12.507 | 12.387 | 12.274 | 12.170 | 12.072 | 11.981 |
| 10.75 | 12.968 | 12.830 | 12.702 | 12.583 | 12.472 | 12.369 | 12.273 | 12.183 |
| 11 | 13.161 | 13.025 | 12.898 | 12.781 | 12.671 | 12.570 | 12.475 | 12.386 |
| 11.25 | 13.355 | 13.220 | 13.095 | 12.979 | 12.872 | 12.771 | 12.678 | 12.591 |
| 11.5 | 13.550 | 13.417 | 13.294 | 13.180 | 13.073 | 12.975 | 12.883 | 12.797 |
| 11.75 | 13.747 | 13.615 | 13.494 | 13.381 | 13.276 | 13.179 | 13.089 | 13.005 |
| 12 | 13.944 | 13.815 | 13.695 | 13.583 | 13.480 | 13.385 | 13.296 | 13.213 |
| 12.25 | 14.143 | 14.015 | 13.897 | 13.787 | 13.686 | 13.591 | 13.504 | 13.423 |
| 12.5 | 14.343 | 14.217 | 14.100 | 13.992 | 13.892 | 13.799 | 13.713 | 13.634 |
| 12.75 | 14.544 | 14.419 | 14.304 | 14.198 | 14.100 | 14.009 | 13.924 | 13.846 |
| 13 | 14.746 | 14.623 | 14.510 | 14.405 | 14.308 | 14.219 | 14.136 | 14.059 |
| 13.25 | 14.950 | 14.828 | 14.717 | 14.613 | 14.518 | 14.430 | 14.349 | 14.273 |
| 13.5 | 15.154 | 15.034 | 14.924 | 14.823 | 14.729 | 14.643 | 14.562 | 14.488 |
| 13.75 | 15.359 | 15.242 | 15.133 | 15.033 | 14.941 | 14.856 | 14.777 | 14.705 |
| 14 | 15.566 | 15.450 | 15.343 | 15.245 | 15.154 | 15.071 | 14.993 | 14.922 |
| 14.25 | 15.773 | 15.659 | 15.554 | 15.457 | 15.368 | 15.286 | 15.210 | 15.141 |
| 14.5 | 15.982 | 15.869 | 15.766 | 15.671 | 15.583 | 15.503 | 15.428 | 15.360 |
| 14.75 | 16.191 | 16.080 | 15.978 | 15.885 | 15.799 | 15.720 | 15.647 | 15.580 |
| 15 | 16.402 | 16.292 | 16.192 | 16.100 | 16.016 | 15.938 | 15.867 | 15.801 |
| 15.25 | 16.613 | 16.506 | 16.407 | 16.317 | 16.234 | 16.158 | 16.088 | 16.024 |
| 15.5 | 16.826 | 16.720 | 16.623 | 16.534 | 16.453 | 16.378 | 16.309 | 16.247 |
| 15.75 | 17.039 | 16.934 | 16.839 | 16.752 | 16.672 | 16.599 | 16.532 | 16.470 |
| 16 | 17.253 | 17.150 | 17.057 | 16.971 | 16.893 | 16.821 | 16.755 | 16.695 |
| 16.25 | 17.468 | 17.367 | 17.275 | 17.191 | 17.114 | 17.044 | 16.979 | 16.921 |
| 16.5 | 17.684 | 17.585 | 17.494 | 17.412 | 17.336 | 17.267 | 17.204 | 17.147 |
| 16.75 | 17.901 | 17.803 | 17.714 | 17.633 | 17.559 | 17.492 | 17.430 | 17.374 |
| 17 | 18.118 | 18.022 | 17.935 | 17.855 | 17.783 | 17.717 | 17.657 | 17.602 |
| 17.25 | 18.336 | 18.242 | 18.156 | 18.078 | 18.007 | 17.943 | 17.884 | 17.830 |
| 17.5 | 18.556 | 18.463 | 18.379 | 18.302 | 18.233 | 18.169 | 18.112 | 18.059 |
| 17.75 | 18.776 | 18.685 | 18.602 | 18.527 | 18.459 | 18.397 | 18.341 | 18.289 |
| 18 | 18.996 | 18.907 | 18.826 | 18.752 | 18.686 | 18.625 | 18.570 | 18.520 |
| 18.25 | 19.218 | 19.130 | 19.050 | 18.978 | 18.913 | 18.854 | 18.800 | 18.751 |

| %<br>Interest | Years | | | | | | | |
|---|---|---|---|---|---|---|---|---|
| | 16.5 | 17 | 17.5 | 18 | 18.5 | 19 | 19.5 | 20 |
| 18.5 | 19.440 | 19.354 | 19.276 | 19.205 | 19.141 | 19.083 | 19.031 | 18.983 |
| 18.75 | 19.663 | 19.578 | 19.502 | 19.433 | 19.370 | 19.313 | 19.262 | 19.215 |
| 19 | 19.887 | 19.803 | 19.728 | 19.661 | 19.599 | 19.544 | 19.494 | 19.448 |
| 19.25 | 20.111 | 20.029 | 19.956 | 19.889 | 19.829 | 19.775 | 19.726 | 19.682 |
| 19.5 | 20.336 | 20.256 | 20.184 | 20.119 | 20.060 | 20.007 | 19.959 | 19.916 |
| 19.75 | 20.562 | 20.483 | 20.412 | 20.349 | 20.291 | 20.240 | 20.193 | 20.151 |
| 20 | 20.788 | 20.711 | 20.642 | 20.579 | 20.523 | 20.473 | 20.427 | 20.386 |
| 20.25 | 21.015 | 20.939 | 20.871 | 20.810 | 20.755 | 20.706 | 20.662 | 20.622 |
| 20.5 | 21.242 | 21.168 | 21.102 | 21.042 | 20.988 | 20.940 | 20.897 | 20.858 |
| 20.75 | 21.471 | 21.398 | 21.333 | 21.274 | 21.222 | 21.175 | 21.133 | 21.095 |
| 21 | 21.699 | 21.628 | 21.564 | 21.507 | 21.456 | 21.410 | 21.369 | 21.332 |
| 21.25 | 21.929 | 21.859 | 21.796 | 21.740 | 21.690 | 21.646 | 21.605 | 21.569 |
| 21.5 | 22.158 | 22.090 | 22.029 | 21.974 | 21.925 | 21.882 | 21.842 | 21.807 |
| 21.75 | 22.389 | 22.322 | 22.262 | 22.209 | 22.161 | 22.118 | 22.080 | 22.046 |
| 22 | 22.620 | 22.554 | 22.496 | 22.443 | 22.397 | 22.355 | 22.318 | 22.285 |
| 22.25 | 22.851 | 22.787 | 22.730 | 22.679 | 22.633 | 22.593 | 22.556 | 22.524 |
| 22.5 | 23.083 | 23.020 | 22.964 | 22.914 | 22.870 | 22.830 | 22.795 | 22.764 |
| 22.75 | 23.316 | 23.254 | 23.199 | 23.151 | 23.107 | 23.069 | 23.034 | 23.004 |
| 23 | 23.549 | 23.488 | 23.435 | 23.387 | 23.345 | 23.307 | 23.274 | 23.244 |
| 23.25 | 23.782 | 23.723 | 23.671 | 23.624 | 23.583 | 23.546 | 23.514 | 23.485 |
| 23.5 | 24.016 | 23.958 | 23.907 | 23.862 | 23.821 | 23.786 | 23.754 | 23.726 |
| 23.75 | 24.251 | 24.194 | 24.144 | 24.100 | 24.060 | 24.025 | 23.995 | 23.967 |
| 24 | 24.485 | 24.430 | 24.381 | 24.338 | 24.299 | 24.266 | 24.235 | 24.209 |
| 24.25 | 24.721 | 24.666 | 24.619 | 24.576 | 24.539 | 24.506 | 24.477 | 24.451 |
| 24.5 | 24.956 | 24.903 | 24.857 | 24.815 | 24.779 | 24.747 | 24.718 | 24.693 |
| 24.75 | 25.192 | 25.141 | 25.095 | 25.055 | 25.019 | 24.988 | 24.960 | 24.936 |
| 25 | 25.429 | 25.378 | 25.334 | 25.294 | 25.260 | 25.229 | 25.202 | 25.179 |

**Table A-1.** Constant Annual Percents Expressing the Sum of 12 Equal Monthly Payments Needed to Amortize a Principal Amount for the Term of Years Shown (*Continued*)

| %<br>Interest | 20.5 | 21 | 21.5 | 22 | 22.5 | 23 | 23.5 | 24 |
|---|---|---|---|---|---|---|---|---|
| 8 | 9.938 | 9.845 | 9.757 | 9.674 | 9.596 | 9.521 | 9.451 | 9.385 |
| 8.25 | 10.127 | 10.035 | 9.948 | 9.867 | 9.789 | 9.716 | 9.647 | 9.582 |
| 8.5 | 10.318 | 10.227 | 10.142 | 10.061 | 9.985 | 9.913 | 9.845 | 9.781 |
| 8.75 | 10.510 | 10.420 | 10.336 | 10.257 | 10.182 | 10.111 | 10.045 | 9.982 |
| 9 | 10.703 | 10.615 | 10.532 | 10.454 | 10.381 | 10.311 | 10.246 | 10.184 |
| 9.25 | 10.898 | 10.811 | 10.730 | 10.653 | 10.581 | 10.513 | 10.449 | 10.388 |
| 9.5 | 11.095 | 11.009 | 10.929 | 10.854 | 10.783 | 10.716 | 10.653 | 10.593 |
| 9.75 | 11.293 | 11.209 | 11.130 | 11.056 | 10.986 | 10.920 | 10.858 | 10.800 |
| 10 | 11.492 | 11.409 | 11.332 | 11.259 | 11.191 | 11.126 | 11.066 | 11.009 |
| 10.25 | 11.693 | 11.612 | 11.535 | 11.464 | 11.397 | 11.334 | 11.274 | 11.219 |
| 10.5 | 11.895 | 11.815 | 11.740 | 11.670 | 11.604 | 11.542 | 11.484 | 11.430 |
| 10.75 | 12.099 | 12.020 | 11.947 | 11.878 | 11.813 | 11.753 | 11.696 | 11.642 |
| 11 | 12.304 | 12.226 | 12.154 | 12.087 | 12.023 | 11.964 | 11.908 | 11.856 |
| 11.25 | 12.510 | 12.434 | 12.363 | 12.297 | 12.235 | 12.177 | 12.123 | 12.072 |
| 11.5 | 12.717 | 12.643 | 12.573 | 12.509 | 12.448 | 12.391 | 12.338 | 12.288 |
| 11.75 | 12.926 | 12.853 | 12.785 | 12.721 | 12.662 | 12.606 | 12.554 | 12.506 |
| 12 | 13.136 | 13.064 | 12.998 | 12.935 | 12.877 | 12.823 | 12.772 | 12.725 |
| 12.25 | 13.347 | 13.277 | 13.211 | 13.150 | 13.093 | 13.040 | 12.991 | 12.945 |
| 12.5 | 13.560 | 13.491 | 13.426 | 13.367 | 13.311 | 13.259 | 13.211 | 13.166 |
| 12.75 | 13.773 | 13.705 | 13.643 | 13.584 | 13.530 | 13.479 | 13.432 | 13.388 |
| 13 | 13.988 | 13.921 | 13.860 | 13.803 | 13.750 | 13.700 | 13.654 | 13.611 |
| 13.25 | 14.203 | 14.138 | 14.078 | 14.022 | 13.970 | 13.922 | 13.877 | 13.835 |
| 13.5 | 14.420 | 14.356 | 14.298 | 14.243 | 14.192 | 14.145 | 14.101 | 14.061 |
| 13.75 | 14.638 | 14.576 | 14.518 | 14.465 | 14.415 | 14.369 | 14.327 | 14.287 |
| 14 | 14.856 | 14.796 | 14.739 | 14.687 | 14.639 | 14.594 | 14.553 | 14.514 |
| 14.25 | 15.076 | 15.017 | 14.962 | 14.911 | 14.864 | 14.820 | 14.780 | 14.742 |
| 14.5 | 15.297 | 15.239 | 15.185 | 15.135 | 15.089 | 15.047 | 15.007 | 14.971 |
| 14.75 | 15.519 | 15.462 | 15.409 | 15.361 | 15.316 | 15.274 | 15.236 | 15.201 |
| 15 | 15.741 | 15.685 | 15.634 | 15.587 | 15.543 | 15.503 | 15.466 | 15.431 |
| 15.25 | 15.965 | 15.910 | 15.860 | 15.814 | 15.771 | 15.732 | 15.696 | 15.662 |
| 15.5 | 16.189 | 16.136 | 16.087 | 16.042 | 16.000 | 15.962 | 15.927 | 15.894 |
| 15.75 | 16.414 | 16.362 | 16.314 | 16.270 | 16.230 | 16.193 | 16.159 | 16.127 |
| 16 | 16.640 | 16.589 | 16.543 | 16.500 | 16.461 | 16.424 | 16.391 | 16.361 |
| 16.25 | 16.867 | 16.817 | 16.772 | 16.730 | 16.692 | 16.657 | 16.624 | 16.595 |
| 16.5 | 17.094 | 17.046 | 17.002 | 16.961 | 16.924 | 16.890 | 16.858 | 16.830 |
| 16.75 | 17.322 | 17.275 | 17.232 | 17.193 | 17.156 | 17.123 | 17.093 | 17.065 |
| 17 | 17.551 | 17.505 | 17.463 | 17.425 | 17.390 | 17.358 | 17.328 | 17.301 |
| 17.25 | 17.781 | 17.736 | 17.695 | 17.658 | 17.624 | 17.592 | 17.564 | 17.538 |
| 17.5 | 18.011 | 17.968 | 17.928 | 17.891 | 17.858 | 17.828 | 17.800 | 17.775 |
| 17.75 | 18.242 | 18.200 | 18.161 | 18.126 | 18.093 | 18.064 | 18.037 | 18.012 |
| 18 | 18.474 | 18.433 | 18.395 | 18.360 | 18.329 | 18.300 | 18.274 | 18.251 |
| 18.25 | 18.706 | 18.666 | 18.629 | 18.596 | 18.565 | 18.538 | 18.512 | 18.489 |

| %<br>Interest | Years | | | | | | | |
|---|---|---|---|---|---|---|---|---|
| | 20.5 | 21 | 21.5 | 22 | 22.5 | 23 | 23.5 | 24 |
| 18.5 | 18.939 | 18.900 | 18.864 | 18.832 | 18.802 | 18.775 | 18.751 | 18.729 |
| 18.75 | 19.173 | 19.135 | 19.100 | 19.068 | 19.039 | 19.013 | 18.990 | 18.968 |
| 19 | 19.407 | 19.370 | 19.336 | 19.305 | 19.277 | 19.252 | 19.229 | 19.208 |
| 19.25 | 19.642 | 19.605 | 19.572 | 19.543 | 19.516 | 19.491 | 19.469 | 19.449 |
| 19.5 | 19.877 | 19.842 | 19.810 | 19.781 | 19.754 | 19.731 | 19.709 | 19.690 |
| 19.75 | 20.113 | 20.078 | 20.047 | 20.019 | 19.994 | 19.971 | 19.950 | 19.931 |
| 20 | 20.349 | 20.315 | 20.285 | 20.258 | 20.233 | 20.211 | 20.191 | 20.173 |
| 20.25 | 20.586 | 20.553 | 20.524 | 20.497 | 20.473 | 20.452 | 20.432 | 20.415 |
| 20.5 | 20.823 | 20.791 | 20.763 | 20.737 | 20.714 | 20.693 | 20.674 | 20.657 |
| 20.75 | 21.060 | 21.030 | 21.002 | 20.977 | 20.955 | 20.934 | 20.916 | 20.900 |
| 21 | 21.298 | 21.269 | 21.242 | 21.218 | 21.196 | 21.176 | 21.159 | 21.143 |
| 21.25 | 21.537 | 21.508 | 21.482 | 21.458 | 21.437 | 21.419 | 21.402 | 21.386 |
| 21.5 | 21.776 | 21.748 | 21.722 | 21.700 | 21.679 | 21.661 | 21.645 | 21.630 |
| 21.75 | 22.015 | 21.988 | 21.963 | 21.941 | 21.922 | 21.904 | 21.888 | 21.874 |
| 22 | 22.255 | 22.228 | 22.205 | 22.183 | 22.164 | 22.147 | 22.132 | 22.118 |
| 22.25 | 22.495 | 22.469 | 22.446 | 22.426 | 22.407 | 22.391 | 22.376 | 22.363 |
| 22.5 | 22.736 | 22.710 | 22.688 | 22.668 | 22.650 | 22.634 | 22.620 | 22.607 |
| 22.75 | 22.976 | 22.952 | 22.930 | 22.911 | 22.894 | 22.878 | 22.865 | 22.852 |
| 23 | 23.217 | 23.194 | 23.173 | 23.154 | 23.137 | 23.123 | 23.109 | 23.097 |
| 23.25 | 23.459 | 23.436 | 23.416 | 23.398 | 23.381 | 23.367 | 23.354 | 23.343 |
| 23.5 | 23.701 | 23.679 | 23.659 | 23.641 | 23.626 | 23.612 | 23.599 | 23.588 |
| 23.75 | 23.943 | 23.921 | 23.902 | 23.885 | 23.870 | 23.857 | 23.845 | 23.834 |
| 24 | 24.185 | 24.164 | 24.146 | 24.129 | 24.115 | 24.102 | 24.090 | 24.080 |
| 24.25 | 24.428 | 24.408 | 24.390 | 24.374 | 24.360 | 24.347 | 24.336 | 24.326 |
| 24.5 | 24.671 | 24.651 | 24.634 | 24.619 | 24.605 | 24.593 | 24.582 | 24.573 |
| 24.75 | 24.914 | 24.895 | 24.878 | 24.863 | 24.850 | 24.839 | 24.828 | 24.819 |
| 25 | 25.158 | 25.139 | 25.123 | 25.109 | 25.096 | 25.085 | 25.075 | 25.066 |

**Table A-1.** Constant Annual Percents Expressing the Sum of 12 Equal Monthly Payments Needed to Amortize a Principal Amount for the Term of Years Shown (*Continued*)

| % Interest | 24.5 | 25 | 25.5 | 26 | 26.5 | 27 | 27.5 | 28 |
|---|---|---|---|---|---|---|---|---|
| 8 | 9.322 | 9.262 | 9.205 | 9.151 | 9.100 | 9.051 | 9.005 | 8.961 |
| 8.25 | 9.520 | 9.461 | 9.406 | 9.353 | 9.303 | 9.255 | 9.210 | 9.167 |
| 8.5 | 9.720 | 9.663 | 9.608 | 9.557 | 9.508 | 9.461 | 9.417 | 9.375 |
| 8.75 | 9.922 | 9.866 | 9.812 | 9.762 | 9.714 | 9.669 | 9.625 | 9.585 |
| 9 | 10.126 | 10.070 | 10.018 | 9.969 | 9.922 | 9.878 | 9.836 | 9.796 |
| 9.25 | 10.331 | 10.277 | 10.226 | 10.177 | 10.131 | 10.088 | 10.047 | 10.008 |
| 9.5 | 10.537 | 10.484 | 10.434 | 10.387 | 10.343 | 10.300 | 10.260 | 10.223 |
| 9.75 | 10.745 | 10.694 | 10.645 | 10.599 | 10.555 | 10.514 | 10.475 | 10.438 |
| 10 | 10.955 | 10.904 | 10.857 | 10.812 | 10.769 | 10.729 | 10.691 | 10.656 |
| 10.25 | 11.166 | 11.117 | 11.070 | 11.026 | 10.985 | 10.946 | 10.909 | 10.874 |
| 10.5 | 11.378 | 11.330 | 11.285 | 11.242 | 11.202 | 11.164 | 11.128 | 11.094 |
| 10.75 | 11.592 | 11.545 | 11.501 | 11.459 | 11.420 | 11.383 | 11.348 | 11.315 |
| 11 | 11.807 | 11.761 | 11.718 | 11.678 | 11.639 | 11.603 | 11.570 | 11.538 |
| 11.25 | 12.024 | 11.979 | 11.937 | 11.897 | 11.860 | 11.825 | 11.792 | 11.761 |
| 11.5 | 12.241 | 12.198 | 12.157 | 12.118 | 12.082 | 12.048 | 12.016 | 11.986 |
| 11.75 | 12.460 | 12.418 | 12.378 | 12.340 | 12.305 | 12.272 | 12.241 | 12.212 |
| 12 | 12.680 | 12.639 | 12.600 | 12.563 | 12.529 | 12.497 | 12.467 | 12.439 |
| 12.25 | 12.901 | 12.861 | 12.823 | 12.788 | 12.755 | 12.724 | 12.695 | 12.667 |
| 12.5 | 13.124 | 13.084 | 13.047 | 13.013 | 12.981 | 12.951 | 12.923 | 12.897 |
| 12.75 | 13.347 | 13.309 | 13.273 | 13.240 | 13.208 | 13.179 | 13.152 | 13.127 |
| 13 | 13.571 | 13.534 | 13.499 | 13.467 | 13.437 | 13.409 | 13.382 | 13.358 |
| 13.25 | 13.797 | 13.760 | 13.727 | 13.695 | 13.666 | 13.639 | 13.613 | 13.589 |
| 13.5 | 14.023 | 13.988 | 13.955 | 13.925 | 13.896 | 13.870 | 13.845 | 13.822 |
| 13.75 | 14.250 | 14.216 | 14.184 | 14.155 | 14.127 | 14.102 | 14.078 | 14.056 |
| 14 | 14.478 | 14.445 | 14.414 | 14.386 | 14.359 | 14.334 | 14.311 | 14.290 |
| 14.25 | 14.707 | 14.675 | 14.645 | 14.618 | 14.592 | 14.568 | 14.546 | 14.525 |
| 14.5 | 14.937 | 14.906 | 14.877 | 14.850 | 14.825 | 14.802 | 14.781 | 14.761 |
| 14.75 | 15.168 | 15.138 | 15.110 | 15.084 | 15.059 | 15.037 | 15.016 | 14.997 |
| 15 | 15.399 | 15.370 | 15.343 | 15.318 | 15.294 | 15.273 | 15.253 | 15.234 |
| 15.25 | 15.632 | 15.603 | 15.577 | 15.552 | 15.530 | 15.509 | 15.490 | 15.472 |
| 15.5 | 15.865 | 15.837 | 15.811 | 15.788 | 15.766 | 15.746 | 15.728 | 15.711 |
| 15.75 | 16.098 | 16.071 | 16.047 | 16.024 | 16.003 | 15.984 | 15.966 | 15.950 |
| 16 | 16.333 | 16.307 | 16.283 | 16.261 | 16.241 | 16.222 | 16.205 | 16.189 |
| 16.25 | 16.568 | 16.542 | 16.519 | 16.498 | 16.479 | 16.461 | 16.444 | 16.429 |
| 16.5 | 16.803 | 16.779 | 16.757 | 16.736 | 16.717 | 16.700 | 16.684 | 16.669 |
| 16.75 | 17.039 | 17.016 | 16.994 | 16.975 | 16.957 | 16.940 | 16.925 | 16.910 |
| 17 | 17.276 | 17.254 | 17.233 | 17.214 | 17.196 | 17.180 | 17.165 | 17.152 |
| 17.25 | 17.514 | 17.492 | 17.472 | 17.453 | 17.436 | 17.421 | 17.407 | 17.394 |
| 17.5 | 17.752 | 17.730 | 17.711 | 17.693 | 17.677 | 17.662 | 17.649 | 17.636 |
| 17.75 | 17.990 | 17.970 | 17.951 | 17.934 | 17.918 | 17.904 | 17.891 | 17.879 |
| 18 | 18.229 | 18.209 | 18.191 | 18.175 | 18.160 | 18.146 | 18.133 | 18.122 |
| 18.25 | 18.468 | 18.449 | 18.432 | 18.416 | 18.401 | 18.388 | 18.376 | 18.365 |

| %<br>Interest | Years | | | | | | | |
|---|---|---|---|---|---|---|---|---|
| | 24.5 | 25 | 25.5 | 26 | 26.5 | 27 | 27.5 | 28 |
| 18.5 | 18.708 | 18.690 | 18.673 | 18.658 | 18.644 | 18.631 | 18.619 | 18.609 |
| 18.75 | 18.949 | 18.931 | 18.915 | 18.900 | 18.886 | 18.874 | 18.863 | 18.853 |
| 19 | 19.189 | 19.172 | 19.157 | 19.142 | 19.129 | 19.118 | 19.107 | 19.097 |
| 19.25 | 19.431 | 19.414 | 19.399 | 19.385 | 19.373 | 19.362 | 19.351 | 19.342 |
| 19.5 | 19.672 | 19.656 | 19.642 | 19.628 | 19.617 | 19.606 | 19.596 | 19.587 |
| 19.75 | 19.914 | 19.899 | 19.885 | 19.872 | 19.861 | 19.850 | 19.841 | 19.832 |
| 20 | 20.156 | 20.141 | 20.128 | 20.116 | 20.105 | 20.095 | 20.086 | 20.078 |
| 20.25 | 20.399 | 20.385 | 20.372 | 20.360 | 20.349 | 20.340 | 20.331 | 20.323 |
| 20.5 | 20.642 | 20.628 | 20.616 | 20.604 | 20.594 | 20.585 | 20.577 | 20.569 |
| 20.75 | 20.885 | 20.872 | 20.860 | 20.849 | 20.839 | 20.831 | 20.823 | 20.816 |
| 21 | 21.129 | 21.116 | 21.104 | 21.094 | 21.085 | 21.076 | 21.069 | 21.062 |
| 21.25 | 21.373 | 21.360 | 21.349 | 21.339 | 21.330 | 21.322 | 21.315 | 21.308 |
| 21.5 | 21.617 | 21.605 | 21.594 | 21.585 | 21.576 | 21.568 | 21.561 | 21.555 |
| 21.75 | 21.861 | 21.850 | 21.840 | 21.830 | 21.822 | 21.815 | 21.808 | 21.802 |
| 22 | 22.106 | 22.095 | 22.085 | 22.076 | 22.068 | 22.061 | 22.055 | 22.049 |
| 22.25 | 22.351 | 22.340 | 22.331 | 22.322 | 22.315 | 22.308 | 22.302 | 22.296 |
| 22.5 | 22.596 | 22.586 | 22.577 | 22.569 | 22.561 | 22.555 | 22.549 | 22.544 |
| 22.75 | 22.841 | 22.832 | 22.823 | 22.815 | 22.808 | 22.802 | 22.796 | 22.791 |
| 23 | 23.087 | 23.078 | 23.069 | 23.062 | 23.055 | 23.049 | 23.044 | 23.039 |
| 23.25 | 23.333 | 23.324 | 23.316 | 23.309 | 23.302 | 23.296 | 23.291 | 23.287 |
| 23.5 | 23.579 | 23.570 | 23.562 | 23.555 | 23.549 | 23.544 | 23.539 | 23.535 |
| 23.75 | 23.825 | 23.817 | 23.809 | 23.803 | 23.797 | 23.792 | 23.787 | 23.783 |
| 24 | 24.071 | 24.063 | 24.056 | 24.050 | 24.044 | 24.039 | 24.035 | 24.031 |
| 24.25 | 24.318 | 24.310 | 24.303 | 24.297 | 24.292 | 24.287 | 24.283 | 24.279 |
| 24.5 | 24.565 | 24.557 | 24.551 | 24.545 | 24.540 | 24.535 | 24.531 | 24.528 |
| 24.75 | 24.811 | 24.804 | 24.798 | 24.792 | 24.788 | 24.783 | 24.779 | 24.776 |
| 25 | 25.058 | 25.052 | 25.046 | 25.040 | 25.036 | 25.031 | 25.028 | 25.025 |

**Table A-1.** Constant Annual Percents Expressing the Sum of 12 Equal Monthly Payments Needed to Amortize a Principal Amount for the Term of Years Shown (*Continued*)

| %<br>Interest | 28.5 | 29 | 29.5 | 30 | 30.5 | 31 | 31.5 | 32 |
|---|---|---|---|---|---|---|---|---|
| 8 | 8.919 | 8.879 | 8.841 | 8.805 | 8.771 | 8.738 | 8.706 | 8.676 |
| 8.25 | 9.126 | 9.087 | 9.050 | 9.015 | 8.982 | 8.950 | 8.919 | 8.890 |
| 8.5 | 9.335 | 9.297 | 9.261 | 9.227 | 9.194 | 9.163 | 9.134 | 9.106 |
| 8.75 | 9.546 | 9.509 | 9.474 | 9.440 | 9.409 | 9.379 | 9.350 | 9.323 |
| 9 | 9.758 | 9.722 | 9.688 | 9.656 | 9.625 | 9.596 | 9.568 | 9.541 |
| 9.25 | 9.972 | 9.937 | 9.904 | 9.872 | 9.842 | 9.814 | 9.787 | 9.762 |
| 9.5 | 10.187 | 10.153 | 10.121 | 10.090 | 10.061 | 10.034 | 10.008 | 9.983 |
| 9.75 | 10.404 | 10.371 | 10.339 | 10.310 | 10.282 | 10.255 | 10.230 | 10.206 |
| 10 | 10.622 | 10.590 | 10.560 | 10.531 | 10.504 | 10.478 | 10.454 | 10.431 |
| 10.25 | 10.841 | 10.810 | 10.781 | 10.753 | 10.727 | 10.702 | 10.679 | 10.657 |
| 10.5 | 11.062 | 11.032 | 11.004 | 10.977 | 10.952 | 10.928 | 10.905 | 10.884 |
| 10.75 | 11.284 | 11.255 | 11.228 | 11.202 | 11.177 | 11.154 | 11.132 | 11.112 |
| 11 | 11.508 | 11.480 | 11.453 | 11.428 | 11.404 | 11.382 | 11.361 | 11.341 |
| 11.25 | 11.732 | 11.705 | 11.679 | 11.655 | 11.632 | 11.611 | 11.591 | 11.572 |
| 11.5 | 11.958 | 11.932 | 11.907 | 11.884 | 11.862 | 11.841 | 11.821 | 11.803 |
| 11.75 | 12.185 | 12.160 | 12.135 | 12.113 | 12.092 | 12.072 | 12.053 | 12.035 |
| 12 | 12.413 | 12.388 | 12.365 | 12.343 | 12.323 | 12.304 | 12.286 | 12.269 |
| 12.25 | 12.642 | 12.618 | 12.596 | 12.575 | 12.555 | 12.537 | 12.519 | 12.503 |
| 12.5 | 12.872 | 12.849 | 12.827 | 12.807 | 12.788 | 12.770 | 12.754 | 12.738 |
| 12.75 | 13.103 | 13.081 | 13.060 | 13.040 | 13.022 | 13.005 | 12.989 | 12.974 |
| 13 | 13.335 | 13.313 | 13.293 | 13.274 | 13.257 | 13.241 | 13.225 | 13.211 |
| 13.25 | 13.567 | 13.547 | 13.527 | 13.509 | 13.492 | 13.477 | 13.462 | 13.448 |
| 13.5 | 13.801 | 13.781 | 13.762 | 13.745 | 13.729 | 13.714 | 13.700 | 13.686 |
| 13.75 | 14.035 | 14.016 | 13.998 | 13.981 | 13.966 | 13.951 | 13.938 | 13.925 |
| 14 | 14.270 | 14.252 | 14.234 | 14.218 | 14.204 | 14.190 | 14.177 | 14.165 |
| 14.25 | 14.506 | 14.488 | 14.472 | 14.456 | 14.442 | 14.429 | 14.416 | 14.405 |
| 14.5 | 14.742 | 14.725 | 14.709 | 14.695 | 14.681 | 14.668 | 14.656 | 14.645 |
| 14.75 | 14.980 | 14.963 | 14.948 | 14.934 | 14.921 | 14.908 | 14.897 | 14.887 |
| 15 | 15.217 | 15.202 | 15.187 | 15.173 | 15.161 | 15.149 | 15.138 | 15.128 |
| 15.25 | 15.456 | 15.441 | 15.427 | 15.414 | 15.401 | 15.390 | 15.380 | 15.370 |
| 15.5 | 15.695 | 15.680 | 15.667 | 15.654 | 15.643 | 15.632 | 15.622 | 15.613 |
| 15.75 | 15.934 | 15.920 | 15.907 | 15.895 | 15.884 | 15.874 | 15.865 | 15.856 |
| 16 | 16.174 | 16.161 | 16.149 | 16.137 | 16.127 | 16.117 | 16.108 | 16.100 |
| 16.25 | 16.415 | 16.402 | 16.390 | 16.379 | 16.369 | 16.360 | 16.351 | 16.343 |
| 16.5 | 16.656 | 16.644 | 16.632 | 16.622 | 16.612 | 16.603 | 16.595 | 16.588 |
| 16.75 | 16.898 | 16.886 | 16.875 | 16.865 | 16.856 | 16.847 | 16.839 | 16.832 |
| 17 | 17.140 | 17.128 | 17.118 | 17.108 | 17.099 | 17.091 | 17.084 | 17.077 |
| 17.25 | 17.382 | 17.371 | 17.361 | 17.352 | 17.343 | 17.336 | 17.329 | 17.322 |
| 17.5 | 17.625 | 17.614 | 17.605 | 17.596 | 17.588 | 17.581 | 17.574 | 17.568 |
| 17.75 | 17.868 | 17.858 | 17.849 | 17.840 | 17.833 | 17.826 | 17.819 | 17.813 |
| 18 | 18.111 | 18.102 | 18.093 | 18.085 | 18.078 | 18.071 | 18.065 | 18.059 |
| 18.25 | 18.355 | 18.346 | 18.338 | 18.330 | 18.323 | 18.317 | 18.311 | 18.306 |

| %  | Years | | | | | | | |
|---|---|---|---|---|---|---|---|---|
| Interest | 28.5 | 29 | 29.5 | 30 | 30.5 | 31 | 31.5 | 32 |
| 18.5 | 18.599 | 18.591 | 18.583 | 18.575 | 18.569 | 18.563 | 18.557 | 18.552 |
| 18.75 | 18.844 | 18.835 | 18.828 | 18.821 | 18.815 | 18.809 | 18.804 | 18.799 |
| 19 | 19.089 | 19.081 | 19.073 | 19.067 | 19.061 | 19.055 | 19.050 | 19.046 |
| 19.25 | 19.334 | 19.326 | 19.319 | 19.313 | 19.307 | 19.302 | 19.297 | 19.293 |
| 19.5 | 19.579 | 19.572 | 19.565 | 19.559 | 19.554 | 19.549 | 19.544 | 19.540 |
| 19.75 | 19.825 | 19.818 | 19.811 | 19.806 | 19.800 | 19.796 | 19.791 | 19.787 |
| 20 | 20.070 | 20.064 | 20.058 | 20.052 | 20.047 | 20.043 | 20.039 | 20.035 |
| 20.25 | 20.316 | 20.310 | 20.304 | 20.299 | 20.294 | 20.290 | 20.286 | 20.283 |
| 20.5 | 20.563 | 20.557 | 20.551 | 20.546 | 20.542 | 20.538 | 20.534 | 20.531 |
| 20.75 | 20.809 | 20.803 | 20.798 | 20.793 | 20.789 | 20.785 | 20.782 | 20.779 |
| 21 | 21.056 | 21.050 | 21.045 | 21.041 | 21.037 | 21.033 | 21.030 | 21.027 |
| 21.25 | 21.303 | 21.297 | 21.293 | 21.288 | 21.284 | 21.281 | 21.278 | 21.275 |
| 21.5 | 21.550 | 21.545 | 21.540 | 21.536 | 21.532 | 21.529 | 21.526 | 21.524 |
| 21.75 | 21.797 | 21.792 | 21.788 | 21.784 | 21.780 | 21.777 | 21.774 | 21.772 |
| 22 | 22.044 | 22.040 | 22.035 | 22.032 | 22.029 | 22.026 | 22.023 | 22.021 |
| 22.25 | 22.292 | 22.287 | 22.283 | 22.280 | 22.277 | 22.274 | 22.271 | 22.269 |
| 22.5 | 22.539 | 22.535 | 22.531 | 22.528 | 22.525 | 22.522 | 22.520 | 22.518 |
| 22.75 | 22.787 | 22.783 | 22.780 | 22.776 | 22.774 | 22.771 | 22.769 | 22.767 |
| 23 | 23.035 | 23.031 | 23.028 | 23.025 | 23.022 | 23.020 | 23.018 | 23.016 |
| 23.25 | 23.283 | 23.279 | 23.276 | 23.273 | 23.271 | 23.268 | 23.266 | 23.265 |
| 23.5 | 23.531 | 23.528 | 23.525 | 23.522 | 23.519 | 23.517 | 23.515 | 23.514 |
| 23.75 | 23.779 | 23.776 | 23.773 | 23.770 | 23.768 | 23.766 | 23.764 | 23.763 |
| 24 | 24.027 | 24.024 | 24.022 | 24.019 | 24.017 | 24.015 | 24.013 | 24.012 |
| 24.25 | 24.276 | 24.273 | 24.270 | 24.268 | 24.266 | 24.264 | 24.263 | 24.261 |
| 24.5 | 24.524 | 24.522 | 24.519 | 24.517 | 24.515 | 24.513 | 24.512 | 24.510 |
| 24.75 | 24.773 | 24.770 | 24.768 | 24.766 | 24.764 | 24.762 | 24.761 | 24.760 |
| 25 | 25.022 | 25.019 | 25.017 | 25.015 | 25.013 | 25.012 | 25.010 | 25.009 |

**Table A-1.** Constant Annual Percents Expressing the Sum of 12
Equal Monthly Payments Needed to Amortize a Principal Amount
for the Term of Years Shown (*Continued*)

| %<br>Interest | 32.5 | 33 | 33.5 | 34 | 34.5 | 35 | 35.5 | 36 |
|---|---|---|---|---|---|---|---|---|
| 8 | 8.648 | 8.621 | 8.595 | 8.570 | 8.546 | 8.523 | 8.501 | 8.481 |
| 8.25 | 8.862 | 8.836 | 8.811 | 8.787 | 8.764 | 8.742 | 8.721 | 8.701 |
| 8.5 | 9.079 | 9.053 | 9.029 | 9.006 | 8.983 | 8.962 | 8.942 | 8.923 |
| 8.75 | 9.297 | 9.272 | 9.249 | 9.226 | 9.205 | 9.184 | 9.165 | 9.146 |
| 9 | 9.516 | 9.492 | 9.470 | 9.448 | 9.428 | 9.408 | 9.389 | 9.372 |
| 9.25 | 9.737 | 9.714 | 9.692 | 9.672 | 9.652 | 9.633 | 9.615 | 9.598 |
| 9.5 | 9.960 | 9.938 | 9.917 | 9.896 | 9.877 | 9.859 | 9.842 | 9.826 |
| 9.75 | 10.184 | 10.162 | 10.142 | 10.123 | 10.104 | 10.087 | 10.071 | 10.055 |
| 10 | 10.409 | 10.388 | 10.369 | 10.350 | 10.333 | 10.316 | 10.300 | 10.285 |
| 10.25 | 10.636 | 10.616 | 10.597 | 10.579 | 10.562 | 10.546 | 10.531 | 10.517 |
| 10.5 | 10.863 | 10.844 | 10.826 | 10.809 | 10.793 | 10.778 | 10.763 | 10.749 |
| 10.75 | 11.092 | 11.074 | 11.057 | 11.040 | 11.025 | 11.010 | 10.996 | 10.983 |
| 11 | 11.322 | 11.305 | 11.288 | 11.272 | 11.258 | 11.243 | 11.230 | 11.218 |
| 11.25 | 11.554 | 11.537 | 11.521 | 11.506 | 11.491 | 11.478 | 11.465 | 11.453 |
| 11.5 | 11.786 | 11.769 | 11.754 | 11.740 | 11.726 | 11.713 | 11.701 | 11.690 |
| 11.75 | 12.019 | 12.003 | 11.989 | 11.975 | 11.962 | 11.950 | 11.938 | 11.927 |
| 12 | 12.253 | 12.238 | 12.224 | 12.211 | 12.198 | 12.187 | 12.176 | 12.165 |
| 12.25 | 12.488 | 12.473 | 12.460 | 12.447 | 12.436 | 12.424 | 12.414 | 12.404 |
| 12.5 | 12.724 | 12.710 | 12.697 | 12.685 | 12.674 | 12.663 | 12.653 | 12.644 |
| 12.75 | 12.960 | 12.947 | 12.935 | 12.923 | 12.912 | 12.902 | 12.893 | 12.884 |
| 13 | 13.197 | 13.185 | 13.173 | 13.162 | 13.152 | 13.142 | 13.133 | 13.125 |
| 13.25 | 13.435 | 13.424 | 13.412 | 13.402 | 13.392 | 13.383 | 13.374 | 13.366 |
| 13.5 | 13.674 | 13.663 | 13.652 | 13.642 | 13.633 | 13.624 | 13.616 | 13.608 |
| 13.75 | 13.914 | 13.903 | 13.892 | 13.883 | 13.874 | 13.866 | 13.858 | 13.851 |
| 14 | 14.154 | 14.143 | 14.133 | 14.124 | 14.116 | 14.108 | 14.101 | 14.094 |
| 14.25 | 14.394 | 14.384 | 14.375 | 14.366 | 14.358 | 14.351 | 14.344 | 14.337 |
| 14.5 | 14.635 | 14.626 | 14.617 | 14.609 | 14.601 | 14.594 | 14.587 | 14.581 |
| 14.75 | 14.877 | 14.868 | 14.859 | 14.852 | 14.844 | 14.838 | 14.831 | 14.826 |
| 15 | 15.119 | 15.110 | 15.102 | 15.095 | 15.088 | 15.082 | 15.076 | 15.070 |
| 15.25 | 15.362 | 15.353 | 15.346 | 15.339 | 15.332 | 15.326 | 15.321 | 15.315 |
| 15.5 | 15.605 | 15.597 | 15.590 | 15.583 | 15.577 | 15.571 | 15.566 | 15.561 |
| 15.75 | 15.848 | 15.841 | 15.834 | 15.827 | 15.822 | 15.816 | 15.811 | 15.807 |
| 16 | 16.092 | 16.085 | 16.078 | 16.072 | 16.067 | 16.062 | 16.057 | 16.053 |
| 16.25 | 16.336 | 16.329 | 16.323 | 16.317 | 16.312 | 16.307 | 16.303 | 16.299 |
| 16.5 | 16.581 | 16.574 | 16.568 | 16.563 | 16.558 | 16.553 | 16.549 | 16.545 |
| 16.75 | 16.826 | 16.819 | 16.814 | 16.809 | 16.804 | 16.800 | 16.796 | 16.792 |
| 17 | 17.071 | 17.065 | 17.060 | 17.055 | 17.050 | 17.046 | 17.043 | 17.039 |
| 17.25 | 17.316 | 17.311 | 17.306 | 17.301 | 17.297 | 17.293 | 17.290 | 17.286 |
| 17.5 | 17.562 | 17.557 | 17.552 | 17.548 | 17.544 | 17.540 | 17.537 | 17.534 |
| 17.75 | 17.808 | 17.803 | 17.799 | 17.795 | 17.791 | 17.787 | 17.784 | 17.781 |
| 18 | 18.054 | 18.050 | 18.045 | 18.042 | 18.038 | 18.035 | 18.032 | 18.029 |
| 18.25 | 18.301 | 18.296 | 18.292 | 18.289 | 18.285 | 18.282 | 18.279 | 18.277 |

| % Interest | Years | | | | | | | |
|---|---|---|---|---|---|---|---|---|
| | 32.5 | 33 | 33.5 | 34 | 34.5 | 35 | 35.5 | 36 |
| 18.5 | 18.548 | 18.543 | 18.540 | 18.536 | 18.533 | 18.530 | 18.527 | 18.525 |
| 18.75 | 18.794 | 18.790 | 18.787 | 18.784 | 18.781 | 18.778 | 18.775 | 18.773 |
| 19 | 19.042 | 19.038 | 19.034 | 19.031 | 19.028 | 19.026 | 19.024 | 19.021 |
| 19.25 | 19.289 | 19.285 | 19.282 | 19.279 | 19.277 | 19.274 | 19.272 | 19.270 |
| 19.5 | 19.536 | 19.533 | 19.530 | 19.527 | 19.525 | 19.522 | 19.520 | 19.518 |
| 19.75 | 19.784 | 19.781 | 19.778 | 19.775 | 19.773 | 19.771 | 19.769 | 19.767 |
| 20 | 20.032 | 20.029 | 20.026 | 20.024 | 20.021 | 20.019 | 20.017 | 20.016 |
| 20.25 | 20.280 | 20.277 | 20.274 | 20.272 | 20.270 | 20.268 | 20.266 | 20.265 |
| 20.5 | 20.528 | 20.525 | 20.523 | 20.520 | 20.518 | 20.517 | 20.515 | 20.514 |
| 20.75 | 20.776 | 20.773 | 20.771 | 20.769 | 20.767 | 20.765 | 20.764 | 20.763 |
| 21 | 21.024 | 21.022 | 21.020 | 21.018 | 21.016 | 21.014 | 21.013 | 21.012 |
| 21.25 | 21.273 | 21.270 | 21.268 | 21.266 | 21.265 | 21.263 | 21.262 | 21.261 |
| 21.5 | 21.521 | 21.519 | 21.517 | 21.515 | 21.514 | 21.512 | 21.511 | 21.510 |
| 21.75 | 21.770 | 21.768 | 21.766 | 21.764 | 21.763 | 21.762 | 21.760 | 21.759 |
| 22 | 22.018 | 22.017 | 22.015 | 22.013 | 22.012 | 22.011 | 22.010 | 22.009 |
| 22.25 | 22.267 | 22.265 | 22.264 | 22.262 | 22.261 | 22.260 | 22.259 | 22.258 |
| 22.5 | 22.516 | 22.514 | 22.513 | 22.511 | 22.510 | 22.509 | 22.508 | 22.507 |
| 22.75 | 22.765 | 22.763 | 22.762 | 22.761 | 22.760 | 22.759 | 22.758 | 22.757 |
| 23 | 23.014 | 23.012 | 23.011 | 23.010 | 23.009 | 23.008 | 23.007 | 23.006 |
| 23.25 | 23.263 | 23.262 | 23.260 | 23.259 | 23.258 | 23.257 | 23.257 | 23.256 |
| 23.5 | 23.512 | 23.511 | 23.510 | 23.509 | 23.508 | 23.507 | 23.506 | 23.505 |
| 23.75 | 23.761 | 23.760 | 23.759 | 23.758 | 23.757 | 23.756 | 23.756 | 23.755 |
| 24 | 24.011 | 24.009 | 24.008 | 24.007 | 24.007 | 24.006 | 24.005 | 24.005 |
| 24.25 | 24.260 | 24.259 | 24.258 | 24.257 | 24.256 | 24.255 | 24.255 | 24.254 |
| 24.5 | 24.509 | 24.508 | 24.507 | 24.506 | 24.506 | 24.505 | 24.504 | 24.504 |
| 24.75 | 24.759 | 24.758 | 24.757 | 24.756 | 24.755 | 24.755 | 24.754 | 24.754 |
| 25 | 25.008 | 25.007 | 25.006 | 25.006 | 25.005 | 25.004 | 25.004 | 25.003 |

**Table A-1.** Constant Annual Percents Expressing the Sum of 12 Equal Monthly Payments Needed to Amortize a Principal Amount for the Term of Years Shown (*Continued*)

| %<br>Interest | Years | | | | | | | |
|---|---|---|---|---|---|---|---|---|
| | 36.5 | 37 | 37.5 | 38 | 38.5 | 39 | 39.5 | 40 |
| 8 | 8.461 | 8.442 | 8.424 | 8.406 | 8.390 | 8.374 | 8.358 | 8.344 |
| 8.25 | 8.682 | 8.664 | 8.646 | 8.629 | 8.613 | 8.598 | 8.584 | 8.570 |
| 8.5 | 8.905 | 8.887 | 8.870 | 8.854 | 8.839 | 8.824 | 8.810 | 8.797 |
| 8.75 | 9.129 | 9.112 | 9.096 | 9.081 | 9.066 | 9.052 | 9.039 | 9.026 |
| 9 | 9.355 | 9.338 | 9.323 | 9.308 | 9.294 | 9.281 | 9.268 | 9.256 |
| 9.25 | 9.582 | 9.566 | 9.552 | 9.538 | 9.524 | 9.512 | 9.499 | 9.488 |
| 9.5 | 9.810 | 9.795 | 9.781 | 9.768 | 9.755 | 9.743 | 9.732 | 9.721 |
| 9.75 | 10.040 | 10.026 | 10.012 | 10.000 | 9.988 | 9.976 | 9.965 | 9.955 |
| 10 | 10.271 | 10.258 | 10.245 | 10.233 | 10.221 | 10.210 | 10.200 | 10.190 |
| 10.25 | 10.503 | 10.490 | 10.478 | 10.466 | 10.455 | 10.445 | 10.435 | 10.426 |
| 10.5 | 10.736 | 10.724 | 10.712 | 10.701 | 10.691 | 10.681 | 10.672 | 10.663 |
| 10.75 | 10.971 | 10.959 | 10.948 | 10.937 | 10.927 | 10.918 | 10.909 | 10.901 |
| 11 | 11.206 | 11.195 | 11.184 | 11.174 | 11.165 | 11.156 | 11.147 | 11.140 |
| 11.25 | 11.442 | 11.431 | 11.421 | 11.412 | 11.403 | 11.395 | 11.387 | 11.379 |
| 11.5 | 11.679 | 11.669 | 11.659 | 11.651 | 11.642 | 11.634 | 11.627 | 11.619 |
| 11.75 | 11.917 | 11.907 | 11.898 | 11.890 | 11.882 | 11.874 | 11.867 | 11.860 |
| 12 | 12.156 | 12.146 | 12.138 | 12.130 | 12.122 | 12.115 | 12.108 | 12.102 |
| 12.25 | 12.395 | 12.386 | 12.378 | 12.370 | 12.363 | 12.357 | 12.350 | 12.344 |
| 12.5 | 12.635 | 12.627 | 12.619 | 12.612 | 12.605 | 12.599 | 12.593 | 12.587 |
| 12.75 | 12.876 | 12.868 | 12.861 | 12.854 | 12.847 | 12.841 | 12.836 | 12.830 |
| 13 | 13.117 | 13.110 | 13.103 | 13.096 | 13.090 | 13.084 | 13.079 | 13.074 |
| 13.25 | 13.359 | 13.352 | 13.345 | 13.339 | 13.333 | 13.328 | 13.323 | 13.318 |
| 13.5 | 13.601 | 13.595 | 13.588 | 13.583 | 13.577 | 13.572 | 13.568 | 13.563 |
| 13.75 | 13.844 | 13.838 | 13.832 | 13.827 | 13.822 | 13.817 | 13.812 | 13.808 |
| 14 | 14.088 | 14.082 | 14.076 | 14.071 | 14.066 | 14.062 | 14.058 | 14.054 |
| 14.25 | 14.331 | 14.326 | 14.321 | 14.316 | 14.311 | 14.307 | 14.303 | 14.299 |
| 14.5 | 14.576 | 14.570 | 14.565 | 14.561 | 14.557 | 14.553 | 14.549 | 14.546 |
| 14.75 | 14.820 | 14.815 | 14.811 | 14.806 | 14.802 | 14.799 | 14.795 | 14.792 |
| 15 | 15.065 | 15.061 | 15.056 | 15.052 | 15.048 | 15.045 | 15.042 | 15.039 |
| 15.25 | 15.311 | 15.306 | 15.302 | 15.298 | 15.295 | 15.291 | 15.288 | 15.286 |
| 15.5 | 15.556 | 15.552 | 15.548 | 15.545 | 15.541 | 15.538 | 15.535 | 15.533 |
| 15.75 | 15.802 | 15.798 | 15.795 | 15.791 | 15.788 | 15.785 | 15.783 | 15.780 |
| 16 | 16.049 | 16.045 | 16.041 | 16.038 | 16.035 | 16.033 | 16.030 | 16.028 |
| 16.25 | 16.295 | 16.292 | 16.288 | 16.285 | 16.283 | 16.280 | 16.278 | 16.276 |
| 16.5 | 16.542 | 16.538 | 16.535 | 16.533 | 16.530 | 16.528 | 16.526 | 16.524 |
| 16.75 | 16.789 | 16.786 | 16.783 | 16.780 | 16.778 | 16.776 | 16.773 | 16.772 |
| 17 | 17.036 | 17.033 | 17.030 | 17.028 | 17.026 | 17.024 | 17.022 | 17.020 |
| 17.25 | 17.283 | 17.281 | 17.278 | 17.276 | 17.274 | 17.272 | 17.270 | 17.268 |
| 17.5 | 17.531 | 17.528 | 17.526 | 17.524 | 17.522 | 17.520 | 17.518 | 17.517 |
| 17.75 | 17.779 | 17.776 | 17.774 | 17.772 | 17.770 | 17.768 | 17.767 | 17.765 |
| 18 | 18.027 | 18.024 | 18.022 | 18.020 | 18.019 | 18.017 | 18.016 | 18.014 |
| 18.25 | 18.275 | 18.272 | 18.270 | 18.269 | 18.267 | 18.266 | 18.264 | 18.263 |

| %<br>Interest | Years | | | | | | | |
|---|---|---|---|---|---|---|---|---|
| | 36.5 | 37 | 37.5 | 38 | 38.5 | 39 | 39.5 | 40 |
| 18.5 | 18.523 | 18.521 | 18.519 | 18.517 | 18.516 | 18.514 | 18.513 | 18.512 |
| 18.75 | 18.771 | 18.769 | 18.768 | 18.766 | 18.765 | 18.763 | 18.762 | 18.761 |
| 19 | 19.020 | 19.018 | 19.016 | 19.015 | 19.013 | 19.012 | 19.011 | 19.010 |
| 19.25 | 19.268 | 19.266 | 19.265 | 19.264 | 19.262 | 19.261 | 19.260 | 19.259 |
| 19.5 | 19.517 | 19.515 | 19.514 | 19.513 | 19.511 | 19.510 | 19.509 | 19.508 |
| 19.75 | 19.766 | 19.764 | 19.763 | 19.762 | 19.760 | 19.759 | 19.759 | 19.758 |
| 20 | 20.014 | 20.013 | 20.012 | 20.011 | 20.010 | 20.009 | 20.008 | 20.007 |
| 20.25 | 20.263 | 20.262 | 20.261 | 20.260 | 20.259 | 20.258 | 20.257 | 20.257 |
| 20.5 | 20.512 | 20.511 | 20.510 | 20.509 | 20.508 | 20.507 | 20.507 | 20.506 |
| 20.75 | 20.761 | 20.760 | 20.759 | 20.758 | 20.758 | 20.757 | 20.756 | 20.756 |
| 21 | 21.011 | 21.009 | 21.009 | 21.008 | 21.007 | 21.006 | 21.006 | 21.005 |
| 21.25 | 21.260 | 21.259 | 21.258 | 21.257 | 21.256 | 21.256 | 21.255 | 21.255 |
| 21.5 | 21.509 | 21.508 | 21.507 | 21.507 | 21.506 | 21.505 | 21.505 | 21.504 |
| 21.75 | 21.758 | 21.757 | 21.757 | 21.756 | 21.755 | 21.755 | 21.754 | 21.754 |
| 22 | 22.008 | 22.007 | 22.006 | 22.006 | 22.005 | 22.004 | 22.004 | 22.004 |
| 22.25 | 22.257 | 22.256 | 22.256 | 22.255 | 22.255 | 22.254 | 22.254 | 22.253 |
| 22.5 | 22.507 | 22.506 | 22.505 | 22.505 | 22.504 | 22.504 | 22.503 | 22.503 |
| 22.75 | 22.756 | 22.755 | 22.755 | 22.754 | 22.754 | 22.753 | 22.753 | 22.753 |
| 23 | 23.006 | 23.005 | 23.004 | 23.004 | 23.004 | 23.003 | 23.003 | 23.003 |
| 23.25 | 23.255 | 23.255 | 23.254 | 23.254 | 23.253 | 23.253 | 23.253 | 23.252 |
| 23.5 | 23.505 | 23.504 | 23.504 | 23.503 | 23.503 | 23.503 | 23.502 | 23.502 |
| 23.75 | 23.754 | 23.754 | 23.753 | 23.753 | 23.753 | 23.752 | 23.752 | 23.752 |
| 24 | 24.004 | 24.004 | 24.003 | 24.003 | 24.003 | 24.002 | 24.002 | 24.002 |
| 24.25 | 24.254 | 24.253 | 24.253 | 24.253 | 24.252 | 24.252 | 24.252 | 24.252 |
| 24.5 | 24.503 | 24.503 | 24.503 | 24.502 | 24.502 | 24.502 | 24.502 | 24.501 |
| 24.75 | 24.753 | 24.753 | 24.753 | 24.752 | 24.752 | 24.752 | 24.752 | 24.751 |
| 25 | 25.003 | 25.003 | 25.002 | 25.002 | 25.002 | 25.002 | 25.001 | 25.001 |

**Table A-2.** Constant Annual Percents for Loans with Annual Payments
To Be Used Only in the Event of 1 Payment Made Annually or Semiannually

| % Interest | Years | | | | | | | | | | | | | | | |
|---|---|---|---|---|---|---|---|---|---|---|---|---|---|---|---|---|
| | 1 | 1.5 | 2 | 2.5 | 3 | 3.5 | 4 | 4.5 | 5 | 5.5 | 6 | 6.5 | 7 | 7.5 | 8 | 8.5 |
| 6 | 106.001 | 71.692 | 54.544 | 44.261 | 37.411 | 32.522 | 28.859 | 26.014 | 23.740 | 21.882 | 20.336 | 19.031 | 17.914 | 16.947 | 16.104 | 15.361 |
| 6.25 | 106.250 | 71.901 | 54.735 | 44.441 | 37.584 | 32.691 | 29.025 | 26.177 | 23.901 | 22.043 | 20.496 | 19.190 | 18.073 | 17.107 | 16.263 | 15.521 |
| 6.5 | 106.501 | 72.112 | 54.926 | 44.622 | 37.758 | 32.860 | 29.190 | 26.340 | 24.064 | 22.204 | 20.657 | 19.351 | 18.233 | 17.267 | 16.424 | 15.682 |
| 6.75 | 106.751 | 72.323 | 55.118 | 44.803 | 37.932 | 33.029 | 29.357 | 26.504 | 24.226 | 22.366 | 20.818 | 19.511 | 18.394 | 17.428 | 16.585 | 15.843 |
| 7 | 107.001 | 72.533 | 55.309 | 44.983 | 38.105 | 33.198 | 29.523 | 26.669 | 24.389 | 22.528 | 20.980 | 19.673 | 18.555 | 17.590 | 16.747 | 16.006 |
| 7.25 | 107.251 | 72.744 | 55.501 | 45.164 | 38.280 | 33.368 | 29.690 | 26.834 | 24.553 | 22.690 | 21.142 | 19.835 | 18.718 | 17.752 | 16.910 | 16.169 |
| 7.5 | 107.500 | 72.954 | 55.693 | 45.345 | 38.454 | 33.538 | 29.857 | 26.999 | 24.717 | 22.853 | 21.305 | 19.997 | 18.880 | 17.915 | 17.073 | 16.332 |
| 7.75 | 107.751 | 73.166 | 55.885 | 45.526 | 38.629 | 33.709 | 30.024 | 27.164 | 24.881 | 23.017 | 21.468 | 20.161 | 19.043 | 18.078 | 17.237 | 16.497 |
| 8 | 108.000 | 73.376 | 56.077 | 45.708 | 38.803 | 33.879 | 30.192 | 27.330 | 25.046 | 23.181 | 21.632 | 20.324 | 19.207 | 18.243 | 17.401 | 16.662 |
| 8.25 | 108.251 | 73.588 | 56.270 | 45.890 | 38.979 | 34.050 | 30.360 | 27.497 | 25.211 | 23.346 | 21.796 | 20.489 | 19.372 | 18.408 | 17.567 | 16.828 |
| 8.5 | 108.501 | 73.799 | 56.462 | 46.072 | 39.154 | 34.221 | 30.529 | 27.664 | 25.377 | 23.511 | 21.961 | 20.654 | 19.537 | 18.573 | 17.733 | 16.995 |
| 8.75 | 108.750 | 74.010 | 56.654 | 46.254 | 39.330 | 34.393 | 30.698 | 27.831 | 25.543 | 23.676 | 22.126 | 20.819 | 19.703 | 18.739 | 17.900 | 17.163 |
| 9 | 109.001 | 74.221 | 56.847 | 46.436 | 39.506 | 34.565 | 30.867 | 27.998 | 25.709 | 23.843 | 22.292 | 20.985 | 19.869 | 18.906 | 18.068 | 17.331 |
| 9.25 | 109.250 | 74.432 | 57.040 | 46.618 | 39.682 | 34.737 | 31.036 | 28.166 | 25.876 | 24.009 | 22.458 | 21.152 | 20.036 | 19.074 | 18.236 | 17.500 |
| 9.5 | 109.501 | 74.644 | 57.233 | 46.801 | 39.858 | 34.909 | 31.206 | 28.334 | 26.044 | 24.176 | 22.625 | 21.319 | 20.204 | 19.242 | 18.405 | 17.670 |
| 9.75 | 109.750 | 74.855 | 57.426 | 46.984 | 40.035 | 35.082 | 31.377 | 28.503 | 26.211 | 24.343 | 22.793 | 21.486 | 20.372 | 19.411 | 18.574 | 17.840 |
| 10 | 110.001 | 75.067 | 57.619 | 47.167 | 40.212 | 35.255 | 31.547 | 28.672 | 26.380 | 24.511 | 22.961 | 21.655 | 20.541 | 19.580 | 18.744 | 18.012 |
| 10.25 | 110.250 | 75.278 | 57.812 | 47.350 | 40.389 | 35.428 | 31.718 | 28.841 | 26.548 | 24.680 | 23.129 | 21.823 | 20.710 | 19.750 | 18.915 | 18.183 |

**Table A-2.** Constant Annual Percents for Loans with Annual Payments (Continued)

To Be Used Only in the Event of 1 Payment Made Annually or Semiannually

| % Interest | Years | | | | | | | | | | | | | | | |
|---|---|---|---|---|---|---|---|---|---|---|---|---|---|---|---|---|
| | 9 | 9.5 | 10 | 10.5 | 11 | 11.5 | 12 | 12.5 | 13 | 13.5 | 14 | 14.5 | 15 | 15.5 | 16 | 16.5 |
| 6 | 14.702 | 14.115 | 13.587 | 13.111 | 12.679 | 12.287 | 11.928 | 11.599 | 11.296 | 11.017 | 10.759 | 10.519 | 10.296 | 10.089 | 9.895 | 9.714 |
| 6.25 | 14.863 | 14.275 | 13.748 | 13.273 | 12.842 | 12.450 | 12.092 | 11.763 | 11.462 | 11.183 | 10.926 | 10.687 | 10.465 | 10.259 | 10.066 | 9.886 |
| 6.5 | 15.024 | 14.437 | 13.911 | 13.436 | 13.006 | 12.614 | 12.257 | 11.929 | 11.628 | 11.351 | 11.094 | 10.856 | 10.635 | 10.430 | 10.238 | 10.059 |
| 6.75 | 15.186 | 14.600 | 14.074 | 13.600 | 13.170 | 12.780 | 12.423 | 12.096 | 11.796 | 11.519 | 11.264 | 11.027 | 10.807 | 10.602 | 10.411 | 10.233 |
| 7 | 15.349 | 14.763 | 14.238 | 13.764 | 13.336 | 12.946 | 12.590 | 12.264 | 11.965 | 11.689 | 11.435 | 11.199 | 10.979 | 10.776 | 10.586 | 10.408 |
| 7.25 | 15.512 | 14.927 | 14.403 | 13.930 | 13.502 | 13.113 | 12.759 | 12.434 | 12.135 | 11.860 | 11.607 | 11.372 | 11.154 | 10.951 | 10.762 | 10.586 |
| 7.5 | 15.677 | 15.092 | 14.569 | 14.097 | 13.670 | 13.282 | 12.928 | 12.604 | 12.306 | 12.033 | 11.780 | 11.546 | 11.329 | 11.127 | 10.939 | 10.764 |
| 7.75 | 15.842 | 15.258 | 14.735 | 14.264 | 13.838 | 13.451 | 13.098 | 12.775 | 12.479 | 12.206 | 11.954 | 11.721 | 11.505 | 11.305 | 11.118 | 10.944 |
| 8 | 16.008 | 15.425 | 14.903 | 14.433 | 14.008 | 13.621 | 13.270 | 12.948 | 12.652 | 12.380 | 12.130 | 11.898 | 11.683 | 11.483 | 11.298 | 11.125 |
| 8.25 | 16.175 | 15.593 | 15.071 | 14.602 | 14.178 | 13.793 | 13.442 | 13.121 | 12.827 | 12.556 | 12.306 | 12.076 | 11.862 | 11.663 | 11.479 | 11.307 |
| 8.5 | 16.342 | 15.761 | 15.241 | 14.773 | 14.349 | 13.965 | 13.615 | 13.296 | 13.002 | 12.733 | 12.484 | 12.255 | 12.042 | 11.845 | 11.661 | 11.491 |
| 8.75 | 16.511 | 15.930 | 15.411 | 14.944 | 14.522 | 14.139 | 13.790 | 13.471 | 13.179 | 12.911 | 12.663 | 12.435 | 12.223 | 12.027 | 11.845 | 11.675 |
| 9 | 16.680 | 16.101 | 15.582 | 15.116 | 14.695 | 14.313 | 13.965 | 13.648 | 13.357 | 13.089 | 12.843 | 12.616 | 12.406 | 12.211 | 12.030 | 11.862 |
| 9.25 | 16.850 | 16.271 | 15.754 | 15.285 | 14.869 | 14.488 | 14.141 | 13.825 | 13.535 | 13.269 | 13.025 | 12.799 | 12.590 | 12.396 | 12.216 | 12.049 |
| 9.5 | 17.021 | 16.443 | 15.927 | 15.463 | 15.044 | 14.664 | 14.319 | 14.004 | 13.715 | 13.450 | 13.207 | 12.982 | 12.774 | 12.582 | 12.404 | 12.238 |
| 9.75 | 17.192 | 16.615 | 16.100 | 15.637 | 15.220 | 14.841 | 14.497 | 14.183 | 13.896 | 13.633 | 13.390 | 13.167 | 12.960 | 12.769 | 12.592 | 12.427 |
| 10 | 17.364 | 16.789 | 16.275 | 15.813 | 15.396 | 15.019 | 14.676 | 14.364 | 14.078 | 13.816 | 13.575 | 13.353 | 13.147 | 12.958 | 12.782 | 12.618 |
| 10.25 | 17.537 | 16.963 | 16.450 | 15.989 | 15.574 | 15.198 | 14.857 | 14.545 | 14.261 | 14.000 | 13.760 | 13.539 | 13.336 | 13.147 | 12.972 | 12.810 |

**Table A-2.** Constant Annual Percents for Loans with Annual Payments (*Continued*)

To Be Used Only in the Event of 1 Payment Made Annually or Semiannually

| % Interest | | | | | | | | | Years | | | | | | | |
|---|---|---|---|---|---|---|---|---|---|---|---|---|---|---|---|---|
| | 17 | 17.5 | 18 | 18.5 | 19 | 19.5 | 20 | 20.5 | 21 | 21.5 | 22 | 22.5 | 23 | 23.5 | 24 | 24.5 |
| 6 | 9.545 | 9.385 | 9.236 | 9.095 | 8.962 | 8.837 | 8.718 | 8.607 | 8.500 | 8.400 | 8.305 | 8.214 | 8.128 | 8.046 | 7.968 | 7.894 |
| 6.25 | 9.717 | 9.559 | 9.410 | 9.270 | 9.138 | 9.014 | 8.896 | 8.785 | 8.680 | 8.580 | 8.486 | 8.396 | 8.311 | 8.230 | 8.153 | 8.079 |
| 6.5 | 9.891 | 9.733 | 9.585 | 9.446 | 9.316 | 9.192 | 9.076 | 8.966 | 8.861 | 8.763 | 8.669 | 8.580 | 8.496 | 8.416 | 8.340 | 8.267 |
| 6.75 | 10.066 | 9.910 | 9.763 | 9.625 | 9.495 | 9.372 | 9.257 | 9.148 | 9.044 | 8.947 | 8.854 | 8.766 | 8.683 | 8.604 | 8.528 | 8.457 |
| 7 | 10.243 | 10.087 | 9.941 | 9.804 | 9.675 | 9.554 | 9.439 | 9.331 | 9.229 | 9.132 | 9.041 | 8.954 | 8.871 | 8.793 | 8.719 | 8.648 |
| 7.25 | 10.421 | 10.266 | 10.121 | 9.985 | 9.857 | 9.737 | 9.624 | 9.516 | 9.415 | 9.319 | 9.229 | 9.143 | 9.062 | 8.984 | 8.911 | 8.841 |
| 7.5 | 10.600 | 10.447 | 10.303 | 10.168 | 10.041 | 9.922 | 9.809 | 9.703 | 9.603 | 9.508 | 9.419 | 9.334 | 9.254 | 9.177 | 9.105 | 9.036 |
| 7.75 | 10.781 | 10.629 | 10.486 | 10.352 | 10.226 | 10.108 | 9.997 | 9.891 | 9.792 | 9.699 | 9.610 | 9.526 | 9.447 | 9.372 | 9.301 | 9.233 |
| 8 | 10.963 | 10.812 | 10.670 | 10.537 | 10.413 | 10.296 | 10.185 | 10.081 | 9.983 | 9.891 | 9.803 | 9.721 | 9.642 | 9.568 | 9.498 | 9.431 |
| 8.25 | 11.146 | 10.996 | 10.856 | 10.724 | 10.601 | 10.485 | 10.375 | 10.273 | 10.176 | 10.084 | 9.998 | 9.916 | 9.839 | 9.766 | 9.697 | 9.631 |
| 8.5 | 11.331 | 11.182 | 11.043 | 10.913 | 10.790 | 10.675 | 10.567 | 10.465 | 10.370 | 10.279 | 10.194 | 10.113 | 10.037 | 9.965 | 9.897 | 9.832 |
| 8.75 | 11.517 | 11.370 | 11.231 | 11.102 | 10.981 | 10.867 | 10.760 | 10.660 | 10.565 | 10.476 | 10.391 | 10.312 | 10.237 | 10.166 | 10.099 | 10.035 |
| 9 | 11.705 | 11.558 | 11.421 | 11.293 | 11.173 | 11.060 | 10.955 | 10.855 | 10.762 | 10.674 | 10.591 | 10.512 | 10.438 | 10.368 | 10.302 | 10.240 |
| 9.25 | 11.893 | 11.748 | 11.612 | 11.485 | 11.367 | 11.255 | 11.150 | 11.052 | 10.960 | 10.873 | 10.791 | 10.714 | 10.641 | 10.572 | 10.507 | 10.446 |
| 9.5 | 12.083 | 11.939 | 11.805 | 11.679 | 11.561 | 11.451 | 11.348 | 11.251 | 11.159 | 11.074 | 10.993 | 10.917 | 10.845 | 10.777 | 10.713 | 10.653 |
| 9.75 | 12.274 | 12.131 | 11.998 | 11.874 | 11.757 | 11.648 | 11.546 | 11.450 | 11.360 | 11.276 | 11.196 | 11.121 | 11.050 | 10.984 | 10.921 | 10.862 |
| 10 | 12.466 | 12.325 | 12.193 | 12.070 | 11.955 | 11.847 | 11.746 | 11.651 | 11.562 | 11.479 | 11.401 | 11.327 | 11.257 | 11.192 | 11.130 | 11.072 |
| 10.25 | 12.660 | 12.520 | 12.389 | 12.267 | 12.153 | 12.047 | 11.947 | 11.854 | 11.766 | 11.684 | 11.606 | 11.534 | 11.465 | 11.401 | 11.340 | 11.283 |

**Table A-2.** Constant Annual Percents for Loans with Annual Payments (Continued)

To Be Used Only in the Event of 1 Payment Made Annually or Semiannually

| % Interest | 25 | 25.5 | 26 | 26.5 | 27 | 27.5 | 28 | 28.5 | 29 | 29.5 | 30 | 35 | 40 |
|---|---|---|---|---|---|---|---|---|---|---|---|---|---|
| | | | | | | | Years | | | | | | |
| 6 | 7.823 | 7.755 | 7.690 | 7.629 | 7.570 | 7.513 | 7.459 | 7.408 | 7.358 | 7.310 | 7.265 | 6.897 | 6.646 |
| 6.25 | 8.009 | 7.943 | 7.879 | 7.818 | 7.760 | 7.704 | 7.651 | 7.600 | 7.552 | 7.505 | 7.460 | 7.101 | 6.857 |
| 6.5 | 8.198 | 8.132 | 8.069 | 8.010 | 7.952 | 7.898 | 7.845 | 7.795 | 7.747 | 7.702 | 7.658 | 7.306 | 7.069 |
| 6.75 | 8.389 | 8.324 | 8.262 | 8.203 | 8.147 | 8.093 | 8.041 | 7.992 | 7.945 | 7.900 | 7.857 | 7.514 | 7.284 |
| 7 | 8.581 | 8.517 | 8.456 | 8.398 | 8.343 | 8.290 | 8.239 | 8.191 | 8.145 | 8.101 | 8.059 | 7.723 | 7.501 |
| 7.25 | 8.775 | 8.712 | 8.652 | 8.595 | 8.541 | 8.489 | 8.439 | 8.392 | 8.346 | 8.303 | 8.262 | 7.935 | 7.720 |
| 7.5 | 8.971 | 8.909 | 8.850 | 8.794 | 8.740 | 8.689 | 8.641 | 8.594 | 8.550 | 8.508 | 8.467 | 8.148 | 7.940 |
| 7.75 | 9.169 | 9.108 | 9.050 | 8.994 | 8.942 | 8.892 | 8.844 | 8.798 | 8.755 | 8.714 | 8.674 | 8.363 | 8.162 |
| 8 | 9.368 | 9.308 | 9.251 | 9.196 | 9.145 | 9.096 | 9.049 | 9.004 | 8.962 | 8.921 | 8.883 | 8.580 | 8.386 |
| 8.25 | 9.569 | 9.510 | 9.454 | 9.400 | 9.350 | 9.301 | 9.256 | 9.212 | 9.170 | 9.131 | 9.093 | 8.799 | 8.611 |
| 8.5 | 9.771 | 9.713 | 9.658 | 9.606 | 9.556 | 9.509 | 9.464 | 9.421 | 9.381 | 9.342 | 9.305 | 9.019 | 8.838 |
| 8.75 | 9.975 | 9.918 | 9.864 | 9.813 | 9.764 | 9.718 | 9.674 | 9.632 | 9.592 | 9.555 | 9.519 | 9.241 | 9.066 |
| 9 | 10.181 | 10.125 | 10.072 | 10.021 | 9.974 | 9.928 | 9.885 | 9.844 | 9.806 | 9.769 | 9.734 | 9.464 | 9.296 |
| 9.25 | 10.388 | 10.333 | 10.281 | 10.231 | 10.184 | 10.140 | 10.098 | 10.058 | 10.020 | 9.984 | 9.950 | 9.688 | 9.527 |
| 9.5 | 10.596 | 10.542 | 10.491 | 10.443 | 10.397 | 10.354 | 10.312 | 10.273 | 10.236 | 10.201 | 10.168 | 9.914 | 9.759 |
| 9.75 | 10.806 | 10.753 | 10.703 | 10.655 | 10.611 | 10.568 | 10.528 | 10.490 | 10.454 | 10.420 | 10.387 | 10.141 | 9.992 |
| 10 | 11.017 | 10.965 | 10.916 | 10.870 | 10.826 | 10.784 | 10.745 | 10.708 | 10.673 | 10.640 | 10.608 | 10.369 | 10.226 |
| 10.25 | 11.229 | 11.178 | 11.130 | 11.085 | 11.042 | 11.002 | 10.963 | 10.927 | 10.893 | 10.860 | 10.830 | 10.598 | 10.461 |

# Final Examination

## The McGraw-Hill 36-Hour Real Estate Investing Course

If you have completed your study of *The McGraw-Hill 36-Hour Real Estate Investing Course,* you should be prepared to take this final examination. It is a comprehensive examination divided into five sections to assist you in reviewing the questions in the book.

## Instructions

1. *This is an "open book" examination,* which allows you to check and recheck your response to the questions. Taking the examination itself is an exercise in helping you discover the ease in using this book as a *reference guide* to assist you in starting your career as a real estate investor.

2. *There is no minimum time period* in which you must complete this examination. It is recommended, however, that the examination be taken *at one sitting* and not spread out over several time periods.

3. This examination is made up of two different types of questions. Parts 1 through 4 contain multiple choice questions. Questions in the final section require fill-in answers. With the multiple choice questions you are to select the *best* answer to the question. Part 5 requires you to fill in blanks, the answers for which will come from your Real Estate Investor's VIP List.

4. To pass this examination you must answer correctly 112 questions. A passing grade entitles you to receive a *certificate of achievement.* This handsome certificate, suitable for framing, attests to your proven knowledge in real estate investing.

5. Carefully fill in your name and address in the spaces provided at the top of the answer sheet, which appears after the exam, remove the

answer sheet from the book, and send it (along with a copy of completed Part 5) to:

Certification Examiner c/o A. Ruiz
*36-Hour Real Estate Investing Course*
Professional & Reference Division
McGraw-Hill Book Company
11 West 19th Street
New York, NY 10011

## The Examination

### Part 1: How to Get Started in Real Estate Investing

### Chapters 1 through 6

1. The two most important qualifications needed to become a successful real estate investor are _____.
   *a.* education and determination
   *b.* determination and attitude
   *c.* money and good credit
   *d.* a winning attitude and lots of capital

2. The following will help build the self-confidence of the real estate investor: _____.
   *a.* clear focus on goal plus a winning attitude
   *b.* more knowledge plus a goal oriented plan
   *c.* positive failure alignment plus successful elasticity
   *d.* all of the above

3. Apparent opportunities are divided into the following two types: _____.
   *a.* dangerous and worthy
   *b.* attainable and not attainable
   *c.* temporary and long term
   *d.* easy and difficult

4. Which of the following statements best describes failure? _____.
   *a.* Failure is not your enemy
   *b.* Failure is the opposite of success
   *c.* Failure is your guide to needed adjustments
   *d.* All the above except *b*

5. Which of the following is *not* one of the five steps to building self-confidence? _____.
   *a.* Pat yourself on your own back when you achieve a goal
   *b.* Concentrate only on your short-term goals

*c.* Believe you will build your own self-confidence

*d.* None of the above

6. Which of the following *least* describes **risk**? _____.

   *a.* Risk can *never* be completely eliminated

   *b.* Risk is relative to the person and the situation

   *c.* Investments that contain any risk at all should be avoided

   *d.* None of the above

7. Which of the following *best* describes **meaningful goals**? _____.

   *a.* These kind of goals are essential to success in real estate investing

   *b.* Without meaningful goals to follow, your path may be at the whim of others or due to indecision

   *c.* Meaningful goals need only be attainable and clearly defined

   *d.* All the above except *c*

8. Goals that are attainable, measurable, tied to a timetable, and are clearly defined are best described as _____.

   *a.* A meaningful goal

   *b.* A long-range goal

   *c.* An intermediate goal

   *d.* None of the above

9. Which of the following *best* defines the reason goals should be clearly defined? _____.

   *a.* So you don't forget the goal

   *b.* So you don't downgrade the goal and shortchange your plan

   *c.* To allow strong focusing of the investment strategy

   *d.* All of the above

10. Which of the following *best* describes real estate terminology? _____.

    *a.* KISS

    *b.* Not universal

    *c.* Communication by example rather than by term is best

    *d.* All of the above

11. How many square feet are there in one acre? _____.

    *a.* 44,000 sq ft

    *b.* 360 sq ft

    *c.* 43,560 sq ft

    *d.* 45,250 sq ft

12. How many acres approximately are in a tract of land that is 390 ft square? _____.

    *a.* 6 acres

    *b.* 4.5 acres

    *c.* One-half acre

    *d.* 3.5 acres

13. Which of the following best describes a **contingency clause**? _____.
    - *a.* A provision one party puts into a contract that always allows that party to get out of the deal no matter what happens
    - *b.* A condition within a contract or agreement that can let one or both parties modify or get out of the agreement
    - *c.* None of the above
    - *d.* All of the above

14. PITI is *best* described as _____.
    - *a.* a mortgage payment that includes all the principal, interest, taxes, and insurance together
    - *b.* a formula used to calculate mortgage amortization
    - *c.* a federal organization to protect consumers from excess charges in lending
    - *d.* all of the above

15. The **basis** of a property is *best* described as _____.
    - *a.* the metes and bound description
    - *b.* a fundamental of an appraisal value
    - *c.* a "book value" used in accounting
    - *d.* none of the above

16. A "code violation" is best described as _____.
    - *a.* something only the seller needs to contend with
    - *b.* something that once a fine is paid is not important
    - *c.* something all buyers would need to know about
    - *d.* something that inhibits a property from being sold until it is resolved

17. Which *least* describes a **balloon mortgage**? _____.
    - *a.* A mortgage that encloses more than one property
    - *b.* A mortgage that can have a required repayment of principal that is different from the amortization schedule
    - *c.* A mortgage with which a borrower can increase the amount of money borrowed
    - *d.* None of the above

18. Which of the following *best* describes a mortgage that has a phrase in it that says "This is a purchase money first mortgage that is secured by the following three properties."? _____.
    - *a.* This is a seller-held first mortgage that is also a blanket mortgage
    - *b.* This may not be a first mortgage unless it was recorded ahead of any other mortgages
    - *c.* This is a blanket mortgage held by an institutional lender who has no relation to either party of the transaction
    - *d.* All of the above

*For the Next Four Questions Review the Following Transaction*

The establishment of a document that allows a buyer to pay 20 percent of the purchase price down and assume the existing first mortgage of

$50,000 and the seller to hold the balance at interest only at ten percent interest due at the end of each year, with a payment in full due on the day before the sixth anniversary of the closing.

19. Which *best* describes the above transaction? _____.
    a. This is an installment sale
    b. The seller is holding a type of purchase money mortgage
    c. The seller held mortgage is a balloon mortgage
    d. All of the above

20. What would be the payment due to the seller the third year following the closing if the total price of the property was $180,000? _____.
    a. $9400 plus the payments due on the first mortgage
    b. $18,888.89
    c. $13,000
    d. None of the above

21. What would the seller collect over the life of this contract if the sales price was $200,000? _____.
    a. $185,000
    b. $165,000
    c. $55,000
    d. $310,000

22. If the buyer paid off the loan held by the seller at the end of 30 months following the closing and the total price paid was $200,000 what is the total amount of the check paid to the seller? _____.
    a. $110,000
    b. $115,500
    c. $165,000
    d. None of the above

23. Which *best* describes a **cost of living adjustment**? _____.
    a. A provision that is used in mortgages or leases that requires an adjustment in one or more terms of the agreement due to an agreed-upon index that measures the cost of living
    b. A provision that allows one of the parties of a contract to take deductions from required payments due to the cost of living adjustments as published by the Federal Government Department of Labor, or other acceptable publication
    c. None of the above
    d. Both *a* and *c*

24. A provision in a mortgage that does not allow automatic assumption by a buyer of the property that secures the mortgage is _____.
    a. a grandfather provision
    b. a due on sale clause
    c. a release of security provision
    d. a subordination clause

25. If a seller agrees to a provision that allows the buyer to put a new first mortgage ahead of the purchase money first mortgage held by the seller, the seller has done which of the following? _____.
    a. Agreed to take a second position on the security of the loan
    b. Agreed to subordinate his or her position to a new loan
    c. Increased his or her risk in the event of a default by the buyer
    d. All of the above

*For the Next Three Questions Review the Following Transaction*

Paula has a six-unit apartment building. Each apartment can be rented for $600 per month. Last year Paula had three apartments vacant for an average of two months each. Her total operating expenses for that year were $15,120. She has a first mortgage of $180,000 that has an annual debt service to amortize fully the loan of $19,800 per year.

26. With no change in rents, what would an investor calculate as the **gross collectable rents** for the next 12 months? _____.
    a. $29,600
    b. $43,200
    c. $28,080
    d. None of the above

27. If an investor paid $100,000 cash to the assumption of the existing mortgage and collected exactly what Paula did last year, what would be the **cash flow** on the investment? _____.
    a. $8280
    b. $4680
    c. $9800
    d. None of the above

28. What would be the NOI if there was a 5 percent vacancy from the same collectable rents and the operating expenses were $16,440? _____.
    a. $24,660
    b. $23,160
    c. $4,860
    d. None of the above

29. What are the *two* ways to increase gross revenue from a fixed number of rental units? _____.
    a. Increase the rent and cut operating expenses
    b. Cut the vacancy factor and reduce debt service
    c. Increase rent and cut the vacancy factor
    d. Cut operating expenses and reduce debt service

30. When two equally sized business zoned lots are located in the same block, but one is on the corner and the other is in the middle of the block, which would be the most valuable? _____.

*a.* The one with the best exposure to traffic
*b.* The lot that was most accessible by the traffic
*c.* The lot on which you could build the most square footage of rental space
*d.* Not enough information known to make a determination

31. What is the most important factor to consider when choosing between two similar lots, each priced similarly, on which the same square footage can be built? _____
    *a.* The setbacks
    *b.* The needs of the user
    *c.* The advertising value of the location
    *d.* Whether this is a "far corner" or not

32. Which of the following may contain the square footage of an odd-shaped lot you are considering buying? _____.
    *a.* The deed
    *b.* The existing mortgage
    *c.* The tax assessor's records
    *d.* The building department records

33. Which *best* describes the term **positive leverage**? _____.
    *a.* A mortgage that has an interest rate that is less than the prime rate
    *b.* A cash flow yield that is greater than the NOI yield
    *c.* All of the above
    *d.* None of the above

34. Which of the following is not one of the four most important areas of the real estate bureaucracy? _____.
    *a.* Planning department
    *b.* Tax assessment office
    *c.* City manager's office
    *d.* Elected officials

35. Alex, a novice investor, makes an appointment to meet his first elected official. Which of the following *best* describes what Alex's goal should be? _____.
    *a.* To make an impression on this official
    *b.* To get the names of several additional people to meet
    *c.* To become a real estate insider by knowing this official
    *d.* To start the process of building contacts

36. Which of the following should you *not* do at the first appointment? _____.
    *a.* Use flattery
    *b.* Look successful
    *c.* Stay as long as possible
    *d.* Be prompt

37. At the start of most public council or county commission meetings the members review and vote on _____.
    a. current ordinances
    b. code violations
    c. the consent agenda
    d. land use regulations

38. When a portion of the value of a property is deducted from the city or county real estate taxes, this is a function of _____.
    a. tax exempt property
    b. homestead exemption
    c. the local zoning office
    d. none of the above

39. When contacting the local government offices to obtain the basic information to get the most out of the public forum, which would be the most important data required? _____.
    a. Time and place of the meeting
    b. The agenda
    c. The names of the members
    d. None of the above

40. Which of the following would contain the most detailed information on property in any subdivision? _____.
    a. A market analysis
    b. The MLS
    c. A deed search
    d. The exclusive listing

41. Which would *best* describe what a **buyer's broker** is? _____.
    a. Any realtor working with a buyer
    b. Any licensed real estate salesperson or broker who takes a buyer to any property and sells that property to the buyer
    c. A real estate agent working under a specific agreement that specifies the buyer and not the seller will pay the agent a fee
    d. All of the above

## Part 2: How and Why Property Values Go Up and Down and What You Can Do About It

### Chapters 7 through 12

42. When a community requires a property owner to pay to improve existing public infrastructure in order to obtain a building permit, this is a result of _____.

*a.* an impact fee being imposed

*b.* the required building permit being collected

*c.* a form of tax shelter being created

*d.* evidence that the property met currency

43. When rent can be increased by updating fixtures in an apartment house, what best describes those fixtures? _____.

    *a.* They have lost their highest and best use

    *b.* They are economically obsolescent

    *c.* They are too old

    *d.* None of the above

44. Many investors argue that paying **impact fees** is a form of _____.

    *a.* a building restriction

    *b.* bureaucratic paperwork

    *c.* a property tax not equally distributed to all property owners

    *d.* all of the above

45. Which of the following is necessary to calculate a taxable gain in the event of a sale? _____.

    *a.* Any depreciation taken over the ownership life

    *b.* The property basis

    *c.* The amount realized by the seller in a sale

    *d.* All the above

46. Which is *not* one of the six reasons property values go up? _____.

    *a.* New public facilities

    *b.* Improved management skills

    *c.* Popular part of town

    *d.* Ample supply of affordable housing

47. Inflation affects all property equally in any given area of the country: _____.

    *a.* True

    *b.* False

48. Inflation is the increased value solely due to the increased cost to replace the item: _____.

    *a.* True

    *b.* False

49. Which of the following can cause property values to increase the fastest over a short period of time? _____.

    *a.* Widen existing highways to allow more traffic

    *b.* Open up new areas by building a bridge

    *c.* Change the use of an apartment building to medical offices

    *d.* All of the above

50. The key to getting the most out of market conditions is to understand the big picture and to concentrate on _____.
    *a.* economic conversions
    *b.* finding the highest and best use of a property
    *c.* developing a comfort zone
    *d.* becoming a real estate investor

51. Changes in property values following development of new roadways can be anticipated because _____.
    *a.* there is a long lead time before the work is started
    *b.* past examples in similar communities can be studied
    *c.* a change from any status quo can have a ripple effect
    *d.* all of the above

52. What are the three things property owners can do to increase value of their property over which they have direct control? _____.
    *a.* Voluntary change, increased bottom line, and new buildings
    *b.* New zoning, higher rents, and remodeling the structure
    *c.* Repainted building, reduced operating expenses, and new management
    *d.* All the above

53. Which statement *best* represents how the investor should approach real estate trends? _____.
    *a.* Review everything possible about what is going on around the world because everything has an effect on values equally
    *b.* Have a good understanding of all the different events that can affect real estate values but pay closest attention to what is going on in your investment community
    *c.* Real estate can be viewed as a national statistic just as gold or the stock market
    *d.* All of the above

54. The development of **new public facilities** will always have a positive effect on the property values in a community: _____.
    *a.* True
    *b.* False

55. Anything causing a reduction of rents in a community can be a prelude to a decline in real estate values for that area: _____.
    *a.* True
    *b.* False

56. A temporary traffic detour while new road work is underway can present the real estate investor with _____.
    *a.* investment opportunity
    *b.* reduced rent during and after the detour

*c.* future value change, which could be up or down

*d.* all the above

57. Investors always have "grandfather rights" under which they can use the property purchased for what it was zoned at the time it was purchased: _____.

*a.* True

*b.* False

58. The attitude of a community toward real estate development is not that important to the real estate investor because it affects all values equally: _____.

*a.* True

*b.* False

59. What is the best way for a real estate investor to take into consideration the age of a roof on a building he or she is considering buying? _____.

*a.* Plan on replacing it as soon as possible

*b.* Anticipate the total cost of the roof and add that expense to the investment cost

*c.* Use a sinking fund to find the loss of revenue to accumulate the cost to replace the roof

*d.* Deduct the cost of the roof from the purchase price

60. "Tight money" can bring new construction to a halt and can therefore prevent the market from becoming overbuilt: _____.

*a.* True

*b.* False

61. What would be the *most likely* result if no reasonable long-term financing was available to finance real estate development? _____.

*a.* A demand for existing property would result and all property values would go up

*b.* The market would stagnate with buyers unable to finance their acquisitions, and property values could go down

*c.* Lenders would step in to provide the needed long-term financing

*d.* Both a and b above

62. Which property represents the *best opportunity* for a future profit with minimal capital improvements? _____.

*a.* A brand new duplex apartment in a good area

*b.* A nice home in a good area that has been neglected for at least two years

*c.* A tract of land in the path of a highway to be built in four or five years

*d.* A restaurant that has been closed for four months because the owner died

63. When a seller has an urgency to sell, which is the *best* technique to sell a difficult property? _____.
    a. Reduce the price until a buyer comes along
    b. Offer the buyer a "nothing down" deal
    c. Consider becoming an aggressive buyer and work an exchange into another property
    d. Place the property up for auction

64. The elements that give property value can *best* be described as _____.
    a. the location, location, location
    b. the importance of the location to the user and the use allowed
    c. the access, traffic flow, and the use allowed
    d. a far corner, prime traffic flow, zoning, and good setbacks

65. Which of the following is an example of a potential hidden cost when buying property? _____.
    a. A zoning violation
    b. A future impact fee
    c. All of the above
    d. None of the above

66. A fast food operator looking for a location would select which of the following sites to build a restaurant (assume the price to be the same per square foot for each): _____.
    a. A near corner with good traffic access for all traffic
    b. A far corner with traffic access from the secondary street only
    c. A "middle of the block" site at the main entrance to a major shopping center
    d. A far corner with great traffic access at an intersection that is soon to undergo major improvement which may triple the traffic

67. Where would you go to find out the number of cars that travel in front of a business location you are considering buying? _____.
    a. The local community building department
    b. The Federal offices of the DOT
    c. The highest authority DOT in control of the road
    d. A local road construction company

68. Which of the following is the best real estate investment strategy? _____.
    a. Buy what you need when you need it
    b. Speculate on long-term value increases
    c. Either of the above based on the goals of the investor
    d. Look for the greatest long-term return for the capital invested

69. The amount of residential units a community will allow in any area can be controlled by _____.

a. the local zoning ordinances

b. setbacks

c. road access

d. impact fees

70. If a property owner wanted to rezone a corner lot to a different zoning that would allow a restaurant, the best chance of success would be if he or she _____.

a. made a good presentation to show why the change in zoning would not affect the other property in the block

b. got all the other property owners in the block together to rezone the entire block

c. requested a variance to allow the restaurant

d. suggested that if the restaurant could not be built he or she would build something ugly, but allowable

71. All property line encroachments can be seen if you know where the property boundaries are: _____.

a. True

b. False

72. Which of the following changes in rules or regulations can a community require the property owner to adjust to? _____.

a. Number of units allowed per acre

b. Setbacks

c. Both of the above

d. None of the above

73. When a property owner has an allowed use in a building that is "grandfathered in" due to building code changes and the building burns down, which of the following would most likely apply? _____.

a. The property could be reconstructed as it was

b. The new building would have to meet all new codes

c. The owner could find a compromise with the building department

d. A rezoning would be the first step for the property owner to take to ensure the use would not be changed

74. If you were selling an apartment building on a site zoned to permit children day-care centers and you lived next door, what could you do to prevent such use? _____.

a. Have the buyer sign an agreement not to do that

b. Put a deed restriction in the deed that would not allow that use

c. Make the buyer subordinate

d. Sell to the buyer under a contract for deed

75. All surveys made are correct: _____.

a. True

b. False

76. When dealing with a **motivated seller** the most important thing for the buyer to know is _____.
    a. how low a price the seller will take
    b. what the seller knows about the property
    c. whether the seller will hold a large mortgage
    d. the primary goal the seller wants to achieve

77. When a buyer makes a change in a property with the end result that the value goes up, this is an example of _____.
    a. getting the highest and best use from the property
    b. an economic conversion
    c. the result of a rezoning
    d. becoming an "insider"

78. One of the best ways to maximize the effect of economic conversions is to _____.
    a. fill a community need
    b. buy a run-down property you can fix up
    c. always look for property you can rezone
    d. close a right-of-way to tie up the property

79. Landscape enhancement is considered a long-term property improvement and has little effect on the short-term value: _____.
    a. True
    b. False

80. One quick and "free" way to get a neighborhood cleaned up is to _____.
    a. organize the neighborhood to pick up the trash
    b. get the city to enforce existing laws
    c. call the Salvation Army
    d. set a good example by cleaning up your property first

81. Baking bread or chocolate chip cookies during an open house of a property you are trying to sell may have the effect of _____.
    a. taking your mind off the real job of selling the house
    b. evoking pleasant memories of prospective buyers
    c. doing nothing to remove "dog smell"
    d. none of the above

## Part 3: How to Find the Right Property to Buy

### Chapters 13 through 16

82. A property that is costing you more than it is making may be a good example of _____.

a. a property that you should consider selling
b. typical of the home you live in
c. an alligator
d. all of the above

83. Which of the following has the greatest risk in a long-term hold for profit property? _____.
a. Vacant commercial lots
b. Single-family homes
c. Multifamily properties
d. Retail shops

84. Which of the following requires the least management? _____.
a. Sales of lots
b. Apartment rentals
c. Triple net commercial rentals
d. Office building rentals

85. When building an investment comfort zone the best geographic area to start with will be _____.
a. an area that is not deteriorating
b. an area that is convenient to the investor
c. where the buying action seems to be directed
d. an area in which the investor can afford to invest

86. When an investor lives in a deteriorating neighborhood it is a good idea for the investor to look for opportunities right there: _____.
a. True
b. False

87. How many property owners should there be in a comfort zone? _____.
a. No more than 600
b. A minimum of 1000
c. Not a criteria for any comfort zone
d. Start with 600

88. The tax assessor's office is one of the best sources for real estate investment information: _____.
a. True
b. False

89. By properly working a comfort zone the investor can be expected to become a real estate expert within a year's time for that area: _____.
a. True
b. False

90. Building a sphere of reference is a good way to become an "insider" quickly. When meeting people the most important long term goal is to _____.

    *a.* make sure you get the name of their secretary
    *b.* make a good first impression
    *c.* make sure that they know you
    *d.* constantly follow up

91. A computer printout that contains many different facts about a property and its current and past ownership history is called _____.
    *a.* property evaluation
    *b.* listing proposal
    *c.* legal description
    *d.* deed search

*For the Next Three Questions Review the Following Metes and Bounds Legal Description of a Property*

> From marker 107 in the center-line of State Road 27, go West 270 degrees a distance of 240 feet to a point of beginning, then North 0 degrees and parallel to the right-of-way of State Road 27 a distance of 1000 feet, then West 270 degrees a distance of 4356 feet then South 180 degrees a distance of 500 feet, then East 90 degrees a distance of 3920.4 feet then South 180 degrees a distance of 500 feet, then East 90 degrees to the point of beginning.

92. The property described can best be described as _____.
    *a.* two rectangles connected at right angles
    *b.* a property that adjoins the right-of-way of State Road 27
    *c.* a property that is 240 ft west of the right-of-way line of State Road 27
    *d.* none of the above

93. How many acres does this property contain? _____.
    *a.* 50
    *b.* 47
    *c.* 102
    *d.* None of the above

94. If the property was for sale at \$1.00 per square foot, and the prospective buyer wants to offer 25 percent less, what would the total offer be? _____.
    *a.* \$1,698,840
    *b.* \$169,884
    *c.* \$226,512
    *d.* None of the above

95. When a property is appraised by the tax appraiser there is nothing a property owner can do to lower the assessment: _____.
    *a.* True
    *b.* False

*For the Next Six Questions Review the Following Case Study*

Andrea is looking at an eight-unit apartment house. The rents average $500 per month. According to the norms for the area the building should experience no more than 6 percent vacancy factor for the year, and operating costs not to exceed 30 percent the gross possible rent.

96. What is the gross rents possible? _____.
    *a.* $45,120
    *b.* $48,000
    *c.* $30,730
    *d.* None of the above

97. What is the NOI? _____.
    *a.* $31,584
    *b.* $30,730
    *c.* $33,600
    *d.* None of the above

98. If there was a first mortgage on the property of $160,000 at 12 percent interest for 12 years remaining (Table A-1 of the Appendix), and Andrea was able to increase the NOI to $34,000, what would the cash flow be? _____.
    *a.* $8,782.40
    *b.* $8,605.60
    *c.* $7,440.50
    *d.* None of the above

99. If Andrea could refinance up to 70 percent of the purchase price at 8 percent interest for a fixed term of 15 years with a 30-year amortization (Table A-1 of the Appendix), what would be the maximum price she could pay and get a 10 percent cash flow return on his investment (assume the NOI is $34,000 and 0 loan cost)? _____.
    *a.* $371,037.00
    *b.* $340,000.00
    *c.* $311,559.00
    *d.* Not enough information to calculate this

100. If the seller refinanced before the sale with a mortgage of $220,000 at the rates shown in the previous question, what would be the total price

Andrea could pay to get a 9.5 percent cash flow return on her investment (assume an NOI of $34,000): _____.

   *a.* $371,037.00
   *b.* $259,726.00
   *c.* $311,559.00
   *d.* $373,989.00

101. If in the situation described in the previous question there was a total of $11,000 of depreciation allowed in the year of the purchase, and Andrea closed on January 1 of the year, what would be her taxable income from this investment (assume principal payments on the mortgage totaled $1,000 for the year)? _____.

   *a.* $4629.00
   *b.* $22,000.00
   *c.* $5629.00
   *d.* None of the above

102. Which of the following expense figures do sellers frequently misrepresent? _____.

   *a.* Gross rents collected
   *b.* Management expense
   *c.* Debt service
   *d.* All of the above

103. Which of the following *best* describes depreciation? _____.

   *a.* An accounting principal that is used by the IRS in finding the amount of a capital gain
   *b.* An allowed annual expense that is based on the declining value of improvements and is a deduction from the NOI from rents to calculate cash flow
   *c.* An annual deduction from the taxpayer's **earned income** based on an IRS allowable percentage of the original value of an income producing property (excluding the land value)
   *d.* A form of tax shelter

104. A sinking fund is *best* described as _____.

   *a.* an accounting principle that enables an investor to deduct the cost of eventual replacements of improvements
   *b.* an IRS provision that is required to enable income property owners to pay their tax over a period of time
   *c.* a fund that is used to pay off debt
   *d.* an accounting principle that is rarely used but which takes into consideration future expenses that will be funded by an annuity paid by the investor

105. Positive leverage is evident when the NOI return percentage is lower than the cash flow return: _____.

*a.* True

*b.* False

106. What is the *best* method of determining the market value of a property? _____.
    *a.* Make an offer with an "out" to see how low the seller will go
    *b.* Do a deed search to find out how much the seller paid and offer 40 percent less
    *c.* Review current properties on the market and those which have sold in the past 12 months
    *d.* Ask lenders what they appraise property at in the area

107. Of the following investment tasks, which is the *most important* to maintain a pulse on the market? _____.
    *a.* Get to know everyone important at the building department
    *b.* Continually inspect property
    *c.* Make a lot of offers
    *d.* Check on deed transfers

## Part 4: How to Buy and Sell Real Estate for a Profit

### Chapters 17 through 20

108. The "G" syndrome *best* describes which of the following situations? _____.
    *a.* A seller who will accept an option payment because he or she doesn't think you will close on the deal
    *b.* A buyer who offers cash and a quick closing
    *c.* A seller who holds out for his or her price no matter how long it might take to get it
    *d.* All of the above

109. The "greener grass" phenomenon is *best* described by which of the following situations? _____.
    *a.* A desire to sell what you have and get something else
    *b.* The sudden value increase that occurs when new landscape is installed
    *c.* A seller who takes back a second mortgage on a property the buyer owns as a part of the deal
    *d.* A seller who accepts an exchange he or she will have no use for

110. The term "I'll pay your price if you accept my terms" is a good example of the way in which the greener grass phenomenon works: _____.
    *a.* True
    *b.* False

111. Which of the following is not an *ideal* time to use the option? _____.
    *a.* Just to tie up a property so that it can be checked out at leisure
    *b.* As a tool to negotiate for other property
    *c.* When time is needed for the property to go up in value
    *d.* To give the seller time to inspect property used in an IRS Sec. 1031 exchange

112. Which of the following techniques can be used with an option? _____.
    *a.* Sweat equity
    *b.* "Out clause"
    *c.* Both of the above
    *d.* None of the above

*For the Next Two Questions Review the Following Case Study*

Frank offered to paint the exterior of Jim's apartment building in exchange for one year's rent in a vacant apartment in the same building.

113. This is an example of sweat equity: _____.
    *a.* True
    *b.* False

114. If Jim were to offer the building for sale, he could include the amount Frank got as credit as part of the NOI: _____.
    *a.* True
    *b.* False

115. Which is the *biggest* advantage to a seller-held mortgage? _____.
    *a.* The mortgage may be assumable by a future buyer
    *b.* The seller is far more motivated than a lender to make a good loan
    *c.* Long-term institutional loans are very difficult to get
    *d.* Sellers are well protected when they take back mortgages on their own property

116. When the mortgage document contains a subordination clause this generally means _____.
    *a.* the seller will allow the buyer to subdivide the property
    *b.* the seller will permit his or her purchase money mortgage to become junior to other debt
    *c.* the buyer must give additional collateral to secure the loan
    *d.* this mortgage has become a balloon mortgage

117. In an exchange if one party was to take a diamond ring as part of the deal, this would be an example of _____.
    *a.* an item that would not qualify as an IRS Sec. 1031 exchange
    *b.* a method to balance equity
    *c.* both the above
    *d.* none of the above

*For the Next Six Questions Review the Following Case Study*

Janet wants to exchange a vacant tract of land she owns that is worth $150,000 and is free and clear of all debt. She offers this property for Cliff's apartment building that he has on the market for $600,000. In Janet's offer she agrees to assume the existing debt of $300,000.

118. What is the balance owed to Cliff? _____.
    *a.* $150,000
    *b.* $300,000
    *c.* $250,000
    *d.* None of the above

119. If Janet owed $50,000 on her property and she knew she could get a new first mortgage of $425,000 on Cliff's property, what would be the total amount of cash that Cliff would get if he took Janet's land subject to the mortgage on it, and Janet paid him off in cash? _____.
    *a.* $200,000
    *b.* $175,000
    *c.* $300,000
    *d.* None of the above

120. This exchange is likely to qualify as an IRS Sec. 1031 tax-free exchange: _____.
    *a.* True
    *b.* False

121. If Janet's basis in the land was $50,000 and she assumed Cliff's original $300,000 mortgage and gave Cliff the land free and clear, what would Janet's new basis be? _____.
    *a.* $350,000
    *b.* $550,000
    *c.* $250,000
    *d.* $500,000

122. Any exchange that moves you closer to a goal is a good exchange: _____.
    *a.* True
    *b.* False

123. The above-noted exchange could be considered as a **like-kind** exchange: _____.
    *a.* True
    *b.* False

124. Which of the choices below best describes a situation in which the seller takes $15,000 credit for legal services as part of a transaction to dispose of a $300,000 property he or she owns? _____.

    *a.* The "G" syndrome
    *b.* A discounted sale
    *c.* A 1031 exchange
    *d.* An accommodation move

125. Any mortgage with a provision that indicates that the mortgage can be assumed providing the buyer meets certain conditions is a fully assumable mortgage: _____.
    *a.* True
    *b.* False

126. A buyer's broker is any real estate agent that the buyer is dealing with: _____.
    *a.* True
    *b.* False

127. Any offer that is titled *Letter of Intent* is not a binding agreement: _____.
    *a.* True
    *b.* False

128. One of the best ways to learn about the other party to an agreement is to _____.
    *a.* have the listing broker tell you about them
    *b.* ask neighbors about them
    *c.* meet them at their home
    *d.* do a deed search on all the property they own

129. Which is not one of the four key factors to consider when structuring an offer? _____.
    *a.* Keep the debt you are to assume within reason
    *b.* Remember that a future sale may depend on the purchase terms you structure when you buy
    *c.* Keep in mind the potential to refinance current short-term debt you put on the property when you buy it
    *d.* Allow the other side to achieve at least part of their goals

130. What is the best way to avoid having a seller fail to negotiate with you because they are insulted at your initial low offer? _____.
    *a.* Tell them they must be really angry at all the people who didn't even make an offer
    *b.* Have a real estate agent who can absorb the frustrations of the seller
    *c.* Wait awhile and make an even lower offer if the property is still on the market
    *d.* Move on to another property and a more cooperative seller

131. The mortgage that has an amortization clause that reads, "The mortgage shall be paid in 11 equal annual installments of principal together with

interest on the unpaid balance at 9 percent per annum" would have an annual payment the second year of _____ (assume the original loan was $110,000).

a. $19,000.00
b. $16,164.50
c. $19,900.00
d. None of the above

132. A mortgage that has more than one property as security is called

_____.

a. a subordinated mortgage
b. a wraparound mortgage
c. a blanket mortgage
d. none of the above

133. If the seller allows the buyer to assume the existing financing and takes back another mortgage on the property, which of the following best describes that event? _____.

a. A blanket second mortgage
b. A subordinated mortgage
c. A wraparound mortgage
d. A purchase money second mortgage

134. When a wraparound mortgage can be used, it can have the following effect: _____.

a. To provide better security to the seller than a regular second mortgage
b. To allow the seller to leverage over existing financing
c. To give the buyer better terms than available in the institutional market
d. All the above

135. A mortgage with an original loan amount of $120,000 at 10 percent interest per year that was scheduled to be paid off at the end of the tenth year that had as the 15th monthly payment $947.00 could *best* be described as

_____.

a. an ARM mortgage
b. equal installment mortgage
c. a balloon mortgage
d. a deficit payment mortgage

136. Which technique is best suited to consolidate a payment schedule for the buyer? _____.

a. A seller-held purchase money second mortgage
b. A wraparound mortgage
c. An ARM mortgage
d. A 30-year fixed interest rate mortgage

137. The *best* way to deal with lenders is _____.
     a. to get to know the secretary to the president
     b. to spend a lot of time with one of their loan officers
     c. to get to know them and bring them projects they like to loan on
     d. to prove to them that your project will be a great success and that the loan will be secure

138. Which lending source is the best for any real estate investor? _____.
     a. The local FHA office
     b. Local private lenders
     c. The seller
     d. The buyer's personal bank

139. An ARM can be one of the most attractive loans available on a short-term basis: _____.
     a. True
     b. False

140. The seller's obligation is to disclose to the buyer anything that may be "bad" about the property he or she is selling. _____.
     a. True
     b. False

## Part 5: The Real Estate Investor's VIP List

*Note:* A spot check of the following may occur and if any of the following is found to be incorrectly answered they all will be presumed to be answered incorrectly.

Complete the following:

141. Name of city: _____

     Phone number of city hall: (_____) _____

142. City manager's name: _____

     Address: _____

     Phone number: (_____) _____

143. Head of the city building department

     Name: _____

     Phone number: (_____) _____

144. Name of county: _____

145. Name of state: _____

146.  Head of county Department of Transportation

Name: _____

Phone number:  (_____) _____

147.  City clerk

Name: _____

Phone number:  (_____) _____

148.  Time of city council meetings: _____

Day of month: _____

Where held: _____

149.  Time of county commission meetings: _____

Day of month: _____

Where held: _____

150.  Name of the county commissioner from your district:

_____

Phone number:  (_____) _____

District: _____

Name of secretary: _____

151.  Name of the president of one savings and loan association:

_____

Phone number:  (_____) _____

Name of secretary: _____

152.  Name of a local real estate lawyer: _____

Phone number:  (_____) _____

153.  Name of a local realtor: _____

Phone number:  (_____) _____

154.  Name of a local surveyor: _____

Phone number:  (_____) _____

155.  Head of the state Department of Transportation

Name: _____

Phone number:  (_____) _____

156.  Head of the county Department of Transportation

Name: _____

Phone number:  (_____) _____

Name _____

Address _____

City _____ State _____ Zip _____

# Final Examination Answer Sheet: The McGraw-Hill 36-Hour Real Estate Investing Course

See instructions on the first page of the Final Examination (p. 325).

| | | | | |
|---|---|---|---|---|
| 1. _____ | 21. _____ | 41. _____ | 61. _____ | 81. _____ |
| 2. _____ | 22. _____ | 42. _____ | 62. _____ | 82. _____ |
| 3. _____ | 23. _____ | 43. _____ | 63. _____ | 83. _____ |
| 4. _____ | 24. _____ | 44. _____ | 64. _____ | 84. _____ |
| 5. _____ | 25. _____ | 45. _____ | 65. _____ | 85. _____ |
| 6. _____ | 26. _____ | 46. _____ | 66. _____ | 86. _____ |
| 7. _____ | 27. _____ | 47. _____ | 67. _____ | 87. _____ |
| 8. _____ | 28. _____ | 48. _____ | 68. _____ | 88. _____ |
| 9. _____ | 29. _____ | 49. _____ | 69. _____ | 89. _____ |
| 10. _____ | 30. _____ | 50. _____ | 70. _____ | 90. _____ |
| 11. _____ | 31. _____ | 51. _____ | 71. _____ | 91. _____ |
| 12. _____ | 32. _____ | 52. _____ | 72. _____ | 92. _____ |
| 13. _____ | 33. _____ | 53. _____ | 73. _____ | 93. _____ |
| 14. _____ | 34. _____ | 54. _____ | 74. _____ | 94. _____ |
| 15. _____ | 35. _____ | 55. _____ | 75. _____ | 95. _____ |
| 16. _____ | 36. _____ | 56. _____ | 76. _____ | 96. _____ |
| 17. _____ | 37. _____ | 57. _____ | 77. _____ | 97. _____ |
| 18. _____ | 38. _____ | 58. _____ | 78. _____ | 98. _____ |
| 19. _____ | 39. _____ | 59. _____ | 79. _____ | 99. _____ |
| 20. _____ | 40. _____ | 60. _____ | 80. _____ | 100. _____ |

| | | | | |
|---|---|---|---|---|
| 101. _____ | 109. _____ | 117. _____ | 125. _____ | 133. _____ |
| 102. _____ | 110. _____ | 118. _____ | 126. _____ | 134. _____ |
| 103. _____ | 111. _____ | 119. _____ | 127. _____ | 135. _____ |
| 104. _____ | 112. _____ | 120. _____ | 128. _____ | 136. _____ |
| 105. _____ | 113. _____ | 121. _____ | 129. _____ | 137. _____ |
| 106. _____ | 114. _____ | 122. _____ | 130. _____ | 138. _____ |
| 107. _____ | 115. _____ | 123. _____ | 131. _____ | 139. _____ |
| 108. _____ | 116. _____ | 124. _____ | 132. _____ | 140. _____ |

# Index

## About the Author

Jack Cummings is a highly successful real estate investor, broker, and developer with nearly 30 years of hands-on experience. He is the author of numerous books on various aspects of the real estate field, including *Successful Real Estate Investing for the Single Person, Cashless Investing in Real Estate, The Real Estate Financing Manual, The Guide to Real Estate Exchanges,* and *$1,000 Down Can Make You Rich.* He is also an international lecturer, having given programs from Australia to Sweden, publishes a real estate exchange newsletter, and has appeared on many television and radio programs nationally and in his hometown of Fort Lauderdale, Florida.